WRITING DEVELOPMENT

STUDIES IN WRITTEN LANGUAGE AND LITERACY

EDITORS

BRIAN STREET
University of Sussex

LUDO VERHOEVEN
Tilburg University

ASSOCIATE EDITORS

FLORIAN COULMAS
Chuo University, Tokyo

DANIEL WAGNER
University of Pennsylvania

EDITORIAL BOARD

F. Niyi Akinnaso (Temple University, Philadelphia)
David Barton (Lancaster University)
Paul Bertelson (Université Libre de Bruxelles)
Claire Blanche-Benveniste (Université de Provence)
Chander J. Daswani (India Council of Educational Research and Training)
Emilia Ferreiro (Instituto Polytecnico México)
Edward French (University of the Witwatersrand)
Uta Frith (Medical Research Council, London)
Harvey J. Graff (University of Texas at Dallas)
Hartmut Günther (Max Planck Institut für Psycholinguistik, Nijmegen)
David Olson (Ontario Institute for Studies in Education, Toronto)
Clotilde Pontecorvo (University of Rome)
Roger Säljo (Linköping University)
Michael Stubbs (Universität Trier)

AIM AND SCOPE

The aim of this series is to advance insight into the multifaceted character of written language, with special emphasis on its uses in different social and cultural settings. It combines interest in sociolinguistic and psycholinguistic accounts of the acquisition and transmission of literacy. The series focusses on descriptive and theoretical reports in areas such as language codification, cognitive models of written language use, written language acquisition in children and adults, the development and implementation of literacy campaigns, and literacy as a social marker relating to gender, ethnicity, and class. The series is intended to be multi-disciplinary, combining insights from linguistics, psychology, sociology, education, anthropology, and philosophy.

Volume 6

Clotilde Pontecorvo (ed.)
Writing Development: An interdisciplinary view

WRITING DEVELOPMENT

AN INTERDISCIPLINARY VIEW

Edited by

CLOTILDE PONTECORVO
Università di Roma "La Sapienza", Italy

JOHN BENJAMINS PUBLISHING COMPANY
AMSTERDAM/PHILADELPHIA

The paper used in this publication meets the minimum requirements of American National Standard for Information Sciences — Permanence of Paper for Printed Library Materials, ANSI Z39.48-1984.

Library of Congress Cataloging-in-Publication Data

Writing development : an interdisciplinary view / [edited by] Clotilde Pontecorvo.
    p.   cm. -- (Studies in written language and literacy, ISSN 0929-7324 ; v. 6)
  Includes bibliographical references (p.) and index.
    1. Language acquisition. 2. Written communication. 3. Literacy. I. Pontecorvo, Clotilde.
II. Series.
P118.W75   1997
401'.93--DC21   97-40728
ISBN 90 272 1799 8 (Eur.) / 1-55619-324-6 (US) (Hb; alk. paper)   CIP

© Copyright 1997 - John Benjamins B.V.
No part of this book may be reproduced in any form, by print, photoprint, microfilm, or any other means, without written permission from the publisher.

John Benjamins Publishing Co. • P.O.Box 75577 • 1070 AN Amsterdam • The Netherlands
John Benjamins North America • P.O.Box 27519 • Philadelphia PA 19118-0519 • USA

ESF remit

The European Science Foundation is an association of its 59 member research councils, academies and institutions devoted to basic scientific research in 21 countries. The ESF assists its Member Organisations in two main ways: by bringing scientists together in its Scientific Programmes, Networks and European Research Conferences, to work on topics of common concern; and through the joint study of issues of stregic importance in European science policy.

The scientific work sponsored by ESF includes basic research in the natural and technical sciences, the medical and biosciences, the humanities and social sciences.

The ESF maintains close relations with other scientific institutions within and outside Europe. By its activities, ESF adds value by cooperation and coordination across national frontiers and endeavours, offers expert scientific advice on strategic issues, and provides the European forum for fundamental science.

Authors' affiliations

Ruth Berman
Tel Aviv University, Israel

Claire Blanche-Benveniste
Université de Provence, France

Brian Butterworth
University College London, U.K.

Giuseppe Cossu
Università degli Studi di Parma, Italy

Michel Fayol
LEAD/CNRS, Université de Bourgogne, France

Emilia Ferreiro
Centro de Investigacion y de Estudios Avanzados, I.P.N., México, D.F.

Uta Frith
Medical Research Council, U.K.

Hartmut Günther
Universität zu Köln, Germany

Jean Hebràrd
Institut Nationale de Recherche Pédagogique, France

Peter Koch
Tubingen Universität, Germany

Georges Lüdi
University of Basel, Switzerland

Serge Mouchon
Université René Descartes, France

Clotilde Pontecorvo
Università di Roma "La Sapienza", Italy

David Olson
University of Toronto, Canada

Ana Teberosky
Universitat de Barcelona, Spain

Liliana Tolchinsky
Universitat de Barcelona, Spain

Colette Sirat
Centre National de la Recherche Scientifique, France

Ludo Verhoeven
University of Nijmegen, The Netherlands

Heinz Wimmer
University Salzburg, Austria

Acknowledgments

This book is the product of a scientific activity that has been supported by the European Science Foundation.

I want to express my personal thanks to ESF and particularly to Dr. Gérard Darmon who greatly helped my work during both the Network activities and the complex preparation of this book.

Particular thanks to Ph.Dr. Alessandra Fasulo, who very cleverly prepared the manuscript for final reproduction, and composed the general bibliography and the analytic index, and to Dr.Hugo Bowles who revised the texts many times with expertise and informed participation.

Rome, 30 July 1997

Table of Contents

Clotilde Pontecorvo
Studying writing and writing acquisition today
A multidisciplinary view   xv
1. *Writing as a scientific field*
2. *Writing versus reading*
3. *Broadening our view of writing*
4. *A literate issue: the complex relationships between literacy and orality*
5. *The need for a multidisciplinary approach to literacy sciences*
6. *Learning a written language, learning a writing system*
8. *Different sociocultural and sociolinguistic contexts of writing.*
9. *The articulation of this book*

Part I Writing and literacy acquisition:
Links between linguistics and psycholinguistics   1

David R. Olson
On the relations between speech and writing   3
1. *Language and writing*
2. *Writing and the discovery of linguistic form*
3. *Children's discovery of "words"*
4. *Writing and knowledge about language*
5. *Writing and cognition*

Claire Blanche-Benveniste
The Unit of Written and Oral Language   21
1. *Unit definition in graphic form.*
2. *The word*
   2.1. *A first definition: the word is an independent item*
   2.2. *The word is an item which may be divided*
   2.3. *The notion of "divisible" differs for each language*
   2.4. *The disequilibrium between the word in the utterance and the word in the system*
   2.5. *The graphic word and the "morpheme" of the linguists*
   2.6 *From the point of view of meaning: one or several words?*
   2.7. *Some principles in writing representations*
   2.8. *"Attached" or "divided" words. Scriptio continua.*
   2.9. *The "real" language words*
3. *Conclusion*

Emilia Ferreiro
The Word Out of (Conceptual) Context   47
   1. Preliminaries
   2. The consequences of the lack of theorization about writing
      for psycholinguistic research.
   3. The tasks attributed to writing.
   4. Historical evolution
   5. Psycholinguistic development: oral and written language
   6. The development of the notion of word: Research about oral language
      or written language?
   7. Final remarks

Ruth A. Berman
Preschool Knowledge of Language: What Five year olds
Know about Language Structure and Language Use   61
   1. Introduction
   2. Form-function relations in language development
   3. The developmental history of linguistic forms
      3.1. Accusatives, Resultative Participles, and Passives
      3.2. Resultative Participles versus Denominal Adjectives
      3.3 Nominalized Forms
      3.4. Null Subjects and Topic Elision
      3.5. Connectivity and Narrative Structure
   4. Conclusions

Liliana Tolchinsky, Ana Teberosky
Explicit Word Segmentation and Writing in Hebrew and Spanish   77
   1. Differences and similarities between Hebrew and Spanish
   2. Development of word segmentation
   3. Development of word writing
   4. Development of word-writing in Hebrew and Spanish
   5. Development of Word Segmentation in Hebrew and Spanish
   6. Word writing and word segmentation in Hebrew and Spanish

PART II. Writing and reading in time and culture   99

Colette Sirat
Orality/Literacy, Languages and Alphabets.
Examples from Jewish Cultures   101
   1. The first period
   2. New developments after the 2nd century BCE
   3. The Islamic period: expansion of literacy and orality
   4. Christian Europe (1000-1250)
   5. The Renaissance and Modern Times

6. *Conclusion*

Françoise Desbordes
The Notion of Orthography. A Latin Inheritance   117
1. The general framework
2. The Greek antecedents
3. The Latin orthographers and their programme
4. Problems: the questionable units
5. Problems: the futility of phonetic transcription
6. Problems: phonetics and phonology
7. Resistance to the idea of a norm
8. From representation to reproduction

Hartmut Günther
Aspects of a History of Written Language Processing.
Examples from the Roman world and the early Middle Ages   129
1. Background
2. Aspects of the history of the book
2.1. Material
2.2. The organisation of the page
3. Aspects of a history of the writing process
3.1. Writing in the Roman world
3.2. The Middle Ages
3.3 Serial organisation: The ABC
  4. Aspects of a history of the reading process
    4.1. Reading in the Roman world
    4.2. The Middle Ages
5. Conclusions and perspectives
5.1. A tentative summary
5.2. Potential and use
5.3. Qui fecit?

Peter Koch
Orality In Literate Cultures   149
  1. Linguistic medium, linguistic conception, and cultural orality/literacy
  2. Oral culture within literate cultures
  3. Phonic distance within literate cultures
  4. Graphic immediacy within literate cultures
  5. Immediacy in relation to distance within literate cultures
  6. Conclusion

Jean Hébrard
The Graphic Space of the School Exercise Books in France
in the 19th-20th century   173

1. Varieties of exercise
2. Copying
3. Making lists and tables
4. Keeping daily records
5. The intellectual function of the graphic exercise

**PART III Written language competence in monolingual
and bilingual contexts** 191

Michel Fayol, Serge Mouchon
**Production and Comprehension of Connectives in the Written
Modality. A Study of Written French** 193
1. Producing connectives in written texts
2. Comprehending connectives when reading texts
6. Concluding remarks

Georges Lüdi
Towards a Better Understanding of Biliteracy. 206
1. What is biliteracy ?
2. Contexts of biliteracy
3. Aspects of individual biliteracy
4. Research needs

Ludo Verhoeven
Acquisition of Literacy by Immigrant Children 219
1. Early bilingualism and emergent literacy
   1.1. Acquisition of bilingual proficiency
   1.2. Bilingual proficiency and metalinguistic awareness
   1.3. Emergent literacy in a bilingual context
   1.4. Role of the environment
2. Learning to read in a second language
   2.1. Processual characteristics
   2.2. Individual variation
   2.3. Causes of class repeating
   2.4. Instructional alternatives
3. Bilingualism and school success
   3.1. Attaining functional biliteracy
   3.2. Bilingual proficiency and school progress
   3.3. Transfer in bilingual development
4. Final remarks

**PART IV Writing systems, brain structures and languages:
a neurolinguistic view** 241

Giuseppe Cossu
Domain-Specificity and Fractionability of Neuropsychological Processes in Literacy Acquisition 243
1. Introduction
2. Historical digression and clinical paradoxes
3. The "extrinsic" factors
4. External boundaries
    4.1. Motor impairment and reading
    4.2. Mental retardation and reading
    4.3. Outstanding intelligence and reading
    4.4. Phoneme awareness and reading
5. A fractionable edifice
6. A domain-specific architecture
7. Conclusions

Heinz Wimmer, Uta Frith
Reading Difficulties among English and German Children. Same Cause - Different Manifestation 259
1. What is dyslexia?
2. German orthography and reading instruction
3. The acquisition of phonological coding in young German and English readers
    3.1. German-English differences in word and nonword reading
    3.2. Conclusions about normal acquisition
4. Phonological coding in German and English dyslexic children
    4.1. Differences in reading strategies
    4.2. Conclusions about dyslexia
5. Evidence for a specific speed deficit in phonological coding among German dyslexic children.
6. Conclusions from German-English comparisons

Brian Butterworth
Neural Organisation and Writing Systems 273

Bibliographic references 293

Analytic index 332

Introduction

Studying writing and writing acquisition today
A multidisciplinary view

Clotilde Pontecorvo

1. Writing as a scientific field

Writing is a specific human activity which can be examined from a number of perspectives. At least two main meanings are associated with it:
  i) writing as the process of tracing symbols on a material surface (papyrus, parchment, wax tablet or paper);
  ii) writing as the process of producing written, permanent, texts.

These two areas have different histories and cultural backgrounds: for instance, the history or histories of the main writing systems are partially independent of the histories of written languages and their genres (prototypical examples of independence are narrative and poetry), although there are genres who develop only if there is a writing system (such as the epistolar one). Similarly the relationship between orality and writing is different when studied in cultures in which oral discussion is more highly valued than writing (such as the Jewish one), or for modern types of orality, such as radio or TV broadcasts, which have some of the organized and systematic features usually thought to be bound to written performance and can be considered forms of "secondary orality" (Ong 1982).

When the psychological and educational aspects of the problems are taken into account, the picture becomes even more complex. The introduction of the word *literacy* - and its present relevance in any discussion about writing and reading (Verhoeven, 1994; Pontecorvo, Orsolini, Resnick and Burge, 1996) - introduces the question of how people, culture, and children specifically learn to use reading and writing in their everyday life and become literate in each of the many meanings of the word. Indeed becoming literate does not only include the technical coding and decoding skills that allow children and adults to use a system of writing successfully, but also the grammatical, discursive, and strategic competences which are the basis of any written text.

From a social point of view the acquisition of a satisfactory mastery of written language is a necessary prerequisite for every work activity, particularly in view of the increasing automation of factories and service industries. Literacy standards have consequently become higher, although the problem of the functional illiteracy of many people, even in developed countries, has not yet been fully resolved (Verhoeven, 1994). However it now seems necessary to go beyond a restricted view of literacy as "learning to decode and transcribe", and take into account that becoming literate requires participating in a complex process of cultural socialization in which a large range of acts of reading and writing have to be regarded as socially positive.

In 1992 the European Science Foundation, aware of the social and scientific relevance of such problems, launched the Network on "Written language and literacy" with a group of scholars who were conscious of the need to explore the cultural and psychological processes involved in the development, acquisition and use of written language from a wide range of disciplines, including the anthropology of writing, the history of culture and of the diffusion and teaching of writing in modern Europe.

Four main perspectives were identified in current research:

1. Historical and socio-cultural approaches to writing systems and written practices contribute to an understanding of the role of social and historical factors in societies and educational institutions.

2. Descriptive linguistic studies are related to the identification of linguistic aspects tandare sensitive to differences and similarities of linguistic structures in oral and written texts.

3. Developmental psycholinguistic research, concerning children's construction of different writing systems and of written language, has been strongly influenced by theories on the psychogenesis and sociogenesis of written language.

4. Studies from a cognitive psychology perspective are focused on the study of cognitive processing involved in the acts of reading and writing, and are aimed at identifying different aspects of the process.

The Network organized a series of three Workshops. At each of them about 20 scholars, mainly European, were actively involved as presenters and/or discussants. The three Workshops were prepared by the Coordinating Committee[1]

---

[1] The Coordinating Committee, chaired by me, was made up of Claire Blanche-Benveniste, Emilia Ferreiro, Uta Frith, Hartmut Günther, Georges Lüdi, Ana Teberosky and Ludo Verhoeven.

which identified the more interesting research trends and took the trouble of organizing the timetable. All papers were circulated in advance, and critically discussed during the workshops. The series of papers and the comments were published after the workshops in three books of Proceedings, which were published by the ESF immediately afterwards and circulated among the researchers of the field[2].

The volume which is presented here is a (necessary) selection of what was presented and discussed in the workshops but does not contain the interesting and lively discussions that were held in the workshops and which are available in the proceedings together with the discussant's papers. Not all the papers presented in the workshops could be included in this volume but all the participants contributed actively to the collective work and I would like to thank here all of those who, for various resasons, do not appear in this book as authors[3].

The main topics of the three workshops and of the relative workshops were the following.

The first proceedings were devoted to "Orality and Literacy: Concepts, methods and data" and edited by C. Pontecorvo and C. Blanche-Benveniste. The essential points that were dealt with concerned the history of the writing systems, the ways in which orality and literacy have been historically linked, the definitions of units and structures in oral and written languages, and the social practices of orality and literacy in diverse cultural contexts. The second proceedings, edited by A.Teberosky and L. Verhoeven, were devoted to "Understanding early literacy in a developmental and cross-linguistic approach" and aimed at clarifying how children acquire their writing strategies, through new insights into the stages of early literacy development. Starting from an interdisciplinary and cross-linguistic approach, the underlying principles in early reading and writing behaviour in children were explored, by comparing oral and written language acquisition, by analyzing processes of emergent reading and writing, metacognition and literacy development, and the acquisition of coherence and cohesion in text. The third proceedings, edited by U. Frith, G. Ludi, M. Egli and C.A. Zuber and devoted to "Contexts of literacy", focused on the influence of environmental factors on children's understanding and production

---

[2] The books with the proceedings can be requested to the European Science Foundation, 1, Quay Lézay- Marnésia, Strasbourg, 67000 France. (Fax: xx33388- 370532).

[3] Besides the authors of the chapters of this book, the other participants in the workshops were: Michael T. Clanchy, Marie Clay, Jean Derive, Mirjam Egli, Nick Ellis, Albertine Gaur, Antonio Gibelli, Annelies Hacky-Buchofer, Bente Hagtvet, .Roy Harris, Amr Helmy Ibrahim, Jean-Pierre Jaffré, Luciano Mecacci, Marina Pascucci Formisano, Marie-José Reichler-Béguelin, Laurence Rieben, Robert Serpell, Raffaele Simone, Traute Taeschner.

of written language, on literate practices in monolingual and plurilingual situations, on the features of the social, family and school literacy contexts, and also on the contributions of neurolinguistic studies for a better theoretical understanding of the normal psychological processes involved in literacy. As will emerge in this chapter, the general assumptions behind the presentations and discussions in the workshops have been transferred as far as possible in the different chapters of this volume, in which, for practical reasons, only a limited amount of authors could be included.

2. Writing versus reading

In the everyday practice of a literate person, it is almost impossible to separate the skills of writing from those of reading. In a sense, if it is theoretically possible to read without writing, it is almost impossible to write without reading. Very young children do it when they begin to practice their symbolic representational skills in early writing development, but even at this very early age they draw considerable feedback from writing, when asked to "read" what they have written. For instance, if they are following the "principle of the minimum quantity" (Ferreiro and Teberosky, 1979) and have written a monosyllabic word, they might decide to delete some written marks after "reading" them because there are "too many to be read". So even with preliterate children reading accompanies and often affects writing.

Although I am aware of this strong interconnection, the aim of this book is to give a particular emphasis to writing: to both the phylogenesis and ontogenesis of writing development; to the history of writing intertwined with that of its material supports; to the way in which multilingual groups have practiced and continue to practice writing; to the difficulties of writing related to the different writing systems.

Research trends on writing and writing acquisition have achieved a degree of maturity that could only be guessed at a few years ago and now the interdisciplinary perspectives are beginning to be developed.

As is well known, psychological research on writing is also recent, even more recent than research on reading. The Ulric Neisser's 1967 book on "Cognitive Psychology" said very little about reading and nothing at all about writing, as if the latter did not involve cognitive processes at all! It was only in the Eighties that early models about the writing process (Hayes & Flower, 1980), the development of early writing (Ferreiro & Teberosky, 1979 [1982]), and the educational study of writing (Bereiter and Scardamalia, 1982) were independently developed. Writing slowly became a matter for psychological research and not simply a problem of teaching methods.

There are two possible explanations for this. One is the fact that learning to read is particularly difficult and complex in a language such as English and the research field has been dominated until now by the perspective of English speaking cultures and scholars. [4]Reading models, particularly the doua route model, and the consequences that can be drawn from these models for evaluating types of acquired or developmental dyslexia, have been constructed out of features and peculiarities of the English language (as Frith and Wimmer underline in their chapter comparing German and English dyslexic and normal reading children).

The second explanation is more sociocultural and not language-dependent. Throughout the history of European literacy, the reading of certain types of texts, namely religious ones, was required - at least since the Reform movement - of all men (and only subsequently of all women), whereas writing is a more modern requirement and was for a long time restricted only to particular professional groups (public employees, important merchants, bankers, priests: see Petrucci, 1995). This interesting possibility is an illustration of the longterm consequences of social values and events even for the development of apparently "neutral" human endeavours.

3. Broadening our view of writing

The multidisciplinary approach to writing concerns many levels of relationship between disciplines and it is also one of the distinctive features of this collection. Some relations are more obvious, others are quite unexpected.

As regards the more obvious ones, let us consider the interface between linguistic and psycholinguistic research. Whereas it seems to be generally accepted that psycholinguistic research needs to refer to a theoretical linguistic background, it is less obvious that the reverse is true, namely that the psycholinguistic results on writing and written language development affects the linguistic domain, as is the case of Claire Blanche-Benveniste's study (this volume) of the units of written and oral language. Ferreiro (this volume) also addresses this question directly.

---

[4] The name of the largest educational association for promoting literacy is the International Reading Association.

Here we touch upon a very delicate point, because the openly declared object of the psycholinguistic research referred to in most of the studies reported in this volume is written language.

Modern linguistics (starting from De Saussure, too often somewhat abusively kinked to this position, see Reichler-Beguin, 1994) has declared (and confirmed many times also by scholars such as Bloomfield and others) that the only language to be studied was oral language, because written language was considered to be a mere trascription of the oral and not deserving of specific consideration by scholars. At the same time, the main linguistic phenomena being studied were for a long time, and in many cases still are, examples of written language only. As Ferreiro argues convincingly in her chapter, although most psycholinguistic research gave little explicit attention to written language, and often declared its intention to study language which was meant to be oral, many psycholinguistic studies still surreptitiously (and perhaps unconsciously) give subjects reading tasks which imply that the subject has to be at least a literate person!

This kind of "double bind" is now starting to be clarified. It involves the shared recognition that a language which is or which can be written is largely different from an oral one (Halliday, 1990), even when taking into account in the largest range of uses of both kinds, as done accurately in some recent literature (reported in the chapter of Koch, this volume).

At this point - and this is one of the pivots of the present book - the distinction between a linguistics of the different forms of oral language and a linguistics of the different forms of written language must reflect a corresponding distinction between a psycholinguistics of oral forms and a psycholinguistics of written forms. The latter distinction is automatic when psycholinguists study the language development of very young and preliterate children, but easily disap pears when the subjects of the research are older children or adults who can *also* read and write.

In other words the issue at stake here is the possible changes that affect the representation of language while the subjects are passing - as native speakers - from a purely oral representation of language to a written one. It begins to be ascertained that lexical representations of young and preliterate children are not identical to those of literate adults. This question is addressed by the studies of Blanche-Benveniste (1994) and of Ferreiro and Pontecorvo (1996), which involve yhe issue about how it is possible to define the units of language and the concept of "word". There is clearly an identification of what an oral word is (even i n young children: Karmiloff-Smith *et al.* 1996) but the representation is not the same when children (and adults) begin to write. The difficulties in over-using the apostrophe shown by poor writers and young children in Italian and

French suggests that "they adopted a pure graphemic procedure, having no equivalence with the parsing of the spoken language" (Blanche-Benveniste, 1994, p. 68). Literacy gives access to a representation of one's language that is largely different from the representation induced by oral practice alone. There is an important and well argued plea, supported by the Prague linguist Vachek (1945 [1989]), against the "transcription view" of writing, which is also present in the chapter of Olson who succeeds in showing, amongst other things, how the structures of languages can be discovered and understood by users through the use of diverse writing systems.

4. A literate issue: the complex relationships between literacy and orality

Before going more deeply into the issue of the need for an interdisciplinary study of literacy, let us consider another old and relevant question concerning the complex relationships that individuals and cultures establish between "their" orality, their oral practices, and their written texts and practices (which Koch , this volume, tries to systematize in general terms). If we consider Plato's discussion in the *Phaedro* of the myth of the Egyptian god Theut (said to have invented writing) about the risk of losing the main cognitive effect of an oral culture, namely a particularly effect memory, one might say that there is a very early symbolic representation of the effects that the relationships between orality and writing can have on the human mind, some 2400 years before cognitive and cross-cultural psychology raised the question!

The sharp opposition between orality and literacy which some anthropologists (such as Goody, 1977), philosophers (Havelock, 1961) and psychologists (Bruner, 1966; Olson, 1977) have proposed and defended was perhaps a necessary transition towards the current more articulated conception which tries to understand the range of relationships between orality and literacy, without presupposing the "great divide" (criticized by Brian Street, 1984).

A peculiar example of the complex relationships between oral and written language is discussed by Sirat (this volume). With reference to the Jewish tradition, particularly during the Middle Ages, she shows how it became accepted that the two Torah - the oral and the written one - both contributed to the existence of a very literate type of orality, characterized by academia discussion and a controlled use of an argumentative oral tradition, which largely accepted stories and quotations. According to the Jewish tradition, the oral Torah had genetic priority but needed to be written down in order to constitute a common point of reference for the infinite chain of future interpretations by the subsequent oral tradition. This subsequent oral traduction was also fixed in writing in various ways, such as the Ghemarà, Talmud, or Midrash, and was kept alive and adaptable by further hermeneutic and creative work by the rabbis which always began with oral discussion. Clearly the orality to which Sirat is referring in her chapter is not the oral language of everyday life and conversation. It is the orality of the cultivated discussion and dispute. Within this kind of orality, however, the arguments were often vivid and in order to be remembered they included not only laws, precepts and internal chaining but also examples, images of scenes of human life, narratives and anedoctes. In other words, typical tools of orality were put at the service of a rational mode of thinking. There is here only a technical - and not conceptual - difference between these types of writing and speaking. It is the same difference that Ochs & Taylor (1992) claim for the dinner table conversations of US middle class families. There, collaborative storytelling becomes a theory-building practice in which facts, statements, and events are evaluated and checked collectively: a way to be orally socialized to the requirements of scholastic and scientific writing.

The orality-literacy distinction can only arise in a culture in which writing is developed. It is one of the first and recurring problems of a literate culture, which needs to distinguish itself from the non written (and not writable) world. In other words there exists a symbolic divide which is continuously being reasserted for reasons of identity and from the point of view of the written universe of literacy.

5. The need for a multidisciplinary approach to literacy sciences

The need for a real multidisciplinary approach to the study of writing and literacy has to be discussed further. First, one needs to clarify why the convergence of different disciplines is even more necessary for writing than for reading. Both phenomena require (at least) a background of linguistics, psycholinguistics, neuropsychology, cognitive anthropology of literacy practices, history and sociology of literate and unliterate social practices. Yet writing has more possibilities than reading. Its largely different products - pictures, tablets, tomb inscriptions, tokens, scrolls and any other support - are visible, long lasting, and have made a history of the cultural tools and practices of writing (such as Gunther, Desbordes, and Olson's contribution to this volume) an easier task. They need to be studied by archeologists, art historians, scholars of the systems of writing and paleographers. Historians of social, popular and school literacy practices have a whole range of artifacts when they study writing, as is shown in Hébrard's (this volume) fascinating reconstruction of the use of graphic layout in the exercise books of French children over the last two centuries.

This kind of multidisciplinary exchange should not be a one way process. It is not only the psychology or the pedagogy of writing that need to be investigated by historians or archeologists. The psycholinguistics of written language development may also be helpful to the historical reconstruction of aspects of writing.

An example of this kind of mutual assistance is the recent large-scale descriptive study of the development of writing in primary school children in the re-writing of Little Red Riding Hood in three Romance languages (Ferreiro, Pontecorvo, Moreira, Garcia-Hidalgo, 1996a, 1996b, and 1996c). This study raises important issues for the psycholinguistics of oral language as concern methodology and transcription conventions. Its results in the area of segmentation development reveal important regularities in children's rules in segmenting words in diverse languages. The way children segment parts of their written texts can be viewed also as possible signs of an evolution in their lexical representation.

This study makes a systematic use of the history of written language and writing. On the other hand understanding children's elaboration of ideographic aspects of mainly alphabetic systems of writing (such as Italian, Portuguese, and Spanish) can have a feedback effect on some historical hypotheses.

This kind of reciprocity is particularly evident in punctuation, an important textual device that has a recent history in Western culture. Indeed, in order to interpret the unique trends of children's puncuation of a narrative text, Ferreiro (1996) largely used insights from recent historical studies (particularly the monumental study by Parkes, 1992). Now that such a large corpus of children's written texts in different languages and cultures has been analyzed and is available for further research, results from punctuation development research (for instance, developmentally speaking punctuation goes from the periphery towards the center fo a text) might be useful for further historical investigation (Petrucci, 1996), particularly for the interpretation of so-called popular writings (Gibelli, 1994) inwhich punctuation is usually scarce and is considered to be random.

In viewing the study of writing and literacy as a multidisciplinary endeavour, I am not assuming that the aim of the ESF Network I chaired was to propose a new transdisciplinary domain. But after four years of such fruitful exchanges with scholars of widely differing perspectives, I now think that a new multidisciplinary focus (or even a transdisciplinary one) should be defined. This might lead to the definition of a new field (since there is no existing terminology for this kind of research a good name for it could be "literacy sciences") within which anthropologists, historians, archeologists, paleographers, linguists, psycholinguists, neuropsychologists, educationalists and others could compare their results and define new research hypotheses.

This proposal is not aimed at eliminating domain specificity but at underlining the fact that beneath this topic there is a complex phenomenon. It is this complexity that requires that each expert of the field (even the neurolinguist or the paleographer) is aware of the scientific results from other disciplines that study the phenomenon of writing and literacy from different perspectives. The "new" history of writing systems (as proposed by Michailowsky (1994) or Sampson (1985), both used by Ferreiro), archeological investigations (e.g. Schmandt-Besserat, 1992, used by Olson), or even the psychogenesis of writing in its more recent discoveries and theorizations (discussed by Cossu and Blanche-Benveniste in their chapters) are examples of these perspectives. The new ethnographic approach can also be a powerful means to struggle against persisting ethnocentric positions, still found in the common sense of some educationalists, who believe that the Western alphabetic writing systems are the maximum of possible cultural progress.

In conclusion, writing and literacy are interdisciplinary objects requiring not only the contribution of different perspectives, but also the interdisciplinary use of critical texts and results from related disciplines. In other words the research questions in each disciplinary domain should still be carried out by using the tools and the methodologies of each discipline . But hypotheses are likely to become more precise and better grounded when defined within the wider perspective of literacy sciences.

6. Learning a written language, learning a writing system

Within the above epistemological framework I would now like to highlight three important aspects of writing research:
a) the distinction and the connection between systems of writing and written language, both from the point of view of child and adult acquisition and of the writer's competence, in which the interaction between linguistic and writing system's differences produces an intereresting variety in acquisition and competence;
b) the affordances of the socio-cultural and socio-historical contexts and tools in suggesting or imposing aims, values and practices for writing of different periods, cultures and places;
c) the more specific role of family and school settings in establishing practices for learning to write, organizing spaces and times, establishing objectives for good writing, and so on.

At the beginnning of this chapter, I mentioned the distinction and the interlinking between systems of writing and written language. It goes without saying that these are two different aspects of a human cultural endeavour. On the one hand, writing means composing a text which is autonomous, permanent and can be read independently of an extratextual context; on the other side, writing means using a writing system, transcribing any possible text, putting permanent marks on a surface.

Writing can today be regarded as being made up of both aspects at the same time, because cases of composition without transcription are either rare, - for example, the traditional manager who still dictates official letters directly to a secretary or to a dictaphone - or extreme, - for example, the illiterate or poorly literate people in less developed countries who are compelled to dictate their letters rto a scribe.

Although I think that it is very important to let young children first negotiate orally and dictate their stories and their first texts to an adult or a peer scribe in order to facilitate their textual production (as has been observed in a number of studies: see Teberosky, 1988; Pontecorvo & Zucchermaglio, 1989; Pontecorvo & Orsolini, 1996; Morani & Pontecorvo, 1995), the distinction between producing a written language and using a writing system cannot be maintained in absolute terms. It is a distinction that is needed only to clarify that not all written texts are in a typically written style - the "sunday language", as Blanche-Benveniste (1982) said - while many orally produced texts (such as lectures, parliamentary contributions, broadcasting pieces) are very close to writing, a matter that Koch discusses in this volume with great clarity.

The above quoted research on LRRH (see Ferreiro, Pontecorvo, Moreira, Garcìa Hidalgo, 1996a, 1996b, 1996c) has shown that when children can write alphabetically,having "broken the code" (Mattingly, 1972; Chall, 1979), but not orthographically - as is the case at the beginning of primary school for most languages - they can be motivated to produce a written text, such as the rewriting of LRRH. Compared to pre-literate and, in the case of Western writing systems, pre-phonographic children, they cope with the task of producing a coherent text by using the conventions of the system of writing of the language in their own ways: for instance, they use capital letters, segmentation, blank spaces, punctuation, although not conventionally The "errors" of children's early text lay-out (Ferreiro & Pontecorvo, 1996) are not random, but give hints as to how children process a text that is to be written and show the possible interactions between unique features of languages and of writing systems.

In other words, writing a text is always carried out within the constraints and the affordances of an overall system of writing, which, in an aphabetic system, is much more than simply understanding and mastering the phoneme-grapheme correspondence. This is particularly evident when one tries to understand why early literate children "need" to use a wide range of awkward *repetitions* (Ferreiro & Moreira, 1996). These latter can have different uses and values but children generally feel it necessary to use them in writing, not because they are still part of an oral genre but rather to give to their texts some of the features of a written text though perhaps not yet of a written language. For instance, they use repetitions to distinguish effectively Quoted Speech from Narrative and, in reported speech, to distinguish the speech itself, the person to whom the speech is addressed and sometimes the speech function ('order', 'recommendation', etc.). It seems as if children use unusual (even unelegant) devices to comply with presumed rules of written text.

It is now evident - from this as well as other studies - that after children have begin to write in a syllabic or in a syllabic-alphabetic way (Ferreiro and Vernon 1995; Pontecorvo & Zuccermaglio, 1990), they produce a text in a *top-down* way, although sometime being very aware of a processing at the level of grapheme and letter graphic form. They do not seem to compose texts by linking words together in sentences and sentences in paragraphs. They do not seem to think to the possibility of dividing the activity into phases recommended by psychologists (such as planning, transcribing and revising) and without proceeding piece by piece[5]. But they seem to be clearly aware of the feature of different genres or registers of written texts, even when they are at the begininng of their writing development and show the emergence of peculiar types of iconicity[6].

7. Cultural artifacts and tools in writing

I consider the mostly ideographic conventions - shared or idyosincratic - of a system of writing as interacting with the evolving representation of what written language is at the aim of constructing a coherent text (see Fayol this volume for a clear definition), because both conventions are constraining and enabling

---

[5] Kintsch (1982) says that a novice writer does altogether what the expert does "in pieces". He refers to the fact that the novice writer (who may or may not be a child) does not divide the task of writing into planning, transcribing and revising. The same can be said to apply to (hypothetical) text composition: the molecular view, which starts from words and goes on to sentences, periods, paragraphs and texts, is not the writing itinerary of the child, except in particular conditions of "playing with words" (awich can now be done with computer software: see Pontecorvo, 1993).

[6] Looking at the features of iconicity in early writings of 4 and 5 years old children, have discovered that they can write a list, a nursery rhyme, a sentence and a story in different graphical ways (Pontecorvo, 1994).

tools at the same time. Historically, the specific ways in which writing and reading were practiced in different times and places determined what was meant by "writing", as Günther (this volume) describes clearly. For example, the idea of an original version of a given text was a late Western acquisition and in ancient times text variants were numerous and accepted (Cerquiglini, 1989). Morevoer, the passage from the scroll to the volume led to drastic changes in the process of composing a book, such as those introduced by Hugo of Saint Victor (Illich, 1993). Viceversa, these changes produced slower but important alterations in the way in which books or pieces of writing were edited.

The history of reading offers extremely interesting materials and suggestions also for writing[7]. There are observations that touch on the relationships between writing and reading; in Roman times for example the two learning activities were neatly separated in time and in people (Cavallo, 1995). Other interesting questions concern the relationships between the way in which text were written and read. For a long time, texts were not segmented in words and not really puncuated (Parkes, 1992): and thus the only possible reading was aloud (Saenger, 1995). However when authors such as Thomas Aquinas, Roger Bacon or William Ockham changed from dictating texts to silent composition using the simpler and less musical style of the scholastic Latin, texts were no longer addressed to a listener but to a reader and reading became more and more an "intimate" apprehension. This not only produced important changes in the way in which texts were composed and divided up into parts, chapters, paragraphs, but also a new kind of textual distribution of punctuation, capital letters, notes and other devices (as Gunther stresses). It also produced a fast development of vulgar writings and a really interesting effect from the psychological point of view, which considers the strict relationships between contents, forms and practices of writing and reading. a new and large production of books expressing devotion, irony, erotism, dissentment, which slowly brought European culture even towards Church reform movements. The suggestive thesis of Saenger (1995) is that the intimacy offered by silent private reading encouraged the expression of personal and free thinking.

A new, big change is now occurring before our eyes. Until now the consequences of the growing use of the word-processor for writing and reading, both in educational and professional settings, has not been entirely predictable. As has already been shown by many studies (Salomon, 1993; Pontecorvo & Paoletti, 1991) the use of the word-processor modifies ways of acquiring literacy of practicing writing for children and adults.

---

[7] The recent book "Storia della lettura (History of reading)" edited by G.Cavallo and R.Chartier (published by Laterza and Editions du Seuil, 1995) offers an outstanding collection of papers on this topic.

As regards acquisition, it seems that the use of a keyboard and the equivalence that a child can establish between different forms of the same letter can facilitate the attainment of the correspondence between the phonological value and the symbolic-graphic appearance of a letter. This correspondence is always the effect of a process of abstraction, because first the learner has to identify the "same" phonetic value in largely variable sound implementations and second the computer keyboard facilitates the other facet of abstraction: the recognition of the same grapheme in largely different instantiations.

Children who use a word-processor in school are also more willing to revise and even completely change their texts (Paoletti & Pontecorvo, 1993); they produce much longer narratives, and they enjoy writing and editing activities more (Pontecorvo, 1993). But, as Salomon (1993) has convincingly shown, the computer affects the cognitive (and social) processes of writing as long as it is used: it is an effect *with*, not an effect *without*, i.e., children's and adults' writing is changed *when* the word-processor is used, because it enhances certain activities which are impossible or very difficult without it.

The word-processor affects the ways adults write, particularly if they are "professional" writers: novelists, journalists, scientists, academic writers in different fields. Some studies have began to tackle this problem for specific professions (see Grossen & Pichon, 1997 for a review). Heath (1997) has analyzed how the use of new computerized editorial tools is changing the job of producing a journal, facilitating collective exchange and collaborative work. However this does not always makes the writtent text better: Fiormonte (1993) has compared the language of different versions and different revisions of four well-known writers (three Italians and one Catalan), studying what changed in their language and in their writing process when they passed from the type-writer to the word-processor. The results are interesting, although not uniform. Linguistic differences were not always evident , because some of the writers when using the word-processor introduce correctives, resulted to be longer and prolix, or to write too long sentences. It was shown that sometimes there is an evident increase in the texts produced with the word-processor of a repetititve use of stereotyped expressions, such as "by means of", "last but no least" or similar, as if the writing with the word-processor was less controlled and did not facilitate conciseness, which is critical for producing a good piece of writing to be read by others.

Writing with a computer will increasingly become a process of screen reading. The diffusion of every type of linguistic, iconic and sound material through the computer - by means of an interactive Cd-Rom encyclopedia, a hypermedia, a computerized dictionary, an internet page, e-mail or any other material that can be consulted on a computer screen, implies that we and particularly our children and grand-children will increasingly "read a screen" even when composing a new text, which may often be based on what is read on the same screen.

The latter situation will surely introduce considerable changes in both learning and practicing of reading-and-writing which we are unable to foresee at this time. Chartier (1992) has tried to guess what these changes will be, by recalling the transformations from the intensive reading (a few books being thoroughly interpreted during the Middle Ages and the Renaissance) to the extensive form of reading (many books being avidly read, as happened with the "reading revolution" of the XVIII century). The clearest transformation is that now the reader can very easily become a writer, a possible co-author of the text he is reading, i.e. one of the authors of a multiauthored writing, or compose a new text from cut and pasted fragments. Perhaps now is the time to improve our understanding of the effects (and the limits) of this change which will involve texts that are not books, journals or newspapers, and will affect the legal and bibliographical norms.

8. Different sociocultural and sociolinguistic contexts of writing.

It is clear that although writing and reading are typical features of our Western culture from its early Greek and Jewish roots, they are not at all an anthropological invariant without historicity (Cavallo & Chartier, 1995)

It is now largely accepted that, if we compare different societies in time and space, the opposition between literate versus illiterate cultures is not the only finding. Dychotomies are no longer useful and we have become aware of a wide range of possible aims, values and methods that appear in writing practices in different periods, cultures, and places. The heuristic studies of Cole, Gay, Glick and Sharp (1971) and of Scribner and Cole (1981), involving different African groups, have shown how it is possible to find different ways of becoming literate and of using literacy that affects specific (not general) functioning of the persons involved, who may or may not develop particular skills.

Heath (1983), using a refined ethnographic methodology in which also teachers and children were involved as "ethnographers" of their own culture, discovered a range of literacy practices in three US communities which differ in various degrees from what is usually to be found in schools. She has also shown how these practices are linked to religious and ideological committments and are socially valued within the family and the community.

These studies suggest that we should be very cautious towards absolutist positions that see expository writing - in the form of academic writing or essay-text literacy[8] - as the final aim of all literate persons. "Literacy has no effects - indeed no meaning - apart from particular cultural contexts in which it is used, and it has different effects in different contexts.", writes Gee (1990:23).

This statement strengthens the claim at the start of this section. One cannot view writing as a generic ability. There is a large range of writing activities that are possible and are differently appreciated in diverse cultural groups. This requires schools to be much more sensitive to the different genres of writing that exist in everyday life, in the professional world, and that are valued in families and communities.

Indeed much psychological and anthropological research (John-Steiner, Panofsky, Smith, 1994) clearly shows that communities, families, schools and work places (as Scribner in Tobach et al., 1997, has shown), all contribute in different ways to establishing practices of writing and of literacy, organizing spaces and times and fixing aims, functions and achievements. Here the presence of more languages and cultures in the horizon of a developing child is critical. Bilingual and multilingual contexts can request rather diverse literate performances according to the language (and culture) which is involved. This can lead to a syncretic literacy (as in the case of Samoan-Americans group (see Duranti & Ochs, 1997) or to a proper biliteracy, which is the ideal aimed for and mostly achieved by different Swiss groups (Lüdi, this volume). Literacy is more easily achieved only in the host language, particularly when children are born and educated in the immigrant country whereas their parents are poorly educated (Verhoeven, this volume).

Modern bilingual (or multilingual) settings are also illuminated by historical studies. The monolingual man is posited by modern scholars, but in early Greece, medieval Europe and modern Java or Sahel (Illich & Sanders, 1988), most people feel at home in several kinds of discourse in different languages . When Romance vulgar speech coexisted with Latin, a uniform written language (such as Latin) was read or pronounced according to the different languages or accents. Then diglossia was common. Current perspectives on the history of writing systems suggest a complex interaction between writing systems and different languages; scholars now think (Michailowsky, 1994) that even the "discovery" of the Greek alphabet is a by-product of adapting the Phoenician graphic system to a language for which it was not suited; this would explain the many ideographic aspects that characterize every alphabetic system and are particularly important in a system of writing like English (Butterworth, this volume).

---

[8] Academic writing is a particular type of writing which begins to be the object of a specific interest of research, which is far from being the object of this book

STUDYING WRITING ACQUISITION TODAY   xxxi

The critical problem now is how schools and educational interventions can deal with linguistic and cultural diversity. This is often a difficult situation, given that the strong cultural differences are hard for a normal teacher to manage. The plan must be to transform a whole range of differences, including linguistic and cultural ones, to educational advantage (Ferreiro, 1995).

9 The articulation of this book

The four parts and the different chapters of this book cover a large range of topics that I have tried to present in my previous discussion.

The first part of the book presents the intertwining between linguistics and psycholinguistics, as it is discussed by some of the most prominent scholars of the two fields: David Olson, Claire Blanche-Benveniste, Emilia Ferreiro, Ruth Berman, Liliana Tolchinsky and Ana Teberosky.

The second part is devoted to the historical and anthropological factors that have characterized writing and reading across times and cultures and presents outstanding contributions of Colette Sirat, Françoise Desbordes, Hartmut Günther, Jean Hébrard. They range from the history of literate practices, which can be both oral and written, to the history of writing artifacts, systems, and graphical conventions. In every case literacy education is involved.

The third part collects important psychological studies of Michel Fayol, Georges Lüdi and Ludo Verhoeven concerning the acquisition and use of written language features by children and students. Putting together problems of written language acquisition in monolingual and multilingual contexts, is aimed at conveying the idea that bilingual and even multilingual situations will be common in present and future societies, as they were in ancient times.

The last part is devoted to the theoretical issues raised by the study of special populations, such as dyslexic, retarded, or aphasic people when faced with different writing systems. The interesting and updated neurolinguistic views of Giuseppe Cossu, Heinz Wimmer, Uta Frith, and Brian Butterworth show how much the study of special behaviors can give light to the normal (but complex) functioning of reading as decoding words and of writing as transcribing.

PART I

Writing and literacy acquisition:
Links between linguistics and psycholinguistics

PART I

Writing and literary expression:
Literature between linguistics and popular culture

On the relations between speech and writing

David Olson

Written words are the signs of words spoken.
Aristotle

A variety of graphic systems have been developed for preserving and communicating information, among them pictures, charts, graphs, flags, tartans and hallmarks. Linguists usually divide the graphic devices used for preserving information into two classes, those which are linguistically based and those which convey visual information more directly. Thus pictures, totems, hallmarks and cattle brands are seen as visual codes while alphabets, syllabaries and character scripts are seen as writing systems - an ideal writing system is taken to be a fully explicit representation of oral language. Yet strict categories are increasingly suspect as no writing system including the alphabet record exactly and fully what is said and furthermore what is said is never identical with what is meant in any case. Hence the relations between speech - what is said - and writing is far from clear and is increasingly a matter of debate. Yet it can be argued, as I will here, that some writing systems, the Roman English alphabet among them, are distinctive in that they bear a rather direct relation to speech (Chomsky and Halle, 1968). That is, the script corresponds in some way yet to be determined, to the linguistic form of an expression rather than to its content or meaning. Indeed, the relation is sufficiently direct that it has fueled the assumption that ideal writing systems "transcribe" speech.

In this paper I review some of the arguments against the assumption that writing is transcription and in its place propose what I take to be a more promising alternative. Revising the assumption about the relation between speech and writing provides the basis for viewing the history of writing systems in a new way, for acknowledging the diversity of writing systems in different cultures, and most importantly for providing an improved understanding of just what children in alphabetic cultures are learning when they become literate. The acquisition of literacy I shall argue is more a matter of discovering the structure of language than merely recording it.

1. Language and writing

The classical assumption about writing is that it is a representation of speech; an ideal writing system is a fully explicit representation of oral language. As I have examined this issue in some detail elsewhere (Olson, 1994; 1996) I shall only briefly review it here. The classical view developed first by Aristotle and seconded in our century by Saussure and Bloomfield and which continues to be held by such modern writers as De Francis (1989) treats writing as completely derivative from speech. Aristotle wrote in *De interpretatione* (1.46): "Words spoken are symbols or signs of affections or impressions of the soul; written words are the signs of words spoken" (b. 384 BC, 1938, p. 115; but see Gunther, 1994). Saussure (1916/1983) attacked as the "tyranny of writing" the fact that linguistic theory took as its object written language rather than spoken and went on to claim that: "The sole reason for the existence of [writing] is to represent [speech]. The linguistic object is not defined by the combination of the written word and the spoken word: The spoken form alone constitutes the object" (pp. 2324). And Bloomfield identified speech with language and saw writing as "a way of recording language" (Bloomfield, 1933, p. 21). Writing was seen as a simple cipher on speech.

There is much to commend this view. It captures the important fact that some writing systems are linguistically based while others are not, it provides some account of the progress or evolution of scripts in the direction of the alphabet, and it captures one of the important understandings acquired in the process of learning to read namely that writing is about words not things. However, in addition to the ethnocentrism of such a view (Boone and Mignolo, 1994), it suffers from what I take to be a critical flaw. Specifically, it assumes that the inventors of writing systems as well as people learning to use writing *already know* about language and its structure-sentences, words, phonemes, literal meanings and the like and that progress comes from finding unambiguous ways to graphically represent those structures. But as Harris (1986) pointed out transcription theory assumes what it needs to explain, namely, that would-be writers already knew about the properties of speech they were trying to transcribe, as if writers were grammarians rather than talkers. Thus it leaves unanswered how knowledge of those properties of speech which subsequently enter into the transcription can arise.

One can imagine an alternative theory. It may be argued, as Gaur (1984/87) and Harris (1986) have done, that writing systems should be viewed not as attempts to transcribe speech but as attempts at unambiguous representation of information. The relation to speech arises from the attempt at unambiguous "readings." In this way, writing systems, rather than transcribing the known properties of speech, provide new concepts and categories for thinking about speech. The development of a functional way of communicating with visible marks was, simultaneously, a discovery of certain representable structures of speech. Simply, writing is a tool of discovery rather than a device for transcription of the known. Or, to adopt an expression from Vygotsky (1962, p. 101), writing brings speech into consciousness.

2. Writing and the discovery of linguistic form

Evidence bearing on the discovery of linguistic form may be gathered in two quite different domains, one the history and ethnography of writing; the other from children's learning to read and write. Consider first the history and ethnography of writing systems. The most striking fact is that writing systems are not necessarily linguistically based. In North America the Iroquois Confederacy used a series of wampum belts to symbolize treaties pertaining to land claims, the interpretation of which is currently the object of a Canadian Royal Commission on Aboriginal Peoples: the two-row wampum, the best-known treaty belt, symbolizes the conditions under which the Iroquois welcomed white people to Turtle Island (North America). The belt features a canoe for aboriginal people and a ship for non-native people, traveling side by side down the river of life. The two-row wampum is often cited as proof that the Mohawks never surrendered their land and rights to self-government (Globe and Mail, April, 1993).

Similar graphic representational systems were employed in ancient southern Mexico (Smith, 1973; Boone and Mignolo, 1994) and are employed to this day by storytellers in India (Gaur 1987, p. 55) and in Ethiopia (Goody, 1987, p. 9).

Two examples of graphic systems used for recording events are illustrated in Figure 1.

The top half of Figure 1 is from a Canadian Blackfoot Indian "Winter Count" from the 18th Century. Each black box represents a year and the depiction indicates some important fact about that year. Beside each drawing is a "reading" recorded by an Anglican priest. At the bottom of Figure 1 is an analogous year count from the Aztecs of precolonial Central America. The year, later identified as 1490 by an unknown source, is the year of "eleven rabbit" (count the circles) and it is the year there was "a hail storm so severe that the fish in the lake died. In the next year, 12 Reed, locusts descend to devour the crops" (Boone, 1994, p. 6566).

Two points to note about such writing systems. The first is their adequacy as notational systems, the second is how they represent. As to their adequacy, a script is to be judged in terms of the tasks it is to fulfil and there is no ground for thinking that these Mesoamerican scripts failed their purpose. Of course it is possible that an altered script would have allowed texts to take on novel purposes. Gombrich (1974) tells of a Greek city state which called on its artists to carve a picture on the city gates announcing to all that their's was a city which had never been captured. Of course the task was impossible. How do you depict a negation without inventing a merely conventional mark representing a *word* rather than the thing? As to what or how these represent, it is clear that such graphic signs convey information, they represent things and events, they do not represent utterances or statements about those objects and events. That is, the signs do not represent words or sentences; they are not linguistically-based scripts.

Those cultures, like ours, had and continue to have an abundance of such representational systems. Any comprehensive list would include such things as totems identifying tribes and carved on tall poles, hallmarks on silver or pewter, colours and patterns of textiles as in Scottish tartans and Mayan robes, as well as cattle brands, crests, coats of arms, religious symbols and icons and the like. The important feature of such signs is that they represent things or events and in some cases the names for things. As such their manner of symbolizing could be characterized as emblematic rather than linguistic. What they do not represent is a linguistic sign, that is, a sign for a word or morpheme. As some paleographers have been at pains to point out, this fact should not be taken as a necessary limitation but rather a simple fact about such writing systems (Boone and Mignolo, 1994). Yet the implications of the manner of representation may have cultural and cognitive implications, some of which we shall explore.

Most linguistically-based writing systems in the West appear to have evolved from the token system developed for accounting purposes in Mesopotamia beginning in the ninth millennium BC (Schmandt-Besserat, 1992). The system, developed by the ancient Sumerians living in what is now southern Iraq about the time that hunter-gatherer societies were giving way to an agricultural way of life, consisted of a set of clay tokens of distinctive shape and marking, used to keep records of sheep, cattle and other animals and goods of various kinds such as oil and grain. Three of the tokens described by Schmandt-Besserat are shown in Figure 2.

ON THE RELATIONS BETWEEN SPEECH AND WRITING 7

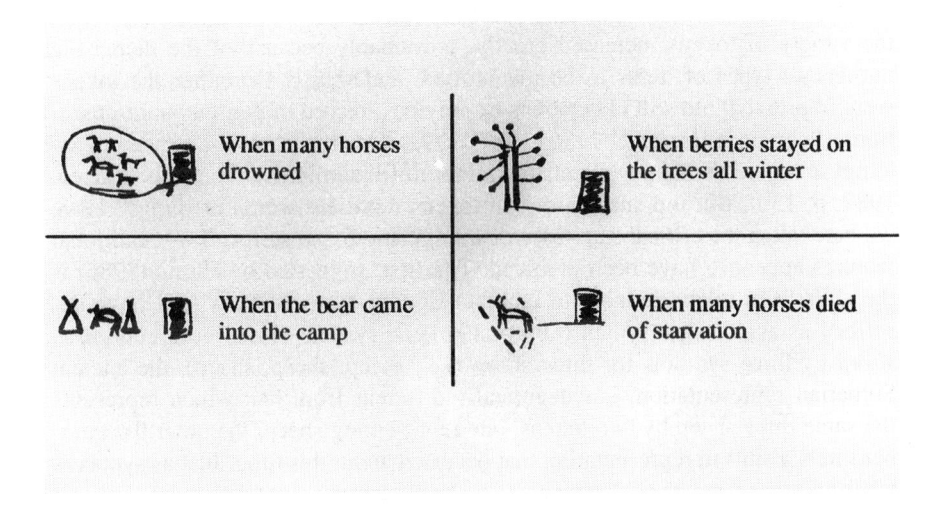

Figure 1a. Blackfoot "Winter Count". Calgary: Glenbow Museum Archive

Figure 1b. Annals for the years 10 House through 2 Rabbit, Codex Mexicanus. Adapted from E. H. Boone and W. Mignolo (eds.) (1994) p.66

About the fourth millennium BC, roughly at the time of the growth of cities, the variety of tokens increased greatly, presumably because of the increasing number of types of items to be inventoried, and shortly thereafter the tokens were impressed into soft clay tablets to provide a record of commercial transactions (Schmandt-Besserat, 1986, 1987, 1992). At this point there was no attempt to record verbal statements but rather to fill administrative needs (Larsen, 1989, p. 130). But did such inscribed tokens represent words or things? Have we here taken the critical step towards a linguistic based script? Two additional features appear to have been involved. The first, suggested by Harris (1986) is the shift from token-iterative to emblem-slotting systems, or what I have described as acquiring a syntax (Olson, 1994). A system which represents *three sheep* by three symbols for three sheep (i.e., sheep, sheep, sheep), the ancient Sumerian representation, is categorically different from one which represents the same three sheep by two tokens, one representing sheep, the other the number three, a shift in representation that occurred about this time. Just as syntax is what makes a language a language, it is the syntax which makes a graphic system "generative" for it permits the combination and recombination of symbols to express a broader range of meanings. And it is the syntax that allows tokens to be taken as word signs. Thus this elementary script has a syntax and could be taken as a model for, that is, as a way of representing the lexical and syntactical properties of a reading of that inscription. Note that on this view, writing did not presuppose an explicit knowledge of words and syntax. Economies of writing led to the scriptal changes which in turn, when read, could be seen as a tokening of the lexical and syntactic properties of that reading. On this view, the concept of a word is the end product of the writing system not a precondition for its development. Writing, historically, brought words into consciousness in the sense that the visible token provides an equivalence class for each occurence of the word.

A second feature is also involved, the so-called phonographic or "rebus" principle, that of using the sound value of a sign representing one object to represent a quite different object - using the sign for "sun", for example, to represent the word "son." Such a substitution can only be made on the basis of the linguistic properties of the sign, in this case the phonetic value and is therefore direct evidence of operating on vocal signs rather than on things. Paleographers (Gaur, 1984/1987; Nissen, 1986) note that by the third millennium BC (2900 BC) the earliest literary texts written in cuneiform appeared and such scripts give clear indications of reflecting the linguistic knowledge of the writer. The sound values for Sumerian signs were detached from their semantic values when Sumerian signs were used to represent a quite different language Akkadian, a Semitic language (Larsen, 1989, p. 131). To represent an Akkadian word such as "a-wi-lu-um," *man*, with Sumerian logographs, the Akkadians simply took the Sumerian graphs which could be read as "a," "wi," "lu," and "um," ignoring the fact that in Sumerian each graph represented a separate word: "a" had meant *water*, "wi" a different word, and so on. Reading Akkadian would then be a matter of pronouncing this series of sounds and the graphs would now be taken to represent syllables of Akkadian rather than the words of Sumerian. Logographs had become syllabics. Note that the argument is not that this use was the product of the application of the phonographic principle of using signs to represent syllables but rather that the new use of old graphs to represent expressions in a new language produced a script in which the constituents *could be seen* as representing syllables. These represented syllables are as much a product of the graphic system as a prerequisite for it. The old script is fitted to the new language as a model is fitted to data; the data are then seen in terms of that model. In this case, the model is that of audible constituents and the flow of speech is heard, perhaps for the first time, as a string of separable, itemizable, syllables. The achievement was less a matter of finding new means for representing phonetic values than a matter of using available means for solving a new problem (see Olson, 1994, Chapter 4).

A similar account has been offered for the transition from consonantal to *alphabetic writing* which occurred, uniquely in the history of the world, when the Semitic script was adapted to represent a non-Semitic language, Greek. The application occurred about 750 BC. Scholars such as Diringer, Gelb and Havelock considered the Greek invention to be the stroke of genius. While not minimizing the significance of the Greek achievement, it is now recognized that the development of the alphabet, like the development of the syllabary, was a rather straightforward consequence of applying a script which was suitable for one language, to a second language for which it was not, namely, of applying a script for a Semitic language in which vocalic differences were relatively insignificant, to the Greek language in which they were highly significant (Harris, 1986; Sampson, 1985; Olson, 1994).

Thus we can dispense with the evolutionary story of writing. Writing systems, rather than being designed to capture or represent deeper levels of structure of language -ideas, words, syllables, phonemes- are pragmatic solutions to communication problems. This is the reason why writing systems do not fall neatly into types-picturewriting, logographs, syllabaries and alphabets, respectively; the classifications are at best rough descriptions and not clearly differentiable types of scripts. Even the claim by DeFrancis (1989) and others that "full writing" systems inevitably record speech is seen by some (Boone, 1994) as too restrictive as important Mesoamerican writing systems function without any attempt to transcribe speech.

Tokens representing jars of oil

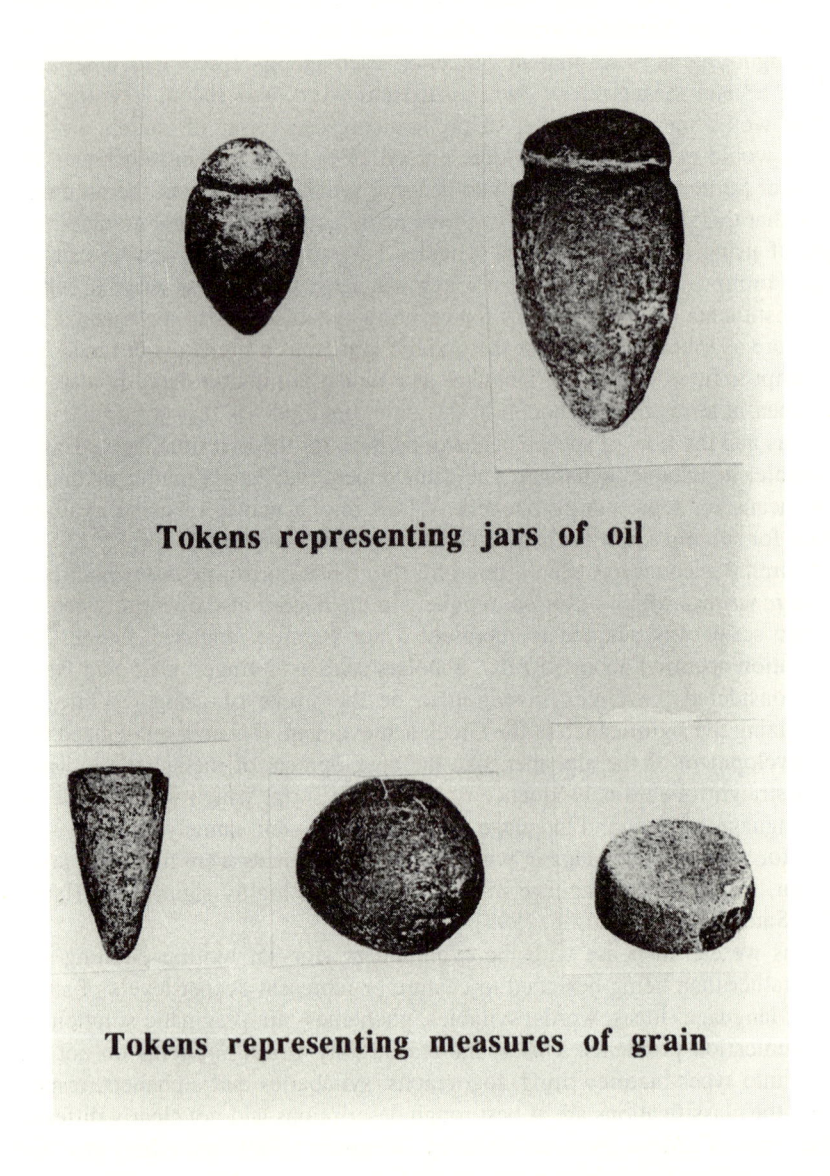

Tokens representing measures of grain

Figure 2. Tokens for record-keeping in Ancient Sumeria. Adapted from D. Schmandt-Besserat, V.I/II, 1992. Reprinted with kind permission of University of Texas Press.

3. Children's discovery of "words"

A story parallel to that of the invention of word or morpheme based scripts can be told about children's discovery of words. It is not obvious to children that writing represents words; they are more aware of the meanings, the story being told or the object referred to. Cute stories abound: On opening a story book and finding no pictures, one 3-year-old cried out: "You can't read that, its only words!" Again, after many rereadings of "Goldilocks", in answer to the question, "Where does it say 'My porridge is too hot'?" the child responded by pointing to the picture of the steaming porridge. Ferreiro and her colleagues (Ferreiro, 1985, 1991; Ferreiro and Teberosky, 1979/1982) showed that non-reading pre-school children entertain a number of hypotheses about what written marks represent. If they are given a pencil and asked to write "cat" they may write a short string of letter-like forms. If then asked to write "three cats" they repeat the same initial string three times, indicating that they take the text to represent objects rather than to represent speech about those objects. In our laboratory we have observed that some pre-reading children when shown the text, *Three little pigs* which is then read to them while the words are pointed out, take each of the written words as standing in a onetoone relation to the things represented. Consequently, if the final word is erased and children are asked, "Now what does it say?" they may reply "Two little pigs." Alternatively, if each of the three words is pointed to in turn and the child is asked what each says, they reply, "One little pig; another little pig; and another little pig." That is, written signs are seen as tokens or emblems rather than as words (Olson, Torrance, and Lee, in preparation; Serra, 1992).

What children know about written words appears to determine what they know or think about spoken words (Downing, 1987; Reid, 1966). Francis (1975) for example, found that children's acquisition of the concepts of *letter*, *word*, and *sentence* were closely tied to their learning to read. Indeed, children first think a word is something you read rather than something you speak. Others, including Piaget (1929), Vygotsky, (1962) and Berthoud-Papandropoulou (1978) have shown that young children conflated orally presented words with things; when asked for a long word they tended to offer a word which represented a long thing and they tend to take words as names, irrevocably connected to objects.

An important achievement in reading, but which tends to pass unnoticed by adults, is that the visual sign has to change in significance for the child; to read is to see that a token is a sign for a word not an emblem for a thing. Children achieve this ordinarily when they learn to read. Thus the conclusion that writing is important in bringing words into consciousness.

It is important to note that the claim is not that words exist only in writing; rather it is that writing is a tool for the discovery of words rather than a device for transcribing them. Writing is, in principle, metarepresentational (Olson, 1991) and hence is a primary means for bringing words into consciousness. Mignolo (1994, p. 258) makes a similar point in arguing that while making graphic signs may be universal, the ways of conceptualizing writing may be culture specific.

A similar story can be told about children's discovery of the phonological properties of speech, a topic much studied under the category of phonological awareness. Learning to read is not so much learning how novel and arbitrary marks represent the already known categories of sound as it is a matter of analyzing the output of the speech mechanism in terms of the categories offered by the script. Schankweiller and Liberman (1972) expressed this relationship in this way:

> In reading an alphabetic language like English, the child must be able to segment the words he knows into the phonemic elements that the alphabetic shapes represent. In order to do this, he needs to be consciously aware of the segmentation of the language into units of phonemic size.... His competence in speech production and speech perception is of no direct use to him here. (p. 309)

Evidence that prereaders lack this segmentation knowledge comes from tasks such as that of counting the "sounds" in a word or adding or deleting phonemes from words: deleting the /f/ from "fish" to yield /ish/, or the /h/ from "hat" to yield /at/, or adding /s/ to /pit/ to yield "spit," for example. Readers find such tasks relatively trivial whereas pre-readers find them extremely difficult (Magnusson and Naucler, 1993).

It now seems clear that this difficulty is not merely developmental (Hakes, 1980). Adult nonreaders have the same difficulty in analyzing their speech that young prereaders do. There is now a great deal of evidence that people familiar with an alphabet come to *hear* words as composed of the sounds represented by the letters of the alphabet; those not familiar do not. Morais, Cary, Alegria, and Bertelson (1979; but see also Morais, Bertelson, Cary, and Alegria, 1986 and Morais, Alegria, and Content, 1987) found that adult Portuguese fishermen living in a remote area who received even minimal reading instruction, often years earlier, were able to carry out such segmentation tasks while those who had never learned to read could not. Similar findings have been reported for Brazilian nonliterate adults by Bertelson, de Gelder, Tfouni, and Morais (1989) and for both child and adult nonliterates in India by Prakash, Rekha, Nigam and Karanth (1993). Scholes and Willis (1991) found that nonreaders in rural parts of the American Southeast had grave difficulties with a large variety of such metalinguistic tasks. Read, Zhang, Nie, and Ding (1986) found that Chinese readers of traditional character scripts could not detect phonemic segments whereas those who could read Pinyin, an alphabetic script representing the same language, could do so. Such findings underline the effects which knowledge of a script can have on one's knowledge of speech. But that is not to say that such awareness is merely a byproduct of learning to read. Rather, to learn to read any script is, at base, to find or detect aspects of one's own implicit knowledge structure or linguistic structure that can map onto or be represented by elements of that script. Consequently, once they are readers, people tend to hear their speech in terms of the model provided by print (Ehri, 1985). Nor is this merely codebreaking, a common metaphor for learning to read. It is less a matter of learning a code, a cipher, than it is a matter of conceptualizing the output of speech in terms of the categories available in the script. Learning to think about the properties of speech rather than the properties of ideas and things is what is required in learning to read a linguisticallybased script.

So how does such knowledge arise? As with words, knowledge of the segmental structure of speech arises from the attempt to map the alphabetic characters onto one's own speech. You can hear this every day as children attempt to spell new words- they slowly articulate speech attempting to hear sounds corresponding to the sounds known to be associated with particular letters of the alphabet. The products are the "invented spellings" such as "lade" for "lady" and "hows" for "house" (Read, 1971). Children are coming to hear their speech in terms of the phonemic categories offered by the *names* and associated sounds of the letters of the alphabet.

My conclusion, then, is that far from writing being the mere transcription of speech, writing provides a model for, that is, a set of categories for thinking about speech, that is, for bringing language into consciousness. Writing is a tool of exploration of the unknown not merely a cipher for recording the known. Some writers, notably Derrida (1976) overstate this point by arguing that writing never was or is a transcription of the sound patterns of a language, indeed, that "phonetic writing *does not exist*" (p. 39, italics in the original). But he captures an important point, namely writing systems including alphabets are not transcription devices.

4. Writing and knowledge about language

Awareness, that is, knowledge about, linguistic structure, I have argued, is a product of a writing system not a precondition for its development. If that is so it will not do to explain the evolution of writing as the attempt to represent linguistic structures such as sentences, words or phonemes for the simple reason that prewriters had no such concepts. The explanation for the seemingly progressive changes in the writing systems of the world is the simple consequence of attempting to use a graphic system invented to be "read" in one language, for which it is thereby reasonably suited, to convey messages to be "read" in another language for which it is not well suited. In each case the development of a functional way of communicating with visible marks was, simultaneously, a discovery of the representable structures of speech. While any graphic device would be taken as saying "the same thing" on each occasion of reading, that is, as a correct representation of a person, object or event, it would not be taken as saying "the same words" on each occasion of reading for there is nothing in the graphic form that can be taken as a model for such linguistic constituents. Critically, only in some writing systems is there anything approximating a onetoone mapping between linguistic element and visual sign.

We may note that emblematic forms of "writing" such as that involved in the use of visual signs to indicate one's totem, one's tribe or one's country do not create a distinction between the name and the thing; the emblem simultaneously stands for the totem and the name of the totem. Furthermore, emblems do not distinguish names from words; names, roughly speaking, are properties of objects whereas words are linguistic entities. We shall later consider the possibility that learning to distinguish the two may have important cognitive consequences -seeing names as mere words may serve to "disenchant" them. For now it is important only that we note that visual symbols may refer without reference to the properties of speech.

As we have seen, in some cultural contexts the tokens and emblems which represent things turned into signs which represent linguistic entities such as words or phonemes and consequently call for reading as we know it. But is is also clear that such a shift is by no means inevitable. The fact that Chinese scripts represent morphemes rather than phonemes is no longer seen as a case of arrested development (Needham, 1969; De Francis, 1989). Further, it has recently been argued that the move from information based writing systems to linguistic based systems never occured in precolonial Mesoamerica and in some cases development moved in the opposite direction (Boone and Mignolo, 1994). Hence, what is required is not a general evolutionary account but rather an account of what may amount to a series of useful historical accidents (Olson, 1994).

Yet the historical shifts in types of script did involve important reconceptualizations. The socalled discovery of the rebus principle of sound equivalences does not merely recruit preexisting linguistic knowledge; the substitution of the signs on the basis of their sound is what "articulates" constituents, that is, brings words or syllables into consciousness. A script which can be taken as representing both syntax and the entities combined by the syntax produces a linguisticallybased writing system, one which is capable in principle of representing everything that can be *said*. And at the same time, it narrows our conception of what such a script says from any suitable paraphrase to "the very words."

Once a writing system has a syntax, the signs can now be seen as representing words rather than as emblems and the construction can be seen as a proposition rather than as a list. The structures present in the *script* now provide the categories needed for recovering some aspects of the implicit structures of language. Such scripts are logographic in that the tokens now represent the major grammatical constituents of the language, namely, words. But, to repeat, it does not follow that the inventors of such a script already knew about words and then sought to represent them in the script. Rather, the scribal inventions dictated a kind of reading which *allowed language to be seen as composed of words related by means of a syntax*. Writing thereby provides the model for the production of an oral reading as well as for the introspective awareness of speech as composed of grammatical constituents, namely, words.

Not all graphic features need be verbalized and not all verbalized differences need appear in the script. The decisive factor in the elaboration of the script will not be the verbal models (for as we have noted such models are not available prior to writing) but rather the attempt at a functional, unambiguous representation (Gaur, 1984/1987; Harris, 1986). In English script, a word beginning with a capital letter is not read any differently than one beginning with a lower case letter; the convention facilitates interpretation not pronunciation; it does not follow a verbal model. Conversely, English script does not employ different graphic signs for long and short vowels; both long /ae/ and short /a/ are written *a*. Furthermore, the script represents only lexicon and syntax; prosodic features and other indications of illocutionary force are lost and have to be inferred from context (Olson, 1994. Ch. 5). Generalizing, we may say that a script is not initially or primarily an attempt at a complete linguistic transcription.

I have been suggesting that the invention of a writing system does two things at once. It provides a graphic means of communication but, because it is then verbalized, that is, read, it comes to be seen as a model of that verbalization. Through borrowing, scripts came to represent deeper aspects of linguistic form and in so doing they provided increasingly precise, that is, narrower models of speech, of "what was said." The conclusion that we are left with is that far from the history of writing being a matter of transcribing speech, it was a matter of inventing graphic codes which in each case served as a model for some aspects of speech. The invention of writing was, at the same time, the discovery of the structures of speech and of seeing language as an object. That discovery, as we have seen, was always fragmentary and incomplete, constrained by function not by theoretical adequacy.

In learning their first language, children clearly have some awareness of linguistic form -they revise their lexicons, their syntax and their pronunciation all of which indicate some kind or level of linguistic awareness (Hakes, 1980; Herriman, 1986; Sinclair, Jarvella, and Levelt, 1978). In addition, all speakers of a language have some stock of metalinguistic concepts such *as ask, say, tell, song, story, poem* and the like which indicate some forms of metalinguistic knowledge. Such "oral" linguistic knowledge is presumably exploited and reorganized in learning to deal with scripts. It is that explication and reorganization that is of concern here.

Explication is not just a matter of bringing implicit linguistic knowledge into consciousness but rather a matter of sorting the output of one system into the categories provided by the script. The theory, the alphabet, "creates" the observables at the same time that it represents them (Ferreiro, 1985, p. 217; Piaget, 1954).

5. Writing and cognition

In this section I will raise the argument that writing, by bringing language into consciousness, may have had and continue to have a significant impact on Western modes of using language and consequently on Western modes of thought.

As we have seen, wordbased scripts provide a model for the language which allows language to be seen as an object or system independently of the things the language is about. But a new understanding of language as consisting of words also has conceptual implications. For one, it may relax the appeal of "word" magic, the belief that one can harm or otherwise affect a person by abusing their name. This is what underlies name calling in every culture and the ritualized "hexes" found in some cultures. Spoken words are taken prereflectively as bearing an intrinsic relation to the object named names are not seen as arbitrary. As mentioned many studies (Piaget, 1929; Vygotsky, 1962; Sinclair, 1978; Berthoud-Papandropoulou, 1978) have shown that children tend to resist the possibiity that a 'dog', for example, could be called a 'cat'. The name is a part of a thing, a relation of metonymy. Similar findings have been reported in traditional cultures (Levy-Bruhl, 1926; Scribner and Cole, 1981). When names are distinguished from things and words from names, words are no longer treated as emblems; they are, as we say, just words.

Harris (1986) has suggested that the failure to distinguish words from names produces a form of emblematic symbolism which may extend to various gods and spirits and

> is often bound up in various ways with word magic and practices of namegiving. It reflects, fundamentally, a mentality for which reality is still not clearly divisible into language and nonlanguage, any more than it is divisible into the physical and the metaphysical, or into the moral and the practical. (pp. 131-132)

Of course, a little of that symbolic word magic exists in all of us; if not a crime it is at least a sin to desecrate a prayer book or the flag (Tambiah, 1990).

A lexically based writing system not only disenchants language, it turns words into objects of reflection. Havelock (1982) and Snell (1960) noted the role of writing in the Greek invention of the concepts of *idea*, *mind*, and *word* and in the way in which words from the common vocabulary suddenly became the subject of analysis and reflection in classical Greek culture. Whereas for the Homeric Greeks notions like *justice* and *courage* were exemplified in the deeds of gods and heroes, for the literate Greeks they became philosophical concepts. My suggestion is that the graphic system may play such a role by providing a model for language in a way that oral narrative and emblematic symbols never could. In this way, writing provided a model for aspects of that form, thereby making the linguistic sign conscious and hence available for analysis into syntactic constituents, the primary ones being words which then became subjects of philosophical reflection as well as objects of definition. Words became things in their own right.

As with words, so, by hypothesis, with utterances. Literacy contributes importantly to the set of distinctions between "what was said," that is, the very words, and "what was meant," that is, the intention or meaning expressed by those words. Goody (1987) and Finnegan (1977) have pointed out that in the oral cultures in which they worked, the notion of word applied to a whole phrase rather than to a particular lexical item. Furthermore, alternative expressions of the same sense were taken as being "the same" whereas literate subjects tend to use the stricter criterion of verbatim repetition as being "the same" (Finnegan, 1977; Goody, 1987). Thus the findings from nonwriting cultures tends to confirm the developmental findings on children's understanding of "the very words"; children tend to regard utterances which meant the same thing as 'saying' the same thing, schooled children do not (Torrance, Lee and Olson, 1992; Olson, 1994).

Unlike knowledge about phonology, knowledge about "actual linguistic meanings," that is, the meaning tied to the actual linguistic form, the "very words," may have implications for the evolution of a literate mode of thought.

The script determines which variants will be treated as equivalent, as "saying the same thing." This is important for formal thinking in that it is the literal meaning expressed by precise wording which enters into formal reasoning. Syllogistic reasoning, deductive proofs and necessary inferences are all based upon the literal meaning of particular expressions. Formal inferences cannot be drawn from metaphorical statements; only those intended literally, cases in which meaning is tied to the precise wording, can enter into such deductions. In this way, literacy contributes to formal thinking and reasoning. Writing, for this reason, appears to have allowed the formation of explicit logics, grammars and dictionaries (Goody, 1987).

Once a script is taken as a model for speech it becomes possible to increase the mapping between the two, allowing one to make a relatively close transcription of speech and conversely, allowing one to speak like a book. Historically, as scripts became more elaborate, their lexicalization or "reading" became more constrained. A more constrained reading confers a more constrained interpretation such as the distinction between metaphorical and literal meaning. There is a long tradition, traceable at least to Levy-Bruhl (1926), which attempted to distinguish the ways of thinking, that is, the modes of thought, characteristic of members of traditional oral cultures from members of educated, literate ones. Some differences were clear: members of traditional cultures tended to accept such statements as "Corn is deer" or "Twins are birds" at face value whereas members of Western literate ones either judged them as false or claimed they were metaphorical. The explanations for these differences are extremely diverse. However, if we note that a strict literatemetaphorical distinction is limited to Aristotelian cultures (Lloyd, 1990) it becomes plausible to claim that such eliptical expression as "Corn is deer" are problems only for those of us committed to these Aristotelean distinctions. For the Huichol Indians who used the expression it was simply a part of a rational inference schema. The Gods require a sacrifice of deer. But as deer are scarce we may sustitute a sacrifice of corn because "Corn is deer." It is achronistic to apply our categories to the speech of those from an earlier period and ethnocentric to apply them to those of a different culture. Yet that is not to deny, either, the importance of the literal-metaphorical distinction to the thought patterns of Western culture.

Not all of the effects of a writing system contribute to thought; writing systems also create blind spots. The fact that alphabetic scripts can be lexicalized in only one way invites the inference that an alphabetic script can transcribe anything that can be said -that it is a complete representation of a speaker's utterance. Just as the readers of a logographic script or a syllabic script may be unaware of what their script does not represent, namely, the phonological properties of their language, so we, alphabetics, may be unaware of what our writing system does not explicitly represent. In fact, our writing system, too, represents only part of the meaning; it is a simple illusion that it is a full model of what is said. An utterance spoken with an ironic tone is represented in writing the same way as the same utterance spoken with a serious tone. Again, a skilled actor can read the same text in many different ways. So the graphic form does not completely determine the reading.

This blind spot which our alphabetic script continues to impart leads us into a particular kind of error. It invites the inference that any meaning we personally see in a text is actually there and is completely determined by the wording-the problem of literalism. Conversely any other "reading" of that text is seen as the product of ignorance or "hardness of heart." How to cope with this interpretive problem attracted the best minds of Europe for a millennium giving rise ultimately to the new way of reading we associate with the Reformation (Olson, 1994; Smalley, 1941).

So what aspects of speech are not represented in a writing system? This question, has many classical answers. Plato thought that writing represented the words but not the author. Rousseau (1754-91/1966) thought it represented the words but not the voice. Some say that it represents the form but not the meaning. These are different expressions of the same point, namely, that while writing provides a reasonable model for what the speaker said, it does not provide much of a model for what the speaker meant by it, or more precisely, how the speaker or writer intended the utterance to be taken by a reader. It does not well represent what is technically known as illocutionary force (Austin, 1962). Writing systems by representing the former have left us more or less blind to the latter.

To sum up. Writing is not the transcription of speech but rather provides a conceptual model for that speech. It is for this reason that typologies of scripts - as logographic, syllabic and alphabetic- are at best rough descriptions rather than types; there never was an attempt to represent such structural features of language. Second, the development of scripts was not, contrary to the common view, a series of failed attempts and partial successes towards the invention of the alphabet, but rather the byproducts of attempts to use a script for a language for which it was at first ill-suited. Third, the models of language provided by our scripts are both what is acquired in the process of learning to read and write and what is employed in thinking about language; writing is in principle, metalinguistics. Knowledge of those aspects of linguistic structure for which our script provide a model and about which it permits us to think, has imparted an important bias to our thought and to the development of our document culture. And finally, the models provided by our script tend to blind us toward other features of language which are also important to human communication but for which the script provides no adequate model. As Blanche-Benveniste (1994, p. 70) says: "literacy gives access to a representation of one's language largely different from the representation induced only by oral practice."

Writing systems in a sense do represent speech. But not in the way that is conventionally held. Writing systems create the categories in terms of which we become conscious of speech. Whorf (1956) had earlier claimed that "we dissect nature along lines laid down by our language"; we could adapt his aphorism to say, "We introspect our language along lines laid down by our script."

Acknowledgment

I am indebted to the Spencer Foundation and to the Social Science and Humanities Research Council of Canada for their support.

The Unit in Written and Oral Language

Claire Blanche-Benveniste

When describing language in our daily lives we use units such as *word* or *sentence*. We have learnt these terms along with the writing process and we apply them to the spoken language, as for example in: "What was that word he used in his sentence?" There are some linguists who consider that these units may not be used scientifically to describe the spoken language because they are simply approximations. Furthermore they are characteristic of "practical know-how" which may indeed accommodate the social rules of writing, but which is fundamentally different from "scientific know-how" (Reichler-Béguelin, 1990).

There are two opposing camps in this often heated debate: those who maintain that the notion of the word may only be acquired through writing, and those who are of the opinion that the word has psychological reality that has already been established prior to the writing experience. The latter opinion is particularly upheld by generativists (Di Sciullo and Williams 1988, G. Miller 1994).

According to the first approach, the word is a term that has been adapted to the writing process and it would doubtless be extremely awkward to attempt a definition of the word within a concept of scientific know-how. There are numerous authors that subscribe to this point of view:

-We should get away from this doubtful notion of the word (Ch. Bally, 1944)
-The word (...) this discredited-but irreplaceable term (E.Benveniste, 1996:123)
-Words are not those ultimate, irreducible signs of language that the extensive interest traditional linguistics has in the word would lead us to believe (Hjemslev,1968:66)
-The pre-theoretical notion of the word is as misleading as it is useful,and linguists would perhaps be better off without it"(Rastier,1990).

The term "practical know-how" may be applied equally well to all types of units[1]. In modern French, Italian, German or Spanish[2] "to write a word" entails the writing of a "short speech"and not a single word. J. Goody has suggested (1979) that in several languages one and the same notion may be expressed by "word, morpheme, sentence, song verse, proverb or general theme". The term word is flexible to some extent. It denotes a part of an utterance which may be the size of a word or a fairly long series of words. J. Goody (1977) and many others have pointed out that certain languages with no written tradition do not seem to have a term corresponding to word or sentence. The vagueness of these terms has suggested that it is a unit without any serious foundation, a simple "artefact" derived from the writing system (Beck, 1964:156).

> Perhaps the most obvious, and the most widely discussed in the literature, is the question of establishing word boundaries, and hence the number of words in a sentence (B.Comrie, 1989:47).

My intention in this paper is to underline some enlightening views on the potential correspondences between certain units of written language and units of spoken language. My observations will be based on those of linguists and historians of writing systems.

I have chosen to base my discussion on a unit with both a graphic and a phonic form, in which meaning may be traced: the word. This choice is justified by two main reasons. Firstly, if we wish to account for writing which corresponds to pronunciation units and ideographic writing which corresponds to meaning units at the same time, it would seem useful to start with what they have in common, that is to say the pronounceable sense units. This is in preference to lower level units such as letters/sounds, which are only appropriate to certain types of writing[3]. Secondly, certain behaviour patterns in young children learning to read seem to reveal (cf. E. Ferreiro, 1987) that they grasp at least as many sense units as pronunciation units. It would seem therefore relevant to take as a starting-point a unit in which all these questions are situated.

No systematic analysis of the status of letters (or characters) in relation to their corresponding phonic itemswill be carried out. The following observations on the word are, as it were, the first stage.

Central to this paper is a hypothesis that I have frequently come across in my reading[4]. What may be understood by *word* should be described at two different clearly defined levels.

At the level where the utterance is produced, the word constitutes an "utterance fragment", with the form and meaning inherent in the specific fragment. The utterances of written language to which we are accustomed automatically yield fragments which are written words. In spoken language, the process of distinguishing an equivalent fragment is far less direct: the utterance appears as a continuous flow. This could be represented in written form by eliminating the graphic boundaries:

ilétaitunefoisuneprincesse
onceuponatimetherewasaprincess

The words of the spoken language which correspond to *fois* and *time*, considered as "utterance fragments" may only be discerned through specific and complex "breaking-down" operations, which will depend to a great extent on the context. This level would then correspond to a "word of discourse", as used within an utterance, in a definite morphological form and "swamped" by the surrounding words. "In order for the sentence to take on a meaning the words should no longer be distinguished one from the other" (G. Guillaume, 1948). In an utterance such as :

the day after election day...

the day appears as a word of discourse, and the group *election day* forms a sort of compound which is valid only temporarily for the utterance in hand (Joly and Paris-Delrue, 1990).

On the second level, we are dealing with the word as it is represented in the language system or as it appears in dictionaries. There we do not find *était* nor *was* but *être* and *to be*. The meaning of the elements *fois* and *time* would be considered as a specific case of the use of the words *fois* and *time* "with multiple meanings and usage". From several points of view this constitutes a type of abstract word.

This second level would seem to correspond to "independent words", as found in lists of directories. These are words that are not being used, but which are potentially available for various uses. They are abstract words, known technically as "lemmas" which subsume (into a single form) many types of morphological operations. This is the case for all the morphological forms of the verb: the first person of the present indicative in Latin, the third person of the perfect tense in Semitic languages, or the infinitive in English and French. This potential word represents its whole paradigm of forms and is what linguists such as G. Guillaume referred to as the *"mot de langue"* (word in the system). It is this word in the system that may be considered as bearing "meaning", since the discourse word may only bear "signification" contingent on the context of its occurrence[5]. The groups formed by a subject, an auxiliary and a verb, as in the French *j'ai marché*, would thus constitute a single *word of discourse* (or *of utterance*). Its signification may only be grasped at a level of group entity.

Thus, from now on, I shall be referring to the word in the utterance and the word in the system. The distinction to be drawn between these two levels would seem to be crucial and has widespread consequences for the comprehension of certain language acquisition mechanisms[6]. This distinction may easily be understood with reference to personal experience. For example, a familiar answer to a question such as "What does *station* mean? "would often take the form of another question: "In what context?" The first question is based on a system word, isolated from any utterance, whereas the reply aims at obtaining the occurrence of the word in an utterance[7].

The gap between the two levels, the utterance word and the system word, varies according to the structure of the languages and the different types of writing. But there is always a gap that needs to be filled.

1. Unit definition in graphic form.

In most Western languages, highly standardised as they are, the printed written language is set up in graphic units:letters, words, sentences, paragraphs, which are in part independent of their pronunciation. Even in an unknown language the units may easily be discerned on condition that they are written in the Latin alphabet. The following example is Irish (from Dillon and ò Cròinìn, 1961:156):

> *Dùirt sé leis féin go mb'fhéidir go ndéanfadh an dà scilling a ghnò. Nì raibh sé ach mìle eile ò bhaile nuair a bhuail bean bhocht uime agus ì cos-nochtaithe.*
> *"Tabhair dhom cùnamh éigin", ar sise, "ar son an tSlànaitheora, agus le hanaman do mmharbh, agus tar cheann do shlìnte".*

Even though we do not know Irish, we are able to list the words in the text by treating the word unit as a series of letters separated by two blank spaces. Hyphens and apostrophes count as variants in this delimiting process. It is equally simple to pick out the sentence unit, which is a sequence of words beginning with a capital letter and ending with a full stop.

If we remain within the domain of the written and do not seek any relation with the spoken language, we may also identify consistencies in the way the words are built up. We note their length, ranging from the longest (*tSlànaitheora*) to those consisting of only one letter (a, ì, ò), the initial and final consonants and vowels and the proper nouns marked by a capital letter. The distributional details of a type of writing can be clearly discerned, even without having to relate it to phonic units in any way. According to the common-sense rule which makes no reference to pronunciation, at least four letters are needed to form a proper noun, three for a common noun and only a grammar word can be formed with two, as exemplified by this short sentence: "Mr. *Inne* is *in* the *inn*" (Halliday 1990:27). Many people explain the double *g* of the word *egg* by this simple rule (G. Sampson, 1985). It would appear that young Portuguese- Italian- and French-speaking children make this type of observation when they claim that at least three different letters are needed to write a word, and that a word may not be made up of several identical letters (E. Ferreiro, 1985). We are able to identify the fact that a text is written in a particular language and become familiar with its word distribution by simply being exposed to the written text, even if we cannot interpret the meaning[8]. Neurolinguistic experiments would seem to indicate that brain response differs when subjects are confronted with words formed correctly, obeying the written rules of the language, as opposed to words formed at random:

> These same areas lit up when the volunteers saw nonwords that nevertheless obeyed rules of English - *"tweal"*- as if the brain was scrambling to assign a meaning to something that by all rights should have one. These semantic areas stayed dark when the volunteers saw consonant letter strings - *"nlpfz"*[9].

2. The word

2. 1. A first definition: the word is an independent item

Let us start with a naive question. If we take the words of the written language as a starting-point can we align the corresponding units of the spoken language with them? Many teachers would be tempted to answer in the affirmative. It is in fact the answer given in the 17th century in the *Grammaire de Port-Royal* (Harris 1990:17): "We call word that which is pronounced separately and written separately".

This simple reply is unacceptable, particularly because it does not take into account the difference between the word in the utterance and the word in the system. In utterances we do not find, or at least only rarely, words "pronounced separately".

The sound flow of the utterance does not allow us to pick out the units corresponding to the written words directly. Well-read adults have learnt to set up links between the written and spoken units. However, we know that children do not manage to do this intuitively, and that it is of no help to them to pick out words which are supposed to be independent within the pronunciation of the utterance, since in fact they are not independent.

> What we transcribe onto the paper with the graphic symbols *loup, wolf,* etc. is simply an abstraction lacking in phonic existence. For example, where does the article end and the substantive begin in the group *le loup* when pronounced without a mute *e*? (P. Naert, 1941:187).

When experiments in automatic word analysis come up against this problem, it has to be taken into serious consideration:

> As opposed to the written word, the spoken word is essentially a continuous phenomenon. Breaking it down into phonemes, words, or meaning groups is one of the fundamental steps in the process of automatic recognition (J. M. Pierrel, 1987:40).

We may believe that we can identify cohesive links between the"pauses" we hear and the commas, semi-colons and full-stops, but, as Nunberg (1990) has so clearly pointed out, they do not in fact correspond to the pauses in spoken discourse. Between the words themselves there are even fewer pauses. Would there indeed be more frequent pauses in an exceptionally slow utterance? Apparently not, since slow delivery picks out groups which do not correspond to the written words. In French, owing to the phenomenon of *sandhi*, we end up with oral production in which the syllables are separated but form a bridge over two words:

> *C'est à Paris qu'ils ont rencontré leurs amis*
> c'est/t-à/Paris/qu'il/z ont/ren-/con-/tré/leur/z a/mis/

When we recite the names of the months in English (Halliday, 1990:51) the underlying compound rhythm groups keep some nouns and bridge over others:
June Ju-/ly/August Sep-/tember Oc-/tober No-/vember De/-cember

In languages bearing word-stress, stress is a means to demarcate spoken units. Thus, in Russian, according to P. Garde (1968) the word should be considered as "a segment bearing meaning which must comprise one single stressed syllable". Here we infer that the unit corresponding to a written word tends in its oral form to have only one stressed vowel. However, this is insufficient as a definition. The criterion of stress does not enable us to count unstressed items as words. These would include prepositions, articles and various particles. Besides this, stress is not always a reliable marker, since it is sometimes more likely to delimit word groups than words. P. Garde quotes Russian examples such as *cetyrëxlétnij* (four years old), which form two phonological words with two stresses, but which is nevertheless written as a single word. Furthermore, when the word comprises more than four syllables, it tends to bear secondary stress, so that it may be mistaken for a string of two words.

D. Bolinger (1975:85) comments that the "er.." of hesitation in French is produced by the speaker before what would correspond to words, and not other elements. Thus we would say:

j'ai un er. . chat j'ai un er. . poisson

but we would not say, for a compound word: *j'ai un poisson-er.. chat*. This procedure enables us to define lexical items but not un-stressed grammatical items such as *le, ne, je*. The natural utterance does not, then, yield real systematic pauses that enable us to mark out words.

2. 2. The word is an item which may be divided

This is the criterion which is most frequently used. A simplistic approach would point out that the word is what we might pick out of an utterance in order to pronunce it by itself, without loss of meaning. However, simple as this operation may seem, it is not what actually takes place in practice. We would be more likely to pick out a group than a word: *ils ont rencontré, leurs amis*[10]. Besides, it is difficult to repeat something that has just been said with the exact wording:

> Speakers and listeners are of course aware that the speaker is speaking; but they are typically not aware of what he is saying, and if asked to recall it, not only the listeners but also the speaker will ordinarily offer a paraphrase, something that is true to the meaning but not by any means true to the wording. To focus attention on the wording of language is something that has to be learnt. For example if you are studying linguistics, it can be a difficult and somewhat threatening task (M. Halliday, 1987:57).

Basing their observations on a series of experiments dealing with the difference between what a text *says* and what a text *means*, Torrance and Olson (1987:138) demonstrated that 3 to 4-year olds who are able to make this distinction are those who, around 10 years old, become the best readers. In one of these experiments it had to be specified whether a character who wanted her new red shoes to be brought, had in fact asked for her *new red shoes* or simply her *red shoes*. Only the best-coached children managed to say what the exact words that Lucy said were[11].

Even people who transcribe recordings of oral discourse and who are used to noting the exact wording fall into the trap. That is to say they repeat the meaning rather than the exact form of what was said, for example, *ma mère* replaces *maman* or *c'était il y a longtemps* replaces *c'était bien avant* (Blanche-Benveniste and Jeanjean, 1986). This semantic shift towards synonyms may be found, in an exaggerated form in certain reading problems distinguished as "alexia":

> When the patients read aloud, they make certain mistakes which consist in uttering synonyms or semantically close words in the place of the words written down. For example, "crab" becomes "lobster", or "cathedral" becomes "church", etc. (E. Andreewsky and Rosenthal, 1990: 104).

The meaning of an item is therefore of great importance within the simplistic operation of word division. Those divided most easily would seem to be those which have a naming function, in particular the proper nouns, which according to all observations have a place apart. Although the context will not always evoke them, proper nouns are easy to discern as divided units even if they are sometimes difficult to pick out.

The proper noun is in some ways the paragon of the "divisible word" and the first that children generally learn to write. In a prototypical approach such as that of Reichler-Béguelin (1990a), it might be said that the proper noun is the prototype of the "word", and that the common noun, certain adjectives and adverbs follow in descending order[12]. Prepositions, articles, and auxiliaries, which are unstressed may not be set apart. If we consider an utterance such as :

les enfants n'avaient pas pu entrer dans la maison

the elements *les, n', pas, dans, la*, which are clitic and unstressed, may not be set apart. It is recognised that young children tend not to think of them as words (E. Ferreiro, 1987). This prototypic scale has been corroborated by various psycholinguistic experiments. In fact children discern the written word best with reference to the proper noun, but "they do not discern the predeterminants, and making them understand them is exceptionally hard to do" (J. P. Jaffré, 1990:102).

> Sentences with two occurrences of the same word (such as the French word "car") are given to the patients to read aloud. In one case the word

will be a substantive (full form), and in the other a conjunction (function word), as in the example: *"Le car ralentit car le moteur chauffe"*. We note that the word is always pronounced in the first case and never in the second one (Andreewsky and Rosenthal 1990: 106).

The history of early writing systems reveals a prototypical series of the same type. It would seem that alphabetic writing was developed on the basis of proper nouns, (Gelb, 1973) since they required more adequate representation than the other words. Sumerian writing was probably forced to develop a system of pronunciation notation by the need to write down Semitic proper nouns, which figured amongst Acadian loan-words (J. Bottéro, 1987:109). Proper nouns are also the most stable words in the transition from one language to another. Thus they may be represented in the same way in different linguistic domains.

Bottéro also notes that in the very early writing of Mesopotamia "recording of words was confined more particularly to the content words" (1987:109). In this way an utterance comprising three elements:

Enki, Isimus, shout

would be read as "Enki speaks to Isimus" without the verb and preposition linking items being written down.

> We would infer from this that only the "content words" which derive from reality are taken into account here. The "non-content words" act as links, which in Acadian were noted by nominal and verbal inflection, and by preposition, conjunction and even pronoun use. These are in fact completely left out (Bottéro, 1987:123).

From this point of view, the proper noun is the word *par excellence*. This is followed by the common nouns that denote things. Moreover,

> These people were convinced that the name originates not in the person denoting it but within the thing itself being denoted. It would thus be an inseparable product of it. And this written name considered as identical to the thing itself constituted material, concrete, extensive data. We might consider this analogous to a substance of which even the tiniest part contains the qualities of the whole, just as the tiniest grain of salt will have all the properties of the heaviest block (Ibidem:125-7)

Proper nouns and nouns which denote things would thus seem to be the two first prototypes of the *word*. The "non-content nouns" which J. Bottéro refers to are prepositions, articles and other clitic items of language to which the "divisible word" definition may not apply.

2.3. The notion of "divisible" differs for each language

We may "divide" different elements within an utterance according to the language being used. A certain "typology" (cf. Schlegel 1818, Pott 1849, Schleicher 1860, Sapir 1921) and the clarifying work by Hagège (1982), have hinged on this criterion to the extent that linguists are divided into two schools of thought. There are those who believe that the notion of the word may not apply to all languages:

> There are large numbers of idioms where the word is a totally different thing from what we are used to considering in these terms. To the extent that it is an improper use of the term to consider, as is sometimes the case, that the Chinese *word* and the French *word* may rank equally (...). Valid, acceptable comparison is only feasible between idioms with a word state that is at least based on the same broad principles even if it is not entirely analogous. (G. Guillaume, *Leçons,* 1947c, 21 nov.)

On the other hand there are those who, like the generativists, argue that the word may nevertheless be considered as the "universal" element of languages[13].

Evidence in favour of the former is provided by languages such as Swahili. A sentence in Swahili may take on the aspect of one single word: *sijamonyeshavyo*, which would be translated into French as: *I have not shown them to him yet.*

"None of the elements may occur alone, for example in reply to a question. In Swahili the reply cannot be *"sija"*, "not yet", which are nevertheless the two elements which correspond to the signified group. Even the verb root is hampered since the shortest form available is *"ona", "vois"*. This is an imperative form in which the verb must go together with what the Bantuists quite often call the thematic vowel, in this case -a" (J. L. Doneux, 1990:2)

Languages such as Chinese or Vietnamese are called "isolating languages" precisely because each item in the utterance may be picked out and written down separately :

- *Thuy ngèo, nhùng anh thìch giùp ban*
- Though poor yet he like help friend
  (Though poor, he likes to help friends, Comrie 1988:451)

In spite of counter-arguments, these languages have often been held up as examples of perfect parallelism between the written and the spoken word.

Languages referred to as "agglutinative" are those like Turkish which have a root that can be isolated but in which the remainder is a series of suffixes which may not form a separate utterance:

-*gel* (to come);
-*geldiyse* (if he had come);
-*geldiyseniz* (if you had come);

-*Tüklestiremediklerizdenmisiniz?*
-*Türk-le-s-tir-e-me-dik-ler-iz-den-mi-sin-iz*
(Are you of those whom we have not been able to Turkify ?)

The latter example is exceptionally long, though easily understood by native speakers according to Bazin (1990). The stem *Türk*, which constitutes a word, may be cut out, but the remainder is a series of suffixes which if they are isolated from the stem do not form an intelligible utterance. The "agglutinative" type of language is thus very different from the evidence of German examples such as: *Autobahnratstättenbesitzer* (motorway lay-by owner) in which each item may be picked out as a series of independent "words": *das Auto, die Bahn* (road), *die Rast* (rest), *die Stätte* (place), *der Besitzer* (owner) (Ramat 1990).

The maximal case of lack of word-division is that of the incorporating languages, also known as polysynthetic, or sentence-word languages, such as Eskimo. In its written form, the sequences of linked items are sometimes so long that, according to specialists you need trained breathing to be able to read them aloud in one go.

The Eskimo word is in fact pronounced in a single breath, however long it is (Cornillac 1993:139):

Nanisivingmunngauqutiginiaqquungitagit (I shall probably not go with you to Nanisivik) (Lowe, 1981:5).

In the second word of the following utterance: *Inuit nunanganniittunut* (to those who are in the the country of the Inuit) only the "word theme" or "stem", *nuna-* (the idea of earth or country) can be isolated. The other elements are all suffixes and endings that cannot function as independent words: the possessive suffix -*ngat/ngan*-; the locative plural -*ni*; the suffix -*it* in its verbal value; the final plural suffix -*nut* (to, towards, for). An even longer verbal construction may be built up on this word: (I will take you to those who live in the country of the Inuit) *Inuit nunangnniittununngauqatiginiaqtagit.* Lowe deduces that "the word then does not exist as such at the level of the language" (Lowe, 1981:7).

2.4. The disequilibrium between the word in the utterance and the word in the system

In languages characterised by wide morphological variation, the element we isolate changes form according to its context. Celtic languages have an initial consonant that varies according to the surrounding context. In Manx (the Isle of Man) the word which corresponds to *friend* takes the form *charrey* (*e charrey*: his friend), *garrey* (*nyn garrey*: our friend) and *carrey* as an independent word. In Breton father is *tad* in its independent form, but *e dad* (his father) and *e zad* (her father). If this word is to be picked out of the utterance, it is likely that it will be quoted in its independent form and not in the form which in fact it had in the utterance itself.

The phenomena of *sandhi* (or *samdhi*) affect the shape of an element, which differs according to whether it is pronounced within the body of the utterance or isolated just before a pause. In Sanskrit, in natural pronunciation where everything is maximally linked, inner *samdhi* occurs at the junction of the morphemes within the word. In a more solemn delivery which separates the elements, this *sandhi* may be eliminated:

- Natural recitation:
sà no mandrésam urjam . . sùstuaìtu. . . sàsvadbhih
- More solemn "pada" recitation:
sà/nah/mandrà/isam/ùrjam sù-stuta/à/etu sàsvat-bhih

The word has several forms, and to pick it out of the utterance is to select a form that is not precisely the one it has when "submerged" in the utterance.

Another variation of great importance is inflection. Which word do we actually use in the French phrases: *"il est parti, il y va"* ? Is it the inflexive verb, *"est parti"*, *"va"*, or the infinitive *"partir, aller"*? The verb in the infinitive, which subsumes all the potential verb forms whilst giving up any specific characteristics pertaining to the context is a type of abstraction. It is in this abstract form, i. e. in its lemma form, that we find the word in a dictionary. Pierre Naert has clearly demonstrated the difference between the inflexive word within the utterance, and the word in the system. He extends his argument claiming that in Indo-European languages there was no word as such for *loup* (wolf):

> In Indo-European there was no word for *"loup"* (wolf). Forms existed such as *lupus, lupum, lupi, lupo*, etc., none of which could claim to quali-

fy more than the other as the very form itself of the word (Naert, 1941:185).

2. 5. The graphic word and the "morpheme" of the linguists

According to the linguists of the Bloomfield school, the basic unit in analysis is not the word, which is a simple graphic convention, but the morpheme. The morpheme is "the smallest unit of form imbued with meaning". It may be smaller than a word, as in the German *kinderchen* (*kind-er-chen*: child, plural, diminutive), or longer than a word as in the French *pomme de terre* or in the English *wild-animal-tamer* (Bloomfield, 1933). Those items which are always linked to other morphemes such as the *-er* of *wild-animal-tamer* or clitic elements *je, ne, te, le* in *je ne te le dis pas* are not words, since they may not appear in an independent form.

K. Togeby (1949) put forward one of the most detailed accounts of the notion of the "word". On the one hand, he distinguished "units" (propositions, word groups, words) and on the other hand "linked forms" (we could equally well refer to them as "linking forms") that always combine with another. He set up a six-level classification chart:

	Linked forms	Units
1°	intonation	period [14]
2°	conjunction	proposition
3°	preposition	prepositional group
4°	article	noungroup
	pronoun	verbgroup
5°	inflexive [15]	word
6°	derivative [16]	theme[17]

The word would thus be defined as "the syntactic unit of which one of the components is a form (or several forms) linked by an inflected". This definition, which is entirely syntactic, implies a certain combinatorial relationship of all the units. But what it yields as a "syntactic word" does not always correspond to the graphic word.

2.6 From the point of view of meaning: one or several words?

In English *black bird* (a bird of black colour) with equal stress on the two terms may be distinguished from *blackbird* (species of bird) with primary stress on the first term. In French *le vin aigre* (sour wine) and *le vinaigre* (vinegar), exist as two completely distinct entities. In this case the writing system accurately reflects the units of analysis. However, it is not always such a simple matter. *Lipstick* is a single word in English but the French *rouge à lèvres* is three graphic words and is not treated as a compound. Hyphen usage symbolises the combining of elements where the components may still be discerned, although it is not systematic in practice (*bricklayer* as opposed to *taxi-driver*)[18].

Automatic word recognition machines are programmed to put forward several different fragments which may be equally plausible for utterances in French such as:

> *un temps froid éventé/un temps froid et venté,*
> *poux rassurés/pour assurer,*
> *il faut des pensées/il faut dépenser* (J. Mariani, 1982:246).

These types of problem have constrained generativists to comment that the assignation of meaning may only take place at the level of the word, and not at the level of the morpheme, as advocated by the structuralists:

> The claim that morphology is based on whole words rather than on morphemes is founded on the fact that it is only at the level of the whole words that form is associated with meaning (St. R. Anderson 1990:162).

2.7. Some principles in writing representations

Certain types of writing may be situated according to whether they are more clearly associated with the "utterance word" or the "system word". A writing system which notes the pronunciation of elements as they arise within an utterance, without dividing the elements that are indivisible in pronunciation, would be closely related to the *utterance word*. This is the case in the above *word-phrases* of Eskimo.

Writing which notes the word in the system would not take into account the pronunciation of the elements in the utterance nor specific significations due to the context. This is the writing tendency of Chinese ideograms.

Homophones may be treated differently according to each of these two tendencies in French utterances such as :

- *il bat sa femme - le meuble est bas - le cheval a un bât*
(he beats his wife - the piece of furniture is low - the horse has a packsaddle)

The monosyllable /ba/ is a verb, an adjective or a noun with entirely different meanings. If it is set apart from the utterance, /ba/ cannot be identified. The only possible reply to the question "What does /ba/ mean?" is another question: "In what context?" Here lies the whole difference between the word within the utterance and the word in the system. Within the utterance itself the segment /ba/ is never ambiguous in meaning. However, French spelling gives it individual status as a "system word", by marking whenever possible the paradigmatic evidence which links it to a "family of words". Thus the verbal /ba/ written as *bat* is the one linked with *battre*; the adjective /ba/ written as *bas* with *basse* and the noun /ba/ written as *bât* with *bâté*.

Within an agglutinative language it is the "words of the utterance" that tend to be written. The three /ba/ would be considered as "linked" morphemes, situated in a specific place within the utterance with no ambiguity of meaning. They could be written in the same way ba, in accordance with the pronunciation. Within an isolating language, where the three /ba/ could be quoted separately, two types of solution present themselves. All three may be written as ba, leaving the distinction to be made through the overall meaning of the utterance and classified in dictionaries under the headings ba N°1, ba N°2 and ba N°3. On the contrary, the three /ba/ may be written in different ways according to their meaning. The pronunciation may be taken into account in varying degrees, or not at all. Chinese writing, which is closely related to the system word, chooses this solution.

> There are large numbers of homophonous morphemes; the three words *shen*, for instance, meaning "to extend", "body" and "deep". These meanings preclude an analysis of one word with three readings. In Chinese writing this is absolutely clear as the words are graphically distinct (Coulmas, 1990: 46)

The three segments transcribed by *shen* are represented by three graphically distinct words, with three significations. The meaning in context provides the means for choosing a particular pronunciation when reading, with differences according to the dialect. This enables system words which are pronounced entirely differently to be written in the same way.

Arabic and Hebrew writing systems basically use system words which are quite abstract with relation to the word as it is actually pronounced. The writing may represent short vowels using a whole diacritic group. However, this is only usual for children's books, books for foreigners or certain types of poetry. In the standard reading of Hebrew these vowel signs are absent, together with the dots which distinguish the reading of certain consonants ([f/p], [ʃ/s]). It is thus extremely difficult, not to say impossible, for someone who does not know the language to read the"non-dotted" words. R. Peereman (1991) quotes a series of words which in their "non-dotted" form may all be written with the same three letters, with the value of the following string of pronounced consonants: [s-f-r or s-p-r]. This simple graphic letter string corresponds to seven possible words:

sefer	sapar	siper	safar	spor	supar	saper
book	barber	he told	he counted	count	was told	tell

Sampson (1985:89-92) analysed the strategies that a non-initiated reader must necessarily use in order to read a letter string in Hebrew. Two stages in this process are made clear: 1) The reader has to ascertain which of the possible words in the language is represented in the string. 2) He must ascertain which vowels are needed between and around the consonants (there is considerable controversy as to whether the first stage is adequate for access to word "meaning", or whether the second one which involves pronunciation is indispensable). I shall re-write below two of the ten examples of "strategies for word reading":

> *1)* <hmlwn> *In a word of several letters beginning with* <h> *the probability is high that, as here,* <h> *represents the definite-article prefix* /ha-/. *In this case the correct reading is* /hammillon/, *"the dictionary" which in context is obvious enough (the succeeding words translate as "contains 30 000 entries in alphabetical order"). Out of context,* <hmlwn> *could equally well read* /hammalon/ *"the hotel" or* /hammelon/ *"the melon".*
> *2)* <hlfwn> *The root [lfn] means "to slander", and* <h> *can be a verbal prefix. But no form taking that prefix has a* <w> *in the last syllable. In any case the context calls for a noun. Therefore the correct reading is the frequent noun* /hallafon/ *the language"; no alternative reading is possible.*

It may be noted that in order to establish the "word in the utterance" and identify its phonic form, a series of strategies must be applied: the root must be rendered independent of suffixes and prefixes; the grammatical category must be chosen (noun or verb); the syllabic distribution must be known and the lexical probabilities within the given context must be assessed.

If we wish to define Arabic, we need to focus on the notion of the root and pattern system (M. Barbot, 1990). The word pronounced as [abjad] meaning "white" has to be understood as the association of a root and a pattern, as may be seen in the following chart:

aBYaD (white)	BaYDä	(white/fem.)
	BaYYaD'a	(to whiten)
	BaYYâD	(whiteness)
	iBYaDDa	(to be white)
aSWaD (black)	SaWWaDa	(to blacken)
	SaWWâD	(blackness)
	iSWaDDa	(to be black)

Following the horizontal line we see the root B-Y-D, which is a carrier of the lexical meaning *white* and, following the vertical line, the pattern a- -a, which marks a set of grammatical values[19]: adjective of colour or masculine singular.

This type of writing system basically records the "system word", but, unlike Chinese, it relies on a pronunciation-linked base, i.e. the consonant-formed stems. It hinges on common knowledge of pronunciation. When the gap is not too great between the language as represented in the system and as pronounced in the utterance, the speakers possess knowledge of this consonant basis. They can thus transfer with ease from the "utterance word" to the "dictionary word". However, if the gap between the standard and the spoken language is wide, this transfer is hard to make. This is the case of most of the Arabic dialects.

> It is true that when they are uttered out of context, you realise that they have not been understood correctly, linguistically speaking. The proof of this lies in the fact that 80% of Arabic-speakers do not know how to use a dictionary since the dictionary is not in alphabetic order but classified by roots. In other words, if people are incapable of analysing the word they are looking up, they cannot find it. The result is that either they have to work like devils and become highly competent, or they remain apart from the language (A. H. Ibrahim, 1990:231).

2. 8. "Attached" or "divided" words. Scriptio continua.

The types of writing which have words with a close relationship to the system have generally had early word-division dating back to their beginnings. Chinese is a case in point. It is the case in Semitic writing: "Most formal Semitic texts of early date used word dividers" (Isserlin, 1991:289). It is also the case for a whole range of types of early writing[20]:

At first sight it may seem slightly strange, but it is in the archaic codes of the syllabic type (Hittite, Mycenaean and Cypriot writing) that delimitation at the level of the word seems to be best accepted within the writing (Reichler-Béguelin, 1990a:28).

It was the practice at an early date for Ancient Greek and Latin:

> From the beginning the Latins knew about and used word division (no doubt owing to the Etruscan influence) up until the 11th century AD (Desbordes 1990:234)

However, after that they abandoned it. This has always been considered a strange form of regression. Writing with attached words, *scriptio continua* was widely practiced up to the 10th century and still evident in the Renaissance epoch:

> *arma uirumque cano, Troiae qui primus ab oris*
> *ARMAVIRVMQVECANOTROIAEQVIPRIMVSABORIS*

Surprise has been shown at the use of *scriptio continua*. Reichler-Béguelin observes: "The only cause for it that we can manage to find is the wish to imitate Greek usage". We might detect here the result of a writing principle closely related to the utterance itself, with the words being attached in the same way as in the speech flow. In actual fact, the Romans had continually set up ways of writing that closely reflected pronunciation. This is exemplified in the rule - preserved in modern script - that " *n* becomes *m* before *p*", as in *im-pello* rather than *in-pello* (Desbordes 1990).

Reading was held to be a far more difficult exercise than we consider it to be nowadays (cf. Dubuisson 1991, Marrou 1965). It was a skill for specialists, with the onus put on the reader. The division of the *scriptio continua* into separate words was a particularly hard task. There were likely to be mistakes in meaning in many cases, as noted by Quintilien:

> We may read *Coruinum,* proper noun, or *cor uinum*, (heart, wine), or *co-rui num*, (raven, is it); we may read *inculto loco,* in an uncultivated place, or *in culto loco,* in a cultivated place (Desbordes 1990: 223).

The practice of *scriptio continua* was not an impediment to the Greek and Latin awareness of word, since their grammatical classification gave instances of it. For whatever reason, it would seem that they considered word division in standard writing to be superfluous.

THE UNIT IN WRITTEN AND ORAL LANGUAGE 39

It is interesting to note that, according to modern-day experiments with six to eight year- olds, children attribute little importance to graphic word division:

> If eight year olds (class CE2) have to read a twenty-word text with no graphic blank spaces, they manage to understand and read it. The only difference that may be noted in the reading of the same text with graphic blank spaces is that it will be read more quickly. (J. P. Jaffré (1990:96)

In France, authors went on using attached words in their manuscripts a long time after printers had adopted fixed norms for word division. Thus Louis XIV wrote (according to F. Brunot 1967, IV-1, pp. 150-167):

Les roys sont souvent obligés afaire deschosescontre leurinclination

and Madame de Sévigné:

jevous feray demeurer dacort quela guerre est vne fort sottechose.

Specific rules were followed in the writing of non-stressable particles such as articles, prepositions and certain negations. Thus, in Indo-European languages, writing has a tendency to bind the particles following the stressed word and to separate the preceding ones[21]. This is shown in Spanish:

- *dàmelo, contarselo (give it to me, to tell it to oneself)*
- *me lo da, se lo conta (he gives it to me, he tells it to himself)*

In all Romance languages in which the article is placed before the noun, articles are written independently. However, in Rumanian, in which the article follows the noun, it is bound to the noun as a suffix[22].

In Galand's (1991) discussion of the Berber language[23] as it was established in the 20th century, he maintains that the most difficult task was not so much to choose an alphabet but to select a system of word division in the utterance. The Berber equivalent of "they bring it to him", *arastidtawin*, can be broken down into the morphemes:

- *ar (unfinished time) -as (to him) -t (it) -id (here) -tawin (they bring)*

Three types of word division were put forward in the writing of this utterance, the most appropriate being the third:

1) arastidtawin -2) ar as t id tawin -3) ar-as-t-id-tawin

If the written form is too compact it is likely to mask the components of the utterance. If it is too broken up, reading is bound to be difficult. A reasonable compromise has to be reached. (Galand 1991)

Although the blank space is the clearest defining agent of the written word, word division through the use of blank spaces does not appear to provide the best explanation of it. As far as Arabic and Hebrew are concerned, there is a secondary tendency which is more revealing on writing types, namely that certain final position letters have specific forms. The basic division that established units as system words was set at the time of the inventory of alphabet forms[24].

2. 9. The "real" language words

In writing systems which record words that are closely bound to the system, language users have frequently tended to consider the only real words to be the written ones. Traditionally the *Académie Française* would justify French orthography claiming that only words within the orthographic system would be clearly "envisaged" and regarded as stable, thus allowing for "high quality" linguistic expression (Liselotte Pasques, 1990).

The "word in the system" imparts a single representation to the word even in the case of varying regional pronunciation . It also implies one written form for each morpheme even if pronunciation varies according to the context (*electric* with /k/, *electricity* with /s/, or *suppress* with /s/ and *suppression* with /ʃ/).

Generativists have justified with this idea by referring to the orthographic recording of underlying forms:

> Our orthography is an almost wholly accurate phonographic spelling-system, but the segments it records are those of the "underlying" level of lexical storage rather than the "surface" phonemes which are actually uttered (Chomsky and Halle, 1968).

> Each morpheme will have only a single spelling regardless of how many distinct pronunciations the morpheme may have in different contexts (M. Halle, 1969).

> The same justification holds good for the recording of monosyllabic homonyms such as *paw, poor, pour, pore* (Halliday 1990:27)

Nevertheless, this type of justification for the differentiation of writing systems, which would allow for the recording of the real word or its underlying form, raises the question of distinguishing the order in which the mutual influence between the written and the oral may be considered to take place. The classical tradition holds that the spoken language blurred meaningful units and that writing remedied the problem. 16th century Portuguese grammarians recounted that the spoken language was the victim of Adam's sins which had caused loss of a large part of meaning in words, and that in a sense writing had expiated these sins (Carvalho Buescu, 1983:90).

Coulmas (1990), in a study on Japanese writing, examines the effects of the written language on the spoken one. He points out that in the 19th century, during the Meiji period (1868-1912), the Japanese language went through a significant crisis. A large number of technical compound words were coined, many of which were homonyms. These could only be distinguished through use of *kanji* writing (Chinese characters). For instance, the term pronounced /kagaku/ corresponds to two types of writing which designate either "science" or "chemistry".

> It is not the case that this writing system is indispensable because of the number of homonyms, but rather that numerous homonyms came into existence in the Meiji period when hundreds of technical terms were needed. They were coined with *kanji* rather than words as the elements of loan translation. This is a special feature of the Japanese use of Chinese characters (...). In a sense, the many homonyms are the price the Japanese paid for overcoming diglossia without giving up their writing system. (Coulmas, 1990:198)

In short, Coulmas shows how this writing system, which assumes a wide measure of independence of the written word versus a spoken one, has had a wide influence on the history of the spoken language in return.

In a provocative study, R.Wright (1982) describes how, throughout the period from the 2nd to the 9th century, the Latin writing system acted as a unifying screen in relation to the different Romance languages. Specialists in Romance languages had habitually taken the view that two sorts of languages would seem to have existed in Western Europe from the end of the Empire up to the 12th century. That is to say, there was Latin which was spoken and written by the scholars, and Early Romance spoken by the uneducated who, up until the 9th century, would not have known how to write it. Wright maintains that, in fact, during the whole of the Early Middle Ages, in France, Spain, Italy and Portugal, people used Latin writing to record their particular Romance language. They would have read texts in Latin with the pronunciation of their already existent Romance language. In Spanish, for instance, the verb form *vienen* (they come) was pronounced almost as it is nowadays, but it was written in Latin form as *veniunt*. Besides, the written Latin *veniunt* was pronounced *vienen*.

Over the territory of Spain, the written Latin *mensibus* was read as *mezes* and people were taught that to record what was pronounced as *mezes*, they had to write *mensibus*. There is evidence to show that in the French domain people had to learn to write *hominem* to record *omne* or *ome* (homme). And furthermore, in order to read this word written as *hominem*, efforts had to be made not to pronounce the final *m* or the *i* between the *m* and the *n*. The reason for this was, as the grammarians of the epoch would say, one should not pronounce what is written: *non debemus dicere ita, quem ad modum scribitur*. In Italy, *hodie* was read as *ozie*: "Solent Itali dicere ozie pro hodie".

> Seventeenth-century French "vierge" or "virge", for example, might be spelt *virgen, virginem, virgine* or *virgini*, in the same way as Modern French [ʃãt]can be spelt *chante, chantes* or *chantent* (p. XI).

It would seem that it was only around the year 800 that the Charlemagne reform carried out by the grammarian Alcuin re-established standard Latin pronunciation. Thus, so it seems, the Romance languages were radically separated and obliged to adopt a different written transcription than that which had been devised formerly by dipping into the Latin writing system. The first written documents that have been handed down to us through history, as far as French, Italian, Spanish and Portuguese are concerned, do not testify the birth of these languages, but rather the date of their new writing systems. It would seem that, through the centuries, written Latin served as a mask which unified the whole set of Romance languages. The latter were able to develop in almost clandestine fashion behind the front of the Latin writing system.

If R.Wright is right, it would mean that during the whole of the Early Middle Ages, Western Europe went through a period of artificial standardisation using the same system for writing words, though for spoken language it was quite the contrary.

3. Conclusion

It is no easy matter to compare the written linguistic analysis units with the oral ones. Linguists, backed by traditions of research, do not always agree as to what the delimitations of the oral linguistic units are. Nevertheless, there is general agreement on the notion that, whatever they may be, they cannot be directly related to the written units. The graphic unit itself is immediately recognisable on sight, and thus delimitation poses no problems. However, since it stems

THE UNIT IN WRITTEN AND ORAL LANGUAGE   43

from a type of "practical" know-how which has been shaped by a historical process, it can in no way be compared to the oral unit.
It is essential to check the validity of the hypothesis, so often mentioned in writing typology research, that writing systems related to the utterance and those related to the system of the language should be distinguished from each other. In the system-related approach, little interest is to be gained from the delimitation of word groups and sentences, whereas there is much interest in the word itself. It is only within the whole issue of the word that the question of the extent to which equivalences between the written and the oral are to be taken into consideration arises.

Notes

[1] J.Bottéro (1987:82)comments that certain characters in Sumerian writing, are equipped with a type of "polyphony". These may serve at will either as syllabic signs or as ideograms. "Thus one may signify in one case the *bovine*, and in another case the syllable *qud*".
[2] The English"word" and German "wort" are etymologically derived from the Latin "uerbum". The Spanish "palabra", Italian "parola" derive from the Greek "parabola", which means literally "a comparison of the phrase". The French "mot", according to Michèle Fruyt (1990:43), would seem to have an etymology stemming from the low Latin "muttum", with the onomatopoeic origin "mu", the mooing of cattle.
[3] "If all we retain from the writing system are the letters and their pronunciation, we efface from the word "writing" its whole existence (...).The true writing system is one of comprehended words, whatever the degree of comprehension may be" (C. Sirat and T. Vinh, 1990:168).
[4] In 1963, James Février exposed this hypothesis in his sub-heading: "The Semites and the alphabet:concrete and abstract writing systems". He commented on an on-going conflict through the centuries between two types of writing systems, and considered Semitic as representative of a major type of abstract writing system (cf. also A. Rosetti, 1947).
[5] This distinction ties up with the one set forward by F. Rastier (1990:65) between signification, "which concerns the independent language word or at least within the lexico-graphical representations that are proposed; and meaning which is bound to word occurrence (and other syntagms within their context). The relation of signification to meaning is that of *type* to *occurrence,* as in German *Sinn* (signification) and *Bedeutung* (meaning).
[6] I could have adopted another type of terminology, such as: "discourse word and language word" in the tradition of Saussure, or again, "surface word and deep word" (as used by certain generativists such as Di Sciullo and Williams 1988). However, I did not wish to take on all the implications of these terms.

[7] It is a well-known fact that the bilingual frequently has trouble in translating "independent words".

[8] Knowledge of graphic material as such may have an effect on the mechanisms of word writing.

[9] According to Sharon Begley in Newsweek, April 20, 1992, p. 43, quoting the work of Marcus Raichle, Washington University in St. Louis.

[10] It can happen that a person challenged on something he has just said has to repeat the whole of his utterance. I have been informed that young waiters learning how to memorize a whole set of orders are generally unable to pick out a fragment. For example, on the order "Two halves of bitter, a black coffee for number three", if we ask "How many beers?", they cannot reply "Two", but have to go through the whole chant.

[11] "Far from being indentified with reading and writing skills, these concepts appear to be part of the general orientation to language and to forms of thought that are of particular relevance to a literate society. Consequently, they are acquired as much from the oral practice of literate parents as from the actual activities of reading and writing" (N. Torrance and D. R. Olson 1987:136).

[12] According to the account of C. Sirat (1981 b:28) a certain type of prototypical word range appears in ancient Hebraic traditions. Thus in the 16th century Cordovero provided this insight: "The letters are bound together in various ways. First they form proper nouns, then common nouns and their derivatives. Later they bind together in a new way in order to form words with a bearing on earthly happenings and material objects".

[13] S. R. Anderson (1988, pp. 162-164) gives a good account of the debate which opposes the more structuralist linguists who uphold morpheme-based morphology to the generative linguists who propound a word-based morphology. It hinges on the fact that there are morphological phenomena which may not be dealt with as segments of a word, but have to be considered as non-segmental patterns. These patterns would be applied to the domain of the "word", and in fact the "word" could be defined as the domain of application for these patterns. Di Sciullo and Williams (1988:110) hold the view that the whole unit hierarchy: "morpheme>word>compound>phrase>sentence may be considered as unbroken, all of a theoretical piece".

[14] "Period" rather than "sentence": Togeby considers that intonation delimits units which do not necessarily correspond to what we understand by "sentence", syntactically speaking.

[15] An inflexive is for example the "s" genitive in English in "The king of England's hat", where it is linked to a noun word group, "the king of England".

[16] A derivative element would be , for example, "-ment" in the English "government".

[17] The "theme" would be the basis as "govern-"in "government".

[18] In writing systems with frequent use of the hyphen, as in French or Portuguese, the question of reforming this point is often raised, either by combining the elements totally or by introducing other hyphens. Total combining is not always feasible as far as the graphic is concerned even if it would be imperative for the meaning. Thus in

French, "arc-en-ciel" (rainbow) is perceived as a unit needing to be written as a single word. This is impossible, however, since the final "c" of "arc" has the value of a /k/, which would be lost and replaced by /s/ if it were written attached to the "e" of the following word: "arcenciel". The same remark holds true for examples such as "bemme-quer" ("marguerite") in Portuguese.

[19] One only writes what is scripted here in capital letters, that is to say:
white: BYD   whiten: BYYD
whiteness: BYD   to be white: BYDD.

The writing system thus reveals the image of an "abstract word". It is interpretation through the enunciative act that is responsible for the major part of the "pattern", allowing for choice of discourse elements.

[20] In the first Phoenician inscriptions (Teixidor 1991:94), the words are carefully separated by a stroke or a stop. It is this practice which led J. G. Février to comment most correctly that the consonant-type writing system was a word writing system.

[21] U. Wandruszka (1992) considers that the Romance languages opt rather for use of the suffix than the prefix, and also tend not to block out the beginning of lexemes in the writing system.

[22] The Slavic languages would seem to be less homogeneous on this point. Kràmsky (1969:56) remarks: "The written norm is often at variance with the delimitations of the word units (...). Thus Czech neznàm vs. Russian ne znayu (I do not know)". The negation which is a clitic item in both languages is written joined in Czech and divided in Russian.

[23] L. Galand (1991:707) explains that the Berber language is written with three different writing systems. Firstly with a writing system composed of traditional "tifnagh" characters (Libyco-berber) recently adopted by militant Berber movements, secondly with Arabic writing, since the 16th century (with extra signs for the vowels) and thirdly with a Latin type alphabet (adopted in 1966 under the patronage of Unesco).

[24] C. Sirat (1981b:28) recounts a series of Hebrew traditions concerning the continuous or interrupted text. According to Moses ben Naahman, known as Nahmanide, who wrote around the year 1200, "The Torah was in a continuous form without division into words. This allowed it to be read both as a series of names (of God) and, in our usual way, as a story ( ) The Torah was handed to Moses in a form where its division into words made the commandments comprehensible. At the same time, he received an oral tradition allowing it to be read as a series of name words".

The Word Out of (Conceptual) Context

Emilia Ferreiro

Several linguists have recently started to elaborate on the consequences of the lack of theoretical reflexion about writing systems for a strictly linguistic analysis (cf. Sampson (1985), Catach, (1990), Blanche-Benveniste, this volume). What, in my opinion, has not yet been analyzed, or sufficiently focused, are the consequences of this lack of theoretical reflection about writing systems for the development of contemporary psycholinguistics. In what follows, I will try to analyze this problem, first in general terms and then with specific reference to research into the notion of word and its psychological evolution. Two authors included in this volume - C.Blanche-Benveniste and D.Olson - will be referred to during the discussion.

1. Preliminaries

Contemporary psycholinguistics, conceived as a truly interdisciplinary field, has suffered from historically ill-defined problems relating to the basic relationship between orality and writing. Several problems have derived from this historical heritage, some of which can be outlined as follows:

(a) Twentieth century linguistics began with consistent and enduring efforts to establish orality as the only object of analysis. As a consequence, psycholinguistic research was almost exclusively devoted to oral language (even though, as we shall see, writing intruded dangerously into experimental designs).

(b) The deficiencies that linguistics attributed to writing correspond to a naïve view (i.e. neither thematized nor theoretically analyzed) according to which writing was merely a technique for transcribing oral utterances. However, it is easy to demonstrate using historical evidence that the function of writing (a social object constructed through cultural encounters) was never to achieve perfect phonetic transcription (nor even an approximate one). The subsequent neglect of writing, conceived of as intrinsically deficient, left it in a "no man's land" (whose consequences will be discussed below). This notwithstanding, writing is an unavoidable object in any study of science and culture.

(c) As a result of the above-described neglect, contemporary psycholinguistics became so convinced that oral language was its unique object of study that it is now necessary to provide explicit arguments to support the view that writing acquisition is not simply a matter of pedagogical enquiry, teaching methods, of books or school environments, but also a legitimate field of psycholinguistic research.

(d) Some linguists and psycholinguists are now, at the end of the 20th century, trying to develop - not only as a program, but with many years of research behing them - three fields of research: a linguistic theory of writing; a linguistic analysis of specific problems related to the syntactic organization of oral utterances that were traditionally considered to be marginal ones; a psycholinguistic theory of the development of written language. These three lines of research developed independently of each other; researchers subsequently found links between them.

2. The consequences of the lack of theorization about writing for psycholinguistic research.

As has already been noted, the 20th century linguistic science began with a consistent and enduring effort to establish orality as the sole object of analysis. Writing was driven out of linguistic territory by Ferdinand de Saussure, who used some particularly violent expressions (cf. Chapter VI of the *Cours de Linguistique Générale*, one of the more controversial and influential chapters of his book)[1]: "L'écriture voile la vue de la langue; elle n'est pas un vêtement mais un travestissement". (For any psychologist, the violence of the expression is evidence of the intimacy of the relationship). A similar view was held by Leonard Bloomfield (1933) who, instead of direct accusations, chose to undervalue written language: "Writing is not language, but merely a way of recording language by means of visible marks". It is not my present purpose to discuss the arguments used by the greatest names of contemporary linguistics to deny writing its citizenship rights. On the contrary, I accept that it was safe to deny them at that moment or, as Ruth Weir (1967) stated: "The victory of accepting the primacy of spoken language has in fact been won so hard that any concession to writing savored of retreat" (cited by Sampson, 1985:13).

In fact, the sharp distinction between oral and written language during the first half of the 20th century had positive consequences at the phonological level. It was established that the phoneme was a conceptual entity that should not be confused with its realizations (phones); it was possible to analyze the distintive features without any reference to graphic representations. The acceptance of de Saussure's extraordinary and powerful characterization of the phoneme as a purely negative and oppositive conceptual entity had great impact: a phoneme is what the other phonemes are not; in other words, a phoneme is no more than a position in a system.

Under the strong influence of Noam Chomsky's proposals, linguistics in the second half of the 20th century established a new but equally strong dichotomy: the competence/performance distinction. This distinction has contributed to a blurring of the importance of the previous distinction between oral and written forms, though in fact, the Chomskyan "ideal speaker-hearer" is already literate (and preferably a linguist...).

It is well known that psychologists reacted immediately to a theory that explicitly built a bridge between linguistic analysis and psychological functioning: "No doubt, a reasonable model of language use will incorporate, as a basic component, the generative grammar that expresses the speaker-hearer's knowledge of the language" (Chomsky, 1965:9). Psychologists tried to prove the psychological reality of the model through a direct equation between transformational operations in the linguistic model and equivalent psychological operations in the speaker's mind.

The important point we wish to emphasize here is the following: the *first* experiment that established the psychological reality of the transformational model (G.Miller and McKean, 1964) used a *reading* task (to read a sentence, to produce the required transformation, to find on a given list the sentence with the required transformation: passive, negative, passive affirmative, and so on). Nobody, to my knowledge, objected that the experiment was not valid due to the utilization of written language. Conclusions were drawn regarding the speaker's competence; the fact that the speaker was acting as a reader seemed totally irrelevant.

Several experiments followed the same line of thought, using various experimental designs and using written language from time to time[2]. The experimental evidence against Chomsky's 1957 model grew and the model was finally abandoned, but, as far as I know, the utilization of writing in some of the more noted and influential experiments was never questioned.

The use of reading tasks is so common in psycholinguistic research that nowadays it is still rather easy to find published research that ask subjects to behave as *readers* while the conclusions are drawn upon *speakers*[3]. It may be that for certain kind of linguistic operations it is irrelevant to work on oral or written stimuli; however, the point to be stressed is the lack of reflection on the use of an oral or a visual medium for a theorization of speakers or knowers of a given language.

Writing intruded not only in the experimental designs but also in the linguistic objects proposed to speakers. The basic unit is the sentence - a unit that several contemporary linguists (P.Achard, C.Blanche-Benveniste, among others) object to as being a typical writing unit, a bad unit for the description and analysis of oral speech. Many of the sentences proposed in the experiments are impossible as oral utterances (and even very strange in writing). Under the irresistible appeal of recursive rules, sentences that could never be proposed as oral utterances were administered to subjects, e.g.: *This is the boy that the man whom the lady whom our friend saw knows hit* (Schlesinger, 1968, cited by Greene, 1972:135).

For obvious reasons, reading tasks were not utilized in experiments with small children. Nevertheless, in many experiments they heard written sentences or a written history. Moreover, as the main aim was always to reach the syntactic level at the "purest degree" (in spite of the unavoidable constraint of realizing syntactic structures through lexical items), the sentences proposed to children suffered, particularly in the 70's, from the same bias of "syntactic gymnastics"[4].

3. The tasks attributed to writing.

The great majority of 20th century linguists shared the view that writing is merely a technical device for transforming oral utterances into visible marks. Among the linguists working in the early decades of this century, very few can be cited as exceptions. The most notable exception was Josef Vachek, of the Prague' school, who published an important article in 1945 about the differences between writing and phonetic transcription[5]. Once established, this distinction seems elementary but even nowadays needs to be established clearly: a phonetic transcription is a technical device. Vachek adds: "On the contrary writing is a system in its own right, adapted to fulfil its own specific functions which are quite different from the functions proper to a phonetic transcription" (1989:7). Therefore, it is senseless to blame writing because it is not a perfect phonetic transcription. Moreover, if one accepts that the phonemic system is only one of the aspects of language considered as a system, "the phonemic system can not claim the exclusive right to be reflected in writing"

Simple though it is, this is a fundamental statement, because writing can only be considered defective under two preconditions: (a) the primacy of the phonological level over all the others; (b) the supposition that writing was invented to represent the phonological level of language analysis.

Vachek goes even further claiming that, while a phonetic transcription is to be regarded as a sign of the second order (i.e. the sign of a sign of the outside world), the text recorded in writing is to be taken, at least in advanced cultural communities, as a sign of the first order (i.e. the sign of an outside world). That is to say, in deciphering a text put down in writing no detour by way of spoken language is necessary to make out its content, as is the case in deciphering a phonetically transcribed text" (1989:4).

This is a major point. In fact, the possibility of conceiving that "la langue" exists as legitimately in written as it does in oral form (two forms totally or relatively autonomous, between which there are no hierarchic or dependency links) is connected to the idea of writing as a prime order system of signs.

This idea might seem a new one, but it has at least one great medieval and hispanic predecesor: Isidore of Seville (c.560-636). Isidore, considered to be the last Father of the Catholic Church, was severely criticized for his "Etymologies". Nevertheless, his influence was wide and profound. Even towards the end of the 9th century he was still carefully studied by the Irish monks and, through the innovations they introduced in transcription techniques, Isidore may now be regarded as a precursor of the great literacy revolution that led to silent reading.

In open opposition to the Aristotelian tradition - supported by Augustine - Isidore regarded the letters of the alphabet as signs *without* sounds. Augustine "followed Aristotle in regarding letters as signs of signs: *'these are signs of sounds, and these sounds in our speech are themselves signs of things we think'*. By contrast, Isidore regarded letters of the alphabet as signs without sounds, *'which have the power to convey to us silently the sayings of those who are absent'*. The letters themselves are signs of things. (...) For this reason Isidore preferred silent reading to ensure better comprehension of the text: *'for the understanding is instructed more fully when the voice of the reader is silent'"* (Parkes, 1992:21).

It is widely recognized that the abandonment of the traditional practice of *scriptio continua* was the first step in a great revolution. The systematic isolation of (written) words, together with a more careful utilization of punctuation marks and various devices for distinguishing of paragraphs and sections (in general, "mise en page" devices, graphic devices with no oral equivalent, "silent" indications for the reader) were the pre-requisites of the great revolution in reading practices that took place around 12th century[6]. In the words of I. Illich (1993): "A new kind of reader comes into existence, one who wants to acquire in a few years of study a new kind of acquaintance with a larger number of authors than a meditating monk could have perused in a lifetime. These new demands are both stimulated and met by new reference tools. Their existence and use is profoundly new. And once these tools are invented they remain fundamentally unchanged until the text composer program of the 1980s. A mutation of comparable depth begins only then." (1980:96)

4. Historical evolution

As we have seen, the presupposition shared by linguists was (and still is) that the main function of writing is to represent (as accurately as possible) the elementary sounds of speech. This presupposition also affected interpretations of the history of writing. It was all too easy to fall into the temptation of considering all writing systems prior to the alphabet as a preparation for it, i.e. as faulty but progressive attempts to represent the basic and elementary level of linguistic structure: the phonological level. Gelb (1952) is the best and most influential example of this line of thought.

During the long development of this "evolutionary" view, the alphabetical writing system, created only once in history, was the only writing system considered not to have any vices. It was regarded as simple, economic, precise, and it was thanks to the alphabet that humanity had achieved rational thought, contemporary science and democracy. Alphabetic writing was the only system that could be considered appropriate for writing down previously unwritten languages, because it was assumed that only an alphabetical writing system could help achieve universal literacy. Although I said it had no vices, it in fact had one fault: the correspondence between phonemes and graphemes was never perfect.

This history of writing that starts with the concrete (pictographs) and moves on towards the abstract (the phoneme), moving step by step inevitably towards the alphabet. Fortunately recent historical research has enabled us to set this kind of interpretation aside.

One of the great conquests of 20th century linguistics has been the study of each language *per se*, rather than considering them in terms of their proximity to the prototypical perfect language: Latin. It is now time to apply the same procedure to written languages. We ought to study each writing system *per se*, instead of considering them in terms of their proximity to a supposedly prototypical perfect writing system: alphabetic writing.

All the original writing systems, as far as we know, were well suited to the language they tried to convey. Those which evolved (Sumerian being the best known example) were transformed by the fact that speakers of languages with

other origins took other people's creations and made them their own. In so doing, they transformed the former language (see Olson, this volume).
On the other hand, it is evident that all the alphabetic writing that are derived from the same Greek origin are somewhat distant from the ideal principles of perfect correspondence between minimal spoken units and minimal writing units. In fact, all historically evolved alphabetic writing is mixed in nature, combining morphological and ideographic marks in various degrees. Is this mixed character an unexpected product of historical development or is it an intrinsic characteristic of any writing system? The answer is not yet available, but discussion of these matters has important consequences. Some researchers argue, for instance, that cuneiform writing, from the very beginning, was a mixture of logograms, phonetic (syllabic) signs and silent categorial determinatives (a kind of ideogram) (Michalowski, 1994). If this proves to be true, it means that phonetism was not the product of evolution but has been present from the very beginning, intimately mixed with other characteristics - as it is nowadays in historically developed writing systems.

5. Psycholinguistic development: oral and written language

The great majority of the population upon which data from psycholinguistic research is made up of university students (mainly students of psychology). The potential bias of data obtained with such a population is never analyzed: university students, by definition, are literate people. Similarly, the children who provided the most influential data on language development theory are children of graduate students or professors (linguists or psycholinguists).

I would not deny the growing importance of culturally based research in linguistic domains. However, data from "exotic" environments and poorly known languages does not have any influence on the general trends of the theory of linguistic acquisition. Data coming from "minority" languages is compared with English, German, Japanese or French in terms of similarities and differences; nobody, to my knowledge, has attempted to build up a new language acquisition theory from a new starting point, regardless of data from "main" languages.

In spite of their tremendous importance, these points are not the main concern of the present argument. The point is that the data that constitutes the bulk of developmental psycholinguistics is provided by children whose parents are highly literate. From the very beginning of their linguistic development, these children interact with written language, orally presented, and with objects that are part of a literate culture (books, magazines, paper and pencils). They grow up knowing that written marks exist and that there is some relationship (although very difficult for them to understand) between these marks and the production of a kind of speech that differs sharply from everyday oral exchanges.

Researchers need to record oral productions with considerable accuracy; recording sessions are technically more successful if the child and his/her caretaker remain in a single place interacting with a single object. It is not surprising that verbal interactions involving a book (naming pictures, talking about the actions of characters or even telling a story) are so often reported in the literature. The problem is that the book is not considered by researchers to be an unusual kind of object, intrinsically linked to written language. More often than not, books are considered to be "toys", on the same level as dolls, cars and balls. The presence of books in naturalistic or experimental settings is extremely frequent, but conclusions are drawn concerning oral language, irrespective of their peculiarity to literate cultures or the degree of parents' literacy.

This lack of attention to the intrusion of written language in the very conditions of naturalistic or experimental settings is discussed in the next section that deals with the presuppositions behind the study of the development of the notion of word.

6. The development of the notion of word: Research about oral language or written language?

The term "word" cannot be taken as a primitive, either in a linguistic sense or in a psychological sense, either historically or ontogenetically (see Blanche-Benveniste, this volume).

The term "word" is not a theoretical term in modern linguistics. 20th century linguists dismissed the idea of finding a definition of "word" valid for all existing (and pre-existing) languages[7]. Regarded as an intuitive and pre-theoretical notion, the word continues nevertheless to have a concrete existence in all alphabetical writing systems and it is unavoidable for any theory of reading in those systems. In spite of theoretical difficulties, the "word" has a practical existence, and a good reader learns to take advantage of its power to organize written material graphically. (I would say: linguists divide into words their statements against the word...)

It is worth emphasizing that psycholinguistic research on the development of the notion of "word" has adopted (implicitly more often than explicitly) the practical notion of "word" belonging to alphabetic writing systems at the present state of their evolution (i.e. strings of letters separated from other strings by empty spaces). However, we have to remember how complex the history of our actual segmentations in writing was and how different the actual solutions for related words in languages with a common origin are[8].

"Word" is without doubt a metalinguistic term and research into it is usually referred to as metalinguistic research or as awareness of "word units". There have been various techniques aimed at examining what is the referent of the term "word" - counting them, reversing the "word order" of a given expression, defining them; detecting a "target word" in a given sentence, saying the first or the last word of a sentence, and so on (cf.Gombert,1990, Chapter IV).

C.Blanche-Benveniste (this volume) proposes an interesting distinction between "words in the utterances" and "words in the system". The former have not fixed limits and are heavily context-dependent. The latter - like the entries of a dictionary - are considered out of context, "abstract" units available to fulfill different functions in actual utterances. Obviously, the operations needed to isolate the "words in the system" are heavily dependent of the possibility of writing them.

If we take this distinction into account psycholinguistic studies of the notion of word can be examined in a new light. We see in fact that, in the absence of a technical definition, researchers took the written definition of word as the "correct" parameter for evaluating children's answers[9].

The problem is that word-units (whose frontiers are defined by several centuries of written practices) are presented in purely oral contexts, as if children could discover these frontiers outside literacy practices.

In fact, there is considerable consensus among researchers: children are able to apply the term "word" to nouns, adjectives and verbs well before they apply it to prepositions, articles and conjunctions[10]. It is only when children are 7 years old (in fact, between 7 and 9 or 10) that they share the written definition of "word" (i.e. they are able to solve all the orally proposed but graphically constructed tasks; see Gombert, 1990, for a review). Since all children interviewed in these experiments attend school, it is not surprising that the age of 7 constitutes the turning point of the studied behavior: at that age children are expected to have had at least one year of literacy instruction[11]

When children are asked to treat the term "word" in relation to written material the task is not considered to be psycholinguistic, but a "reading readiness task". To my knowledge, the only experimental setting where written material as well as writing instruments were used to study the children's "concept of word" is the one we reported in 1992 (Ferreiro and Vernon). This has remained unnoticed as usually happens with articles published in Spanish. The interest point of this research - carried out with 4-5 year old children - is that it showed that the term "name" was understood by the majority of the children as having a very clear meaning: a string of letters associated with the object[12], while there was no such consensus for the term "word" (for some children, it was the same as to a story, for others, it was the same as letters or minimum sounds without meaning; in between, all kind of intermediate answers). In a recent experiment using proverbs (Ferreiro, in press) we were able to show that normal children who already write alphabetically but have not yet grasped all the conventions of graphic segmentation into words have difficulties in matching the oral counting with the written counting, using in both cases the same term "words".

What can we conclude from the available evidence? It is not true that pre-literate children do not have a "word concept" or that they cannot make explicit segmentations into words; the problem is that their way of analyzing them does not correspond with the written definition of word. In fact, they do not find good reasons to apply the same term ("word") to such heterogenous entities as, for instance, "house" and "a". They easily distinguish between "word" and other pieces of language that are there "to put the words together".

The reluctance of children to put everything that we say under the common term "word" is not surprising. In the classical Roman and Greek tradition, the linguistic terminology was polysemic (*rema, lexis* and *logos*, in Greek, as well as *uerbum, dictum, dictio, uox*, in Latin, are not equivalent to our present concept of word) (Fruyt and Reichler-Béguelin, 1990). Moreover, the traditional analysis of *partes orationis* made specific use of terms for sub-categories (for instance, the opposition between *uerbum/nomen*, that corresponds to verb/noun) without having a generic term for all the sub-categories. It seems to us that, in children's minds, the situation is closer to that of the traditional grammarians than to the literate practices of today.

7. Final remarks

It is not easy to work against the strong tradition that we have inherited from Aristotle and Augustine, which claims that writing signs are second grade signs, signs of signs, visible signs of pre-existing oral signs. However, for many reasons this view is of no help in understanding either writing as such or its psychological and historical evolution. There are two main ideas within this tradition that constitute a real obstacle to our understanding: the idea of *transposition* and the idea of *substitution*.

According to the former, the same units that "naturally" exist at the oral level are merely transposed (technically) to the written level without any process of reconstruction. According to the latter, the mechanics of the process is conceived of as being similar to a Pavlovian chaining of stimuli: the sight of food is substituted by the sound of the bell; a light can substitute the sound of the bell and so on.

I would suggest that it is more convenient to think about the relationships between oral and written units in terms of Piaget's theory of hierarchical systems that are constructed on the basis of preceding ones. In such a case, units at a previous level do not automatically become the units of the subsequent level: each level defines its own units. Thus, we do not have a chain of symbols that can substitute one another but a new level of organization. With regard to writing, language is an object "at another level". As a consequence, the units of writing should not be conceived of as pre-determined by oral utterances. They need to be discovered anew.

Notes

[1] We are aware of the discussion concerning the attribution of all the assertions included in the *Cours* to de Saussure. Nevertheless, the *Cours* is the fundamental text of linguistic structuralism, the authorship of which was attributed to de Saussure, though based on the notes of two of his students. It is considered here in this light.
[2] For instance, H.Clark (1965), Wason (1961), and Wason and Jones (1963) used written language in their experimental designs.
[3] For instance, a survey of volumes 19 to 24 of the *Journal of Psycholinguistic Research* that correspond to years 1990 to 1995, shows that 25 of the 163 published articles (i.e. a little bit more than 15%) used written material in the experimental tasks, without further analysis of the consequences of the intrusion of written sentences or words. More often than not, there is lack of justification; sometimes the justification is on practical grounds: for instance, Hickock (1993:244) said that "The sentences were presented visually (in order to eliminate any influence of intonation in auditory speech) one word at a time in the center of the screen". In addition, in several research designs the subject's answers consist of a writing task. Authors indicate that they were conducting "all-visual" or "self-paced reading experiments"; that "subjects made lexical decisions to visual targets"; that subjects were asked "to read target sentences", "to read stories" or to react to "verbs presented in their written infinitive form"; they evaluate differences in "reading time", etc. However, conclusions are drawn about the "human sentence processing mechanisms" or whatever expression is used to indicate language comprehension.
[4] I include myself in this critique. When, with other colleagues of H.Sinclair's team, I carried out a cross-linguistic study of the comprehension and production of relative clauses, the sentences used for the comprehension task were also impossible at the oral level: *El conejo que el gato empujó lavó al oso / The squirrel that the pig pushes licks the bear / Le cochon que le singe pousse lèche la vache*. (Ferreiro, Othenin-Girard, Chipman and Sinclair, 1976). Fortunately, we also studied the production of relative clauses, the more informative part of the research results.

[5] Various articles of J.Vachek are included in a recent volume (Vachek, 1989). The other names that share Vachek's concern about writing are: the Finn Aarni Penttilä (1932) and H.J.Uldall, disciple of Hjemslev (1944).

[6] It is worth noting that Isidore, a promoter of silent reading, also paid great attention to punctuation marks.

[7] "Le mot, unité maîtresse incontestée de la grammaire et du lexique avant l'apparition de la linguistique moderne, est banni sans pitié et ne trouve plus nulle part droit de cité (c'est d'ailleurs la seule unité primaire de la grammaire traditionnelle qui soit chassée aussi impitoyablement du vocabulaire et de la prise en considération des linguistes)" (Pergnier, 1986:15).

[8] For instance, comparing the present orthography of three languages of Latin origin, we see that written Spanish has a tendency to separate adverbial expressions that are kept as a "single word" in Portuguese and Italian. For instance (in the above mentioned order) we have: *entre tanto / entretanto / intanto; con todo / contudo / inanzitutto; sobre todo / sobretudo / soprattutto; tal vez / talvez / talvolta.* (Cf.Ferreiro, Pontecorvo et al, 1996, Chapter II).

[9] For instance: "The children confused the first two words of the *all much only* string with such single words as *almost, also, always, already,* etc." (Tunmer et al., 1983:577).

[10] Adverbs do not constitute an homogeneous class; some adverbs seem to be treated like the nouns, i.e. accepted as "words", while others are not so easily accepted.

[11] In a recent paper (Karmiloff-Smith and al., 1996) it is argued that 4 and a half-5 year old children are able to isolate words in an on-line task, which consists of repeating the last word said by an adult who is *reading* a story. (The article states that "The child listened to a story which is interrupted at times. Each time the experimenter stops mid-story, the child is asked: "What was the last word I said?". However, given the text presented in Appendix 2, one can only imagine that reading aloud was used, so as to maintain a sufficiently consistent procedure). As usual, children were interviewed in a school setting ("They were all from two classes of what is known in the UK as 'infant school'"). Several questions remain unanswered. (A) Children are not listening to a tape but a real person reading aloud; nothing is said about the control of particular intonation contours - or even stress - that could serve as cues. As any one knows, it is difficult to keep the stimuli under such conditions constant. (B) The analysis is made in terms of "Open and closed class words", without further justification of this choice. Why choose a dichotomy that is applicable only at the start of language acquisition? Do the authors imagine that the mental lexicon is organized in such a way in 4-5 year old children? It is difficult to give an affirmative answer to this question. In addition, half of the items of the "closed class" could be analyzed as "content words". (C) Instead of testing their actual knowledge of the written language, which would never have produced a clear reader/non reader distinction but a continuum, children were automatically assumed to be 'non-readers'. (D) Correct answers, as usual, were defined by written criteria, but the conclusions did not consider the influence of the literate environment. After saying that "There seems to be an intricate interplay between metalinguistic awareness and reading", the last sentence of the arti-

cle insists on a purely developmental view: "metalinguistic awareness could turn out to be part of language acquisition itself rather than the mere product of literacy".

[12] In fact, a string of letters fulfilling children's formal criteria of interpretability, i.e. minimum quantity of letters and internal variability (Ferreiro and Teberosky, 1979)

Preschool Knowledge of Language:
What Five year olds Know about Language Structure and Language Use

Ruth A. Berman

1. Introduction

The knowledge of language attributed to children of five to six years of age, just prior to literacy instruction in most Western cultures, depends critically on how one chooses to characterize "linguistic knowledge". This study aims to show that, on the one hand, five-year-olds know a great deal but, on the other, certain aspects of their language use reflects knowledge that is markedly lacking compared with adult members of their speech community. The point of departure for this chapter is thus Karmiloff-Smith's observation that age 5 "can be considered as a frontier age psycholinguistically" (1986a:455).

Two extreme views can be discerned regarding the level of linguistic knowledge attained by 5-year-olds. One identifies language acquisition with acquisition of generative grammar as a "cognitive system ... that develops in early childhood" (Chomsky 1972:4). Researchers in this paradigm point out that children "master a rich and intricate system of rules for language production and comprehension by the time they reach school age" (Crain 1991:597), and they emphasize the rapidity of this process as consistent with a strongly nativist bias, and as "the expectation that would come most directly from linguistic theory, which envisions a rapid and effortless transition from the 'initial state' to the 'final state'" (Crain and McKee 1985:94). This view has dominated developmental psycholinguistics since its inception in the 1960s, and has tended to limit the age-range of language acquisition research. From this perspective, "children are presumably engaged in the process [of learning to speak the language of their community] at the ages when we most often try to tap their abilities, from 1 to 5 years" Pinker (1984:6).

At the other extreme is the prescriptive tradition which was predominant in child language studies in the pre-Chomskian era (e.g. McCarthy, 1954). The language of the preschool child, like that of any illiterate, is an imperfect version of the desired adult form. Children need to be taught to improve their language, to acquire the skills of reading and writing, to learn the correct usage and the standard dialect, in order to become fullblown and worthy members of the speech community. From this perspective, what the child learns after age 5 is the crucial part of language development.

The present study seeks to navigate between these two extremes, in line with developmental psycholinguists who regard partial knowledge as a legitimate and interesting subject of inquiry, spreading over a time period from infancy to well beyond age 5. In a Piagetian, constructivist view of development, children are characterized as knowing a good deal at each phase of their general cognitive and linguistic development, but as needing to extend and reorganize this partial knowledge to reach a mature level of proficiency. In contrast with the Piagetian paradigm, however, language here is treated as a system in its own right rather than as fully determined by general cognitive processes and structures shared by other domains of knowlege. Nor is development anchored in age-bound, invariant, domain-neutral stages; rather, linguistic development manifests different sequential points in emerging grammatical abilities (Brown, 1973), definable as recurrent phases in acquisition, reorganization, and integrative mastery of different linguistic systems (Berman, 1986, 1987, 1990) and of other cognitive domains (Karmiloff-Smith, 1986b, 1992). Also in contrast to the Piagetian model, this view does not accord privileged status to metalinguistic knowledge; the "fully proficient" type of knowledge discussed here need not entail speakers' ability to reflect metacognitively on the grammatical structures and the form/function relations available to them.

This intermediate view can also be accommodated with the idea of "weak continuity", i.e. that the principles of U(niversal) G(rammar) are available from the outset, even though children's grammars may deviate from the target grammar of what will be their native language (Weissenborn, Goodluck, and Roeper, 1992). However, UG in this sense applies only to a generative grammar, whereas the view defined here would include not only (possibly rather different) formal principles but also "substantive" or "naive" universals (Chomsky, 1965; Keenan, 1975): categorial distinctions which must, may, or cannot be marked in a particular language (by morphology: Bybee, 1985; by clause structure: Slobin, 1982; and by lexical semantics: Talmy, 1985).

These divergent views on whether 5-year-olds know everything, very little, or quite a lot but by no means all of their language derive from different definitions of what constitutes "knowledge of language". A highly constrained view identifies language acquisition with acquiring **grammar**, typically some current model of a generative grammar. Language acquisition research since the 1960s has shown that children "acquire" simple clause structure by around age 3 to 3 and a half, and more complex constructions and interclausal relations by age 5. Beyond these two major breakoff points, certain "difficult" structures are added in early school years, defined variously as complex categories (Karmiloff-Smith, 1986a:457-458), syntactic developments in school-age speech and writing (Scott, 1988), and "late acquisitions" (Slobin, 1985).

In contrast to these structuralist, form-based analyses, are studies which analyze children's knowledge of language in terms of language use. Some such research is anchored in pragmatically motivated descriptions of young children's communicative skills in conversational turn-taking, negotiating, and pretend-play in social interaction context (Snow, 1989). Other research is concerned with skills related to the development of literacy - not only reading and writing, but also acquisition of a literate lexicon, verbal reasoning, and use of figurative language (Nippold, 1988). A third motivation, and the one underlying the present study, is thus the interrelation between linguistic form and language function in development.

2. Form-function relations in language development

A "linguistic form" refers here to any kind of linguistic device: bound morphemes, closed class items, syntactic structures, lexical expressions, and grammatical processes such as subject elision or left-dislocation (Berman and Slobin, 1994:18-19, 109-126). A "language function" refers to the way such forms are used to express referential content and in managing the flow of information in extended discourse (Berman, 1996; Budwig, 1991). For example, pronouns may be deictic or anaphoric, and they may serve for topic maintenance or for topic shift in discourse; adjectives may be attributive or predicating, and serve for noun modification or object-specification; relative clauses may serve a presentative function to introduce new referents, or a continuative function in relating different events in an ongoing narrative.

The burden of this chapter will be to show that linguistic forms have long developmental histories. In addition, language functions also start out with restricted or even unconventional forms. For example, to express a relation of **simultaneity**, where two events co-occur or overlap in time, 3 to 4 year old children telling a story based on a picture booklet use words meaning 'also, too' (e.g. German *auch*, Hebrew *gam*, Turkish *da*) to describe two things happening at the same time (e.g. *the boy fell and the dog also (fell)*. Five to six-year-olds use subordinating conjunctions like English 'when', verbless clauses (e.g. *the boy fell with the dog next to him*), or (in Turkish) nonfinite gerundives. Schoolchildren aged 9 to 10 years occasionally use explicit lexical markers of simultaneity, e.g. English *while*, Hebrew *benatayim* 'meanwhile'. And adults use semantically specific terms in a range of syntactic constructions, e.g. English participial *while running alongside of him* or Hebrew nominalized *tox kdey ricato* 'in the course of his-running'.

A second example is of **retrospection**, referring back to situations mentioned earlier in the discourse, which are relevant at a later point. In the same picturebook, the first picture shows a jar with a frog inside it, the next shows the frog getting out of the jar, then an empty jar is shown, and two pictures later the dog is shown with its head stuck inside the jar. Some 3- and 4-year-olds were able to refer to the jar's former state by using a possessive phrase, e.g. *the frog's jar, the jar of the frog*, showing that they have conceptualized this complex temporal notion. Older children used complex syntax for this purpose, e.g. *the jar the frog was in* or *the jar that belonged to the frog*. And mature narrators (in our sample, adults) used an array of means for expressing retrospection, e.g. they combined relative clause syntax with pluperfect morphology, describing the jar as *the place that had been the frog's home*, or *where the boy had kept the frog*. Such use of complex syntax for condensing elaborate arrays of events and participants is well beyond the abilities of preschool children. Discourse-motivated "syntactic packaging" of this kind is manifested only by proficient narrators; and adults, too, may demonstrate individual differences in this respect.

3. The developmental history of linguistic forms

As evidence for how much, or how little, is known by 5-year-olds, this section traces the developmental history of different linguistic systems: marking of verb-argument and voice relations (3.1), adjective formation (3.2), nominalizations (3.3), null subjects (3.4), and markers of connectivity (3.5). Analysis centers on data from Hebrew, but the general idea applies to acquisition of any language. On the one hand, linguistic forms are acquired at an early age, and the passage from non-use to grammatical mastery may appear to last only a few months. On the other hand, however, these forms have a long developmental history, and the passage from early grammatical mastery to proficient, discourse-motivated use may last beyond school-age into adolescence. Data from other languages are noted, to demonstrate how this universal pattern of overall development interacts with factors of target-language typology, to determine which particular subsystems are mastered earlier or later in the process.

Findings are presented from three types of data, in the belief that different research procedures are important complementary sources of evidence for one's claims. The data-base includes (a) *Structured elicitation tests* comparing adults with children aged between 2 and 9 years required to comprehend and produce novel forms based on familiar lexical items (noun compounds, denominal verbs, and resultative participles) and other procedures for deriving action nominals and syntactic passives (Berman 1995a); (b) *Naturalistic speech output* including longitudinal records of 5 Hebrew-speaking monolingual children, aged 18 months to 3 years in conversation with their parents, and a corpus of nearly 1000 innovative lexical usages of children aged 18 months to 7 years from diary and parental records (Berman, 1993a); and (c) *Narratives* elicited from Hebrew-speaking children aged 3 to 9 years compared with adults, including accounts of personal experience in a quarrel or fight and accounts based on a picture booklet and on a short film without words (Berman, 1995b).

3.1. Accusatives, Resultative Participles, and Passives

These three disparate forms are related by alternations between Hebrew verb morphology, as illustrated for the verb-roots sh-b-r 'break' and t-k-n 'fix, repair' in (1) a,b, and c.

(1) a. **Active Verb with Accusative Marker** *et:*
        Ron <u>shavar</u> ve Boaz <u>tiken</u>   et   ha-berez:
        Ron broke   and Boaz mended   Acc the tap

(1) b. **Resultative Participle**:
        ha-berez eyno <u>shavur</u>, hu   <u>metukan</u>
        the tap   isn't broken,   it's mended

(1) c. **Syntactic Passive**:
        ha-berez nishbar   al ydey Ron ve   tukan   (al ydey B)
        the-tap   was-broken (by Ron)   and mended   (by Boaz)

Details of Hebrew verb-pattern morphology are not of present concern (Berman, 1993a). What matters here is the contrast between the developmental history of three related linguistic forms. First, children master use of the prepositional *et* as a unique marker of accusative case, illustrated in (1a), by the young age of 2;6. This involves complex, abstract knowledge which is not always semantically motivated: *et* marks direct objects only if they are definite; it is used with stative as well as activity verbs; and some verbs of transitive activity govern prepositions other than *et*, e.g. compare *Ron shavar et ha-berez* 'Ron broke ACC the-tap' with *Ron ba'at ba-berez* 'Ron kicked in=at the-tap'.

Second, children show productive command of resultative participles forms expressing endstates, like those in (1b) and others, corresponding to English *broken, torn,* or *lost*, from age 3 to 4 years. Evidence derives from children's "creative errors" in spontaneous speech output from as young as age 3, and from the fact that they produce morphologically appropriate versions of such forms over half the time in a structured elicitation task (Berman, 1994). In contrast, syntactic passives like those in (1c) are avoided by children as late as age 6 years of age, around the middle of first grade. This is the case even when children are given obligatory contexts for passive-formation, whereas 12-year-old 6th-graders regularly provide such forms. This difference between resultative participles and syntactic passives is remarkable, since (a) both sets of forms derive from alternations in verb-pattern morphology, and this system has generally been mastered by age 4 years[1]; and (b) both the resultative participles like those in (1b) and many tensed passive verbs like *tukan* in (1c) are formed with the same passive-marking vowel *u*.

This delay in use of passives into school-age cannot be due to semantic opacity nor to morphological complexity, since younger, preschool children show early command of form/function relations in direct object marking and in use of resultative participles. One factor which can account for this delay in passive formation is that Hebrew speakers have alternative expressive options for performing the discourse functions associated with passive voice, i.e. downgrading of the agent to present an "undergoer perspective" on events. (a) Speakers can use verb-morphology to construct middle-voice forms, which is what Hebrew-speaking children do from as young as age 4 - as do adults - in picturebook narrations (Berman and Slobin, 1994, 515-538); (b) they can downgrade agency by subjectless impersonal constructions, used by children as young as 2 years old in their naturalistic speech output; and (c) they can topicalize nonagentive nominals by fronting to pre-subject position or by left-dislocation. Thus, Hebrew displays a rhetorical preference for other devices to fulfil the discursive functions of passive voice in a language like English.

An additional factor is that of register. Passive voice forms are typical of academic discourse in learned journals and from lecture podia, on the one hand, and of journalistic reporting in the media, on the other. In these contexts, activities are said to be "conducted" and events are "caused" or "expected" rather than described in direct, active terms. These two contexts are readily accessible to educated, literate speakers, but they are inappropriate and hence irrelevant to the everyday colloquial discourse which governs the speech input and output of preschool children.

3.2. Resultative Participles versus Denominal Adjectives

Consider, next, the case of adjective-formation. From around age 3, children speaking languages which have a class of adjectives enrich their vocabulary by adding to their stock of basic attributive terms, e.g. words for (Clark, 1993). As noted in the preceding section, Hebrew-speaking 3-year-olds also have productive command of the corresponding *-u* marked resultative participles. This is shown by the creatively innovative errors they make in producing a form like unconventional *takun* 'fixen' for required *metukan* 'fixed' [Keren, aged 2;11] or *meshutaf* 'rinsed' for conventional *shatuf* [Hagar, aged 2;10]. Slightly older children also innovate such forms by coining them from nouns, e.g. Hila, aged 4;2, describes her icy-cold hands as *krux-ot* 'iced-Plural' from the noun *kerax* 'ice', and Erez, aged 4;8, asks whether his tea is *meluman* 'lemoned', from the noun *limon* 'lemon'.

Hebrew has another highly productive device for forming adjectives from nouns: by adding the stressed suffix *-i*, e.g. *xashmal/xashmali* 'electricity/electric', *tsava / tsva'i* 'army/military', *ta'asiya/ta'asiyati* 'industry / industrial'. Yet our large corpus of unconventional lexical usages of preschool children shows very few such forms, mostly from older children, e.g. Ran, aged 5;4, describes his father's metal gun as *barzel-i* 'iron-y', and Tal refers to a glass bottle as *zxuxit-i* 'glass-y' = 'made of glass, transparent'. This contrast between the early, and robust, mastery of resultative adjective formation with the later, only occasional, use of denominal adjectives is not immediately obvious. Morphologically, resultative participles are more complex, since they are marked by a stem-internal vowel compared with a suffixal vowel at the end of the word, and they differ much more from the related active verb or base-noun than denominal adjectives differ from their source nouns. (Compare *meluman* with *limon-i* as possible versions of English 'lemoned' or 'lemony'; and lexicalized *metu'as* 'industrialized' from the verb *le-ta'es* versus *ta'asiyati* 'industrial' from the noun *ta'asiya*).

Semantically, too, it is not obvious that attributing resultant endstates to an object is more accessible to children than attributing associated properties to nouns. Besides, English-speaking children produce denominal adjectives with the suffix *-y* freely from as young as age two, both conventional *dirty*, *soapy* and innovative forms like *cracky*, *nighty* (Clark, 1993). This contrast between earlier and later acquisitions in different languages can be explained by two related typological distinctions: speaker preferences for productive new-word formation, and levels of usage and register. English denominal adjectives are formed from the basic, everyday wordstock of Germanic origin, available to English-speaking children from an early age, as a preferred, highly transparent method for attributing properties to nouns. In contrast, English denominal adjectives with Latin-based stems, e.g. *military* or *industrial*, are associated with later, schoolage vocabulary. In Hebrew, denominal adjective-formation is typical of academic and journalistic discourse, types of language usage which are neither relevant nor accessible to preschool children.

This analysis suggests that what children will learn relatively late depends on the nature of diglossia in the target language. Its source may be dialectal, as in the standard language of school compared with the local dialect of the home; and/or historical, as in the strata of English vocabulary; and/or contextual, as in register differences between everyday colloquial usage, standard intermediate-level usage of newspapers and academic discourse, and the normative requirements of the official language establishment (Ravid, 1995).

Another typological factor is structural. Hebrew as a Semitic language typically creates new words synthetically, by associating affixal patterns with consonantal roots. For children, this means that deriving verbs and adjectives from the system of verb-pattern alternations is a highly productive and hence accessible option. English prefers syntactic means such as zero derivation for creating verbs from nouns or the linear device of stem-suffixation. Crosslinguistic research has shown that children are sensitive to the favored devices of their native language from an early age, and that they have a good idea of "how things are done" in it well before attaining literacy. (See, for example, in expressing spatial notions, Choi and Bowerman, 1991; in new-word formation, Clark, 1993; and in marking tense/aspect and connectivity in extended discourse, Berman and Slobin, 1994). Typological preferences may speed up acquisition of general structural features of the target language; but they may also restrict and hence delay command of the full range of expressive options available for performing certain rhetorical functions in the target language.

3.3 Nominalized Forms

Nominalizations and nonfinite verb forms are another area where language typology interacts with level of usage to determine early versus late acquisitions. In a large scale crosslinguistic project, children of different ages were asked to tell a story based on a wordless picturebook depicting the adventures of a boy and his dog in search of a runaway frog (Berman and Slobin, 1994). We labeled as "late acquisitions" forms which were absent from the narrations of the preschool 3- to 6-year-olds in our sample, which appeared only occasionally in those of 9- to 10-year-old schoolchildren, but which were well represented in the texts of our adult narrators. The children's texts were quite typically lacking in nonfinite and nominalized verb-forms. In English, for example, participial -

ing, used widely for progressive aspect by the youngest children, and in complement constructions by the older children, appeared in an adverbial or other modifying function only in mature narrations (e.g. *And the deer carried him off to the edge of a cliff, with his dog chasing after*). In Hebrew, high-register gerundive forms (e.g. *be-hagio liktse ha-matsok* 'in-reaching-his to-the-end the cliff' = 'upon his reaching the edge of the cliff') did not appear in a single text, in keeping with the colloquial style suited to a children's adventure story. And only a few adult narrators made use of the highly productive, morphological mechanism of Hebrew for deriving abstract nominals from activity verbs (e.g. *ha-yeled haya asuk be-xipus axarey ha-tsfardea* 'The-boy was busy in-search after the-frog' = 'in searching for the frog'; *hem mamshixim bi-meruca-tam* 'They continue in-flight-their' = 'with their flight, fleeing').

Avoidance of nominalized forms in Hebrew children's narrative texts is consistent with findings from structured elicitations: Preschool 5-year-olds generally understood such forms in context, 9 year old schoolgoers produced them consistently in a completion task, but only 11-year-olds in the last class of primary school could coin novel nominalizations from unfamiliar verbs (Ravia and Avidor, in press). This avoidance of such forms until well into school age cannot be due to morphological complexity, since alternations between source verbs and their related nominalizations are akin to other derivational processes in Hebrew which are largely mastered by children as young as age 4 (Berman, 1995a). I suggest, rather, that the difficulty has several sources. One of these is syntactic complexity in the sense of "degree of deformation" of simple clause structure entailed by a particular syntactic process. Compare the three different levels of complexity illustrated for English nominalizations and their Hebrew counterparts in (2a) to (2c).

(2) a. **Simple Clauses with Finite Verbs**:
He'll build/construct the castle. It'll be easy for him.
hu yivne et ha-migdal. yihye kal bishvilo

(2) b. **Infinitival Extrapositioned Subjects**:
(For him) to build/construct the castle will be easy.
(bishvilo) li-vnot et ha-migdal yihye kal

(2) c. **Gerundive / Nominalized Subjects**:
(His) building/constructing (of) the castle /
(His) construction of the castle will be easy.
bniyat(-o) et ha-migdal tihye kala.
building+FM (-his) ACC the castle will-be easy+FM

In both languages, the examples are ranged on a cline of decreasing transparency. In English, the nominative-initial, SVO order of the simple clause is violated in (c) by a possessive pronoun followed by a gerundive or nominalized form, with genitive *of* and no overt tense marking; and in the Germanic wordstock, gerunds and derived nominals take the same *-ing* form as in building, but the Latinate *construct* splits between *constructing* and *construction*. In Hebrew, normal SVO word order is further violated, since the possessive suffix *-ó* 'his' follows the nominalized form, accusative case-marking is retained, but verb-tense is neutralized in the feminine gender derived nominal *bniya* 'building, construction'.

It is thus not surprising that children defer use of these forms till a literate stage in their development. Besides, possibly because of their syntactic complexity, nominalizations tend to be restricted to more formal registers of expository and academic discourse in both English and Hebrew. Yet here, too, structural complexity and opacity interact with factors of language typology to determine what options children will select for combining two or more tensed clauses in a single syntactic package. In our elicited narratives, preschool children typically string simple, tensed clauses one after another across their texts. Schoolage children use the typologically most accessible options for syntactic packaging. Children of Spanish- and Hebrew-speaking backgrounds rely heavily on subordination with *that-* for this purpose. Turkish children, on the other hand, use some of the nonfinite nominalized forms which correspond to finite subordination in their language from preschool age (Slobin, 1988). English-speaking children, in contrast, who are able to use both *to* infinitives and *-ing* forms of verbs correctly in simple clauses by age 2, fail to use these same constructions for the complex purposes of nominal embedding illustrated in (2b) and (2c). These represent more formal, literate rhetorical options for English speakers/writers.

This set of examples demonstrates how the factors of syntactic complexity and of typological preferences interact with the ***expressive options*** available in developing form/function relations in the domain of clause connectivity: by strings of separate simple clauses, as in (2a), favored by the preschool child, possibly by casual spoken in general; by infinitivals, readily available to children by late preschool age - although not when extraposed, as in (2b); or by finite subordinate clauses used increasingly by 9-year-old schoolage children, more so in Spanish and Hebrew than in English and German, while structurally unavailable to Turkish-speakers. These interrelated factors together combine to explain the finding from Hebrew experimental elicitations combined with extended narratives in different languages, that nominalizations are a late acquisition, not readily accessible to the preschool child.

3.4. Null Subjects and Topic Elision

The syntactic question of how children learn whether their language does or does not allow "null subjects" has generated much research in the past decade. Children clearly need to learn constraints on where their language requires, permits, or prohibits, a surface subject. English, like French, requires an overt subject in nearly all clause-types; Spanish, like Italian, allows (and in coordinate or complex clauses requires) no surface pronoun subject in many different syntactic environments. Hebrew allows null subjects in some but not all types of clauses, both simple and complex. This continuum was clearly reflected in our crosslinguistic narrative sample. Across age groups, English speakers used a surface 3rd person subject pronoun in the vast majority of all clauses in their texts; Hebrew speakers did so around 40% of the time; while Spanish speakers rarely used one (only 14 instances in 60 different texts). The fact that there were no significant age-related differences for each language in this respect demonstrates that the youngest children in our sample, aged 3 to 4 years, have already gained command of the grammatical construct of "null subjects" at the level of the simple clause.

Qualitative analysis of the distribution of subject pronouns in English and Hebrew narratives, however, reveals a more complex picture, of a U-shaped type of development. The youngest children, aged around 3 years, occasionally omit subjects ungrammatically; in contrast, older preschoolers, aged 4 to 6, may over-use surface subjects where not required, e.g. *And then the boy and the dog they both fall in the pond*. By school-age, 7- to 9-year-old children increasingly apply subject ellipsis correctly in coordinate and subordinate clauses, e.g. *The boy climbed up a tree and [0] looked in the hole*. That is, children proceed from initial ungrammatical ellipsis to correct use of subject pronouns in simple clauses; this is followed by a period of over-marking of subjects, typical of the phase when a particular device is being consolidated (Karmiloff-Smith, 1986b); subsequently, early school age children gain command of the grammatical constraints at interclause level. An even more proficient, or mature, mastery phase is achieved only later, when subject-ellipsis serves the discursive function of topic maintenance across stretches of text.

In different types of Hebrew narrative texts, some schoolage children, 7- and 9-year-olds, were able to use subject-elision for this discourse function at a relatively local level of two or three adjacent clauses. Adult narrators sometimes did so across entire lengthy stretches of text. However, not all adults use this device equally in Hebrew where, as noted, subject elision is optional. This introduces yet another factor which distinguishes preschool children's language use from that of fully proficient speakers: individual choice in deploying a particular grammatical structure as an optional rhetorical device. This is particularly notable in regard to the next topic: text connectivity as indicative of discourse-level abilities.

3.5. Connectivity and Narrative Structure

The final set of data concerns devices for marking discourse connectivity: the coordinator *and* and temporal markers of sequentiality such as *(and) then, after that*. Again, analysis focuses on findings from Hebrew (Berman, 1988, 1996); but closely parallel findings have been documented for other languages (e.g. for English, in Peterson and McCabe, 1988, 1991; for French, in Jisa, 1985, 1987; and for Spanish, in Sebastiàn and Slobin, 1994).

Development of form/function relations in use of the basic connective *and* in conversational and in different narrative contexts is outlined in (3).

(3) **Phase Position/Function**   **Intention Signalled**

1 - Utterance-initial "announcing"   I have more to say
(in the same conversational turn)

2 - Clause-initial "chaining"   Something else/more happened
(in chronological sequence)

3 - Text-embedded "chunking"   Events or states are related
(within a discourse theme)

To start with, children prefix *and* to consecutive utterances in the stream of speech, e.g. *and we went, and I saw, and it was empty, and ...give Danny some too*, announcing they have more to say. Here the form functions as a conversational "filler", or as "discourse glue" (Peterson and McCabe, 1988); early uses of *and* fail to mark either normative syntactic structure or conventional semantic content. For 2-year-olds, its function is primarily interactive, communicating to the hearer that more is to come. This is replaced, by around age 3, by grammatical use of *and* for coordinating clauses. Semantically, use of *and* develops between ages 3 to 5 years from expressing mere addition of events or states to expressing sequential and, later, causal relations between events (e.g. *Danny fell and hurt himself*). That is, preschoolers' use of the connective <u>and</u> develops from a communicative, to a syntactically wellformed, and to a semantically more elaborative function.

Beyond age 5, some schoolchildren between ages 7 to 9 may <u>overuse</u> it to precede nearly every clause in the narrative texts which they produce. Adults, in contrast, use <u>and</u> sparingly, primarily as a connective device specifying two or more parallel events, performed by the same participant at different times or places (e.g. *the boy climbed up a tree and looked into a hole inside its trunk*) or by different participants at the same time and place (e.g. *the boy climbed up a tree to look for the frog and the dog ran from the bees that were chasing him*). Proficient narrators rarely initiate a sequence of clauses, with coordinating *and*.

Use of explicitly sequential connectives such as *(and) then* or *after that* demonstrates an even more marked U-shaped curve across different types of narratives. They occur only occasionally in the texts of the youngest children in our samples (aged 3 to 4 years), are very common among the children of late preschool and early schoolage (5 to 7 or 9 years), and rare among adults. Five-year-old narrators, like early schoolage children, produce strings of narrative text, with nearly every successive clause introduced by *and then* or its equivalents. This shows that they have mastered the concept of sequentiality, of one event following another, which forms the backbone of narrative chronology, and that they prefer to mark it overtly. Proficient narrators, in contrast, use such markers sparingly, showing their understanding that temporal sequentiality is the default case for events in narrative discourse. Their use of sequential connectives is subordinated to the overall frame of discourse, to mark episode boundaries, the initiation of a new episode, or reintroduction of a prior theme.

Thus, preschool children still need to master discourse-motivated selectivity in using linguistic devices for marking grammatical relations between clauses and of semantic relations between events and states. It is not enough that they can organize discourse at the local level of adjacent clauses or utterances in on-going speech output. They must command cognitive control at a global level of hierarchical organization, which in narratives means overall, plot-level action-structure.

Findings from Hebrew narrative productions (Berman, 1995b) confirm results of other research on the development of narrative structure (see, for example, Hickmann, 1995; Hudson and Shapiro, 1991). For example, we compared the proportion of children speaking five different languages who made explit reference to all three major plot components of the picturebook-based "frog story" - the initiating event (the boy wakes up to find his pet frog has disappeared), the elaboration or central thematic structure (repeated attempts to find the frog, a sustained search for the missing pet), and resolution (the boy finds his frog). Only 10% of the children aged 3 and 4 years had such fullblown narrative organizations, compared with one-third of the 5 year olds (34%), two-thirds of the 9-year-old fourth-graders, and all (92%) of the adults (Berman and Slobin, 1994, pp. 46-57). Five-year-olds typically bridge the gap between lack of a general narrative schema manifested by 3- and 4-year-olds and the well-developed narrative competence achieved by early schoolage (7 to 9-year-olds).

Five-year-olds are also at a transitional phase, a bridge between younger preschool and older schoolchildren, in how they construe the task of storytelling. The narratives of 3- to 4 year olds are largely interactive: they are concerned with "talking to" someone, they rely on heavy input scaffolding, and include personal digressions, and a strongly affective component (Reilly, 1992).

Schoolchildren, between 7 to 10 years of age, tell well-constructed stories, with an organized flow of information (often with props like *and then*); but their accounts tend to be stereotyped, even boring. They construe the situation of (elicited) storytelling as essentially informational, concerned with getting the facts across, and as a school-type task, requiring an efficient, rather than a personalized account of events. Ongoing research suggests that this early schoolage construal of the task is not merely an artefact of the structured elicitation setting (Berman and Reilly, 1995). Rather, it is cognitively determined, the product of the conventional, structured patterns of thought of the pre-adolescent child, the way 9-year-olds "know" how to tell a story. But it is also culture-bound, the product of the conventionalized output induced by adaptation to school-based requirements, the way 9-year-olds have been "taught" how to tell a story.

Proficient narrators, the adults in our samples, share with school-age children a good command of narrative structure, but they elaborate the plot-based information with evaluative comment far more than the children. That is, they treat storytelling as communicatively motivated, as a means for impressing, or entertaining, or amusing the interlocutor, even for telling the interlocutor something about themselves as people, and/or as narrators on a metacognitive level. Proficient narrators are concerned not only with "telling a story", but with "telling a good story" (Reilly, 1992). To this end, they also show a degree of selectivity not found among younger, or less proficient storytellers: both in the means they use to lend textual cohesiveness to their narratives and in how they construe the task of narration in a given setting. Some prefer packaging of events by subordination, others use nonfinite forms or nominalizations, others combine these with null subjects as a means of topic maintenance; some adopt a highly subjective, interactive mode of storytelling (like young preschoolers), others choose to objectivize the task (like our 9-year-olds), and so inform more than entertain. Individual selectivity with respect to the narrative stance adopted in particular settings is far less evident in the oral narratives of 9- and 10-year-olds, who have already achieved a fair degree of literacy.

Five-year-olds are at a "frontier age" in this as in the other domains considered here. On the verge of becoming proficient story constructors, they are crucially affected by discourse setting. When asked to give an account of a personal experience, such as a quarrel, they perform on a par with 7-year-old and

9-year-old schoolchildren. When asked to relate the contents of series of four to six pictures, some are like 4-year-olds, others are moving towards 6-year-old abilities. In telling the longer, more complex picturebook-based "frog story", their language is like that of older schoolgoing children in many respects, but not many display command of narrative action structure. In a cognitively even more demanding task, when asked to tell the contents of an event without words which they had just witnessed, 5-year-olds were unable to produce any kind of coherent text, and in this they differed markedly from 8- to 9-year-olds. As is generally the case when knowledge is not yet fully consolidated and coordinated as an integrated system, the narrative abilities of 5-year-olds are still vulnerable, and highly sensitive to external factors and constraints imposed by task-related demands.

4. Conclusions

In sum, children know a great deal in their native language by the time they enter school, as was established by early research in developmental psycholinguistics (Brown, 1973), and as emphasized by current research in generative syntax (e.g. Weissenborn et al, 1992). Crosslinguistic research has also shown that children are attuned to the typological features peculiar to their native language by early preschool age. Three-year-olds have excellent command of simple clause-structure: word order, case-marking, and grammatical inflections for tense/aspect and agreement. By age five, preschool children are adept at combining clauses and have mastered a good deal of complex syntax; they have command of a large vocabulary; they can express varied perspectives on events; and they can construct narratives which are sequentially well-organized. By the time they start primary school in Western cultures, children know an impressive amount about both language structure and language use.

Yet, and here is the paradox, there is a long developmental route to follow before children become fully proficient users of a language. The major problem is not merely adding more formal principles, further structures, or new words. Rather, the proficient language user needs to integrate different types of knowledge: command of a full range of linguistic forms in the native language, for example, rote-learned adjectives, resultative participles, and denominal adjective formation; and mastery of language functions, for example, that objects can be specified by adjectives, by prepositional phrases, and by relative clauses, for different discourse purposes. Coordinating these forms and functions to meet the requirements of extended discourse imposes great cognitive demands, in managing the flow of information in online language production (and comprehension), and in constructing texts as coherent and cohesive at both global and local levels of organization. The proficient speaker-writer also needs to gain command of the rules and the conventions which govern different types and levels of usage, in order to meet conditions of appropriateness for different discourse modes - informing, arguing, negotiating, narrating, describing and, eventually, in producing expository and academic discourse. It also involves sensitivity to the different registers appropriate for different contexts of use: intimate conversation, everyday colloquial usage, formal speech or writing, and literary style. When one considers the enormity of the task, it is not surprising that learning a language proceeds well beyond preschool age, on through to adolescence at least.

Language knowledge after 5 thus involves a complex configuration of interrelated types of knowledge: (1) linguistic - command of the full range of expressive options, the grammatical and lexical forms, available in the target language; (2) cognitive - the ability to integrate forms from different systems of the grammar, and to deploy these options to meet different discourse functions; and (3) cultural - adapting the favored options of a given speech community to particular discourse settings at particular levels of usage. Chomsky, Piaget, and Vygotsky were all right about what is involved in learning a language. Each, however, was concerned with only certain facets of this complex enterprise.

Notes

[1] This is proved by preschoolers' performance on a range of structured elicitation tasks, summed up in Berman, 1995a, and by the fact that the same 6-year-olds who failed to give passive forms did change intransitive verbs to their morphologically related causative counterparts over two-thirds of the time.

Acknowledgments

This chapter is a revised version of a paper entitled "The developmental paradox: How much and how little five-year-olds know about language structure and language use" presented to the Second Workshop of the European Science Foundation Network on Written Language and Literacy - "Understanding early literacy in a developmental and cross-linguistic approach" - held at the Netherlands Institute for Advanced Study in the Humanities and Social Sciences, Wassenaar, the Netherlands, in October, 1993. I am grateful to Prof. Claire Blanche-Benveniste for her illuminating discussion, to other participants in the workshop for their interesting comments, and to an anonymous reviewer for further helpful input.

Explicit Word Segmentation and Writing in Hebrew and Spanish

Liliana Tolchinsky, Ana Teberosky

Learning to write in an alphabetic system influences the way people conceive of language and plays an important role in the ability to segment the speech stream. Studies have shown that adult literate Chinese found it natural to segment a sentence into syllables whereas literate Englishmen found it more natural to do it in words and then in terms of individual sounds (Bugarski, 1993). In general, in the process of acquiring literacy, 5 year old English, Portuguese, Japanese, Chinese or Indian speakers have no problems with rhyme recognition and syllable detection but only speakers raised in an alphabetic system will attain subsyllabic levels of segmentation (Morais, Alegria, Content, 1987; Read, Zhang, Nie, and Ding, 1986). Yet how is this ability to analyze words into their components affected by particular features of alphabetic systems? How similar or different would word segmentation be among children who have acquired literacy in scripts which, though alphabetical, differ in other features? One way of examining this question is by comparing word segmentation in children who have acquired literacy in different alphabetical scripts. This is addressed in the present study which compares word segmentation in Hebrew and Spanish, two languages that use different alphabetical scripts.

1. Differences and similarities between Hebrew and Spanish

Why these two languages? Comparison between Hebrew and Spanish is particularly useful because despite the discrepancies in script and morphological structure, the two languages share important phonological features. We assumed that this interplay of similarities and differences would help us to discriminate the influence of the scripts from that of the languages.

Let us consider the differences between the two scripts. First, Hebrew and Spanish scripts differ in the shape of their letters and in the directionality of their writing. Spanish uses the Latin alphabet and is written from left to right and Modern Hebrew uses an alphabet derived from Aramaic and is written from right to left. Spanish orthography includes letters for consonants and vowels. Although the degree of transparency of Spanish orthography is controversial - Green, (1990:91) shows that "only six letter-sound correspondences can be considered strictly biunique" (a, e, o, l, f and d)- it is more transparent than English or French. Without doubt the vowels are the most consistent subsystem of Spanish orthography. Spanish orthography thus provides an exhaustive representation of the phonemic structure of Spanish words and a stable representation of their vowel structure.

Hebrew functions rather differently. The Hebrew alphabet includes only consonants. Hebrew alphabetic orthography, however, has two varieties, one non-vocalized and the other vocalized ("punctuated"). The non-vocalized orthography represents the consonantal skeleton of words which carries most of its lexical values (Berman, 1987, McCarthy, 1981). Four letters of the Hebrew alphabet - *yod, vaw, hey* and *aleph* - (called *matres lectionis*, see appendix 1 and note 3) designate both semivowels and glottal/pharyngeal segments as well as partially representing vowels (Coulmas, 1989; Gesenius, 1910, Ravid, 1996).[3]

The vocalized orthography portrays all the Hebrew vowels through a system of diacritics (*nikud,* 'pointing') which are small dots and dashes placed under, above or within the letter (Jensen, 1969).The use of vocalized ("punctuated") script, however, is rather specialized. It appears in Biblical texts, when writing poetry and foreign names, in children's books and when learning how to read. Texts for adults, except for new immigrants, are not vocalized. Vocalized orthography seems to be more transparent than non-vocalized since it provides a more exhaustive representation of the phonemic structure of Hebrew words. However, there is no one to one correspondence between the 5 Hebrew vowels and the diacritics. There are 2-4 diacritics for each vowel and the same diacritic may have different readings. These and other reasons may explain why the diacritic marking system has never been established in Hebrew writing. Adults still prefer to rely on grammatical knowledge and contextual cues to disambiguate words written in non-vocalized script.

The above mentioned differences are also reflected in the way people speak about elements of the writing systems. In Spanish, it is very common to refer to any letter by its name (e.g. *la ese* 'the s'; *la te,* 'the t'). Moreover, the name of the vowels coincides with their sound (e.g. la a 'the /a/'). In Hebrew, only the consonants are named and the correct name of the vowels is high specialized knowledge.

There are also important differences in the structural features of both languages. Spanish is far from being an isolating language: very few words other than interjections, conjunctions, prepositions and a subset of adverbs consist of one morpheme or are immune to both inflection and derivation (Green, 1990); rather morphosyntactic markers are usually affixed to the lexical root for derivation and/or inflection, and, except in the case of certain verbs, there are no internal stem changes. In Hebrew, as in most Semitic languages, nonconcatenative morphology prevails. Hebrew morphology works on roots with four, three or occasionally two consonants which cluster around a semantic field. The morphosyntactic system sometimes operates on these roots to derive words by juxtaposition, but generally speaking a variety of purely morphological alternations internal to the stem are applied. The vowel patterns are fixed, as are the systems of infixes, suffixes and prefixes (Berman, 1978, Aronoff, 1985).

Despite the differences between the two languages with respect to scripts and morphology, they display important similarities in phonological structure. The first concerns vowel structure. Both spoken Spanish and modern Hebrew can reasonably be claimed to have only five vowels (/i/, /e/, /a/, /o/, and /u/) (Bolotzky, 1978). Second, in both languages the distribution of vowels and consonants shows an overall distribution close to 50%[4] and the scale of frequency of vowels is also similar. In both languages the vowels /a/ and e/ are the two most frequent ones followed by /o/, /i/ and /u/ (Bosch, Costa, and Sebastian, 1994). The vowels /o/, /i/ and /a/ and /i/ may form diphthongs, whereas /a/ and /e/ and /u/ and /e/ do not.

Finally, although Spanish is a syllable-timed language since the syllable, rather than the morpheme or the word, is the unit of linguistic organization on which the phonemic constraints operate, both languages are similar in their average number of syllables per word and the type of syllables they allow[5]. Syllables may be open - CV - or closed - CVC - and single vowels may form a syllable. In Spanish, onset (+consonant) is the optional and unmarked element, whereas the rhyme nucleus (+vowel), which contains the height of sonority, is obligatory.

These differences in script and morphology together with the similarities in phonological structure mean that a comparison between Hebrew and Spanish is particularly suitable for discerning the relative influence of each of these factors on children's ability to segment words. If phonological structure is a determining factor in word segmentation we ought on the whole to find similar performance in the two languages before children learn to write conventionally. If, on the other hand, segmentation is affected by morphological structure, we ought to find that preliterate forms of segmentation are different in the two languages.

How are we to account for the possible influence of scripts? The problem is that it is not easy to posit a clear *before* in the acquisition of literacy since knowledge about writing starts long before children are able to read or write conventionally (e.g. Ferreiro and Teberosky, 1979). We decided that in order to account for the influence of scripts on segmentation we should explore the way in which they segment throughout the process of acquiring writing. Hebrew-speaking and Spanish-speaking children from preschool up to second grade were asked to write and to segment a set of words and we analyzed both their written products and their segmentation responses. In this sense we have taken a different stance from other researchers who have concentrated either on the development of phonological segmentation or on the development of writing.

2. Development of word segmentation

Experimental evidence for the development of the ability to analyze words into components comes from a variety of tasks (for a review see Adam, 1991; Treiman, 1985; Stanovich,1986). For example, tapping-tasks,in which 4 to 6 years old are required to count the number of syllables or segments in a given word (Liberman, Shankweiler, Fisher and Carter, 1974); tasks in which they are asked to pronounce "the phoneme in isolation" or to say what is left after deleting one phoneme (Vellutino and Scallon, 1987; Share, Jorm, Maclean, and Matthews, 1984) or to pronounce the word components "bit by bit" and "the smaller bits" (Fox and Routh, 1975). Despite the fact that test items are generally preceded by ample training or modelling, the majority of these tasks produces similar results: at 4 hardly any child is able to perform the tasks successfully, at 5 only a small percentage (usually less than 20%) can do them, and at 6, the majority. After a number of repetitions and task variations, most of the researchers have come to conclude that children "become aware" of the syllable, before becoming aware of phonemes (Fox and Routh, 1975; Hardy, Stenett, and Smythe, 1973; Treiman and Baron, 1981).

Further investigations have demonstrated, however, that the hierarchical structure of the syllable has important effects on the segmentation capabilities of children and adults. If 5;6 year olds are asked to judge whether spoken syllables begin with a specific phoneme, for example /s/, they show more difficulty in recognizing /s/ at the beginning of a syllable like #spa# than at the beginning of syllables like #sap# or #sa#. It has become clear from the work of Treiman (1981; 1985; 1992) that children go through intermediate stages at which they are able to isolate consonants occupying specific positions in certain classes of syllables. It seems easier for the children to decompose a syllable into Onset and Rhyme and then delete (or isolate) one of these constituents than it is to decompose the Onset into its constituents and delete one of them. This sort of finding suggests that prosodic categories such as the syllable are more important than was originally supposed for analyzing children's segmentation performance.

Although most of the evidence pertaining to the development of segmentation abilities copme from with English speaking subjects, data from speakers of other language has begun to be collected. Cross-linguistic studies suggest that segmentation strategies may be language specific (Mehler, Dommergues, Frauenfelder and Segui, 1984). Italian children found it much easier to segment into syllables than into phonemes or morphemes (Devescovi, Orsolini, and Pace, 1990) and French speakers listening to French words resort to syllabification. However, this kind of syllabic segmentation is very rare in English speakers listening to English words. Cutler suggests that the influence of nuclear syllable boundaries may induce listeners to ignore the syllabic structure of the word (Cutler, Mehler and Segui, 1986). More recent studies have shown, however, that English speaking adults tend naturally to think of sounds in speech in terms of semisyllabic segments, but that minimal instruction can serve to make them analyze words in individual sounds. Before instruction the majority of these speakers said there were two sounds in "cat", some said there were three, and a few that there was just one (Scholes, 1993, p. 45). We will return to these findings because they question the nature of the ability we are describing.

Accessibility of vowels and consonants may also differ from one language to another. Vowel identification may be easier in Spanish than in English, because they are more stable, form syllables or are obligatory constituents, whereas in English vowels are often neutralized in normal speech (Shimron, 1993). Consonant identification may be as easy in Hebrew than in English, but for different reasons. In Hebrew, the identification of the consonantal skeleton out of which a word is formed is essential for interpreting and producing unfamiliar words and this ability is well-established by age 4 (Badry, 1983; Berman, 1985; Clark and Berman, 1984; Levy, 1988, Berman, 1993).

The reviewed studies suggest that between 4 and 6 years of age there is an increase in children's capacity to delete, to count and to pronounce the individual sounds that make up a word. The ability to analyze words goes through an intermediate stage in which children are still unable to segment into phonemes but can isolate consonants in certain classes of syllables. Moreover, these processes may differ from one language to another. But what is the nature of the capacity we are describing? In the literature it is usually described as "metalinguistic" a capacity that requires conscious access to otherwise implicit knowledge, including sensitivity to rhymes or categorization of sounds. For some researchers the latter abilities differ only in their general cognitive demands but otherwise tap the same capability as segmental awareness. They see in children's ability to detect rhyme (Bradley and Bryant, 1983) or to know nursery rhymes (Maclean, Bryant, and Bradley, 1988) part of a continuous development of phonological awareness. Studies with Portuguese illiterates have shown, however, that illiterates can detect rhyme and manipulate syllables but not phonemes (Cary, 1989). This evidence would argue against a continuity hypothesis. The above quoted study by Scholes (1993) shows that even literate adult English speakers do not naturally carry out "phone-level segmentation" (p. 52). It seems that analysis of words in terms of individual sounds requires special training or at least minimal instruction, i.e. certain circumstances facilitate conscious access to levels of analysis that otherwise remain implicit. Moreover, rhyme recognition and syllabic segmentation are developed spontaneously whereas "phonemic awareness is linked not to literacy in general but to alphabetic literacy in particular" (Prakash, Rekha, Nigam and Karanth, 1993). It is reasonable to consider alphabetic literacy as one of these facilitating circumstances.

The fact that most children succeed in the segmentation tasks at an age at which formal instruction on reading usually starts and the failure of illiterate adults to perform these tasks has led psychologists to posit a link between literacy and segmentation. For more than ten years we have witnessed a vigorous debate in the literature as to whether explicit segmentation is a necessary precursor, a causal condition (e.g. Bradley and Bryant, 1983) or just important to successful literacy acquisition, or whether it is the other way around, that it is learning to read that fosters phonological awareness (Read, et al. 1986).

The former view came under strong attack when it was found that Down syndrome children who perform badly on traditional tests of phonological awareness can, nonetheless, read and write Italian fluently (Marshall and Cossu, 1991); deaf children who have poor phonological structures before they learn to read and write can develop phonological awareness with the help of literacy (Hanson and Fowler, 1987) and cases of a deficit in phonological segmentation combined with a mastery of reading have begun to be reported (Campbell, 1991). Most researchers are currently discussing the occurrence of mutual facilitation or reciprocal interaction between print and speech (Ehri and Wilce, 1980, 1984). "The novice begins with phonetics insights based on articulatory and acoustic cues" (Ehri, 1993 p.39). These initial insights become fixed or modified in interaction with the particular features of the scripts. On the one hand, this would explain children's preference for syllabic segmentation. On the other hand it stresses the shaping effects of reading and spelling acquisition on segmentation.

Although empirical research into the links between literacy and segmentation came initially from reading, quite a few studies have also looked at spelling. Researchers have explored the influence of segmentation on learning to spell (Bradley and Bryant, 1983; Fox and Routh, 1983; Frith, 1979; Smith, 1980; Perin, 1983; Rohl and Tunmer, 1988) or on predicting reading skills (Mann, Tobin and Wilson, 1987) and also the effect of learning to spell on improving segmentation skills (Hohn and Ehri, 1983; Torneus, 1984). Increasing support for the claims of reciprocal interaction is coming, in our view, from studies of the development of 'invented spelling' from preschool on (cf., Chomsky, 1972; Ehri, 1986; 1989; 1993; Ehri and Wilce, 1980; Frith, 1980; Gentry, 1982; Read, 1971; Templeton and Bear, 1992;Treiman, 1993). In these studies children who are not supposed to know how to spell conventionally are asked to write in their own way. Analysis of these spelling strategies reveals how much implicit knowledge the children have about the phonological structure of language - a kind of knowledge that might differ from the one implied in oral segmentation tasks.

Although we are not very sympathetic to the term "invented spelling" since children do not seem to be inventing but rather exploring features of a script, we have taken a similar approach in this study, asking very small children to write in their own way without a model, and then analyzing the developmental path toward conventional writing.

3. Development of word writing

The supposition that children's knowledge about writing starts with formal reading instruction is implicit in most of the research on segmentation. Nevertheless, one of the most significant contributions in the field of literacy in the last twenty years has been the demonstration that, at least for children from urban environments, this supposition is untenable. Knowledge about writing starts prior to formal instruction and evolves through a number of domain specific stages before attaining conventional spelling. With respect to the development of word writing, researchers who have studied this evolution in Romance language (Besse, 1991; Camean Gorrias, 1990; Ferreiro, 1986; Ferreiro and Teberosky, 1979; Staccioli and Andreucci, 1989; Pontecorvo and Zuccermaglio, 1988) have shown that 4 year olds written production already abide by the formal constraints of writing. When 4 year olds are asked to write isolate words they usually produce linear strings of discrete or linked units -simile print or simile cursive- in a limited number and variety. At this stage, however, the number and type of marks the children use has nothing to do with the acoustic length or the phonological structure of the words children are asked to write. They may produce similar strings for monosyllabic or tetrasyllabic words. Children usually use the letters of the writing systems they are exposed to, but the letters are not used according to their conventional value. They use them because they are letters, not because they describe specific phonological segments. Only at a later stage do children look for correspondences between the number and type of letters and the acoustic length of words. At this stage children usually try to segment words in order to guide their writing. The first unit of segmentation they seem to rely on is the syllable. During this "syllabic period" the number of letters children use maps onto the number of syllables of the words they are asked to write. Later on children will look not only for "quantitative correspondences" (between the number of syllables and the number of letters) but also for "qualitative correspondences" (Ferreiro, 1988), i.e. they will not use any letter but select them for their conventional value. This is still not conventional orthography but phonographic correspondence according to the range of possible alternatives allowed by a specific script. In Romance languages children tend to use vowels to represent syllables. As they grow older, and after a series of cognitive conflicts between segmentation while writing and spelling, they grasp the alphabetic principle, i.e. they look for correspondences between letters and individual sounds.

Although a similar developmental progression was found in Hebrew (Tolchinsky Landsmann, 1991), it may be the case that this development is well supported only for certain languages and scripts. In a case study of literacy development in an English speaking child, there is no mention of a syllabic period (Bissex, 1980). Moreover, although other authors have also noted that preschoolers' writing of words is typically characterized by the use of consonants (e.g. VKT for *vacation*), they have interpreted this behavior as "omission of vowels" (Shimron, 1993) and not as syllabic mapping. Kamii (Kamii, Long, Manning and Manning,1993) have suggested that in English there must be a sort of consonantal stage rather than a syllabic one. In the literature on 'invented spelling' there is no mention of a syllabic period - researchers have identified a semiphonetic stage (e.g. Gentry, 1982; Templeton and Bear, 1992) at which children use only part of the letters required to write the word alphabetically. But again this is interpreted as partial representation rather than as a representation regulated by another unit of segmentation. The basic assumption of the syllabic period is that children are analyzing words into syllables and looking for a correspondence between them and letters. Syllabic correspondences are therefore possible by using consonants, vowels or even non-conventional letters. If one follows this line of reasoning, children who use only vowels or consonants - one for each syllable in the word - are not "omitting letters", they are assuming that the rule of correspondence is one letter per syllable. The interesting question is on what basis do they decide to use consonants or vowels. It is in this sense that the comparison between Spanish and Hebrew is particularly interesting.

4. Development of word-writing in Hebrew and Spanish

We asked 56 Spanish-speaking and 59 Hebrew-speaking children from preschool through second grade to write a series of words dictated by an adult native speaker in each of the respective languages. The words were said one by one and the child was asked to write them without providing any model. To make the comparison between languages easier, we looked for a set of nouns as similar as possible in both languages. The words varied in number of syllables, from mono-syllabic to tetra-syllabic, were part of the typical out-of-school vocabulary and very familiar. Appendix 2 shows the test materials used in the tasks (for details in administration and coding procedures see Teberosky, Tolchinsky Landsmann, Zelcer, Gomes de Morais and Rincon, 1993 and Tolchinsky and Teberosky, submitted). The purpose was to get a picture of the evolution of word writing in these languages. With this purpose in mind we analyzed the written outputs for both letter-sound mapping and use of conventional letters, i.e. whether any analysis of the word guided children's writing and whether they use the letters according to their conventional value. On the basis of these criteria children's written outputs were analyzed according to a system of categories ranging from: 1) Formally constrained writing; 2) Syllabic mapping without conventional value; 3) Syllabic mapping with conventional value using mainly vowels; 4) Syllabic mapping with conventional value using mainly consonants, 5) Alphabetic-syllabic mapping; 6) Non exhaustive-alphabetic and 7) Exhaustive-alphabetic, for each word separately.

Both in Spain and in Israel formal instruction in reading and writing starts in first grade. Therefore, for preschoolers and first graders, and even for quite a few second graders, it was a novel, sometimes embarrassing situation. They were asked to write words from the social environment not the ones typically learned at school, and to do so on the spot. In these circumstances children clearly struggled with the many dimensions involved in writing (e.g. formal constraints, the shape of the letters, the attempts to map letters to sounds). Thus, although the development of word writing is depicted through the written products, details of the writing process were always taken into account.

Figure 1, which shows the same word *mandarina* written in Hebrew and in Spanish by children with different levels of conventionality and letter-sound mapping in their writing, illustrates the development of word writing in the two languages.

On top, we see what we have termed *formally constrained writing* because children's outputs are constrained by the general features of writing (linearity, discontinuity, minimal number of elements and internal variety) but not yet by the specific constraints of orthography. Children use conventional Hebrew and Spanish letters, but they use any letters. For example, Shay (5;7) (a) uses the letters S*TY to write Mandarina, and Cristopher (b) use ERISTO for the same word. There is no relationship between letters and sounds. Moreover children use an almost fixed number of marks for monosyllabic or multisyllabic words. Needless to say this assertion can not be made on the basis of one written output but rather must take into account what children write for all the words.

In examples (c) and (d) below (in Figure 1), the number of letters maps the number of syllables in the word (the same children wrote two letters for *pi#ca*, four letters for *co#ca#co#la,*) but they still use any conventional letter, with no relationship to the sounds in the word.

We have termed this form of writing *syllabic mapping without conventional value*. One should note that in Hebrew the child uses both consonants and *matres lectionis*, the letters than can function as vowels, and that Spanish speakers use both consonants and vowels (or rather what *we* call consonants and vowels because the child is using them still without their conventional value).

In the example below, it is possible to appreciate that not only the number of letters correspond to the number of syllables but also that the letters are used according to conventional sounds. In order to write *mandarina* the child uses *mem*, for #man#, *dalet* for #da#, *resh* for #ri# and *nun* for #na#. In Spanish, however, the child uses [a] for #man#, [a] for #da#, [i] for #ri# and [a] for #na#, i.e. just vowels. Children are carrying out a syllabic mapping using consonants only in Hebrew and vowels in Spanish. We have noted before, when describing previous levels of writing, that children may use consonants in Spanish and *matres lectionis* in Hebrew. One should remember that at that level children are not looking for correspondence between sounds and letters. At the level we are describing here, when they do look for correspondences, the selection is already language specific.The discrepancies between scripts are thus more evident.

In examples (g) and (h) we find a more exhaustive representation of the sound structure of the word. We termed this *syllabic-alphabetic mapping* because children produced a sort of mixed mapping. In the figure, Maricarmen (h) exhaustively noted the first and the last syllables in MANDARINA, but for the second and the third she only put the vowels. For Hebrew, but not Spanish, this kind of mapping (disregarding spelling rules) is already conventional writing.

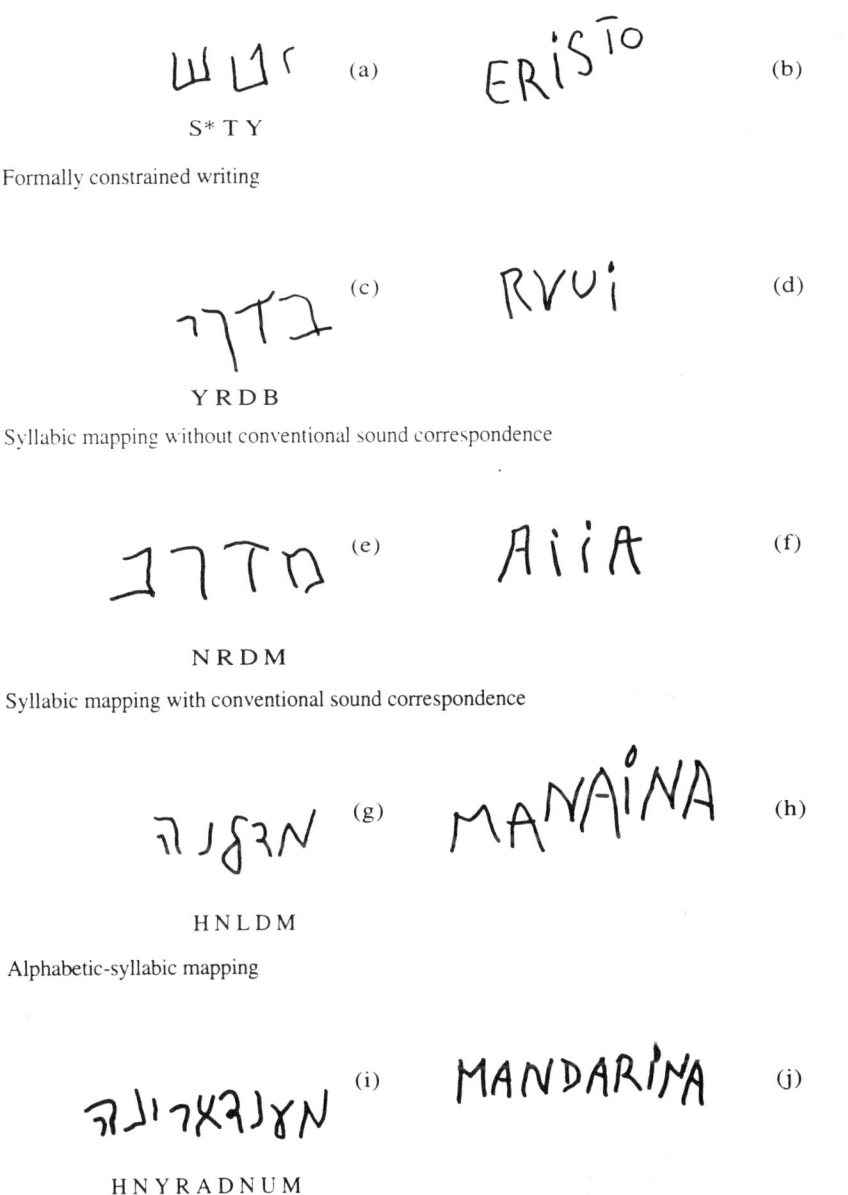

WORD SEGMENTATION AND WRITING IN HEBREW AND SPANISH   87

ש ט ר (a)   ERiSTO   (b)

S * T Y

Formally constrained writing

בדר   (c)   RVUi   (d)

Y R D B

Syllabic mapping without conventional sound correspondence

מדר   (e)   AiiA   (f)

N R D M

Syllabic mapping with conventional sound correspondence

ןנצגה (g)   MANAiNA (h)

H N L D M

Alphabetic-syllabic mapping

ןנצגאריה (i)   MANDARINA (j)

H N Y R A D N U M

Alphabetic mapping

Figure 1. Hebrew-speaking and Spanish-speaking written representation of the word mandarina at each writing level

At the bottom, (i) and (f) are examples of writing constrained by *alphabetic mapping*: one letter for each consonant and vowel in the word. In Spanish this is conventional writing - disregarding spelling mistakes- but in Hebrew it is not. Hebrew-speaking children take advantage of the *matres lectionis* to produce this kind of mapping and very seldom use diacritics, despite the fact that they are present in books for learning to read.

If we look at the most frequently used category across words, there is a clear developmental pattern in the forms of writing from preschool to second grade in both language groups. This is shown in Figure 2a and 2b.

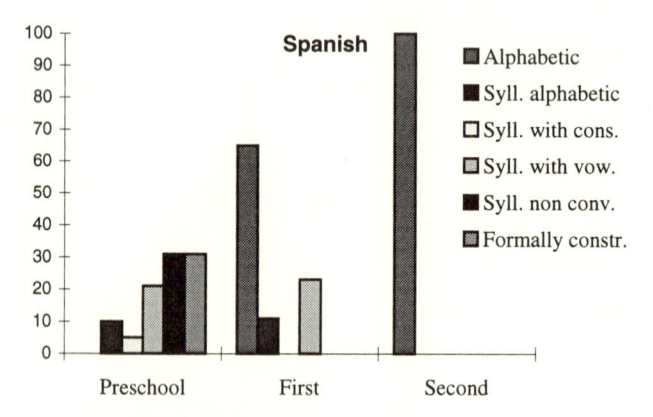

Figure 2a. Written product scores in Spanish

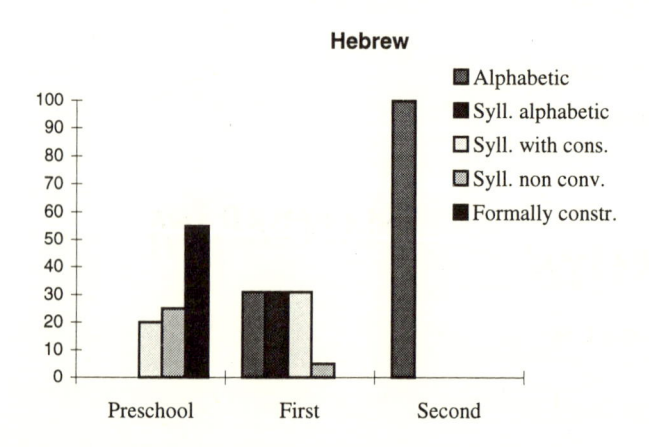

Figure 2b. Written product scores in Hebrew

WORD SEGMENTATION AND WRITING IN HEBREW AND SPANISH   89

Only preschoolers' outputs were scored as *formally constrained* or as *syllabic mapping without conventional value* in both language groups. These two categories of writing have disappeared in first grade.

In first grade most written products were scored as *syllabic mapping using letters with conventional value, syllabic-alphabetic* or *alphabetic*.

Note that none of these forms of writing involves analyzing the word and looking for letter sound correspondences. In syllabic mappings the unit of segmentation is the syllable whereas in syllabic-alphabetic or alphabetic mapping children are performing subsyllabic analyses. There is, however, a strong discrepancy in the type of letters children used to achieve letter to sound mappings. In Hebrew they used consonants whereas in Spanish they used mainly vowels. In second grade all written products were alphabetic, exhaustive or non-exhaustive.

Within this overall developmental picture, it is important to clarify that children's forms of writing are sensitive to word structure[6]. In Hebrew exhaustive-alphabetic mapping except for *pizza, Coca Cola* and *te* (tea), was used only, perhaps, because in these words the use of *matres lectionis* is orthographically compelling. In cases when their use is optional or not allowed, they used neither *matres* nor diacritics. This is the reason why *salami* or *mandarina* were not written alphabetically. Hebrew orthography does not allow the use of any of these devices to denote vowels in the first two closed syllables. In the Spanish group, on the other hand, words like *salami, Coca Cola* and *te* (tea) were written alphabetically by most first graders.

Interestingly, the word *Coca Cola* did not elicit better spelling despite its being so pervasive in the children's environment. This finding suggest that visual information is not playing an important role for a child who is attempting to write by searching for phonographic correspondence. The only word that no child could write with the correct spelling was *pizza*. Children produced a variety of non-conventional spellings (e.g. *PISA, PISSA, PICSA, PITSA, PICHA, PITZA, PIZA, PIZAZA*). Though not as much as *Coca Cola*, the word *pizza* has a strong visual presence in Barcelona. So, the reason for such a variety of spelling might be that the word *pizza* includes a sound which is not represented in the Spanish alphabet by a single letter. Hebrew speaking children were more successful in the correct spelling of the same word due probably to the fact that there is a letter in the Hebrew alphabet for the corresponding sound.

In sum, at every grade of school, even prior to formal instruction, children displayed knowledge of writing and sensitivity to the conventions of the respective scripts. Moreover, in second grade all of them wrote alphabetically and in order to do that they must clearly have analyzed the words into their sound-components. Let us see what happened when the same children are asked to segment a series of words orally - a task that also involves analyzing and pronouncing word components.

5. Development of Word Segmentation in Hebrew and Spanish

In the oral segmentation task we showed the children a picture (e.g a piece of chocolate), asked them to say what was in the picture and then to say it again "bit by bit", and again "in smaller bits". Using the same procedure children were then asked to segment 6 words (see Appendix 2). No examples or feedback were provided because we wanted to tap spontaneous segmentation. This task, as carried out, is an artificial, metalinguistic one, but it served our purpose because it seemed to tap the kind of ability required for writing more closely (van Bon and Duighuisen, 1995).

To score children responses, we considered constructing a system of categories using the criterion of exhaustiveness in pronounciation of word components. It was immediately clear that there was a group of responses that could not be scored according to this criterion because they differed substantially from the rest. Instead of pronouncing the word components in any fashion, children said the names of the letters in which the words had to be written. We called this form of response 'oral spelling', and children who only produced this type of response were treated separately. For the rest of the children we used an ordinal scale ranging from: 1) *Unsegmented*, the word is said in a single breath; 2) *Pronounciation of syllables*, the word is said by pronouncing only syllables in isolation (e.g. sa#la#mi); 3) *Pronounciation of vowels in isolation and syllables*, the word is said by pronouncing syllables but includes the pronunciation of some vowels in isolation (e.g. ra#di/o/); 4) *Pronounciation of consonants and syllables*, the word is said by pronouncing syllables but this includes the pronunciation of some consonants in isolation (e.g., te#le#fo/n/); 5) *Pronounciation of consonants, vowels and syllables*, the word is said by pronouncing some consonants, some vowels and some syllables in isolation (e.g. pi/ç/a); 6) *Pronounciation of consonants*, the word is said by pronouncing some or all the consonants in isolation but some or all of the vowels are deleted (e.g. ʃ/k/l/d) and 7) *Exhaustive pronunciation of consonants and vowels*, the word is said by pronouncing every consonant and vowel (e.g. s/a/l/a/m/i).

To get a developmental picture of oral segmentation in each language group children were scored according to the most frequently used category of response for multisyllabic words.

As shown in Figure 3a and 3b, there were two clear cut findings. First, the syllable is by far the most significant segmentation unit in preschool and first

WORD SEGMENTATION AND WRITING IN HEBREW AND SPANISH   91

grade in both languages, although significantly more so in Spanish (at a p<0.001 level). In preschool, 95% of Spanish-speaking and 65% of Hebrew-speaking children utilized syllabic segmentation as their most frequent form of response. The popularity of syllabic segmentation tended to decrease with school-grade, but it was still utilized by 35% of Spanish-speaking second graders.

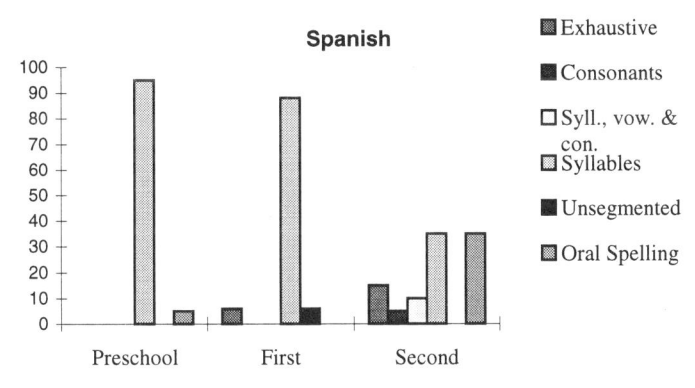

Figure 3a. Word segmentation scores in Spanish

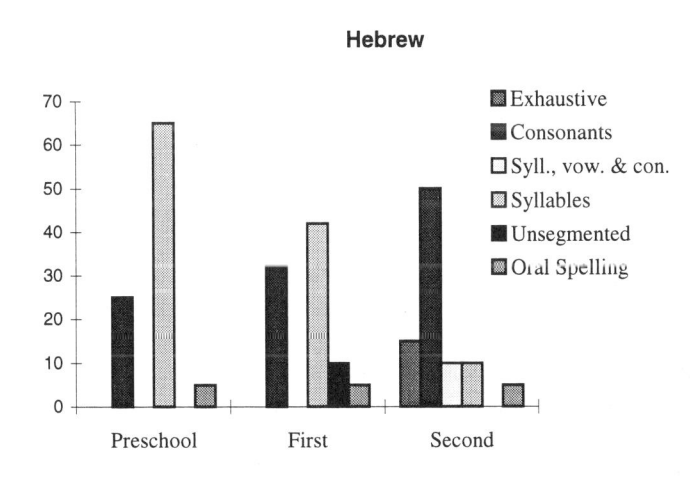

Figure 3b. Word segmentation scores in Hebrew

A second important finding is that very few children had exhaustive segmentation as the most frequent form of response - in the Spanish group, 1 first grader and 3 second graders and, in the Hebrew group, 3 second graders. In other words, there are important cross-linguistic similarities both in the preferred unit of segmentation in preschool and in the evolution toward subsyllabic segmentation with grade. Nevertheless, there were important differences between languages as to the ways in which words were analyzed. One form of response, pronunciation of consonants in isolation, appears almost exclusively in Hebrew. It starts in preschool and becomes the most frequently used form in second grade. Another form of response, oral spelling, appears exclusively among Spanish-speaking second graders.

As in the writing task, the categories utilized for segmenting each word show clear differences in children's response to word structure in the two languages. In the Spanish group, the three words eliciting more syllabic segmentation were *salami*, *chocolate* and *teléfono*, perhaps due to the regular syllabic structure of the words (CV-CV-CV). In the Hebrew group, the word eliciting most syllabic segmentation was *salami*, probably because of its regular syllabic structure. The three words eliciting more isolation of consonants were *shokolad*, *radio* and *télefon*. In each case the isolated consonant was the coda in the open syllable. By contrast, we found no monosyllable effects in consonant isolation - for example in *tei* (tea) children could isolate the vowel /i/. In sum, differences in the number and structure of the syllables elicited different ways of segmentation.

6. Word writing and word segmentation in Hebrew and Spanish

We started this chapter by considering the effect of particular scripts on the ability to analyze words into their components. We suggested that children's evolving knowledge of writing may account for this effect, assuming that literacy penetrates and co-mingles with children's phonological knowledge to determine how words are analyzed.

Our study has shown that in both language groups, prior to formal instruction, preschoolers display knowledge of the respective scripts. Even though written products are formally constrained or regulated by syllabic mapping using letters without conventional value, we can still point to script specific differences: as a rule, children use the letters of the script they are exposed to, they rarely invent graphic marks. Later on, the representation of the sound structure of the words is achieved in each language by making use of the respective orthographic options available in each language. Hebrew-speaking children use consonants while Spanish-speaking children mainly use vowels. We believe that these preferences can be explained by the way each script reinforces linguistic features of the languages.

The primacy of consonants is a major typological property of Hebrew. The three-consonantal roots carry the bulk of semantic information and form the skeletal basis of word structure. Moreover, this morphological feature is reinforced by the script since the alphabet includes only consonants, and diacritics are socially less available. This fact may explain Hebrew children's preference for consonants. As for Spanish, although the use of vowels suggests a choice between equally viable options, it turns out that the script reinforces a very stable vowel system. The above mentioned coincidence between vowel names and sounds may also be a contributing factor to children's preference for vowels.

The increasing influence of the scripts is also evident in the developmental pattern of word segmentation. In preschool, when children' writing is still formally constrained or children use letters without conventional value, the syllable is the preferred unit of segmentation in both languages. This preference may, on the one hand, reflect the phonetic-acoustic similarities between the two languages bu, may also support the claims for the psychological reality of the syllable as a unit of segmentation (Treiman and Zukowski, 1988).

With school grade, however, the discrepancies between the two language groups increases. The use of oral spelling is present in Spanish and absent in Hebrew whereas the possibility of isolating consonants is present in Hebrew and absent in Spanish. We think that both are the result of the particular features of the scripts children's are exposed to. In oral spelling children said the names of the letters instead of the individual sounds of the words. In a sense, oral spelling is a kind of exhaustive segmentation, though supported by the graphic elements of writing. Following a long standing European tradition (Harris, 1992, p.27), children seem to conceptualize the units of speech in terms of the writing system. Written units exist in advance, as notation, and they can be part of a list of names and shapes that children can memorize. At an oral level there is no such previous inventory transmitted by tradition. In Spanish the names of the letters are common social knowledge and in the case of vowels the name coincides with the sound, thus providing important cues for analyzing the words. Neither social knowledge nor coincidence between names and sounds provides such cues in Hebrew. The names for consonants do not provide cues for sounds and the names for vowels require a rather specialized kind of knowledge. Features of the respective scripts are influencing the way people speak about the elements of writing and this, in turn influences children's ways of segmenting words.

As to the second main difference - pronunciation of consonants in isolation - two reasons can again be given for it: the role of consonant roots in Hebrew and the features of Hebrew writing. One could even argue that the script is mirroring the morphological structure of Hebrew thereby influencing segmentation behavior. Since the relationship between the linguistic structure of languages and the features of writing systems is still a matter of controversy, we consider the first interpretation to be more prudent.

As regards the relationship between word writing and word segmentation, knowing how to write in an alphabetic system did not cause any great change in the preferred unit of segmentation. Children's increasing knowledge about writing only introduced new segmentation behavior and did not necessarily produce explicit segmental analysis. The different performance in word writing and segmentation can be explained by the different level of accessibility implied in each of them. When writing a word children must access the sound structure of the words *for* writing it. In this case, segmentation is a means of performing a task with the support of external monitoring. In oral segmentation, children must access the sound structure of the words *per se* without any external support.

Children's preferences do not imply, however, that they are unable to segment words exhaustively. Since the task was proposed to the children without providing examples and without corrections, it is clear that we are not tapping children's performance limits but only their preferences. Children may know how to segment into consonants and vowels and still not display this knowledge in the word segmentation task. We should therefore constrain our evidence within this limit. Segmentation into syllables precedes the ability to produce an alphabetic written product, but knowing how to write alphabetically does not lead to exhaustive segmentation when the word is presented orally. This finding speaks in favor of a high specificity of exhaustive segmentation. It requires specific demands and exemplification (or training). An additional finding of our study concerns the non-homogeneity of writing and segmentation. In line with previous research by Treiman (1985; 1992), our study showed the strong dependence of writing and segmentation performance on word structure.

The development of word segmentation and word writing in Hebrew and Spanish illustrates the way in which literacy shapes native linguistic intuitions. It occurs through the way scripts reinforce certain phonological and morphological features of particular languages but also through social uses and ways of speaking about writing.

Notes

[1]Uppercase italics will be used for the written form of the words in each language and lowercase italics for the spoken form. In the examples the words will be presented in the Spanish reading. The rules for transliteration from Hebrew writing appear in appendix 1. (#) is used to indicate separation between syllables; it may indicate nor-

mative boundary or pausing done by the children when pronouncing. (/) indicates separation between subsyllabic units.
²For example, the following words all share the same consonantal tier q-l-T , meaning 'take in, absorb': kalat 'absorbed', hiklit 'recorded', *huklat* 'was recorded', *klita* 'absorption, (radio) reception', *haklata* 'recording', *miklat* 'bomb shelter', *maklet,* radio receiver, *taklit,*'record', *kaletet,* 'tape cassette', *koltan,*'(biological) receptor' *kelet,* 'input'. (Ravid, 1996). In non-vocalized script most of them would only partially represent the vowels 'i' and 'o' by *matres lectionis*.
³In Spanish: 47.12% and 52.88%, respectively (Rojo, 1991) and in Hebrew: 42.9% and 57.1%, respectively (Nali, 1957; Tene, 1968).
⁴The most frequent syllables in Spanish are CV (#ca#); CVC (#cal#); V (#a#) and VC (#ar#). There are others, such as CVV (#teu#); CVVC (#cuen#), CVCC (#cons#), CCVCC (#trans#) and VVC (#aun#), but never CCCVC, as in the English word *scream*. Intrasyllabically, the onset may be simple, C+V, or compound CC+V, and the rhyme may comprise from one to three vowels (e.g. the word *buey,* (ox)).(Harris, op. cit., pp. 18). Similarly in Hebrew the most frequent syllables are: CV (#sa#); CVC (#gur#); VC (#ab#). Single vowel sounds may form a syllable. In general, Hebrew has more monosyllables than Spanish.
⁵Children's written productions were scored separately for each word, and the use of consonants or vowels in the case of syllabic mapping was coded separately. However, the two categories were combined for the purpose of statistical analysis since it was not possible to attribute a different position on an ordinal scale to the use of vowels or consonants since the use of vowels is privileged in one script, and the use of consonants in the other. Results showed that the differences between words are significant F(4,436)=5.93; p<.0001; there are significant interactions between language group and word F(4, 436)=7.29, p<.0001, between word and grade F(8, 436)=4.79, p<.0001, and between language group,word and grade F(8, 436)=4.97, p<.0001.

Acknowledgements

Part of this paper was presented at the Second Workshop of the European Science Foundation Network on Written Language and Literacy - Understanding early literacy in a developmental cross linguistic approach - held at NIAS (the Netherlands Institute for Advanced Study in the Humanities and Social Sciences), Wassenaar, the Netherlands, 7-9 October 1993. We are very thankful to Juan Guàrdia for his constant help and advice in the statistical treatment of the data , to Arthur Gómes de Morais and José Matas for their participation in data collection and discussion of different parts of the paper, to Jana Zelcer for her participation in data collection and to Ruth Berman for the bibliography search and advice.

Appendix 1

List of Hebrew letters as transcribed by Latin letters in describing written forms

A- Alef

B- Beth

C- Gimmel

D- Daleth

H- Hey

W- Waw

Z- Zayin

X- Het

T- Teth

Y- Yod

K- Kaf

L- Lamed

M- Mem

N- Nun

S- Samekh

U- Ayin

P- Pey

C- Tsadiq

Q- Qof

R- Reish

S*- Shin

T- Tav

a: slightly modified from Levin, Korat and Amsterdamer (1996)

b: Teth and Tav are pronounced alike in standard Hebrew but are orthographically different, therefore Teth will be transcribed with an asterisk.

Appendix 2

Test materials used in the writing task

Spanish	Hebrew	Relevant differences
TE (te) cv#cvv	TH (tei)	Structure of the syllable: in Hebrew, rhyme with two vowels
PIZZA (pitsa) cvc#cv or cv#ccv	PYÇH (piça) cv#cv	In Hebrew /c/ is a consonantal phoneme different from /ts/ and is represented in the orthography
SALAMI (salami) cv#cv#cv	SLMY (salami) cv#cv#cv	No relevant differences
MENTA (menta) cvc#cv	MNTH (menta) cvc#cv	No relevant differences
COCA-COLA (Coca Cola) cv#cv#cv#cv	QWQH QWLH (Coca Cola) cv#cv#cv#cv	No relevant differences
MANDARINA (mandarina) cvc#cv#cv#cv	MNDRINH (mandarina) cvc#cv#cv#cv	No relevant differences

Segmentation task

TE (te) cv#cvv	TH(tei)	Structure of the syllable: in Hebrew, rhyme with two vowels
PIZZA (pitsa) cvc#cv or cv#ccv	PYÇH(piça) cv#cv	In Hebrew /c/ is a consonantal phoneme different from /ts/ and is represented in the orthography
SALAMI (salami) cv#cv#cv	SLMY (salami) cv#cv#cv	No relevant differences
TELEFONO (Teléfono) cv#cv#cv#cv	TLFWN (Télefon) cv#cv#cvc	Structure of last syllable and different stress
CHOCOLATE (chocolate) cv#cv#cv#cv	SWQWLD(shokolad) cv#cv#cvc	Structure of last syllable CVC and different stress
RADIO (radio) cv#cvv or cv#cv#v	RDJW (radio) cv#cvv or cv#cv#v	In Spanish /io/ is a diphthong

PART II

Writing and reading in time and culture

Orality/Literacy, Languages and Alphabets
Examples from Jewish Cultures

Colette Sirat

The purpose of this study is to describe the distinctive roles of orality and literacy in the history of the Jewish people. This history is characterized by complementarity and multiplicity: the complementarity of oral and written, the multiplicity of spoken languages, alphabets, cultural environments and opinions among the Jewish people itself.

Writing has been part of some cultures (Mesopotamian, Egyptian) from the beginning; for others (Greek, for example) it has not. This has also been the case for the Jewish people. The idea of writing is present throughout the text of the Bible, with 529 words being used in relation to writing or books; the word *sefer* (book), for example, is used 177 times; writing is mentioned when God gives His law to the People of Israel on Mount Sinai. He speaks, but also writes down the contents of the first Tablets which are then destroyed; Moses hears the words of the Lord and writes them down on a book, i.e. a scroll, and also on stone tablets as a sign of the Covenant.

1. The first period

The first period of the history of the book in Israel dates roughly from the 9th to the 3rd or 2nd centuries BCE Hebrew was the language spoken by the inhabitants of Judah and Israel from at least the 12th c. BCE, when they entered the land of Canaan, up until the destruction of the First Temple and the Babylonian Exile in 586 BCE It seems that Hebrew continued to be spoken by those who remained in Judah (Naveh and Greenfield, 1984). However most of the educated class was then in exile and by the time they returned to Judah, a province of the Persian Empire, their descendants were speaking Aramaic

(Barr, 1989). From the conquest of Canaan until the 3rd or 2nd c. BCE the Palaeo-Hebrew alphabet, which had evolved from the West-Semitic-Phoenician-Canaanite alphabet (Naveh, 1982), was used in Israel for the writing of Hebrew.

Scholars disagree as to the importance of writing in this period. The debate hinges on three questions: 1) Were there schools for scribes or aristocratic children before the Babylonian Exile? 2) What was the level of literacy? 3) Had the text of the Pentateuch already been canonized? (Demsky and Bar-Ilan, 1988).

Some people had learned how to write at home, as shown by the many names, lists and seals which served administrative and economic purposes (Ahituv, 1992) and by the biblical text, which quotes the titles of twenty-four books which may, or may not, be part of the actual Bible. From some of these names we learn that the events referred to in the books ranged from the Mosaic period to the Exile, and there is no indication that they were authoritative for religious practice or doctrine. Other titles of books are cited in the Bible as canonical laws for all generations and it is likely that these are part of the Pentateuch as we know it.

However, when books are quoted in the biblical text, it is always as a single copy read by one person to the people. Moses states that the "Book of the Torah" was to be read to the people once every seven years from the copy kept by the Priests (Deut. XXI, 9-13). One book and one reader for all the people was also the situation at the time of Jehosh'aphat's reform (II Chronicles XVII, 3-9) and when King Josiah tried to eliminate the pagan cults that flourished prior to the Exile to Babylonia in the 6th c.B.C.E.(II Kings XXII, 8-11, XXIII, 1-3).

When Israel returned from the Babylonian Exile the law was once again read to the people by Ezra the Scribe (Nehemiah VIII, 1-8). Since most Jews' mother tongue was Aramaic, the text was translated and explained by the Elders and the Levites (Sirat, 1991). The Jews in Egypt used the Paleo-Hebrew alphabet as well as the Aramaic one and many documents were found in both languages. Letters and literary and historical texts are dated from the 7th to the 5th c. BCE (Porten and Yardeni, 1986, 1990).

2. New developments after the 2nd century BCE

A new period began during the 3rd-2nd c. BCE, roughly one century after the conquest of the Middle East by Alexander the Great and the establishment of the Seleucids' rule. The number of books was greater, and the Bible took on a new importance with the creation of the synagogue and regular weekly reading from the Book. From that time on, the influence of the Pharisees grew and a sharp distinction can be noted between oral and written texts.

The ancient Paleo-Hebrew alphabet was associated with the Priests and the Monarchy. It was taught in scribal schools which catered to official and administrative professions. Nationalistic connotations and bonds with the Maccabean ideology of a Jewish free state are clear. Hebrew coins, with just one exception, were minted using the Paleo-Hebrew alphabet up until the Bar-Kokhba revolt in 132-135. Until the first centuries AD, the name of God, the Tetragram, was often written in this Palaeo-Hebrew alphabet in the biblical books written in Hebrew or Greek (see Figure 1).

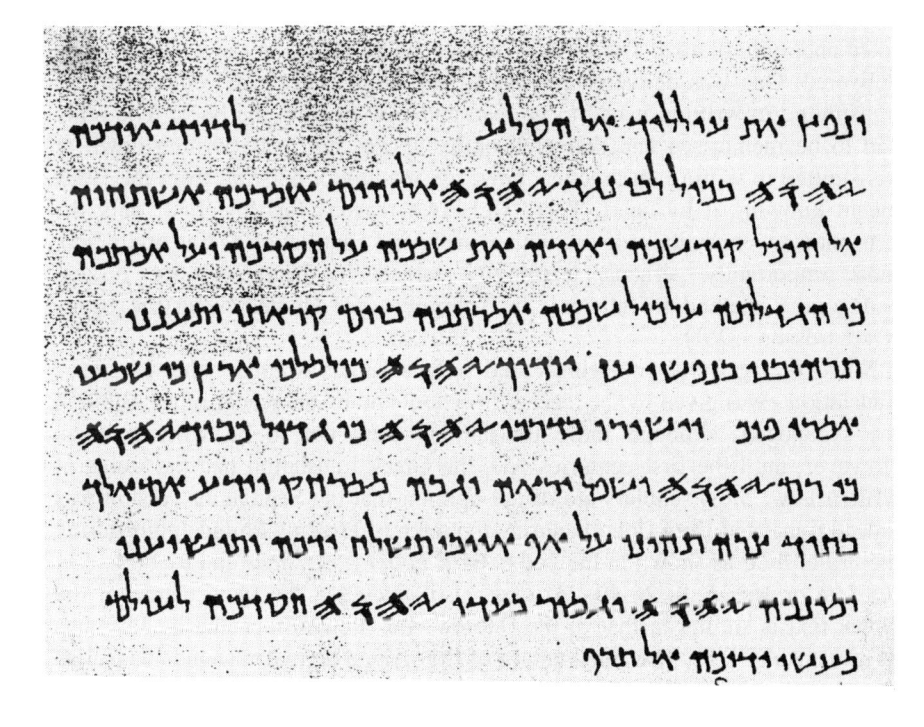

Figure 1. In this Hebrew Psalms scroll God's name is written in paleo-hebraic letters (cfr. J. A. Sanders, The Psalms Scroll of Qumran, Cave 11, Oxford, 1965, col. XXI, plate XII).

The new Hebrew alphabet, derived from the Aramaic one, came to the fore with the Pharisees who promoted the study of the Law. In the first period, religious teaching was conducted orally, by a father to his children (Deut IV, 9 and XI, 19). The Pharisees founded schools based on the Hellenistic model - in these schools reading and writing was not only carried out in an alphabet other than Paleo-Hebrew, but had a different aim. The schools were not professional but a substitute for the father in teaching children the Law of God. There were schools in Jerusalem before the Common Era (Morris, 1977) and the Mishnah affirms that they were of two kinds - one for the teaching of written texts and one for oral texts. This distinction was essential for rabbinical Judaism.

The terms used for the two types of study were also different. For the study of written text the Rabbis used the term *miqrah* from *qarah* (to read) as opposed to the study of the oral text called *mishnah*, from *shanah* (to repeat). The two Laws were said to have been received by Moses on Mount Sinai, and were fixed and authoritative. The difference between them was in the way they were delivered. One was delivered by way of the written word and could only be transmitted in writing; it had to be read and written from the book. The other had to be memorised and delivered orally; it was not to be written down or transmitted in writing. In practice, however, reading or copying from the Book meant knowing it by heart. There were two reasons for this: first, only the consonants were written down, with vowels and cantillation learnt orally and, more importantly perhaps, learning a subject by heart was the normal pedagogical method for all texts in Antiquity - for Homer as for the Bible. (Gerhardsson, 1961).

Since the text was in Hebrew and people spoke Aramaic, the Targum - translation - was given by the teacher in school and by the reader of the Bible in the synagogue, although these translations were not to be written down. However, until the first centuries AD, the Greek translation had the status of written Law. Most scholars are of the opinion that the Septuagint version was indeed translated from Hebrew during the reign of Ptolemy Philadelphus during the 3rd c. BCE as shown in the 2nd c. BCE *Letter of Aristeas* and by Philo (*On the Life of Moses*, II, 26-40). Aristeas also states that the fixed nature of the Greek text is similar to that of the Hebrew one, a claim repeated by Josephus (*Against Apio*, I, 8). The fixed nature of the written text corresponds to that of the oral one. The *Mishnah* and the *Beraithah* (the part of the oral tradition which was not included in the canonical edition) were memorised word for word. They were "edited" on the basis of oral traditions (and perhaps students' private notes: *megillot setarim*) by Rabbi Judah the Prince around the end of the 2nd or the beginning of the 3rd c. His Mishnah was virtually canonized and it is this text which is used nowadays. The public presentation was oral. The *Tanna*

ORALITY/LITERACY, LANGUAGES AND ALPHABETS 105

(repeater, reciter) memorised the text of certain portions of the Mishnah which he then recited in the presence of the Rabbis. These *Tannaim* were chosen for their extraordinary memory, although they were not always particulary intelligent: "The magian mumbles and understands not what he says; the *tanna* recites and understands not what he says" (Babylonian Talmud, *Sotah* 22a).

The decision to keep the oral Law oral was deliberate. The Pharisees condemned the Sadducees who used the *Sefer Gezerot*, a book of *halakhah*, which was deposited in the Temple. The reason for this decision seems to be the fundamental distinction made between the categories of biblical book and sages' decisions. The biblical books were "holy" (in terms of purity they were said to "defile the hands") the oral works of the Rabbis were not. Like the Scripture, they were divinely inspired but in a different way, whose difference had to be maintained. Prayers were also to be kept oral to avoid being on a par with written biblical prayers.

From the time of Rabbi Judah the Prince until the middle of the 7th c. the *Amoraim* explained the *Mishnah*, sometimes using the *Beraithah*, their explanations and many earlier traditions. The ensemble of these interpretations make up the *Gemarah; Gemarah* and *Mishnah* together are called *Talmud*. There are some differences between the text of the *Mishnah* as explained in Babylonia and the text of the *Mishnah* as explained in Palestine. However, these differences are minor when compared with the *Gemarah* which is another text altogether. And if we look at the text of Bible commentaries called *Midrashim* we see what is generally thought of as an oral text, with all its variations.

Here, however, the difference between the *Mishnah's* text on the one hand and the *Gemarah's* and *Midrashim* texts on the other is not the one generally found between a written and an oral text. The more stable text is the canonized oral text, whereas the more varied one is the freer explanation. The attitude to the text is one of "interpretation". The question "Why?" is found in the *Gemarah* hundreds of times.

The oral law was eventually written - a final step in the process of editing it orally - but it continued to be taught and studied orally in the Academies (*The Literature of the Sages*, 1987). Once written, it was not published until the 8th or 9th c. and the first copies we know of were sent to Spain during the 9th c. The fact that Oral Law was kept oral for so many centuries is particularly noteworthy because the spread of literacy began in the 1st c. BCE and flourished in the first centuries AD. There is mention of this in Eccl. XII, 12: "My son beware of anything beyond these. Of making many books there is no end and much study is a weariness of the flesh".

During the many centuries that oral Law was kept oral, literacy in many alphabets was widespread as shown by the books, inscriptions and graffitti that have been preserved. Indeed, as regards books, the scrolls found near Qumran have some connection with the Qumran Community and even if they cannot be called "a library" they give an indication of the books possessed by the members of that community. This Qumran Community may have been large, yet the number of books is astonishing - there are the remnants of at least 823 rolls (Tov, 1994). Most of the rolls are in the Hebrew language and in Hebrew script; a few are in Palaeo-Hebrew script, some are in Aramaic script and language and others are in Greek characters and language.

Hellenized Jews wrote many treatises in Greek, not all of them apologetic. With the rise of the Church, this Greek literature was rejected by the Rabbis who tried to impose the supremacy of the Hebrew alphabet over all other writings. They did not, in fact, ever succeed and Greek, written in Greek letters, was used by Jews until it was replaced by Arabic during the 1st c. of the Hegira, i.e. 7th c. AD (Loewe, 1994).

As regards inscriptions, which are also numerous, a 1st c. monumental tomb discovered in Jericho belonging to the Goliath family shows 32 inscriptions written or inscribed on 14 ossuaries. Of these inscriptions, 17 were in Greek, 15 in Hebrew. Three ossuaries bear bilingual inscriptions and one appears to have been executed by the same hand (Hachlili, 1979). In the Diaspora, votive inscriptions in synagogues were mainly in Greek. In Palestine, some inscriptions were in Greek and others in Aramaic and Hebrew. In one synagogue in the Yemen the monumental inscription was in the Sabean language and alphabet with another smaller one in Hebrew (Navëh, 1992). In Rome, 535 inscriptions were found in three catacombs, dating from the 1st c.B.C.E. to the 4th c.: 405 of them are in Greek (76%), 123 in Latin (23%), 3 in Hebrew, 1 in Aramaic, 2 bilingual (Greek and Latin, Aramaic and Greek) and 2 were illegible (Leon, 1966). In Southern Italy, knowledge of Greek writing lingered until the 10th c. It is probable that most simple Jews could also read the Hebrew Bible, for during this period, the "Word of God" became the "Text written by God", with "the eye" taking precedence over "the ear" among the Jews. The Law was looked at and the Sepher Torah was created.

The *Sepher Torah* is a book and it is not a book. It is a book if a book is defined as an object from which a text is read, since it was used to read the Pentateuch during the synagogal service. It is not a book if a book is thought of as the variably shaped object familiar to us today: the Torah in fact has changed very little since the beginning of the Common era. If we consider any other religious or non religious text that has been faithfully transmitted for as long as the *Sepher Torah*, the actual book we read from now is very different from the one in Antiquity. Homer's Iliad was first written on papyrus rolls, as was the practice in Greek and Roman times; during the Middle Ages and the Renaissance it was written on a parchment codex; later, the text was printed on paper and new editions were made, using the first editions as well as any ancient manuscripts which could be found. This does not apply to the *Sepher Torah*. Nowadays, it is still handwritten on a parchment scroll: the preparation of the parchment and the ink, the layout and ruling, the manner of sewing the skins, and graphic features of the text aim to comply with the instructions established in the first centuries of the era. However, during the 6th-8th c. the *Masorah*, including the division into verse, vowels and the cantillation (the traditional way of reading the Sepher Torah) was put into writing not on liturgical rolls but on codex bibles. These were adopted as the standard book for study and other purposes (Sirat, 1994).

3. The Islamic period: expansion of literacy and orality

The Islamic period (650-1250) was, at first, favourable to an expansion of both literacy and orality. The cultural climate has been described by Ibn Haldun as one in which: a) scientific and artistic production, i.e. the art of writing and other related arts such as calligraphy, the art of the copyist and book production, increased; b) people were eager to put down their views in writing; c) people were eager to hold discussions about all sorts of problems.

Jewish culture was a part of this climate and Jewish people quickly learned the new language. They spoke colloquial Arabic as their mother tongue and classical Arabic as their literary language. There was never any opposition in rabbinic circles to the use of Arabic as a literary language. The Hebrew language, and script, was used for the Bible, liturgical poetry and prayers. Aramaic (in Hebrew letters) was the language of rabbinic law and Talmud. From the 9th c. on even the Talmudic Academies *Responsa* were written in Arabic (in Hebrew letters). The Bible was translated into Arabic by Saadia Gaon (882-942) and Yefet b. Eli (active during the second half of the 10th c.), the Hebrew text being studied with the help of the Arabic translation. Education in Arabic literature and letters was generally provided in the family and not in the community school (Reif, 1990) and, until 1200, almost all Jewish works of Jewish thought and all scientific texts were written in Arabic. This participation by the Jewish people in contemporary Islamic intellectual life is particularly important because all previous currents of thought were still active in the intellectual life of the Near East. In contrast to Europe where the Norman invasions destroyed most Greco-Roman culture and where only a few clerics could read and write, the basis of Greco-Roman civilization had survived in the Near East with no break in continuity (Byzantine and Arabic philosophers took over from the last commentators of Aristotle) and had been enriched by Manichean, Zoroastrian and Indian culture. Widespread translation made most Greek scientific works available to the Arabic-speaking world. These translations, which took place, broadly speaking, between 850 and 1050, were generallly carried out by Christians from a Syrian text under the patronage of the Caliphs.

Oral Law, in whatever way it was written, continued to be orally discussed. The Talmudic Academies answered queries from communities all over the world. There are tens of thousands of these replies, *Responsa*, some very brief and some explaining of an entire book, chapter, or topic. We quote here I.Ta-Shema (Encyclopaedia Judaica, s.v. Responsa):

> The Yeshivot [Academies] followed a set procedure for dealing with queries. In general, hundreds of such questions were read and discussed at the Yeshiva during each of the two months of *kallah* in the presence of the full forum of its scholars and pupils. At the conclusion of the discussion, the yeshivah scribe wrote the decision of the head of the Yeshivah at his dictation and all the senior members of the yeshivah signed it.

The decision followed an oral discussion and was transmitted in writing. As Head of the Academy, Saadia Gaon (882-942) followed this oral procedure. However, he composed his own works alone and in writing, as did Maimonides (1138-1204), "Chief of the Jews" in Egypt, who answered many queries about religious questions in his own hand. Some of these replies are extant.

The scribes, in Hebrew as in Arabic, transcribed the text - be it the Word of God or a secular book - without any addition or correction. They transcribed it exactly without altering the author's words. This prevalence of exact textual transmission, linked to a growing awareness of personal creativity and responsibility, was not the case in Christian Europe.

4. Christian Europe (1000-1250)

Religious texts were the only ones studied by Jews in Ashkenazic countries. Science and philosophy were studied in Latin in Christian universities where Jews were not accepted. Very few Jews knew Latin - Hebrew and Aramaic were their literary languages and these were written in Hebrew letters.

ORALITY/LITERACY, LANGUAGES AND ALPHABETS

Jews spoke French in France, England and the Rhineland and, later, German in Germany. All these languages were written in Hebrew letters, hence the fact that Hebrew manuscripts are important testimonies of the French language during the centuries when Latin alone was written. The exchange of ideas between the Christian and Jewish communities was essentially oral. Discussions and disputes were numerous and some of them were written down, sometimes in Latin and sometimes in Hebrew.

Although all Jewish boys learnt to read, orality was an important factor and attitudes to texts were "open". A good illustration is provided by the commentaries on the Bible and the Talmud by Rabbi Salomon b. Isaac, *Rashi*, from Troyes (1040-1105). There are hundreds of manuscripts and printed editions of these commentaries in our possession, for Rashi has been the most studied Jewish author from the Middle Ages till modern times. These manuscripts can be divided into two groups - the Sephardic-Italic and the Franco-Ashkenazic. The manuscripts in the second group offer significantly different versions. They show that to French and Ashkenazic medieval sages Rashi's commentaries were works of continuous literary evolution. It was therefore legitimate to add or omit phrases, providing those additions or omissions did not alter the basic meaning or concept (Grossman, 1988, 1995). Rashi himself would have agreed - he omitted, amended or added to the Talmud he was commenting on, but not to the Bible.

Until the close of the 13th c. oral study was the norm in the French and Ashkenazic world. It was based on the reading of a text, either the Bible, the Talmud or the Midrash. The written text was not always the one known by heart and it could be different from other texts, in which case scholars would not hesitate to "correct" the text they were reading. Translation into the vernacular and commentary by the rabbi were carried out with the help of oral traditions and customs "heard from the mouth of his teacher". Scholars went from rabbi to rabbi and from town to town in order to learn from different masters and they jotted down what they heard in their *quntressim* - personal notebooks. Some of these notebooks from the 12th and 13th c. have been preserved. These notes were supplemented by extracts from books, stories heard or seen and examples given by rabbis. A few of these *vademecum* became "books" such as the *Mahzor Vitry* or the *Mordekhai*.

Another feature of Ashkenazic books before 1300 was a tendency towards non-linearity. They might be written in fanciful layouts using the four directions of space or the text could be part of a drawing or written as ornamentation in micrography. The *Masorah*, written in very small letters in the margins of Bible codices, was naturally used for drawing. All these non-linear texts, even those which seem purely ornamental, are legible, yet it is doubtful that they were read very often. They were probably written for the mutual pleasure of the scribe and the reader. The book was there to be read but also to be looked at. It functioned as a work of art, whose figurative layout did not hold a necessary relation with the meaning of the text (micrographic ornamentations are not calligramms!) but the playful drawing of an infinite variety of animals and grotesques (Sirat, 1994).

It was during the 13th c., probably in Paris, that the Hebrew religious book was given the layout which is so well suited to its form of study, and which it has retained to this day. The glossed book has both a central text and commentaries on the same page. The eye can wander back and forth from text to commentaries (see Figure 2). This method of reading is certainly not the fast scanning advocated for information selection, being much more akin to problem-solving, and it is hardly surprising that in today's Talmudic Academies students read the glossed Talmud aloud with a companion, asking each other questions, raising objections and disputing words and meanings.

5. The Renaissance and Modern Times

Beginning in the 14th c. (some precursors date from the 13th c.) more and more Jews learned to read, understand and copy Latin books, although their number was never great. This situation changed with the increasing numbers of books available in vernacular languages, and by the 15th c. many Jews were writing in Spanish or Italian. Most Italian rabbis wrote in Italian as well as Hebrew.
The printing of Hebrew books began in Italy and Spain in about 1470. Printed books resembled manuscripts in most respects - in layout as well as in the form of letters, yet the proliferation of books did not modify readers' manner of thinking, or the kind of texts read. We have a reasonably good picture of the libraries in the Duchy of Mantua in 1595. Following a Church edict ordering the expurgation of books, Jews were required to submit a list of books to be censored.
The 430 lists preserved in the Mantua community archives reflect the content of the private libaries of most of the community members. The books, which total 21,142, are mostly printed Hebrew books and there is a small number in Yiddish and Italian. Average sized libraries numbered about 50 volumes, while some scholars could boast collections ranging from 100 to 350 books. 11% of books were owned by women. The bulk of these libraries consisted of prayers-books, Bibles and books on the commandments. Half of the community members were also interested in ethics, grammar and *Mishnah* and a third of them read philosophy, mysticism and fiction. Medicine and sciences were read

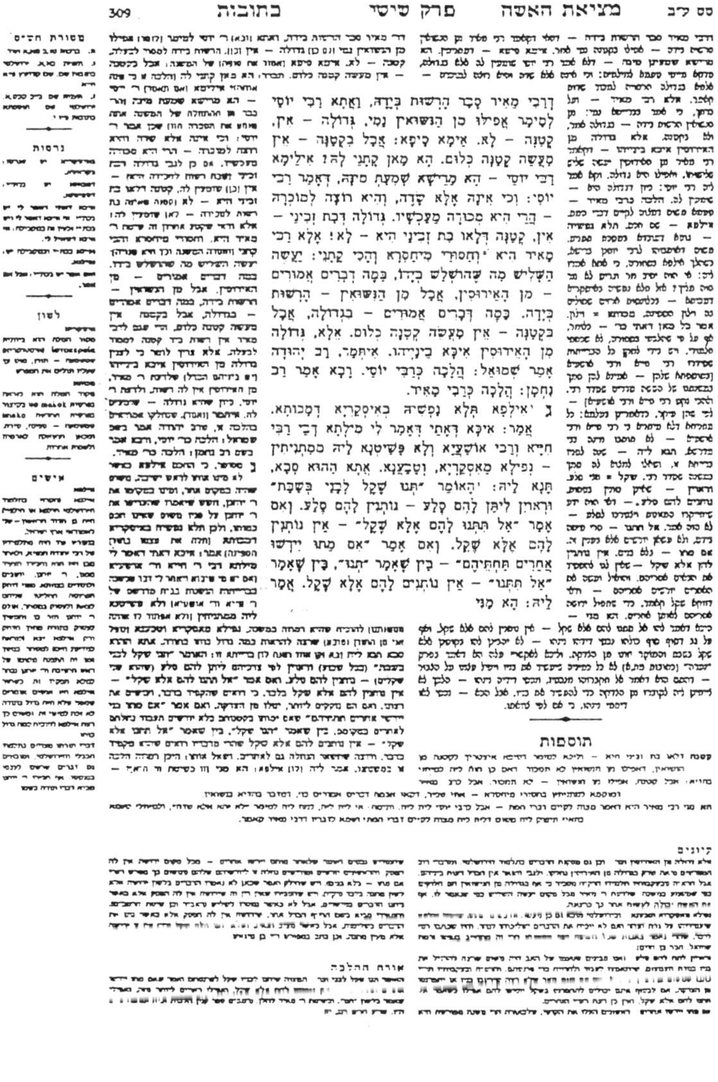

כתובות פרק שישי מציאת האשה

309

דרבי מאיר סבר הרשות בידה, ואתא רבי יוסי
לסיקר אפילו מן הנשואין נמי. גדולה – אין,
קטנה – לא. אימא סיפא: אבל בקטנה – אין
מעשה קטנה כלום. הא מאן קתני להז אילימא
רבי יוסי – הא מרישא שמעת מינה, דאמר רבי
יוסי: וכי אינה אלא קדה, והיא רוצה למוכרה
– הרי היא מכורה מעכשיו. גדולה דבת זביני –
אין, קטנה דלאו בת זביני היא – לא! אלא רבי
מאיר היא וחסורי מיחסרא והכי קתני: עשה
השליש מה שהושלש בידו, במה דברים אמורים
– מן האירוסין, אבל מן הנשואין – הרשות
בידה. במה דברים אמורים – בגדולה, אבל
בקטנה – אין מעשה קטנה כלום. אלא, גדולה
מן האירוסין איכא ביניהו. איתמר, רב יהודה
אמר שמואל: הלכה כרבי יוסי. רבא אמר רב
נחמן: הלכה כרבי מאיר.

ג אילפא תלא נפשיה באיסקריא דמכותא.
אמר: איכא דאתי דאמר לי מילתא דבי רבי
חייא ורבי אושעיא ולא פשיטנא ליה ממתניתין
– נפילנא מאסקריא, וטבענא. אתא ההוא סבא,
תנא ליה: האומר "תנו שקל לבני בשבת"
וראוין ליתן להם סלע – נותנין להם סלע. ואם
אמר "אל תתנו להם אלא שקל" – אין נותנין
להם אלא שקל. ואם אמר "אם מתו יירשו
אחרים תחתיהם" – בין שאמר "תנו", בין שאמר
"אל תתנו" – אין נותנים להם אלא שקל. אמר
ליה: הא מני

תוספות

Figure 2. Modern Edition of the Talmud. Jerusalem, 1950

in Hebrew and sometimes in Italian. Italian books make up only 2.4% of the total and are mostly literature and poetry. Yiddish make up 2% of the books (Baruchson, 1993).

Printing, however, lent the texts a uniformity which they had not previously had. The printing of the complete Babylonian Talmud by Daniel Bomberg in 1523-1524 determined the external form of the Talmud for all time, including the foliotation, the inclusion of Rashi's commentary in the inner margin, the choice of supplementary commentaries in the outer margin and the division of the *Mishnah* as well as that of the *Gemarah*. Since 1517, when Daniel Bomberg published two Hebrew Bibles (a quarto and a folio) divided as the Vulgate (with 2 books of Samuel, 2 Kings, 2 Ezra-Nehemiah and 2 Chronicles), all Hebrew Bibles have been printed in similar fashion, with numbered chapters following the Vulgate number. In Bomberg's great Bible of 1547-48, the verses are numbered at every fifth verse. These divisions were slowly accepted and today the Bible is universally quoted by chapter and verse, even amongst the very orthodox (and anti-Christian) Jews. Medieval Prayers, although written, had been very different: every city, even every synagogue had had its own variant readings. The oral tradition of prayer was not forgotten in the age of manuscript. Printing changed this situation and unified whole countries; only liturgical rites which were not worth printing kept their individuality and diversity.

In our own times, multilingualism as well as multigraphism is the norm for Jews in Israel as well as in other countries. In spite of the proliferation of books and the uniformity of traditional texts provided as printing, orality is as alive as it ever was.

6. Conclusion

The brief historical outline presented here (a more detailed one would have required many volumes) has, I hope, substantiated the claim in the introduction regarding the complementarity between literacy and orality, and of the multiplicity of both. Since the first millenium B.C.E., Jews have spoken at least two languages and diglossia often existed in one or two of these languages. From the 1st c. B.C.E. most male Jews knew how to read the Hebrew alphabet. Educated people, whose number is unknown but which was certainly not restricted to a small class of scribes, knew how to write not only in the Hebrew alphabet but in two alphabets: Hebrew/ Greek, Hebrew/Arabic, Hebrew/Latin. The terms "orality" and "literacy" have thus had so many different meanings in the course of Jewish history that, in my opinion, to use any of them without describing their circumstances would be of no interest at all.

In the course of this history, the notion of "text" has included oral texts. The Mishnah, for example, was a fixed text, although oral for many centuries. Texts, whether oral or written, were open or closed and this difference was not simply a consequence of "technology" but also of ideology or philosophy. The Bible's written text was fixed very precisely for religious reasons. It was given by God and every letter or accent is of paramount importance. Philosophical and scientific texts were fixed because their authors gave them the stamp of individuality. Prayers and the texts related to the Oral Law were fixed when a mechanical process (printing) made them identical and cheaply available to the whole community or communities.

Whether oral or written, open or closed, the texts were always thought of as "texts" and, at least for a part of the readers, interpretation was recognized for what it was, that is: interpretation. This is the kind of thinking which D. Olson (1977) attributes specifically to the written text. However, what this scholar compared is not an oral text versus a written one, but conversations, "small talk" versus a written text.

Another important point pertains to the aspect of "orality" being described. Orality has been studied as a source of history - inferior to writing - or as a mode of poetic composition - superior to writing. Its role as a way of furthering knowledge has not been investigated outside the Jewish tradition where students of the Oral Law emphasize its importance.

In Talmudic Academies, current studies continue to be essentially oral. The page of the text is read aloud by two students and is followed by discussion and explanation. Disputing the Talmudic text is facilitated by the glossed layout, where text, commentaries and sources are arranged on the same page. Is the situation really very different in scientific subjects? Reading scientific texts silently and selectively does not constitute scientific activity in its entirety. The number of congresses and colloquia in scientific fields indicates that oral dispute is as necessary to us as it was to our predecessors in medieval universities.

Learning or group discussion is conducted through speech. Knowledge is arrived at by confronting numerous ideas presented by different people; each person may draw his own conclusion and put it in writing. When writing alone, a person can compare different ideas, read from different books and decide for himself what he will write as his opinion - he is limited by his own knowledge and the information he can obtain. As we know, this is a question of the availability of sources as much as the scholar's personal curiosity. Individuality is more pronounced when a person composes alone and writes alone.

Information is certainly greater when people discuss collectively and propose different points of view.

The two approaches, collective and oral, personal and written are necessary for the construction of science. Nevertheless, the need for oral discussion is not acknowledged in modern studies, the presence of orality is denied and writing is equated with science. (Havelock, 1991; cf. Fleishman Feldman, 1991).

The complete expulsion of the oral mode of communication from what is called "science" has, in my view, two main causes, although there are probably many more that I am not aware of: a) the desire to equate knowledge with physics, as defined before the discovery of the quanta: i.e. the study of unchanging "things", or letters in our case. b) ignorance of the history of science and philosophy.

R.Saljö (1988:179-180) recalls that:

> the very beginning of empirical research on cognition in the modern sense, can be identified with the ingenious contribution by Hermann Ebbinghaus (1885/1964): the nonsense syllable... the research subject became an ahistorical and asocial being whose ways of interpreting the world were consciously disregarded... In the laboratory version of thinking, knowledge was conceived of as a fixed entity and defined as discrete units of information."

This view of human learning has been dramatically enhanced by MacLuhan's idea that: "Societies have always been shaped more by the nature of the media by which men communicate than by the content of the communication" and also by using the terms "learning" and "intelligence" when speaking of computers (one example among many is Y.S. Abu-Mostafa, 1995). In many subsequent studies "the meaning of words" has been forgotten: academic fashion has perpetuated the "great divide" in what seems a more palatable form (Street, 1988). However, not only has the *meaning of words* been excluded from most studies, investigation of the different modes of thinking and the history of learning have also been overlooked. If we accept the "general claim", also called "the autonomous model of literacy", the Greeks adopted the alphabet during the 8th c. BCE Modern science began in the 16th c. AD What was happening during the 24 centuries that it took *"literacy"* to influence human thinking?

These centuries saw the growth of philosophy and science. This is a very intricate history and much will have to be done if we wish to understand even a small part of of the role played in it by orality and literacy. What we do know, however, is that philosophical and scientific ideas were transmitted and expanded through many cultures, languages and scripts.

For many Muslim (Pines, 1986; Daiber, 1990) and Jewish medieval philosophers, (Sirat, 1990a, 1990b) scientific truth was based more on logical and demonstrative thinking than on observation of facts. However - like sixteenth-century European intellectuals - they did distinguish in both scientific and religious texts *"meaning* from *interpretation.* The former were seen as objective and interpretations were seen as subjective, personal, invented or fabricated of... hermeneutics, the interpretation of texts provided the conceptual categories needed for scientific epistemology". However, these attitudes to text, which flourished during the 10th-13th c. in Islamic as well as in Jewish philosophy, do not prove Olson's simplistic hypothesis (1991, p.152) "that the contrast between texts and their interpretations provided the model, and more than that, the precise cognitive categories or concepts needed for the description and the interpretation of nature, that is, the building of modern science".

In fact, scientific ways of thinking predate modern science by many centuries, and modern science emerged in a chaotic context where, as shown by Koyre's, Yates' and many other studies in the history of sciences, scientific ideas were mixed with astrological and kabbalistic ideas and some very 'muddy' thinking. In our own times, scientific ideas are also translated into many languages, written in many modes of writing, adopted by many cultures, through books. Yet they are also transmitted by lectures, congresses and colloquia. Is this muddy thinking too?

The Notion of Orthography
A Latin Inheritance

Françoise Desbordes

Suetonius was able to examine the writings of the Caesars and that of Augustus in particular detail. One of his comments on August's writing was the following:

> He does not really respect orthography, that is to say the rules of writing formulated by the grammarians (*formulem rationemque scribendi grammaticis institutam*). He would seem rather to agree with the opinion expressed by those who believe that one should write as one speaks. He often inverts or misses out letters or even syllables. These are errors that everyone commits, thus I would not have mentioned it if it had not been claimed, to my great surprise, that he had removed from office a consular legate, accusing him of ignorance and lack of culture.The dismissal would appear to have been justified by the fact that this man had written *ixi* instead of *ipsi*. (Augustus, 87)

This text draws our attention to an important aspect of the way that the Romans viewed the relationship between written and oral - the notion of orthography, with its necessary corollary, the error, and the problems of practical application that it raises.

Following the Latins, we too make a distinction between writing and correct writing. It is not enough to know how to write, but we need to know how to write correctly: is this widely accepted postulate really indispensable? What then is the correct form for alphabetic writing? The Latins did indeed pose the question but handed it down to us without any definitive solution.The whole notion of orthography may have a sting in its tail.

1. The general framework

We are indebted to the Latins for many aspects of writing. For the alphabet, of course, and also for the variety of text types (from the epitaph to the personal letter) which illustrate the wide range of possible uses for the written word. Besides these, we are indebted to the Latins for their ideas of writing. The Latins had a secular and utilitarian view of writing. They regarded it as a memory system enabling information to be stored and communicated at a distance across time and space. Learning to read and write was for them a necessary first step in the intellectual (and social) skills that needed to be inculcated from an early age. They also held the view that "live"speech had emotional, persuasive qualities lacking in writing, which they regarded as completely distanced from the writer. These and similar ideas are derived from the same origin and have something in common, namely the idea that writing is a secondary artefact aimed principally at representing spoken language.

The origins of orthography should be placed within this "representation" perspective. Two distinct objects are being presented: the "represented" (oral) and the "representant" (written).We may ask what conditions must be fulfilled for the latter to be "correct" and other representations to be "incorrect". Indeed the term *orthographia* belongs to this vast family of words grouped around *orthos, orthotès*, which means linking in a straight line, and subsequently accuracy, exactness, appropriateness. All these meanings are based on the idea of the *only* possible right answer to any question: there can be only one right answer in the same way as there can only be one straight line between two points.

2. The Greek antecedents

It is of course true that the Latins simply took over the Greek view of orthography. Orthography is a Greek invention. It became evident at the turn of the 2nd and 1st century BC when grammar (another Greek invention), was becoming the science of linguistic correction. Orthography was part of this grammar. Once *orthoepy*, i.e. correct oral expression, was established, orthography set out what was supposed to be the correct representation of this correct oral expression. Only a few of the numerous works which the Greek devoted to this issue have survived. There are, however, sufficient for us to grasp the general direction of their views.

The origin of orthography is the wish to reduce the diverse written forms that a word may be given by a writer to a single correct form. The history of alphabetic writing systems explains the reasons for this diversity of forms. Some of these reasons, such as clumsiness, incompetence or simply slips on the part of the writer are connected. There are other reasons which prevent writing from being simply the mechanical application of the alphabetic code: the original imperfection of the alphabet, language variations over time and a general tendency to write not just by perpetually reproducing an analysis of the oral, but, as far as possible, by reproducing, to a more or less exact degree, what one has already *seen* written down. The sheer weight of this wide variation of graphic production attracted the attention of Alexandrian philologists who set out to establish definitive texts, working on several and often differing copies. This led to research into the criteria necessary for correction. The grammar system *stricto sensu* which was produced from their observations was to be normative. The idea of correction of language as a whole, which was based on this system, became widespread through the doctrine of *hellènismos*, and was extended to the graphic representation of correct language. The issue was no longer to "correct" (establish) texts, but to set up rules for correct production of texts.

The grammarians spoke about the imperfection of the alphabet with regard to the very principle which was supposed to have governed its creation, that of a univocal and integral representation of oral units. However, there could be no doubting the alphabet, just as there could be no question of suddenly reforming the written forms to which people had already become accustomed. The grammarians thus viewed orthography as a science which guided the search for a suitable written form in cases where the ear was no longer a satisfactory guide. For example, they discussed the problem of *iotacism*, the passage to [i] of sounds that were formerly dipthongs and vowels. The alphabetic principle would have required a uniform transcription of *iota*, but the former written forms tended to hold their own (even nowadays the question of *iotacism* is highlighted in modern Greek spelling). The multiplicity of the written forms corresponding to [i] was thus ratified. The circumstances in which one form or the other were to be used were also established. In order to do this the discussed word was bound to a series of other words by means of certain criteria which quickly became standard: etymology, analogy, language history and dialect. Greek orthography is thus, to a certain extent, a supplement to the alphabetic code and constitutes the rules for the representation of "difficult" words rather than of minimal oral units.

3. The Latin orthographers and their programme

The story begins again in Rome. The Greek alphabet was adopted by the Romans through the Etruscans. There was a "mobile"period when the alphabet was improved, followed by a fixed period in which it was set on a pedestal as sacred. The language, however, continued to evolve. The continual lament of the grammarians over "missing letters" and "superfluous letters" had no effect, and even though the Emperor Claudius invented three new letters, they did not survive his reign. (It is said that the same thing happened later on for the Merovingian king Chilperic). However, reflections as to what might or should be the usage of the alphabet appeared as early as the end of the 2nd century BC and were systematized during the Augustan era by the introduction of the Greek notion of *orthographia*. There is a vast literature on this subject, since it was of great interest to the scribes and copyists of the Middle Ages..

Two complete treatises by Terentius Scaurus and Velius Longus from this period of original production, i.e. the first two centuries AD, have survived as well as the account by Quintilian in book 1 of the *Oratory Institution*. There are also other fragments, particularly by Cornutus, and the chapter *De orthographia*, from the *Ars grammatica* by Marius Victorinus. (The latter is from the IVth century, but the doctrine may date back to Verrius Flaccus, a contemporary of Augustus). The authors' comments and the problems they addressed are still highly instructive for us nowadays.

Suetonius contrasted the grammarians' orthography with the type of writing that we would refer to these days as "phonetic writing", i.e., "writing as we speak". The most striking fact about the orthographers of the Upper Empire is that they all explicitly advocated "phonetic writing". Quintilian sums up their position well:

> In my opinion, apart from exceptions sanctioned by usage, we should write in accordance with what is pronounced. The role of letters is in fact to preserve sounds and restore them, entrusting them to the reader. Letters should thus represent what we will have to say. (1.7.30)

Suetonius's contrasting idea thus seems not to be confirmed. According to the orthographers, writing should be considered a secondary phenomenon whose sole function was to provide an exact image of what it represented. Their view of orthography was that it needed to be justified and not arbitrary, stemming from the nature of writing itself and from its relation to speech. Their highly reasonable programme may be summed up in three points: 1) to distinguish carefully the written from the oral, 2) to classify the oral units and 3) to place them so as to correspond to the written units. Up to a certain point they managed to do this relatively successfully.

Orthography did not need to deal directly with speech, but aimed simply to teach how to note down orally produced forms, whatever they might be. It was not supposed to make a choice between contemporary oral forms, such as between *forcipes* and *forpices* (pincers). This was the business of orthoepy. Nor was it supposed to choose between ancient and modern form; for example, orthography was not supposed to decide on the two written forms *absorbui* and *absorpsi*, but simply on the choice of *absorbsi* or *absorpsi*. Nor was it supposed to disambiguate homophones, because the role of writing was not to "improve" the oral form. Orthographers were particularly bitter about this point:

> Pay no attention to the question of ambiguity and write both the nominative plural and the genitive singular with *-ae* . Anyone who is incapable of distinguishing the number and the case in the words quoted above is a total fool. (Victorinus, GL[1] VI, 14)

Once the difference between the oral and the written had been established, the oral (*enunciatio*) had to be analysed precisely. This was a task for which a form of experimental phonetics was used when needed (albeit to a limited extent!)

For example, metrical theory was used to show whether the sound represented by 'I' was a consonant. To demonstrate that the sound corresponding to Z was not "double", we have the following example:

> It is clear that if someone happens to arrive whilst I am pronouncing the sound of this letter, he will find that it continues as it began. On the other hand, if it is a ψ or a ξ, he will hear the final S, but nothing more of the sounds which begin these double letters. (Longus, GL VII, 51)

The remaining task was to establish correspondences between the identified sounds and the letters of the alphabet, which remained unalterable. A compromise viewpoint consisted in recognising the fact that the alphabet was not perfect and that on the whole it was sufficient for one to realise this fact and write accordingly. We should note that the vowel signs were "dichronic" (that 'A' represented [a] or [a]), that 'I' represented a vowel, a consonant or two consonants, that 'X' was a "double letter", that 'K', representing the same thing as C, had to stay "silent" etc. These were the very same facts that the later Arts would teach.

4. Problems: the questionable units

Nevertheless this reasonable programme was marked by points of divergence between specialists. The alphabet functioned on an all or nothing principle: either it was 'A' or it was not 'A', with no acceptable intermediary. What should an orthographer do when in doubt as to which letter to attribute what he thought he had heard? When we read orthographers' works it is clear that they were frequently up against an imperceptible evolution of the phonological system in which certain opposing forms tended to disappear, to a lesser or greater extent according to location and social class (similar, for example, to the current French faltering surrounding the opposition between *un brin d'herbe* and *un beau brun*). Thus, the scholars of the Lower Empire came up against the problem of the opposition /b/ /w/, for example. Even at that time Longus observed:

> We may not set aside the idea of linking orthography to ortheopy in certain cases where both the pronunciation and the written form is put into doubt. (GL VII, 72)

Should one write *arispex* or *aruspex*; *mensor* or *mesor*; *coniunx* or *coniux*; *sumptus* or *sumtus*? It was at this point that the orthographers resorted to criteria which had been established by their Greek predecessors, namely etymology, analogy and history. Thus, when Scaurus recommends the written form *sed* as opposed to *set* referring to history (following the supposedly ancient form *sedum*!), he draws attention indirectly to the fact the the sounds [d] and [t] may not be clearly distinguished from each other. In other words, he is observing that the opposition of /d/ and /t/ is cancelled in final position.

5. Problems: the futility of phonetic transcription

Resorting to criteria of *ratio* is more significant than it might seem at first sight. It means that the orthographers supported a concept of writing that we would call phonological and non-phonographic. In fact the Ancients seem to have contrasted the essential and the superficial, the intelligible and the perceptible. Clearly it is legitimate to establish a differentiated representation of the nuances picked out by hearing and the Latins had made a fair amount of progress as far as phonetic analysis was concerned. To say nothing of the question of vowel length, stress or intonation, that gave rise to a number of observation, they had identified a velar nasal [ŋ], three variants of /m/ and three of /l/, and different forms of /k/ according to the vowel following it, etc. Suggestions had been made to represent [ŋ] by the digraph gg, to convey the dropping of the phoneme of final [m] by only writing half of the letter M (ʌ) ! and to contrast *ka* and *ce*. Attention was also paid to the number of oral units:

> Cicero seems to have ordered the written form with relation to speech. It was indeed he who thought that *Aiiacem* and *Maiiam* should be written with two I. (Longus, GL VII, 54)

In fact contemporary phoneticians confirm that in the word which is normally written *Aiax* and *Maia*, there are indeed two consonants, one on each side of the syllabic boundary. Caesar used the same idea when he even suggested writing the genitive of *Pompeius* as *Pompeiii,* with three I's (according to Priscion, GL II, 14).

However, these suggestions aimed at a true *phonetic transcription* met with hardly any success. Above all they were accused of being useless, e.g. in giving a differentiated representation to positional variants which are produced automatically:

> Those who write *Troiam, Maiam,* with a single I say that the written form should not be weighted down with a surplus of letters, whilst the sound is enough in itself. Indeed, it is part of the very nature of certain letters to have a certain length and for their sound to be drawn out in pronunciation. This is also the case in *hoc est,* where the thickness of the letter itself is filled out in the pronunciation [hoccest]. It is part of the nature itself of the letter 'I' to be pronounced more openly when it comes between two vowels, since the preceding letter is bound to it, and the following one is too. (Longus, GL VII, 54)

In the same way, Varro considered that it was of no use to add an H before the initial Y of Greek loan-words, since aspiration is automatic. The same applied to words beginning with R:

> The reader should understand by himself that *Rodus,* even without an H, is the equivalent of *Rhodus* and *retor* of *rhetor.* (Quoted by Cornutus, GL VII, 154)

Even then Lucilius (frg. 9 GRF), refused to accept the idea of differentiated representation of long and short vowels. He maintained that the onus was on the reader, since vowel length was immediately determined by the word where it was situated.

6. Problems: phonetics and phonology

How far can one legitimately analyse nuances of speech? From the viewpoint of the Ancients, at least since Plato, the great and surprising quality of the writing system was to have reduced the infinite diversity of human speech to a handful of units. Writing was also the means by which speech was realised as *uox scriptilis*, over and above the contingencies of individual production. To have multiplied the differences would have meant regression and not progress. For example, although the Latins generally agreed on the issue of "useless" letters (the alphabet could be reduced to 17 letters), there was never any consensus concerning the "missing letters". Indeed, any suggestions or attempts to add letters (as by Claudius) came up against a refusal to take the contingent, irrational oral occurrence into consideration. It was true that assessment through what one heard was considered to play a role in identifying oral units, but a differential function also had to be set up with regards to meaning. Thus, within the heated debate as to whether the letter H could be regarded as a "useless letter" since aspiration simply modified certain oral units, we find the following extremely "up-to-date" argument based on the difference in meaning between a "minimal pair":

> H is a consonant which works towards signification [*adsignificans*], since the signification is changed when it is added or taken away. Thus *hīra* [intestine] differs from *īra* [anger]. (Longus, GL VII, 52)

However, even though we may concede that all the varieties of production of /m/ which do not imply a change in meaning may be represented by a single M, we are faced with another problem, which was of great concern to the Latins. That is the *quaestio*, the traditional and unresolved problem set out by Quintilian:

> Here is a question frequently posed: should one when writing prefixes, conform to the sound occurring in the compound form or in their free form? For instance, in the word I pronounce as *optinuit*, the *ratio* [=analysis] requires the second letter to be B, whereas the sound heard is rather a P. Or in the word *immunis*, the N required by *ueritas* [=etymology], is influenced by the sound of the following syllable, and changes to another M. (1. 7. 7.)

Optinuit is a compound that includes the verbal prefix *ob*. In the same way *immunis* is a compound that includes *in*. On the one hand we may claim the merits of *aures*, and on the other hand those of *ratio* and *ueritas*. In *immunis* we may detect an [m], an item of a class of sound duly identified elsewhere. However might we not consider that it is simply a question of a specific and automatic production of /n/ in a particular position? On this point opinions were divided:

> There are those who believe that we should trust to the sound and write in accordance with what we hear. We might say, indeed, that nearly the whole of the debate on the correct written form amounts to the question of whether we should write what we hear [*quod audimus*] or what we ought to write [*quod scribi oporteat*]. As far as I am concerned, sound does not resolve everything. Cornutus, GL VII, 149.

This same Cornutus believed in fact that one should write *tamtus* and not *tantus* [so large], with reference to *tam* [so much], and *exsilium*, and not *exil-*

ium, [exile] in accordance with "etymology" *ex solo* [away from the earth]. However, he preferred to conform to the sound heard in the case of the verbal prefixes (he could not "hear" *ad-* in *accedo, attuli, assidus*).

On a more general level, this whole debate concerning the sound heard and *ratio* was highly confused. Even today reference books bear traces of it, with, for instance, *colludo*, but *adludo* in the Gaffiot dictionary, etc. Attitudes to compounds or to etymology were extremely diverse, and there were sometimes preconceived ideas on audibility. For instance, Scaurus, unlike Quintilian, was convinced he could hear a [b] in *obstitit*. Once again the question was how far one should go. If indeed the written form ignored the effects of assimilation, why not those of apophony as well? Should one not write *exaestimo* instead of *existimo*, on the pretext that the simple verb was *aestimo*. This is an example quoted and strongly condemned by Victorinus.

7. Resistance to the idea of a norm

The search for an orthography ended up, paradoxically enough, by casting doubt on the whole alphabetic principle. Several concurrent written forms could be justified: *coniunx* (referring to the verb *iungo*) and *coniux* (referring to the genitive *coniugis*), *Aiax* and *Aiiax*, *immunis* and *inmunis*. Practically speaking, this is a demonstration of the fact that plurality of written forms is made possible through a *word writing system*, which will accomodate quantities of variants so long as the meaning does not change. Perfection, the *orthotès* of representation, was both useless and impossible. Cratylus in his time had already complained about the situation. He observed:

> When by the help of grammar we assign the letters A and B, or any other letters to a certain name, then, if we add, or substract, or misplace a letter, the name which is written is not only written wrongly, but not written at all; and in any of these cases becomes other than a name. (Plato, *Cratylus*, 432)

This is the morality of the same and the different - of all or nothing. In reply to this Socrates gave a little lesson on the status of the image. He maintained that it could not be perfect, unless it were identified with its model, and thus had ceased to be an image of it. Conversely it did not cease to be an image "if some detail were added or taken away".

In the text I quoted at the start of this paper, Suetonius, in his own way, was saying very much the same thing when he defended the idea of "writing the way one speaks". The accused consular legate in question had written as he spoke: *ixi* instead of *ipsi*. Probably we are faced here with evidence of the confusion already triggered off between [ps] and [ks]. Augustus wrote as he spoke. He certainly left out or inverted letters and syllables and although we might have regarded him as somewhat dyslexic, Suetonius maintained that these were normal errors, *communis error hominum*, and simply showed people's generally casual approach to writing, which should not be punished. "Writing the way one speaks" was a slogan for "writing the way one wishes", with no check being made on it. This is evidence of reticence towards the normative claims of grammarians, though not the content of their doctrine. Suetonius was writing at a time when grammarians were still a rather discredited class. That is to say, in opposition to their rules on spoken language, spontaneous usage was supported and in opposition to their rules on writing, spontaneous writing was supported.

The Greek Sextus Empiricus was more or less a contemporary of Suetonius. It was he who expressed the arguments pertaining to this type of resistance most clearly. In his critical account of grammarians, Sextus devotes a brief chapter to orthography (*Aduersus mathematicos*, I, 169-175). There are two main points. Firstly, grammarians do not agree amongst themselves. If orthography were indispensable the absence of general agreement would prevent the writing of anything at all. However, this is not the case:

> all of us, grammarians or not, use the letters which must necessarily be used to indicate the noun, and we are not concerned with those which are not necessary. (Sextus Empiricus, ibidem)

Secondly, as long as a word does not change in meaning, the way it is written does not matter. For instance, *smilion* [lancet] when written as *zmilion* remains the same and does not become *drepanon* [sickle]! "Of what use is this lengthy, vain and stupid chattering on the subject by grammarians?"

8. From representation to reproduction

"Latin orthography does not exist, "said Louis Havet (REL 2, 1924). Nothing could be more true if we give 'orthography' its present precise meaning of a unique and official form of written language. The ancient Greek concept did not become embodied in a State institution before the 19th century. However, the dying world of latinity paved the way for the future.

To a certain extent, and undeniably quickly, the grammarianas won the battle. The influence of the School became widespread, and with it the adherence to the idea of a norm. Thus one had to speak correctly and write correctly. If one did not manage to do so, it was a fault and deserved reproof. Without going into details, let us mention a significant example. Eucherius the bishop of Lyon (circa 450) sent to Agroecius the *De orthographia* of pseudo-Caper. In reply

Agroecius sent him his own *De orthographia,* with a letter in which he traces a comparison between the bishop's power to reprove morals and his concern with checking his followers' writing practices. (*Nihil ergo quod in nobis est alienum a castigatione tua credis*: it seems to you that nothing of what concerns us ought to be free from your correction.) Here is an example of the assimilation of moral rectitude to orthography, of the spelling mistake to sin.

However, this type of correction was no longer the object of debate. Later grammarians did not discuss the subject, for they believed and taught dogmatically that orthography consisted in *writing as one had written previously*. There was no longer an issue over the relation between the written and the oral because this had been put into the hands of the authority that had supplied the example of the correct written form. *Auctoritas* was the criterion that the first orthographiers had rarely and reluctantly used, since a true grammarian always preferred the intelligible *ratio* to the concrete attestation. *Auctoritas* was a means of putting an end to all the hesitating and of replacing justification by prescription, representation by identical reproduction. In this way a written form was considered correct if it was identical to the standard form, whether this form was justified or not. This is not to say that suddenly everyone began to write in a uniform, correct fashion. Indeed, this is not the case in late Antiquity! Nevertheless, there was at least the satisfaction of at last being able to separate the wheat from the chaff.

My intention here has been to highlight some of the questions handed down to us by the Latins. Is alphabetic writing an integral phonography and does it have to be? What are we to understood by this expression? Can we, or indeed, must we rely on the reader to reproduce the words on the basis of a minimum of information (and in that case, what is a minimum?). Or on the contrary, should we assume that written communication, with fewer contextual clues than oral communication, requires further information? Can for example, distinguishing homophones be part of a general tendency that allows for "improvement"? Should the written form be modified as fast as the oral one, and, if so, when and how should the alphabet be changed? Or should we take it as a rule to write as has been done previously?

Finally, we may pose the following questions. Can we do without an orthographic norm and consequent concomitant errors? Can we go back to the good-natured attitude of Suetonius, who remained unshocked by the dyslexia of Augustus?

In 1975 on the occasion of another quarrel over French orthography, R. Barthes suggested that we should write as we speak, and without rules or reproof:

If I wish to write"correctly", that is to say "in conformity", I am free to do so, just as I may find pleasure even now in reading Racine or Gide. Lawful orthography has its charms since it can even be perverse. However, "gaps" in knowledge or "slips" should no longer be penalised, and should cease to be regarded as aberration or foolishness. Society should accept at long last, (or should we say, once more) that the writing system opt out of the State system which it is now part of. In short, being dismissed "on the grounds of spelling" should no longer exist. (R. Barthes, in *Monde de l'Education*, 1975:17)

This is a simple proposal that has not met with much success. . .

Notes

[1]GL = *Grammatici Latini* (ed. H. Keil), 8 vols, Leipzig, 1855-1880 (repr. Hildesheim, 1961); GRF = *Grammaticae Romanae Fragmenta* (ed. G. Funaioli), Leipzig, 1907 (repr. Stuttgart, 1969).

For further details, see F. Desbordes, *Idées romaines sur l'écriture*, Lille, Presses universitaires, 1990, or (if necessary!) *Signes graphiques et unités linguistiques:textes latins sur l'écriture, des origines à la fin du II°siecle de notre ère*, thèse d'Etat (Higher Doctoral thesis) defended at Université Paris IV, Sorbonne in 1985.

Aspects of a History of Written Language Processing.
Examples from the Roman world
and the early Middle Ages

Hartmut Günther

1. Background

Most research done on written language and literacy during the last 200 years has focused on the history of scripts and writing systems. Within this type of research, decipherment has been of special importance. To decipher a text meant solving the problem of the "reduction of language to writing" The predominant perspective taken in most of these studies was thus the phonographic one. The seminal *Study of Writing* by Gelb (1963) is presumably the most advanced account of this position: Writing, we are told, is at its best if its relation to speech is optimised. The study of the history of writing from this perspective is teleological, its only objective being the description of the writing system in relation to the inner form of language. Neither the real form of writing and written signs plays an important role, nor the activities of writers and readers, the materials they use or the way they perform these processes: It is just language that matters, not language use.

How is it possible to write a history of reading and writing processes faced with the fact that they are no longer observable? Many linguists hope that from the description of the evolution of the linguistic structure of writing systems conclusions can be drawn about the processing devices used when a language is written or read. Others rely on observation of the form and organisation of written documents. Again, it is hoped that specific aspects of the development of the form and the organisation of written utterances and texts will shed some light on the way they were produced and processed. A third type of data is contemporary utterances about the reading and writing process. The considerable number of such utterances has not attracted the attention of many scholars; Balogh (1927) and Saenger (1982) are notable exceptions, focussing their papers on the problem of whether reading was silent or aloud in the ancient world and in the Middle Ages.

Predominant up till now has been the examination of the linguistic aspects of reading and writing processes. Because of this predominance, I will restrict myself to the following general remarks. The great bulk of scientific literature on the history of writing and literacy in the West is devoted to the development of writing from its Sumerian origins up to the present day. The predominant perspective, already alluded to above, was the phonographic one: The development of writing systems was seen as a progression from pre-writing (i.e. cave paintings, tokens on pottery, etc.), pictographic approaches, logographic systems, rebus-principle, syllabic writing to full phonographic writing, i.e. the alphabet. The motor for this development, according to the teleological view, was economy in terms of learnability, easy description and elegance (Gelb 1963).

There are two problematic features in the teleological view. Since the alphabetical principle is seen as the point of no further refinement, a history of writing (in this sense) might safely stop at the Greek invention of alphabetical writing with a final chapter outlining how this ultimate principle spread around the world. From an abstract point of view, English, Finnish, Indian and Korean modern writing are more or less satisfactory adaptations of the principle, but nothing of theoretical interest has been added to the Greek idea that one letter should somehow fit one sound, phoneme or the like.

Related to this is the second problem: Why does the extensive use of this best of all writing systems lead to the evolution of non-phonographic features of writing systems, e.g. schema constancy, homonymic differentiation, abbreviations without phonographic counterpart, capitalising etc.? From the phonographic perspective such new features should be regarded as deviations from a better past or an impossible ideal orthography (one grapheme = one phoneme), resulting in a never ending need for reform in every language that uses an alphabetical system.

In the following paragraphs, aspects of a history of written language processing will be discussed by examining the history of the book (§ 2), and reports on writing (§3) and reading processes (§ 4).

2. Aspects of the history of the book

> **book**, n.1. Portable written or printed treatise filling a number of sheets fastened together (forming roll, or usu. with sheets sewn or pasted hingewise & enclosed in cover); literary composition that would fill such a set

of sheets (or several) if printed... (Concise Oxford Dictionary (COD) 1964, 134)

The book is the major medium of literacy in the Western world. For many centuries it has been the major medium of transfer of knowledge, and has still not been completely replaced in this function by modern media such as radio, television, the internet etc. The dictionary entry printed at the beginning of this paragraph is characteristic in not explicitly distinguishing between its material aspects (paper, bound) and linguistic content (treatise, literary composition).

2.1. Material

When writing appeared some 5000 years ago in Sumer and Egypt, the first examples we know of were inscriptions on solid materials. Very early on, however, papyrus was also used. The Egyptian hieroglyph showing a roll of papyrus can already be seen on stone inscriptions of the 4th millennium.

The description of papyrus which follows is taken from Mazal (1994). Papyrus was produced from the marrow of the papyrus plant cut into thin stripes; these were then laid upon a table, two or more with each other transversely across; they were glued together by the drying liquid of the plant. By the direction of the stripes, one side (*recto*) was easier to write on than the other (*verso*) where the movement of the writing tool (*calamus*, made of reed) was disturbed; in fact, the back side was not used very often. For larger documents, single pages were glued together to yield rolls up to 40 feet long, as a rule about 10 inches high. To facilitate reading, writing soon was carried out in columns, the precursor of the page of a book.

In a sense, papyrus was a rather good choice. It can easily be reproduced, it is not heavy and can be carried around. It also has its disadvantages, however. First, its production presupposes certain climatic conditions; hence, the production of papyrus was the chief article of commerce in ancient Egypt. Second, the best form for documents written on papyrus is the roll (for reason of the material); however, rolls are difficult to handle, particularly if specific information is being sought. Raible (1991b) compares this to the difference between a musical tape and a CD: To find a specific point is simple in the latter medium, but difficult (and time consuming) in the former. Third, papyrus rolls are rather short lived compared with parchment or paper, particularly if they are used (i.e. read). In fact, one of the major occupations in the famous library of Alexandria was the continuous copying of older papyri which were about to become difficult to read or to disintegrate. In Northern countries, the transient character of papyrus was an even more severe problem.

Such problems did not arise when parchment was used. The name of the material (lat. *pergamentum*) is derived from the name of the city of Pergamon. Its invention is attributed to Eumenes II's wish to establish a library at Pergamon and it was introduced when the availability of papyrus was restricted because of political differences with Egypt. However, the production and use of (first leather, later untanned) parchment for recording purposes can be traced back to earlier uses in Persia and in other Asiatic countries.

Parchment is a specially prepared animal skin. First, the hair is removed from the skin, then it is stretched and dried. Finally, it might be treated with some chalk or a similar substance for whitening. Parchment is made from the skin of sheep, goats, and young cattle; top quality parchment, *vellum*, is produced from very young or even unborn calves. It is a long lasting material. It is much more likely to be destroyed during production than during writing or reading. Parchment is heavier than papyrus; its production takes time, and is far more expensive. For this reason, writing was a very special process, not just an everyday job. Similarly, books were very expensive objects, not intended for everyday use by anyone.

Once parchment began to be used for writing, the new form of the book (called *codex*) emerged quite quickly, derived from earlier wooden wax tablets strung together with cords. As in later developments, the use of parchment did not alter writing conventions immediately. Indeed, rolls are used even now for deeds and some official documents. Papyrus was used for shorter documents for quite a long time; it was only in the third century AD that nearly all writing was done on parchment. Writing of notes or other short texts not intended to be preserved for a longer period was done on wax tablets already developed in the Roman period. Parchment remained the main writing material for more than 1000 years. Writing and reading processes as well as the form of books changed when paper became the major writing material.[1]

2.2. The organisation of the page

Observing children entering school, it is obvious that as well as all the other problems they encounter when learning to write letters and words, they have considerable difficulty in organizing written symbols on the page. It takes quite some time until they learn to write on the line, to produce letters of equal size, to anticipate the end of a line etc. It seems that a similar development can be observed in the history of writing (cp. Ludwig 1994, 50-54).

Raible (1991a) gives an impressive outline of the development of the organisation of the page from the Hellenistic period to early modern times. Figure 1 models the major aspectsof this development achievements.

(1)
MOSTDOCUMENTSWRITTENINANTIQUITYDISPLAYCHARACTERISTICSSIMIL
ARTOTHISEXAMPLEONLYCAPITALLETTERSAREBEINGUSEDTHEREISNOPUN
CTUATIONANDNOSEPARATIONOFWORDSPARAGRAPHSORHEADLINESAREM
ISSINGETC
(2)
CLEARLYSUCHAWAYOFWRITINGMAKESREADINGVERYDIFFICULT
INFACTSILENTREADINGOFSUCHATEXTSEEMSNEARLYIMPOSSIBLE
HENCETHEINDICATIONOFBOUNDARIESOFLONGERSEGMENTSWAS
INTRODUCEDBYLARGERINITIALSSTARTOFANEWLINEANDOTHERD
EVICES
(3)
THE BREAKTHROUGH HOWEVER WAS THE SEGMENTATION OF THE LINE
INTO MEANINGFUL UNITS (WORDS) THIS NEW WAY OF ARRANGING
MATERIALS ORIGINATED FROM DEMANDS IN THE PROCESS OF COPYING
TEXTS
(4)
Presumablyatthesametimethedistinctionofupperandlowercaselatersspreadf
romtheCarolingialminuscule.Theuseofuppercaseletterswasrestrictedtohea
dlinesinitialsandspecialeffectssuchasthenameofGODimportantwordsetc.
(5)
This was followed / and accompanied / by the invention of punctuation
marks of several sorts / used to indicate syntactic boundaries. The first
mark used was the full stop / indicating sentence boundaries / followed
by the *virgula* (slash) to separate syntactic phrases / question marks / etc.

Figure 1. Abstract demonstration of layout development from Roman times to the late Middle Ages

My example is clearly an oversimplification. Whereas, in a very abstract sense, the five examples can be taken as representing some kind of a chronological order, this is not true in strict, historical terms. For example, in Ugaritic cuneiform writing, a sign was used to indicate word boundaries; this was also true of some Latin texts of special character (see Raible 1991a). Detailed accentuation and punctuation was used by the philologists of Alexandria to help find the right interpretation of difficult texts, etc. What these observations - individual facts that have been well known for years - amount to in the present context is this.

The first example, i.e. writing capitals in *scriptio continua* without further textual organisation, implies that as a rule, reading was *reading aloud* (Balogh 1927, Saenger 1982). Texts written this way simply cannot be read silently in the way we read nowadays. In fact, reading these texts is not reading in a modern sense at all; after all, it takes a long time to read. I shall come back to this point later. Texts of the sort of example (1) are thus typically *phonographic*.

The development shown in examples (2-5) can be explained by reference to the reader - *Is fecit cui prodest,* as Raible (1991a) puts it. The introduction of structuring devices into written texts facilitates reading in the sense of quickly extracting information from texts. This is in fact already present in the development from rolls to the codex, the latter being much easier to handle than the former. The Greeks, writing on papyrus, divided their texts into several parts (chapters), each written on a separate roll. Raible (1991a) points to several other new features, i.e. introduction of headlines, chapters, paragraphs, initials, illustrations etc. which developed during this period, i.e. between roughly 400 and 1400 AD.. All these developments point in the same direction: Written texts, which also became quite long,were shaped according to the reader's needs. The invention of a new script format, the Carolingial minuscule, can also be interpreted in this spirit, since it is definitely easier to read (see Brekle 1994 for elaboration). The major development taking place between 400 and 1400 AD is the *grammatical* organisation of texts: Separation of larger units like paragraphs, verses, sentences (2); indication of beginnings and end of words (3) and clauses (5).

This development is not a natural one. All the above mentioned features are present in earlier stages of the history of writing but are not generally used. For example, Ugaritic cuneiform writing, an early Semitic consonantal writing system (app. 1400 BC), shows regular use of a separation mark between words. Early Greek texts also show it; it only disappears in the 6th century. Furthermore, the development is not uniform; some innovations occur and are then forgotten, others are restricted to certain areas. To cite another example: Cursive writing, which was so important in ancient Egypt that it became completely distinct from the official hieroglyphs, was not developed in Greece, the Roman world or the early Middle ages. It is the aim of the following two sections to find some explanation for the changes in the development of writing and reading processes.

3. Aspects of a history of the writing process

> **write**, v.i. & t. 1. Trace symbols representing word(s) esp. with pen or pencil or typewriter on paper or parchment, ... 3. Compose for written or printed reproduction or publication, put into literary form & set down in writing, ... (COD 1964, 1511)

In discussing writing as a process, it is useful to distinguish a broad sense of the expression from a narrow sense, as in the dictionary entry above[2]. In the narrow sense, writing is the activity of producing written characters on a surface. In the broad sense (which implies the narrow one), writing is the production of texts, from very short ones to book-length ones. In relation to the times we are dealing with, there is a difference between the scribe (narrow sense) and the author (broad sense). The following considerations borrow heavily from Ludwig (1994; 1996) and Saenger (1982).

3.1. Writing in the Roman world

Writing in the narrow sense was considered an inferior activity in the Roman world. Whereas the ability to read was widespread among the educated, writing was not. Ludwig (1994, 56f) distinguishes the following types of writing: (1) Short notes, personal letters etc. were written by the author himself. (2) Longer texts were dictated to scribes, mostly slaves. (3) Being basically an oral culture, a common practice was to write down speeches, transactions etc. The spoken texts were written down on wax tablets by so called *notarii*, sometimes in a form of shorthand (Tironean notes, named after Cicero's secretary Tiro who was said to be the inventor of this system); sometimes only key words or central sentences were written[3]. These *notae* were later edited and then written down for publication. Some of these speeches were themselves based on written composition. (4) The most frequent writing process was copying. Usually, one person dictated a text to several scribes. Sometimes, one person produced just one copy; in this case the writer loudly dictated the text to himself. As Saenger (1982, 373) points out, this means that all writing in the Roman world involved speech.

Clearly, writing in the narrow sense defined above was in fact always writing to oral (self-)dictation; however, writing as text production presumably was not. As Ludwig (1994) points out, the final version of a text, i.e. the fair copy, was produced after a number of stages including revision in both content and form. In this respect, it seems that, the general difference between producing a written text and delivering a speech was already felt in Roman times (in the sense of modern psycholinguistic models of writing, e.g. Hayes and Flower 1980). A case in point is Saenger's remark (1982, 371) that Quintillian held (direct) dictation responsible for careless style, and that St. Jerome complained in later years that being forced to dictate led to the detriment of his style; both held that "one could only compose proper sentences when one polished them by hand" (372). A useful description of the way writing was carried out in the Latin world is provided by Pliny (Epistolae IX, 36): The writer concentrates very hard on the text, he memorises and afterwards, some portion of text is vocally dictated to the scribe[4]. Indeed, the etymological development of the word *dictare* itself shows that dictation was the act of bringing some form of composed work to writing; indeed, in later times, the Latin word appears as a loan-word (e.g. German *dichten*) which only means "composing", i.e. writing in sense (2) above (cp. Ernout 1951, Ludwig 1996).

To sum up: as a rule, production of a written text was based on, so to speak, a "division of labour". The author dictates to a scribe or edited/revised what had been written down by scribes (*notarii*), and a final version was produced by somebody else. This kind of division was also necessary since texts written by even well educated writers were themselves marred by "orthographic" mistakes, as Suetonius notably remarks of Augustus (see Desbordes 1993 for a discussion of the notion of orthography in these times). As regards a psycholinguistic interpretation, it would seem that this division of the writing process in the modern sense point to quite different psychological/psycholinguistic processes, which might only later become unified (or which indeed might not).

3.2. The Middle Ages

The changes in the form of written texts mentioned above (*scriptio discontinua*, punctuation marks, organisation of the page by paragraphs, headlines etc.) indicate that some changes in the writing process occur during the Middle Ages. Let us first look at the change from continuous to discontinuous writing, which takes place at the *scriptoria* of monasteries. Saenger (1982) mentions three reasons for this development: (a) the organisation of the text for reference purposes, (b) reading problems in the foreign language, and (c) facilitation of the process of copying. I shall come back to point (a) below. There are many documents which describe the production of a codex on dictation. In Kirmaier et al. (1994, 96), a reprint of a very clear example can be found. In the middle of the picture is St. Jerome, the "author" of the Vulgate. Down on the right, on a much smaller scale, one can see a scribe with the wax tablet, listening to dictation or preparing a text for selfdictation. Down on the left one can see an illuminator drawing on the roll which stretches from St. Jerome´s hand to him.

As regards copying, Saenger (1982) discusses an interesting problem. Reading and dictation both involve speaking; however, labour in the monastery had to be silent. Hence,

> the separation of words provided the sine qua non for the silent copying of texts by medieval scribes. The rule of Saint Benedict had set forth the ideal of silent labour, but early monastic scribes, like their pagan predecessors, had been forced by the undivided written lines to enunciate as they copied. (Saenger, 1982:378)

As a first attempt at silent copying, manuscripts of extremely short lines can be found - lines which can be held in memory without being spoken. A more powerful way was to place blank spaces between words. This development, however, points to a foregoing or at least parallel different dictation technique, i.e. dictation by word units rather than syllable-like units (Saenger 1982:371,384). Presumably, this change is directly tied to the fact that Latin became extinct as a spoken language. It was still the international language of writing - writing in vernaculars is very unusual and does not appear at all in the literate culture of the Middle Ages[5]. This means that all writing occurred in a foreign language which was more (in Italy and France) or less (in the Germanic countries) similar to the native language of the writer. Writing to dictation by means of letters or syllables seems to be a rather difficult task in a foreign language (as is reading *scriptio continua*, see below). The central unit in foreign language learning is in fact the lexical unit, the word.

If this idea is correct, the course of development fits quite nicely with the approach of Olson (1993; see also his contribution to this volume) to the history of "how writing represents speech". The third, grammatical phase in the development of writing systems would again be tied to some foreign influence - this time the discrepancy between the spoken mother tongue vernacular and the written foreign language. Note that what we find first in most vernaculars is glosses, i.e. translations of single words written between the lines over the Latin word in order to give a hint of its meaning.

Silent copying, however, has another aspect. The copyist is no longer dependent on the speed of the dictator. He is able to grasp the meaning of the text and give it more structure. It seems to me that all the new developments found in early medieval codices (rubrication, illumination, structuring of the text by headlines, running heads, paragraphs etc.) are (at least partially) also a consequence of the new technique of silent copying. As a result, a new type of division of labour arises: There is the writer, the rubricator, the illuminator, the binder etc.[6]

The general organisation of texts in terms of chapters, headlines, running heads, numbering of paragraphs, illumination, coloured initials, separation of text and commentary, indices, tables of contents etc. presupposes a certain coordinating power. Raible (1991a,b) relates these solutions (which took some 400 years to develop) to the concept of *ordinatio*, i.e. the attempt to show content organisation through formal organisation (here of the book).

> What matters is the attempt at absolute clarity, the visualisation of the fact that the whole is composed out of single elements in such a way that by looking at the whole its parts can be perceived, and that the parts point always to the whole (Raible 1991a, 27; my translation)

As an extraordinary example, the gospel book of Henry the Lion might be cited (Kötzsche 1990). On the one hand, for some time at least, this kind of result could only be produced by the above described division of labour; but it also requires some kind of organisational centre, the head of the *scriptorium*. Organising texts in such a sophisticated way required enormous knowledge.

So far, it was mainly writing in the narrow sense which was shown to have changed. More importantly, though, as a consequence of changing copying habits, writing as text production also underwent changes. This can already be seen from the texts that were being produced. In the early Middle Ages, the major writing activity was the production of copies of already existing texts. Writing in the sense of composing, of text production (if it occurred), was oral dictation, which include all aspects of oral activity (for what follows see in particular Saenger 1982, Ludwig, 1996). Because of the limited space of note materials like wax tablets, composition of larger works was extremely difficult because the text, once written (i.e. once dictated), was not supposed to be changed again. In the early Middle Ages we rarely find several versions of the same text as a result of consequent revision or editing - changes, as a rule, come about through different writing hands. It is only later, when authors no longer restrict themselves to merely reformulating the truth of the past, that the author is obliged to write himself. Authors realise the epistemic potential of writing, i.e. that writing something down, revising and editing is a device for shaping and enlarging knowledge (e.g. Hayes and Flower 1980 for modern modelling). This is one of the most important steps in the history of literacy: Writing, an instrument for recording or documentation in the first instance (as an external memory), also becomes an instrument for the production of knowledge.

Interestingly, the division of labour continues to exist in various ways. It is known that texts that Saint Thomas had written himself were quite illegible; hence, he had to dictate from his own manuscript to a scribe; again, from this manuscript (!), reading copies were produced (Ludwig, 1996). What is the main development is that texts are connected to an author as his personal work.

3.3 Serial organisation: The ABC

The organisation of pages and books is an indication of some change in the general spirit. Reading a book no longer implies incorporating some general truth, but rather getting information. This change in the attitude of the reader requires the writer (and the scribe, later the printer) to arrange the materials in such a way that the reader need not go through the text from the beginning to the end in order to find what he wants; rather, he or she needs some index which enables her or him to find the required information directly. However, no general device was available to meet this need.

The arrangement of materials in a book presupposes certain ordering principles. For instance, a description of a cow might start from anatomy proceeding from head to feet or tail, or it might start from functional aspects such as the birth and feeding of calves, production of milk, etc. As long as there exist strong traditions as far as external ordering principles are concerned, it might seem that the arrangement of materials in a book is the direct consequence of the nature of the material[7]. Scientific interest, however, might focus on special kinds of information which just do not follow from such a tradition. A useful example is a library. Once the number of books exceeds a certain level, knowledge of subtopics implies knowledge of the information sought. Hence, what is needed is an external ordering principle which is not related to the content of the book. First attempts had already been made in the Roman world, e.g. Saint Jerome's writing *per cola et commata*, which resulted in the received organisation of the Holy Bible in chapters and verses.[8]

Nowadays, the most widely used external ordering principle is the so called alphabetical ordering principle. Since it seems to be "as easy as ABC", few attempts have been made to explain its functioning. Alphabetical ordering works like this: The letters of the alphabet in their received order ABC ... XYZ are equated to the series of natural numbers indicating their position within this order. Words are ordered in such a way that they are treated as numbers, the composing letters being digits in a system to the base N, where $N = 1 +$ the number of letters in the alphabet used (for reference see Günther, 1996). Take the following simplified example, the alphabetical order of the English words BAD, ICE, DEAD, EACH. Transforming letters to a set of digits (and filling up zero at the end of shorter words), we get: BAD 2140, DEAD 4514, EACH 5138, ICE 9350. Although this might seem strange at first glance, every reader of this paper could use a dictionary using this ordering principle. However, it takes a long time for children to come to grips with this system - watch them trying to find a number in the telephone book of, say, Nice (and perhaps watch some adults, too). This is also true for the historical perspective. The order of the alphabet, i.e. the ABC, is very old - it is attested earlier than 1900 BC in the north-west Semitic area. The Greek took over this order from the Phoenicians; they also used the characters of the alphabet for the writing of numerals (Ifrah 1989, Günther 1996). Nevertheless, alphabetical ordering of words does not occur very often in ancient Greece. Furthermore, usually only the first letter was taken into account (acronymic principle), see Daly (1967) for reference. In Rome, alphabetical ordering (initial letter only) was at best used for scientific purposes

(Pliny). It is hard to believe, but even in an organisation as big as the Roman army, alphabetical ordering for lists of soldiers, goods etc. was not used!

The development of absolute alphabetical ordering is similar to other developments discussed above: The principle itself might have been known to some individuals - Daly (1967) cites Galen's Hippocratic glosses as the first example - but its use spreads only much later; see Miethaner-Vent (1986) for several attempts during the time between 1000 and 1300 AD. At least three problems can be mentioned which are responsible for the fact that such an apparently simple principle was hardly used by anybody.

(1) As Daly (1967) points out, parchment was far too expensive to be torn into strips - the most simple technical way of putting an unordered list into an absolute alphabetical order. Wax tablets do not hold enough materials at one time.

(2) There was no generally valid orthography of the language of the books, i.e. Latin (see above). Moreover, with writing and reading still mainly phonographic, even the existence of just one orthography of medieval Latin would have produced similar problems since the pronunciation of Latin differed greatly from language to language, resulting in many "dialects of Latin". In Miethaner-Vent's interesting article, several examples are cited from authors quarrelling about the proper place of a word in an alphabetical order just because they were not sure about its pronunciation (usually in the preface explaining the ordering principle to the user). To give just one example: The letter V was used for writing of the consonant [v] and of the vowel [u]. Consequently, the position of a word containing it differed according to its phonetic value (vowel or consonant). Yet, this value was different in different versions of medieval Latin. Hence, even though the principle of absolute alphabetical ordering might have been understood, its application was difficult for the writer and even more problematic for the reader, since in order to work, it presupposed the non-phonographic analysis of words.

(3) Furthermore, one might doubt if the principle itself was really understood by most people at that time. As shown above, absolute alphabetical ordering implies the treatment of words as a string of digits. In particular, it implies the interpretation of letter strings as if they were numbers. However, numbers were written and used in the cumbersome Roman way. Whereas in Greece, the use of the same characters to write numbers and words made such an interpretation somewhat easier, the Roman way of writing numbers concealed this kind of relation. Moreover, the Greek and Roman numerical system was an addition system lacking a sign for zero. In such a system, the idea of a digit, i.e. a number sign of different value according to its position, is unknown. But it is just this idea which is needed if words are to be ordered by analogy to the order of

numbers. It was the invention of a positional system in ancient India, which became slowly known via Arabic influence in Europe around 1000 AD which caused a revolution in mathematics (Krämer 1988). Only on this basis did the idea of strict alphabetical ordering really gain ground, involving, by the same token, a new interest on Latin orthography (see Günther 1996 for more details and speculations).

Alphabetical ordering is a phenomenon which is impossible without written language of a certain kind. Its consequences for everyday life are perhaps more important than many other implications of literacy since it brings the division of text, writer and reader down to the level of the elements of texts, i.e. words. Alphabetical ordering is in fact rather unlikely to occur in periods of phonographic reading and writing since there is no ABC of speech.

4. Aspects of a history of the reading process

read, v.t. & i., 1. Interpret mentally, declare interpretation or coming development of, ... 2. (Be able to) convert into the intend words or meaning (written or printed or other symbols ...) ... 3. Reproduce mentally or ... vocally, while following symbols with eyes ..., 4. Study ... (COD 1964, 1027)

The dictionary entry for reading reveals an even larger number of different readings (!) than the entry for writing cited above. Yet, even here we might distinguish (among others) two different general meanings of the word: Reading in the narrow sense of interpreting visual signs in relation to some language, and reading in the broader sense of trying to understand a text. Again, the broad sense entails the narrow one.

The above discussion of the historical development of the writing process already implies aspects of its reading equivalent. For a general outline of the history of reading see Ganger (1994). Again, I draw heavily on Saenger (1982), see also Raible (1991a,b).

4.1. Reading in the Roman world

As far as I am able to understand my sources, the picture seems to be clear: Reading up to 500 AD is almost exclusively reading aloud (see Balogh, 1927; Saenger, 1982 with lots of references). This is easily seen from Figure 1 above: Reading a text written in capitals only, without word separation, punctuation etc. is extremely time consuming, and it is definitely helpful to sound out (parts of) what is written in order, lets say, to hear if it makes sense:

Roman grammarians considered the letter and syllable to be basic to reading. The Roman reader, reading aloud to others or softly to himself, approached the text syllable by syllable in order to recover the words and sentences conveying the meaning of the text. ... For all Romans, the proper co-ordination of the eye and the tongue was an indispensable part of the activity of reading. A written text was essentially a transcription which, like modern musical notation, became an intelligible message only when it was performed orally to others or to oneself." (Saenger 1982, 371; with particular reference to Quintillian, *Institutio Oratoria*).

However, this does not mean that quiet reading was not possible - we are informed by several sources that it did in fact occur (see Balogh 1927, 84-91 for reference). Augustinus' astonishment at seeing his teacher Ambrosius reading while his lips were closed is justly famous. However, it was an exception to the rule. In fact, as Balogh (1927) points out on several occasions, the observation of silent reading in those days was noteworthy simply because it was a deviation from the common practice, i.e. reading aloud.

How was it possible to exercise silent reading given the nature of the texts? One possible explanation might be that there were not as many different texts as there are today. In fact, it might be claimed that reading in antiquity and in the early Middle Ages was much more a question of relying on a memory aid for a text more or less known by heart than a device for extracting information from a (hitherto unknown) text (see Clanchy 1992). Moreover, silent reading in Augustinus' sense meant that he watched his teacher reading with his lips sealed and producing no sounds (*vox autem et lingua quiescebant*; Confessiones VI, 3). As Saenger (1982, 383f) points out, Isidore of Sevilla "recommended that the tongue and lips be moved quietly" during reading, i.e. that "silent" reading meant reading aloud without making a noise.

In terms of modern psycholinguistics, such silent reading does not exclude subvocalization or phonological recoding which, according to some researchers, always occurs even in actual silent reading. To strengthen the point somewhat further: The argument that *scriptio continua* implies reading aloud is as often claimed as it is invalid. There is no need to believe that reading aloud in antiquity has anything to do with what modern psycholinguists call phonological recoding. The general theory - derived, to be sure, from theories of structural linguistics - requires us to believe that this process of reading uses graphemephoneme-correspondences (GPC), letter units that are translated into sound units. If Saenger's description of the process in antiquity and in the early Middle Ages is correct, than we do not find any process by which the string of letters is transformed into a string of phonemes which is then identified with some phonological address in the reader's mental lexicon; rather, some units of syllablic size are sounded out, and the lexicon is searched for the best fitting analogy.[9]

4.2. The Middle Ages

Reading in the Roman world and up to the early Middle Ages is usually reading aloud; furthermore, it was much more common to read together, i.e. in groups, than to read alone. In fact, this habit was still dominant at a time when silent copying was already common in the *scriptoria* (Saenger 1982, 379f). It seems to me that this time lag is perhaps best explained by the same factor already described above as being (partially) responsible for the introduction of the separation of words: the fact that Latin was only a written language, and a foreign language for all writers and readers. Consider the way the Romans read and how reading was still taught in the early Middle Ages, i.e. by letters and syllables - a method which was abandoned at the end of the Middle Ages to be taken up again later when reading in the vernaculars was taught. Learning to read by such a method seems to be an extremely difficult task: the alphabetical relation between letter and sound had been defined on a basis which was no longer available since the "spoken" Latin of that time differed greatly from classical Latin (see Illich 1991). Reading such texts aloud, it seems, is the root of later silent reading, since the units brought together are really spoken words of "new" and written words of classical Latin, which bore only a very loose alphabetical relation (see also above on the ABC). Paradoxically, then, "logographic" reading of an alphabetical script was developed because phonographic reading did not work anymore (Saenger 1982, passim).

It is only in scholastic times (from about 1150 on), with the needs of readers to study in the modern sense (reading to acquire knowledge), that true silent reading developed, although centuries were to pass before this became the usual way of reading for everybody and not limited to specialists. In the late Middle Ages, public lectures involved both kinds of reading. the lecturer read aloud, and the students were asked to read silently with his text in their hands, cp. Saenger (1982, 391): "While professors read aloud from their autograph texts, students followed the lectures by silently reading from their own books"; in fact they were obliged to take these books into the lectures[10]. One might safely assume that the roots of modern "normal" silent reading are indeed found in this development. However, it has to be acknowledged that only specialists were readers of that sort. Although societies were what is called "literate cultures", they were still oral cultures as well.

5. Conclusions and perspectives

5.1. A tentative summary

Reading and writing both involve speaking for a long time, if only for technical reasons. The development of page layout in the broadest sense is a prerequisite for modern reading and writing habits; it constitutes a further "grammatical" stage in the development of writing. The modern concept of the author of a text is one of the results of such developments.

Writing and reading were time consuming, arduous tasks. They were exercised much more often together, i.e. by groups, than by individuals. The abundance of different texts, which is typical of our daily life, was unknown. Those who wrote and read were professionals, able to exercise a technique which had not been mastered by very many people. Reading a text was essentially a way to refresh memory of what one had written. It took a long time for writing to become an instrument for distributing information, and for reading to become the process of extracting information from a text rather than re-cognizing knowledge which was already more or less present in the reader's head.

5.2. Potential and use

The large body of written texts on writing and literacy and the importance of literacy in the development of Western culture seems at times to have exaggerated the true role written language and literacy played in western history. The alphabet by itself does not lead to complete alphabetisation, the knowledge of the ABC does not lead directly to the widespread use of this formal ordering system, and the separation of words (*scriptio discontinua*) does not lead directly to silent reading. To put it slightly differently: the existence of the alphabet, the ABC, the separation of words etc. do not by themselves bring about a realisation of their potential. Word separation was known in Greece from the start; Galen knew the principle of absolute alphabetical order - but nobody else used these principles.

Related to this rather general statement is another point: As in the history of phonographic script (Olson 1993), the motor of historical developments seems to have been the influence of peripheral, unrelated events: the use of the ABC was achieved when the numerical system changed to the positional system. Separation of words arose when there was a demand for the silent copying of texts in a foreign language. Silent reading developed when reading shifted from a rather general linguistic recognition of better or less well known texts to the extracting of information from texts.

This implies, however, that in comparing different literate cultures one should be extremely careful. Literacy, as all other cultural goods, can only be defined in relation to a specific culture at a specific historical moment. There is thus no concept of "literate culture" - for there exist many quite different literate cultures. Literacy is to be defined in relation to these.

5.3. Qui fecit?

In a very bold piece of research, Wolfgang Raible (1991a; see also 1991b, 1994) used data of the sort just outlined and other sources to substantiate his thesis that the development of (alphabetical) writing systems in the West is driven by the reader: *Is fecit cui prodest* (literally "He made it who takes advantage of it") is the programmatic (deliberately enigmatic) subtitle to his outline of this development. Seen from this perspective, every development cited above can be taken as positive evidence for his argument: *scriptio discontinua*, page layout, alphabetical ordering, as well as data not cited such as the development of minuscule writing, punctuation marks, the invention of abstract mathematical notation, capitalising of the beginning of sentences etc. Modern fast normal reading presupposes all these developments.

Whereas this sounds reasonable, there are several problems with this kind of approach. The most significant, perhaps, is the teleological nature of Raible's approach: Phonographic teleology is replaced by "the reader" looking carefully at what is useful for him and what hampers his goal of extracting information from a text. However, this notion of "reading" is inadequate for the early Middle Ages in which reading was much more re-reading, recalling texts from memory by means of a written document.

Moreover, it is rather difficult to conceive of the process in Raible's terms. Clearly, on a trivial interpretation, the statement does not make sense: A text is not changed by reading it. Even the 'feedback' theory of change seems problematic, as the following caricature shows: a reading monk enters the *scriptorium*, calling to the scribe "Hey brother, reading your stuff is awfully difficult; just go ahead and invent some techniques for easier reading; otherwise, I won't read anymore".

Even if one follows the very cautious interpretation that the needs of the reader, inferred from the development of the form of written texts, lead to developments in writing technique, such an approach is still teleological, and is not warranted by the data provided above. As we have seen, one major reason for the (general) introduction of the separation of words was the need for silent copying of a foreign language. Its usefulness for reading is presumably not immediately acknowledged. Similarly, being guided by the concept of *ordinatio* is not so much an attempt to make something clear for somebody else, but above all to make it clear to oneself. In fact, all the developments Saenger (1982) and Raible (1991a) discuss lead not only to texts which can be read more easily, but also to the change from the dictator to the author of a text. What is interesting, though, is that the development takes time and that for quite some time the emerging division is not clear-cut (see also Ludwig 1996). Clearly, the page layout is not the composer's work, but is made by the scribe; but, in order to develop it, the scribe cannot simply be a dumb secretary.

Thus, it is not the reader who furthers development. It is always and only the writer who is doing the work and trying to do it better. Writing, as it were, offers the possibility of using speech but without needing to communicate. *Scriptio discontinua* is invented for the benefit of easier copying, clarity of writing (minuscule, punctuation) and is developed for guiding oneself (and only then, perhaps, the potential reader). It is the cognitive function of language which becomes dominant in written language and writing; by developing the written form, it becomes possible to make it work for communicative functions also. The aim of *ordinatio* (see above) is not for telling something to somebody else but above all for explaining it to oneself, just to understand things. The modern reader, trying to extract information from texts, is the product of this kind of writing.

Notes

[1] The invention of paper in China dates back to the 2nd century A.D. It started to be used in Europe app. in the 10th century by Arabic mediation. In a sense, paper, being produced from rags, combines the virtues of papyrus and parchment: It is more easily reproducible, it is not as heavy as parchment, and it is less expensive; on the other hand, it is more stable than papyrus and can be used to form books. The spread of paper as a writing material (and later as the surface for print) has no doubt far reaching consequences for the development of modern literate cultures, in particular for the reader and his habits; however, this is beyond the scope of the present paper.
[2] Omitted in my quotation is sense 2 "Fill, draw up, or fill in with writing" which is, in my view, not different from sense 1.
[3] This point needs further clarification. Saenger (1982, passim) notes that composing from notes or delivering a speech from a number of key words was an unknown technique up to the end of the Middle Ages.
[4] Here is the citation in full: "Clausae fenestrae manent; mire enim silentio et tenebris ab iis, quae avocant, abductus et liber et mihi relictus non oculos animo, sed animum oculis sequor, qui eadem quae mens vident, quotiens non vident alia. Cogito, so quid in manibus, cogito ad verbum scribenti emendatique similis, nunc pauciora, nunc

plura, ut vel difficile vel facile componi tenerive potuerunt. Notarium voce et die admisso quae formaveram dicto."

[5] Of course, the beginnings of vernacular writing have attracted the attention of many scholars simply because they are the oldest documents in these languages. By this very fact, the importance of vernacular writing up to the 13th century is extremely exaggerated. There is just one medieval literate culture: Latin writing.

[6] A very clear outline of book production in the Middle Ages can be found in Trost (1994), including some contemporary illustrations of the production process.

[7] There still exist several schools of thought, which claim that there exists some *ordo rerum* which arranges things in the world by itself, only Man in his stupidity has (not) yet found out the exact plan of the arrangement ...

[8] The exact meaning of this expression is not clear, see Saenger (1982, 374f), Raible (1991b, 8).

[9] In fact, there is an approach in modern psycholinguistics which is compatible with this interpretation: Reading aloud may, but need not, imply prelexical phonological recoding (see Henderson 1985 for a review): It could be that in reading aloud we first recognize words or cohorts, which are then (postlexically) recoded into speech.

[10] Saenger (1982, passim) several times refers to some changes in pictures of the reading and the writing process, observing e.g. if the mouth of the reader is open or closed, if the words enter via the ears or the eyes, etc. An exhaustive collection and discussion of such visualization of the reading and writing process during the ages remains a desideratum.

Orality in Literate Cultures

Peter Koch

When dealing with 'orality in literate cultures', we must first examine several terminological and conceptual questions. From the distinctions proposed in section 1. it follows that 'orality in literate cultures' does not constitute a unitary problem and has to be discussed from at least four very different angles: these are addressed in sections 2.-5.

1. Linguistic medium, linguistic conception, and cultural orality/literacy

Over the last two decades, insights from cognitive psychology have revealed the internal prototypical structure of perceptual and conceptual categories (cf. Rosch 1978). This applies to everyday concepts, but frequently - at least in the humanities - to academic concepts as well[1]. 'Orality' and 'literacy' seem to be fairly good examples of the latter. It goes without saying that intimate, spontaneous conversation is an instance of prototypical orality and that statutes are instances of prototypical literacy. The university lecture and the private letter might be regarded as instances of less prototypical orality and literacy respectively. But what about oral poetry in nonliterate cultures? Although literacy does not by definition exist in non-literate societies, we would hesitate to call oral poetry prototypical orality - especially when compared to spontaneous conversation in those same societies.

I am convinced that prototypical concepts are legitimate in linguistic research inasmuch as they reflect the prototypical organization of the object under consideration. Let us now examine the prototypical nature of the concepts 'orality'/'oral' and 'literacy'/'written'.

1.1. Unfortunately, 'oral'/'written' are polysemous terms covering two different - though related - aspects of communication that have to be strictly distinguished:

the **medium** and the **mode** of communication. This discrimination is not entirely new in linguistics and has been discovered and rediscovered by a number of scholars, in part independently of each other: Behaghel 1899; De Mauro 1970; Nencioni 1976, 1; Akinnaso 1985; Chafe and Danielewicz 1987; Halliday 1987, 66; Horowitz and Samuels 1987 etc.

Chafe (1982, 36) distinguishes four styles of language within the data used in his investigation on speaking and writing: (1) informal spoken language, from dinnertable conversations, (2) formal spoken language, from lectures, (3) informal written language, from letters, (4) formal written language, from academic papers.

In my opinion, however, the most straightforward approach to the problem dates back to 1974, when the romanist Söll proposed his distinction between linguistic medium (*code phonique* vs. *code graphique*) and linguistic conception, i.e. mode (*langue parlée* vs. *langue écrite*)[2].

In the medial sense[3], 'oral' (= 'phonic') and 'written' (= 'graphic') are clearly dichotomous, non prototypical concepts. A given discourse can only either be uttered acoustically or written down. *Tertium non datur*. Certainly, it is always possible to read a written discourse or to write down a spoken discourse. But these are cases of the so-called medium-transferability (Lyons 1981, 11), typical of human language. In any concrete act of communication we have to choose one of the two existing media or to combine them, but there is no "compromise" between the phonic and the graphic realization.

In contrast to this, linguistic conception only involves the communicative mode of a given discourse. What is at stake here, is a higher or smaller degree of textual coherence, of syntactic complexity and of lexical refinedness as well as the selection of different language varieties. In this sense, 'oral' and 'written' are clearly prototypical concepts. It goes without saying that a spontaneous conversation is a more prototypical instance of oral conception than an interview with a politician and that a statute is a more prototypical instance of written conception than an editorial.

Even the combinations of medium and conception are of a prototypical kind: in present-day societies at least, we observe clear affinities between oral conception and the phonic medium on the one hand (e.g. spontaneous conversation) and between written conception and the graphic medium on the other hand (e.g. statutes). But at all times, the two other logically possible combinations have existed: oral conception in the graphic medium (e.g. the private letter) and written conception in the phonic medium (e.g. the university lecture). In certain cultures and epochs, these combinations are of paramount importance and perhaps more "prototypical" than the others (see below 2.1. and 3.2./3.). At all events, the above-mentioned medium-transferability of human language always assures the possibility of such combinations, including extreme and somewhat "artificial" cases like the transcription of a spontaneous conversation (= utmost degree of oral conception in the graphic medium; see below 4. and 5.6.) or a statute read aloud (= utmost degree of written conception in the phonic medium).

1.2. A very interesting approach in this respect is the one proposed by Biber (1988), who factorizes the "prototypical" situational characteristics [i.e. linguistic conception] of each mode [i.e. linguistic medium]. He uses "the term 'oral' discourse to refer to language produced in situations that are typical or expected for speaking, and the term 'literal' discourse to refer to language produced in situations that are typical for writing" (161).

Now, a terminological problem arises. If we have to split the field of orality and literacy into the two aspects of linguistic medium and linguistic conception, why on earth should we continue to use the etymologically "medial" terms 'oral' and 'written/literate' to denote the aspect of conception? It would be more sensible to choose neutral terms such as the ones proposed by Wulf Oesterreicher and myself: communicative 'immediacy' for oral conception and communicative 'distance' for written conception. Thanks to their metaphoricity, these terms encompass a series of different situational characteristics or communicative parameters that are highly relevant at the level of linguistic conception:[4]

I. physical immediacy vs. distance:
face-to-face interaction of partners vs. distance in space and time;
II. social immediacy vs. distance:
1. private vs. public setting of the communicative event,
2. familiarity vs. unfamiliarity of the partners,
3. emotional involvement vs. detachment,
4. context embeddedness vs. contextual dissociation of a discourse;
III. referential immediacy vs. distance:
reference to the EGO-HIC-NUNC and to elements of the immediate situational context vs. reference to elements that are far from the EGO-HIC-NUNC and from the situational context;
IV. elocutional immediacy vs. distance:
1. dialogue vs. monologue,
2. maximum vs. minimum cooperation of partners,
3. free topic vs. fixed topic,
4. spontaneity vs. reflection.

Each of these parameters, except I., is of a scalar nature. So the varying degrees of privateness/publicness, of familiarity/unfamiliarity etc. and the interaction between varying values of the different parameters produce a continuum of overall values of immediacy vs. distance, that can be represented as follows:

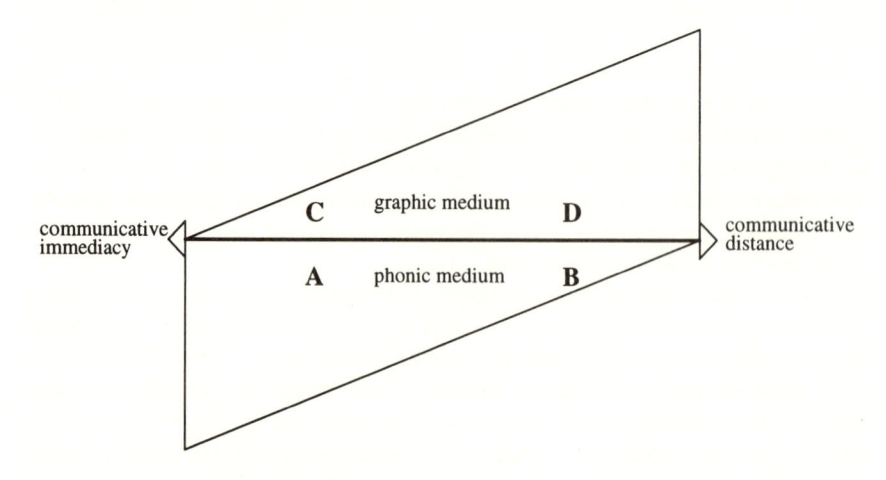

Figure 1. Medium and conception

This parallelogram symbolizes not only the immediacy-distance continuum, but also the more or less prototypical combinations between conception and medium, as described above: A = phonic immediacy; B = phonic distance; C = graphic immediacy; D = graphic distance.

Furthermore, Fig. 1 symbolizes the centrality of linguistic conception. In contrast to current opinion, not only our strategies of verbalization, but also the medium of realization itself are chosen as a function of parameters I.-IV., i.e. of the position on the immediacy-distance continuum in a given situation. Obviously, physical parameter I. is most important in this respect. If your partner is absent, you have to rely on the graphic medium (and write a letter, for example). In the age of the telephone, you can certainly choose the phonic medium as well. Even in this case, however, your medial choice depends, once more on parameters of linguistic conception, especially II.1.2.3. and IV.1.4.: for a spontaneous, dialogic communication with a friend, in a private, emotional setting, you will in general prefer the phonic medium (phone call) despite the physical distance; on the other hand, a communication between strangers in a more public, non emotional setting will favour the choice of the graphic medium (letter).

1.3. In view of our heading 'orality in literate cultures', there remains a fundamental problem with Fig. 1: it shows us the situation in a fully fledged literate culture, where both the phonic and the graphic medium are present. But what about the so-called oral cultures? We have to acknowledge that in primary orality people have only the inferior triangle of Fig. 1 at their disposal, because members of those cultures move exclusively within the phonic medium[5]. Note that there is a radical asymmetry between communication in primary oral and in literate cultures: the graphic medium is inconceivable in oral cultures (which doesn't mean that communicative distance is inaccessible: see below 2.1.), whereas literate cultures still comprise communication in the phonic medium (and, of course, communicative immediacy).

Consequently, we may distinguish, after all, three senses of 'orality'/'literacy' that are logically independent, though interwoven with each other:

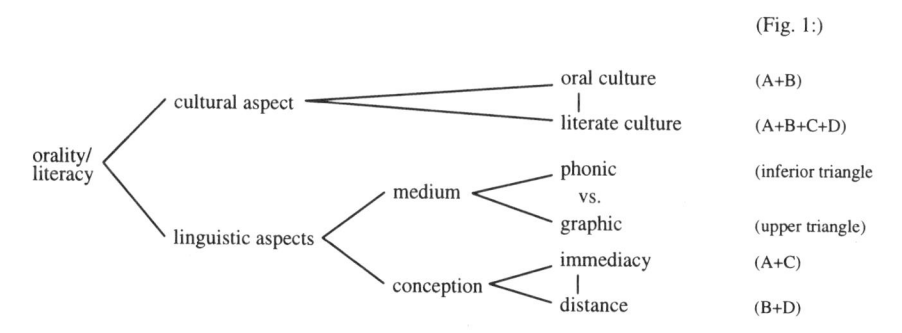

(Fig. 1:)

orality/literacy
- cultural aspect
  - oral culture (A+B)
  - literate culture (A+B+C+D)
- linguistic aspects
  - medium
    - phonic (inferior triangle)
    - vs.
    - graphic (upper triangle)
  - conception
    - immediacy (A+C)
    - distance (B+D)

Figure 2. Orality and literacy; cultural, medial, conceptional.

Thus, the question of 'orality in literate cultures' turns out not to be a unitary problem. 'Literate culture' clearly concerns cultural literacy, but 'orality' may refer either to 'oral culture' or to 'phonic medium' or to 'immediacy'. Hence, we can deduce from Fig. 1 and 2 that there are a number of different problems to be treated here:

– the problem of oral culture (A+B) within literate cultures (A+B+C+D): chapter 2.
– the problem of phonic distance (B) within literate cultures (A+B+C+D): chapter 3.
– the problem of graphic immediacy (C) within literate cultures (A+B+C+D): chapter 4.
– the problem of immediacy as a whole (A+C) in relation to distance as a whole (B+D) within literate cultures (A+B+C+D): chapter 5.

2. Oral culture within literate cultures

2.1. In 1. we noted that poetry in primary oral cultures could not be regarded as 'orality' in the same sense as spontaneous conversation. On the basis of Fig. 1, we now become aware of the fact that primary oral cultures are certainly confined to the inferior triangle (i.e. to the phonic medium), but they nevertheless include a considerable range of variation at the level of linguistic conception. On the one hand (sector A), there is everyday spontaneous conversation, on the other hand (sector B), there are discourse traditions like oral poetry, riddles, proverbs, ritual utterances etc., which clearly belong to phonic distance (cf. Chafe 1982, 49-52; Schlieben-Lange 1983, 78-80; Akinnaso 1985, 332 ss.).

As we see, our decision to choose the "medially" neutral terms 'immediacy' and 'distance' to denote linguistic conception proves to be of great advantage. Speaking of 'written' conception for sector B in primary oral cultures would be absurd, whereas we can easily recognize the existence of some kind of communicative distance in them.

Undoubtedly, sector B traditions in a primary oral culture ($B^{[A+B]}$) differ from sector B traditions in a literate culture ($B^{[A+B+C+D]}$). Firstly, $B^{[A+B]}$ traditions rely entirely on mnemotechnical resources to realize communicative distance, independently of the graphic medium: music, rhythm, assonance, rime; formulas and stereotypes. Secondly, taking the performance of oral epics (by a singer) as a paradigmatic case (cf. Oesterreicher 1997, 207-211), we can state with regard to the level of linguistic conception that it is of a - temperate - distance type, implying, it is true, face-to-face communication (parameter I. in 1.2. above), involvement (II.3.), and a certain cooperation with the public (IV.2.), but also public setting (II.1.), contextual dissociation (II.4.), referential distance (III.), monologue (IV.1.), formal rendition of a fixed topic (IV.3.), and reflection in the composition or memorization of (the rules for producing) poems (IV.4.).

Consequently, sector B communication in primary oral cultures ($B^{[A+B]}$) is not simply 'orality', but represents a special kind of phonic distance that could be denominated elaborated orality (where 'orality' refers to the phonic medium and 'elaborated' to communicative distance; cf. Koch and Oesterreicher 1985, 29-31; 1994, 588, 593.)

2.2. We may now compare in a highly schematic way primary oral societies to literate societies by characterizing their members and their communicative habits (according to Fig. 1) as follows:

		primary oral societies	literate societies
members		nonliterate	literate
communicative habits	sector A	phonic immediacy	phonic immediacy
	sector B	$B^{[A+B]}$ = phonic distance of the elaborated orality type	$B^{[A+B+C+D]}$ = phonic distance, dependent on the existence of the graphic medium
	sector C	—	graphic immediacy
	sector D	—	graphic distance

But in real cultural history, things are much more complicated, and - once more - we come up against prototypical concepts. As we know, the transition from oral to literate culture is a very slow, non unidirectional process with many intermediate stages, regressions and much historical variation (cf. Graff 1987; Burns 1989; Günther and Ludwig 1994, articles 33., 34., 36.-38., 40., 66.-74.). The Sumerian society and pharaonic Egypt were only "protoliterate" or "oligoliterate" (Goody and Watt 1968, 34). During the Greco-Roman Antiquity, script remained the privilege of a small, though increasing minority. In the Dark Ages "both Western Europe and the Byzantine East reverted to conditions of severely restricted literacy under theocratic governments and caste systems reminiscent of the ancient empires of Mesopotamia and Egypt" (Burns 1989, 193). Levels of literacy rose again from the 12th century on, but it still remained the privilege of a minority, even after the invention of print, until the systematic alphabetization campaigns of the 19th and 20th century.

What about the members of the society and the communicative habits in the transitional stages between a primary oral culture and a fully fledged literate culture? Are we to suppose that elements of oral culture continue to play a certain role in literate cultures?

2.3. During the millenia of transition from primary oral to literate culture, the societies concerned were made up of different groups of members as regards their participation in (medial and cultural) literacy. In the European context, we have to distinguish not only literates and nonliterates, but at least four groups (cf. Grundmann 1958, 8; Havelock 1976, 2 ss.; Bäuml 1980, 246 s.):

-full literates (*litterati*).
-quasi-literates, participating in literacy without being (fully) acquainted with the graphic medium - a situation typical of the Middle Ages (see below 3.3.).
-semi-literates: especially in periods of expanding alphabetization, there is a growing proportion of persons acquainted (more or less) with the

graphic medium, but with limited experience in communicative distance (see below 4, 1)).
– illiterates (*illitterati*).

At no moment of the long transitional phase to fully fledged literacy is the status of the *illitterati* in such a cultural context to be simply identified with that of the nonliterate members of a primary oral society, because the *illitterati* within a literate culture are in contact with the institutions of literacy to some degree.

The implications of this contact may be judged differently in psychological terms and in terms of cultural history. From a psychological point of view, the results of Luria's investigations into illiterate subjects in Uzbekistan and Kirghizia (1976) urge Ong not to overestimate the influence of literacy on illiterates' thinking: "Writing has to be personally interiorized to affect thinking processes" (1982, 56). From the point of view of cultural history, we have to consider every epoch separately in order to assess the impact of literacy on illiterates. In the Western European Middle Ages - a particularly instructive example (cf. Grundmann 1958; Graff 1987, 34-52) - it was the church that represented the central agency of literacy (juridical and political literacy, too, was incumbent on the clergymen, who, up to the 12th century at least, were virtually the only *litterati*). So, the sphere of contact between medieval *litterati* and *illitterati* comprised sermons, prayers, confession forms, oaths etc. - in short the communicative habits of public lecture and recitation that all belonged to sector $B^{[A+B+C+D]}$ in Table 1. In other words, specific types of phonic distance managed by the *litterati* constituted a crossroads that led *illitterati* in medieval literate societies to a certain participation in cultural literacy without having command of the graphic medium[6]. Thanks to this form of acculturation, called "ungeschriebene Verschriftlichung" by Ivan Illich (1984, 49), medieval *illitterati* had a not neglegible access to communicative and cultural domains inconceivable for nonliterates in a primary oral society.

2.4. Even though *illiterati* in a literate society can participate, at least to some extent, in phonic distance of the $B^{[A+B+C+D]}$ type and thereby in cultural literacy, communicative habits and discourse traditions of elaborated orality ($B^{[A+B]}$; see 2.1. above) do not fail from one day to the next. What is particularly interesting in this respect, is the ancient Greek and the medieval heroic epos[7]. If the research of the last few decades in this field is accurate, the form of these texts resembles very much the form of real oral poetry: formular style, stereotypes, redundancies, "mouvance" (Zumthor 1983, 253) etc., according to the requirements of the singer and to the performance in front of an audience.

We are faced, however, with the fact that all these texts have come down to us only in a graphic form. This is not a purely medial problem, because we now seem to be in sector D of Table 1, typical of literate cultures. Actually, the above-mentioned epic poems belong to the oldest written documents of the languages concerned. So they all have undergone certain transformations due to the literate culture that enables people to write them down. At the moment of their "redaction", they already represent declining discourse traditions, that are consciously preserved (and sometimes exploited for ideological purposes), but also partly (not totally!) reshaped at the level of linguistic conception. The French *chanson de geste*, e.g., constitutes "le legs d'une tradition essentiellement orale à une société basculant vers l'écrit" (Martin 1988, 159)[8].

For a long time, there remain certain transitional zones between culturally oral traditions of distance B[A+B], literate phonic distance B[A+B+C+D] and literate graphic distance (D). When literacy begins to expand and we get to a higher rate of - sometimes rather modest - alphabetization and instruction, oral traditions still furnish many a matter for the new reading public as well as for the analphabetic audience to whom the texts can be read (cf. the *Bibliothèque bleue* from Troyes in Ancien Régime France; see Martin 1975). But independently of the oral or literate origin of the reading matter, (modestly) alphabetized people often treat it like oral material, reading it again and again and learning it by heart (cf. Schlieben-Lange 1983, 69).

Indeed, (culturally) oral traditions and communicative habits possess a certain tenacity, but become more and more residual in a developed literate culture. Nevertheless the example of the Serbo-Croatian *guslari* (cf. Lord 1960; Foley 1977) shows that traditions of oral improvisation can survive even in an - at least partially - literate society of the 20th century.

3. Phonic distance within literate cultures

As we saw in 2.3., sector B was the crossroads of *litterati* and *illitterati* within medieval literacy. Generally speaking, the importance of sector D[A|B|C|D] in "oligoliterate" societies is much greater than in fully fledged literate societies. Thus Ong seems to be right in saying that "manuscript culture in the west remained always marginally oral" (1982, 119). However, what is meant by 'manuscript culture' (3.1.) as well as by 'oral' (3.2. and 3.3.) needs to be specified.

3.1. It is well known that in Antiquity and during the Early and most of the High Middle Ages graphic documents used to be read aloud or at least with minimal phonation (cf. for instance Chaytor 1945, 10 ss.; Saenger 1982; Illich

1993); i.e. the medial transfer D ⇒ B (according to Fig. 1) was almost indispensable for the realization of communicative distance. Typically, texts with a culturally highly important (religious, literary or political-ceremonial) content, belonging to the domain of communicative distance, were recited in the presence of an audience ("recitation literacy" according to Havelock 1976:21).

From the medial point of view, *scriptio continua* (that was given up only between the 8th and the 11th century A.D.) considerably hampered the visual recognition of linguistic units (words, sentences etc.) within texts, and this had to be compensated for by reading aloud as a kind of acoustic "scanning" (cf. Saenger 1982, 371).

It was not until the 12th/13th century A.D. that silent reading was fostered by the medial achievements of "modern" layout (word separation, punctuation, sentence-initial capitals, chapter headings etc.; cf. Raible 1991b, 6-10; Frank 1994; Günther 1994). So these innovations already culminated w i t h i n manuscript culture in the age of scholasticism (parallelled by an increase in - handwritten - book production and by the appearance of urban booksellers and lay stationers in the 12th century[9]).

Consequently, we can say that the shift from reading aloud to silent reading as normal realization of communicative distance took place long b e f o r e the invention of printing. Printing may have further encouraged silent reading, but was not crucial for its development[10].

3.2. Ascribing certain 'oral' characteristics to manuscript culture (especially in the Middle Ages) would certainly be much to simplistic. The transfer D ⇒ B as a particular mode of being of communicative distance in an (oligo)literate culture has to be distinguished not only from silent reading as the mode of being of communicative distance typical of fully fledged literate societies (D[A+B+C+D]), but also from elaborated orality B[A+B] (see 2.1.) and from the residues of elaborated orality B[A+B] within a literate society A+B+C+D (see 2.4.).

Thus, the *Chanson de Roland*, as rooted in elaborated orality (B[A+B]), cannot be put on a par with, say, the *roman courtois* or the poetry of the troubadours (cf. Koch 1993a, 53 s.). Despite their reliance on recitation and/or their - partially - phonic diffusion, these latter came in to being in the very lap of literacy (A+B+C+D).

Nevertheless it is worth taking into account the importance of the phonic medium for these and other medieval literary discourse traditions. Thanks to Zumthor, we have become aware of "vocality" as an essential feature of medieval literature, based on recitation and performance (cf. Zumthor 1987; Schaefer 1992).

These communicative characteristics inevitably impinged upon the level of conception. Since recitation of medieval literature implied the presence of an audience (cf. I. in 1.3.), some kind of emotional involvement (cf. II.3.), and the impossibility of total reflection (cf. IV.4.), certain concessions to communicative immediacy are not surprising: redundancies, reduced syntactic complexity, apostrophes to the audience, author's interventions, references to the situation of performance etc.[11] This yields a special type of "théâtralité" (Zumthor 1987, 289).

On the other hand, we have to keep in mind that in a literate society this "theatricalism" cannot be altogether spontaneous, but may result to some degrees from conscious design (cf. e.g. Stempel 1993). Furthermore, typically vocal techniques such as rhythm and assonance or rhyme are particularly well suited to support communicative distance. So, the vocality of medieval literature is distance, albeit attenuated distance.

Vocal distance was an indispensible element not only of medieval literature, but also of some nonliterary quasi-ritual discourse traditions fundamental for medieval communication: the preambles of charters and the exordia of official letters, redacted in rhythmic prose (*cursus*) and making appeal to stereotyped moral values, were meant to be declaimed in a solemn setting as a kind of monarchal or ecclesiastical propaganda. In this case, vocality conveyed an extreme degree of communicative distance ("repräsentative Öffentlichkeit" according to Habermas; cf. Koch 1992a, col. 880).

3.3. Note that the importance of sector B (in Fig. 1) for ancient and medieval literacy was not confined to the reception of distance type texts (along the path D ⇒ B). Sector B was involved on the production side as well: we know that literate people used to dictate their texts, transferring them along the path B ⇒ D (cf. the references cited above in 3.1. as well as Ludwig 1994, 56-60).

The fact that autographs of Rome's ruling class members contained misspellings, proves that they were more familiar with dictation to a secretary than with the direct use of the graphic medium. But even when writing by themselves, they stuck to a kind of self dictation in a low voice, analogous to minimal phonation on the reception side (cf. Saenger 1982, 371 s.).

In the Middle Ages, besides the groups of medieval *litterati* and *illitterati*, there was a group of quasi-literates (see 2.3. above), who were not (fully) acquainted with the graphic medium, but had access to full literacy including text production in the realm of distance, whether in sector B or via B ⇒ D (which is not the case with the *illitterati*). Charlemagne, for example, who knew Latin and Greek, was able to make speeches, probably knew how to read, but never really learnt to write.

But even within the group of medieval *litterati*, we find a systematic distinction between the *dictator*, who formulated the text, and the *scriba* (or *amanuensis*), who wrote it down. Interestingly, it is the *dictator* that should be regarded as the exponent of medieval literacy. In a metonymical sense, *dictare* is 'compose a distance type text (called *dictamen*)', which is restricted either to poetry[12] or - more typically - to prose, especially to legal documents and letters (as for the *ars dictandi*; see below).

Now a somewhat paradoxical problem arises: although medieval distance type texts were typically produced by dictation, this medial practice did not necessarily fit to all the requirements of maximal distance according to parameters I.-IV. in 1.3.: without (direct) access to the graphic medium one has to cope with certain spontaneity effects (IV.4.), and it is much more difficult to plan one's text coherently and concisely (a fact those of us who dictate letters are still aware of nowadays). There were two possible strategies for dealing with this problem.

On the one hand, people could make concessions at the level of conception, producing texts that did not avoid all features of immediacy, such as redundancies, reduced syntactic complexity etc. (cf. Mair 1982) - a production strategy that was partly in harmony with features of typically medieval vocal reception (see 3.2. above).

On the other hand, the *dictator* of very formal, official texts needed aids for formulation in order to assure maximal communicative distance. That is why *ars dictandi*, as a central branch of medieval rhetoric (12th-14th century), offered to the user of its manuals rules for standardized text patterns and collections of model letters or documents and official forms (cf. Murphy 1974, 194-268; Camargo 1991).

3.4. At first glance, the situation of a *dictator* dictating his text (B ⇒ D) and that of an *orator* formulating his speech (B) seem to be quite different. After all, the *orator* acts in front of an audience, whereas the *dictator* is separated in space and time from his recipients (cf. parameter I. in 1.2.). In the last analysis, however, the two situations have many features in common: public setting (II.1.); (presupposed) unfamiliarity with the recipients (II.2.); contextual dissociation of the text (II.4.); referential distance (III.); elocutional distance (IV.1.-4.).

So the *dictator* as well as the *orator* had to face a considerable degree of communicative distance within the phonic medium (B),[13] and, consequently, both tended to rely on an *ars* providing them with - more or less - standardized text structures, models, tropes, *topoi* etc. Not very suppprisingly, then, we observe osmotic processes between these and other communicative activities involving sector B: when justifying the canonical parts of medieval letters, masters of the above-mentioned *ars dictandi* were inspired - rightly or wrongly - by the *partes orationes* pattern of classical rhetoric; vice versa, 13th century *ars arengandi*, providing models of political speeches in Italian *comuni*, took up elements of *ars dictandi*, but also of *ars predicandi*, the art of preaching (cf. Koch 1992b, col. 1035-1038).

4. Graphic immediacy within literate cultures

We should note the fact that writing was not "invented" specially for distance type texts (sector D in Fig. 1). The early graphic records in Babylonia, that paved the way for writing, were made up of book-keeping lists accessible only to a small group of users and largely embedded in economic activities and non-verbal contexts. In short: they were characterized by central - though certainly not all - elements of communicative immediacy (in particular II.1., 2., and 4. in 1.2.; cf. Koch 1997, 51-54). In other words: from the outset of writing, the graphic medium and elements of communicative immediacy were not incompatible.

Admittedly, the graphic medium implies a reification of the written text that later fostered a development of communicative distance unknown in primary orality, producing an apparently "natural" affinity between the graphic medium and distance (cf. Jechle 1992; Ehlich 1994; Koch 1997, 62-64).

But even though, from then on, it was the combination of the graphic medium with immediacy (sector C in Fig. 1) that seemed to require justification, sector C has never, since the beginnings of literacy, been something out of the ordinary. We are able to identify recurrent motives that continually induce literates to realize - at least partial - immediacy in the graphic medium: C[A+B+C+D]. Oesterreicher proposes a typology of communicative constellations in which linguistic elements of immediacy occur in the graphic medium (cf. Oesterreicher 1995 and 1997, 200-206; see also Koch 1993b, 235-237, and the references cited there):

1) *Writing by semi-literate persons*. Semi-literates (see above 2.3.) are more or less acquainted with the graphic medium (or at least in a position to dictate their texts), but due to their limited experience in the realm of communicative distance, they cannot help using linguistic elements typical of immediacy and inappropriate to the target discourse tradition (or producing hypercorrections). Examples of such writing include common people's inscriptions, diaries, autobiographies, accounts of journeys, and private letters, merchants' letters, spell

tablets etc. (cf. e.g. Bruni 1984, 187-236, 486-517; Gibelli 1993; Oesterreicher 1994).

2) *Writing by bilingual persons in a triglossic situation.* In certain speech communities, a dominant language L_1, comprising a 'high' variety for distance and a 'low' variety for immediacy, coexists with the 'low' (immediacy) variety of a dominated language L_2. In this situation, semi-literate persons may have command of 'low' L_1 and 'low' L_2, but not of 'high' L_1 and write their texts in a language close to 'low' L_2 (possibly with interferences from 'low' L_1). We find examples of this type - with L_1 = Greek and L_2 = Latin - in the private letters of Roman soldiers in Egypt (2nd century A.D.).

3) *Relaxed writing.* Even literate writers do not strive for communicative distance, when addressing close friends in a private setting and with emotional involvement and/or when writing in a hurry (cf. II.1.-3. and IV.4. in 1.2.), e.g. in very private letters or personal notes and records.

4) *(Subsequent) records of spoken utterances.* In everyday life, exact recording of spontaneous spoken utterances is quite unusual (and literal recording is, strictly speaking, unrealizable before the invention of the tape recorder). Nevertheless, in certain juridical contexts (actions for defamation) it has always been indispensable to take down the - putative - wording of insults and injuries, even in ancient times (cf. Koch 1993a, 46 and n. 21). What is much rarer than this is a merely documentary, quasi-scientific motivation for recordings of spontaneous spoken utterances (in this respect the meticulous records of the French dauphin's spontaneous spoken utterances in the *Journal d'Héroard*, 1601-28 (cf. Ernst 1985), constitute an extraordinary document).

5) *Writing adjusted to lower competence of readers.* When addressing people that are less familiar with communicative distance (like children, pupils, even certain adults), highly literate authors feel compelled to produce texts characterized by features of immediacy in order to facilitate comprehension.

6) *Writing subjected to 'simple' discourse traditions.* In the case of 5), adjustment to communicative immediacy was an individual decision of the author. In other cases, this kind of adjustment is an inherent characteristic of a given discourse tradition, especially in popularizing texts on religious subjects (cf. the *sermo piscatorius* of Roman Christian authors) or in practical disciplines (medicine, architecture, agriculture, cookery etc.).

7) *Writing according to plain style rhetoric.* Even when addressing highly literate people, authors of certain literary genres adhere to the old rhetoric and poetic tradition of *stilus humilis/planus*, adopting a "simple", "natural" manner of writing, that is not aimed at imitating true communicative immediacy proper (see 8)), but at avoiding any excess of communicative distance (as for example in manneristic styles).

8) *Mimesis of immediacy or simulated orality.* In several literary or quasi-literary discourse traditions, the simulation of communicative immediacy for mimetic-realistic or satiric purposes is widespread: in stage plays (especially in comedies), in realistic novels, in parodies, in comic strips (back to their earliest precursors in inscriptions), in "speaking" inscriptions, in advertising etc.

With respect to spontaneous phonic immediacy (sector A), these text types provide only indirect and selective evidence, because they are characterized by inexactness and/or by concessions to communicative distance, to the prescriptive norm (see below 5.1. and 5.4.), to the standard of the discourse tradition concerned etc. This holds even for those text types that seem to have a particularly high "fidelity": note that subsequent records of spontaneous speech (4) cannot be more accurate than human memory and that literary "orality" (8) is always simulated and filtered through the artistic will of the author (cf. also Koch 1993b, 237).

It is only with the invention of tape and video recordings that we are able to store genuine phonic immediacy and to transfer it exactly into the graphic medium (sector C). But this is not a usual communicative practice. It is limited to the secret services and - at a metalinguistic level - to conversational analysts (see below 5.6.).

5. Immediacy in relation to distance within literate cultures

5.1. The existence of the graphic medium creates a fundamental asymmetry in the communicative "space" of a given speech community. Literacy splits the totality of utterances into two classes: on the one hand genuine phonic immediacy (sector A) and on the other hand everything that is organized in a certain sense around graphic distance:

- sector D, i.e. graphic distance itself.
- sector B: phonic distance is a central part of cultural literacy, in certain historical situations an even more prototypical form of communicative distance, as we saw in 3.2.-3.4. In any case, phonic distance in a literate society ($B^{[A+B+C+D]}$) relies heavily on the possiblity of developing and recording communicative distance in the graphic medium (sector D).
- (parts of) sector C: even though graphic immediacy in the form of constellations 4) - 8) seems to be a less prototypical part of "literacy" due to its particularities at the level of conception, it is widely diffused, as we saw in 4., and, thanks to its graphic realization, constitutes an integral part of cultural literacy from the outset.

The division of the literate communicative "space" into A vs. D(+B+C) has important consequences for language varieties and language history (5.2.-5.4.), linguistic consciousness (5.5.), and linguistic investigation (5.6.).

5.2. It would be wrong to think that oral societies have no special language norms for communicative distance: even in primary orality we meet with archaic varieties reserved for poetic or ritual purposes and alien to everyday communication, as e.g. Homeric epic language (cf. Browning 1982, 49; Ong 1982, 23, 47; Zumthor 1983, 137 ss.; Akinnaso 1985, 350 s.).

But it is not until the beginning of literacy that the reification achieved by the graphic medium enables literate people to establish what we might call a prescriptive norm, i.e. a language variety designed to assure an ideal stability required by maximal - graphic and phonic - distance (cf. Koch 1988, 331 s., 340 s.; Koch and Oesterreicher 1990, 16). By overruling diatopical variation, the prescriptive norm lends itself to communication across a larger speech community (spatial distance: I. in 1.2.). By overruling diastratical and diaphasical (low) variation, the prescriptive norm enhances the prestige of a speaker/writer in public communication between strangers (social distance: II.1. and II.2. in 1.2.). By overruling diachronic variation and - ideally - language change, the prescriptive norm lends itself to communication not only with contemporaries, but also with posterity (temporal distance: I. in 1.2.).

The prescriptive power of a distance norm in literacy may be implicitly - but not unconsciously - based on exemplary (literary, religious etc.) texts. Sooner or later, however, the prescriptive norm will be supported by explicit codification (grammars, dictionaries, antibarbari etc.). The higher the degree of literacy is, the more urgent is the need for codification. The invention of printing combined an additional reification of language in the graphic medium with the printers' and publishers' economical interests and thus simultaneously encouraged the expansion of literacy and the standardization of European vernaculars, which definitively codified their prescriptive distance norms from the Renaissance on: upper-class London dialect for English; Parisian *bon usage* of the 17th century court for French; Meißen chancery language for German; 14th century literary Florentine for Italian; etc.[14]

5.3. Now, a feature that characterizes literate speech communities are the permanent conflicts and interactions between the prescriptive distance norm on the one hand and the varieties reigning in the realm of immediacy on the other (dialects at the diatopical level, popular speech at the diastratical level, low registers at the diaphasical level etc.).

Establishing a prescriptive norm is a paradoxical kind of language change, because it is aimed to overriding language variation and language change (see above 5.2.). It follows from this that, once a prescriptive norm has been established in a literate speech community, a fundamental tension arises between the ideal stability of the prescriptive norm, applying to the whole realm of communicative distance (sectors B+D), and the kind of unplanned language change that permanently takes place in the immediacy varieties (sectors A and even C)[15].

There are two fundamental reactions to such norm conflicts to be observed in the history of all great cultural languages: puristic defence and re-standardization.

Purists tend to cut off the realm of distance from all influences of immediacy varieties. This results in a total petrification of the prescriptive norm, a process that can be clearly seen in the history of French, where the strict adherence to the 17th century prescriptive norm produced a real bipolarity, setting *français écrit* (for distance) against *français parlé* (for immediacy) as two very divergent varieties (cf. Koch and Oesterreicher 1990, 140 s., 150-165).

In the long run, such a petrification of the prescriptive norm leads to a situation of diglossia, as defined by Ferguson (1959): in a diglossic speech community, there are two extremely divergent varieties, a 'high' variety (H) for distance and a 'low' variety (L) for immediacy (without any functional overlapping). Famous examples of this type of diglossia are: the Latin-Romance world of the Middle Ages (H = Latin; L = Romance vernaculars), the Arabic world (H = Classical Arabic; L = regional Arabic dialects), Swiss German (H = *Hochdeutsch*; L = *Schwyzertütsch*); Modern Greek (H = καθαρεύουσα; L = δημοτική; but see below)[16] etc.

A quite opposite reaction to norm conflicts between distance and immediacy consists in a process of re-standardization, in which the prescriptive norm assimilates elements of immediacy varieties. In the history of Spanish, for instance, we observe a sort of continuous re-standardization; more drastic processes of re-standardization can be observed between Old and Middle/Modern French and - even more radically between Old and Middle English (cf. Koch 1993b, 238). Diglossic situations are likely to end up, sooner or later, in a process of re-standardization: cf. the emergence, since 1974, of a Standard Modern Greek on the basis of δημοτική, but absorbing καθαρεύουσα elements, too (cf. Browning 1982, 57 s.).

Re-standardization is a dynamic typical of literate speech communities (and fostered by social upheavals). Firstly, elements of immediacy varieties may invade the prescriptive norm via the graphic medium, because there are transitional zones between graphic immediacy (sector C) and distance (sector D), including the activities of semi-literates (see above 4, 1) and 2)), certain types of literature (see 4, 7) and 8)) and - especially nowadays - journalism. Secondly, elements of immediacy varieties may invade the prescriptive norm via the phonic medium, because there are transitional zones between phonic immediacy (sector A) and phonic distance (sector B), which in turn is closely related to graphic distance (sector D).

This latter path of innovation is open to even more radical changes like language replacement in the realm of distance. It is no coincidence that the earliest vernacular texts, in which German and Romance languages began to replace Latin, were largely designed for a "vocal" realization in sector B, the crossroads of medieval *litterati* and *illitterati* (see 2.3. and 3.2.): oaths, forms of confession, prayers, benedictions and incantations, sermons, religious poetry, religious theatre (cf. Feldbusch 1985, 169-200; Koch 1993a, 49-54).

5.4. Note that the tensions and dynamics characterizing literate speech communities are not unidirectional. Besides the effects of immediacy varieties on the prescriptive distance norm (5.3.) we have to consider effects in the opposite direction.

We already saw in 4. that under normal conditions - disregarding modern transcriptions - graphic immediacy (sector C) never is perfect, extreme immediacy. Among other things, it is through the graphic medium that prescriptive norm has a partial, often clandestine effect upon texts of the types 4, 1) - 8). But even phonic immediacy (sector A) does not always remain immune to influences of the prescriptive norm.

Thanks to the fundamental social, economic or cultural changes of the last two centuries (industrialization, urbanization, migration, administrative centralization, military service, compulsory education, boom of the press etc.) literacy pervaded many speech communities, so that a lot of newly alphabetized illiterate people came into contact with graphic distance (sector D). For the most part, this was only passive contact (by reading), but many people even got used to writing by themselves (often producing, however, texts of type 4, 1). in sector C). Be this as it may, a large proportion of the speech community acquired an at least passive competence of the prescriptive norm.

We may add to this the more recent impact of the modern audiovisual mass media (radio, cinema, television). Their national (sometimes international) diffusion requires a unified language norm, and the prescriptive norm presents itself quite naturally, all the more so since much, though not all audiovisual media communication pertains to phonic distance (sector B: e.g. news, reports, documentaries, talks). Furthermore elements of the prescriptive norm can easily invade even the realm of immediacy, because especially in the audiovisual media there are transitional zones between sectors B (distance) and A (immediacy): for example, interviews with politicians (cf. 1.), discussions etc. All in all, contact with graphic distance (sector D) and the path B → A within the audiovisual media led to an infiltration of prescriptive norm e l e m e n t s into phonic immediacy (sector A) and produced novel varieties of immediacy in the speech communities concerned:

- regional dialects: *Modified Standard, français régional, regionale Umgangssprache, italiano regionale, español regional, kyo-otuu-go* (Japanese) etc.
- nationwide popular sociolects: *italiano popolare, español popular* etc.
- nationwide low registers: *colloquial English, français familier/populaire, Umgangssprache, italiano familiare, español coloquial* etc.
- nationwide 'spoken' varieties: *spoken English, français parlé, gesprochenes Deutsch, italiano parlato, español hablado* etc.

By replacing the old local dialects above all, these novel varieties involve a complete reorganization of the realm of immediacy typical of modern literate societies (cf. Koch and Oesterreicher 1990, 138-141, 172-176, 206-208; 1994, 600.). In some speech communities this reorganization is already going to extinguish local dialects (centre of Northern France, Northern Germany) and even autonomous vernacular languages (think of the precarious situation of Irish or Occitanian, threatened by English or French even in the realm of immediacy). Once a vernacular language is extinct, we can speak of language replacement in the realm of immediacy (cf. the case of Manx in the English speech community, of Vegliotic in the Serbo-Croatian speech comunity etc.).

5.5. Literacy restructures consciousness (Ong 1982, 78 ss.) and, thus, the split A vs. D(+B+C), described in 5.1., restructures linguistic consciousness. Literate people usually identify language with the graphic manifestation of language (C+D), with communicative distance (B+D), or, more commonly, with the prototypical combination of both (D). Consequently, literate people are usually taken in by two typical fallacies:

At the level of the medium, literate people speak of the "pronunciation" of a word, overlooking the fact that a *signifiant* is primarily a phonic reality and only secondarily a graphic representation.

At the level of conception, linguistic varieties and even languages pertaining exclusively to the realm of communicative immediacy (dialects, popular speech, vernacular languages etc.) are considered deformations of the "only", "correct" variety or language reserved for communicative distance (standard language or vehicular language), even though this is absolutely false on phylogenetic, ontogenetic, pragmatic, and/or historical grounds. From a historical point of view, this fallacy proves to be a corollary to the development of a prescriptive norm in literate societies (see above 5.2.).

The attitude resulting from these two fallacies can be denominated **scriptism**.

5.6. Inasmuch as literacy restructures linguistic consciousness and produces scriptism, it also impinges upon the conditions of **linguistic investigation** - or rather creates them. The reification achieved by the graphic medium is the prerequisite of systematic reflection on language, and scriptism is its legacy[17]: from the beginnings, reflection on language essentially has been reflection on language in the graphic medium and/or on communicative distance. It is not until about 1800 that linguistics is established as a real empirical and historical science, which respects language in its graphic a n d its phonic realization and in all its varieties, including distance and immediacy.

But since authentic phonic immediacy (sector A) is ephemeral, the investigator is faced with considerable technical problems. So the traditional dialectologist, for instance, had to content himself with questionnaires, which potentially reduce spontaneity and authenticity, or with dialect texts in the graphic medium, that, at best, belong to text types 4, 1), 2), 4), or 8) in sector C.

Things improved with the availability of tape and video recordings that could serve as a basis for transcriptions. Today's dialectologists, sociolinguists, and conversational analysts have a more direct access to sector A in its authentic manifestations via exact transfer to the graphic medium (A → C), but we should not cherish the illusion that we succeed in capturing e v e r y linguistic and nonlinguistic element of a spontaneous conversation - even by means of video recordings and their subsequent transcription.

At any rate, the foregoing considerations hold only for the investigation of modern contemporary immediacy. In case we want to study authentic phonic immediacy of the past, we have to cope with the fundamental division A vs. D(+B+C), produced by literacy (see above 5.1.); in other words: a division between those texts that (can) come down to posterity through a written record and those that do not.

As we saw in 3.2.-3.4., on the side of communicative distance the phonic sector B and the graphic sector D often are so closely interwoven with each other that many texts of sector B are reflected in written documents of sector D. In contrast, spontaneous phonic immediacy belonging to sector A generally leaves no direct traces in sector C. The text types described in 4, 1) - 8). provide only indirect, distorted evidence of a past state of affairs in sector A (see above 4.)

In a methodological perspective, this is a very important point for linguistics. Authentic phonic immediacy of the past is lost for ever and therefore inaccessible to direct scientific observation (whereas our sound and video recordings will constitute a most interesting material for future researchers). The lack of authentic material compels present-day linguists to get their informations about sector A in the past - with all reservations - from indirect documents:

- sector C texts of the types 4, 1) -8).
- metalinguistic sources:
  - linguistic material stigmatized by purist grammarians or lexicographers, a profession that is accustomed to condemning everything close to immediacy (elements marked diatopically, low on the diastratical or diaphasical scale, belonging to the 'low' variety in diglossia etc.). Take the well-known example of the Latin *Appendix Probi* (5th/6th century A.D.).
  - glossaries and phrase books from the past, inasmuch as they are destined for private use (II.1. in 1.2.; e.g. certain glossaries as the *Glossario di Monza*, 10th century A.D.) or contain dialogical parts (IV.1.; e.g. the French *Manières de langage* of the Middles Ages and the early Modern Times).

Whenever linguists study varieties of immediacy in the past, they inevitably resort to the above types of sources: investigating, for example, vulgar (i.e. spoken) Latin or the history of spoken French and Italian (cf. e.g. Ernst 1980; Radtke 1984; Koch and Oesterreicher 1990, 137, 173; Koch 1993b, 235 s.; 1995; Oesterreicher 1994; 1995).

6. Conclusion

The heading 'orality in literate cultures' does not refer to a unitary question, but to a ramified complex of problems. In the light of our threefold distinction between cultural orality/literacy, medium (phonic/graphic), and conception (communicative immediacy/distance), we have been obliged to discuss quite different aspects of "literacy":

- In (partially) literate cultures, illiterate members and residual oral traditions coexist with literate members and literate traditions, and the former are naturally in contact with the latter (chapter 2.).
- Even in (cultural) literacy, the phonic medium can play an important role in the realm of communicative distance, as for example in reading aloud, dictation, and especially medieval "vocality" (chapter 3.).

- An integral part of (cultural) literacy is made up of certain types of texts in which - relative - communicative immediacy appears in a graphic format (chapter 4.).
- Cultural literacy splits the communicative space into texts belonging to the graphic medium and/or communicative distance on the one hand and texts belonging neither to the graphic medium nor to communicative distance on the other. This split, and the resulting tensions and interactions between distance and (phonic) immediacy, decisively affect language varieties and their history, linguistic consciousness and linguistic investigation (chapter 5.)

To sum up: cultural literacy is characterized by multiple interactions between oral and literate cultural traditions, between the phonic and the graphic medium, and between communicative immediacy and distance.

Notes

[1] As regards the necessary distinction that has to be drawn between these two types of prototypical concepts, cf. Koch 1996, 224-226.

[2] Cf. Söll 1974, 11-19 (^{3}1985, 17-25); see also: Koch and Oesterreicher 1985, 17-19; 1990, 5 s.; 1994, 587 s.; Raible 1994, 4-6.

[3] For the aspect of the medium cf. several contributions to Coulmas and Ehlich 1983 and to Pontecorvo and Blanche-Benveniste 1993; numerous contributions to Günther and Ludwig 1994; see also Glück 1987; Günther 1988; Raible 1991a; Olson 1994.

[4] Cf. Koch and Oesterreicher 1985, 19-23; 1990, 6-12; 1994, 587 s. —Frith's discussion in Pontecorvo and Blanche-Benveniste 1993, 246-248, suggests that autistic individuals seem to be impaired in communicative immediacy, whereas some of them can achieve high standards in communicative distance.

[5] As for the fundamental step from primary oral culture to literate culture, cf. several important publications by Goody (e.g. Goody and Watt 1968) and by Havelock (especially 1976); cf. also Ong 1982; Schlieben-Lange 1983, 52-64; Finnegan 1988. But note the pleas against the simplificative "Grand Dichotomy", against the "Great Divide", and against the "threshold" thesis: Graff 1987, 2-14, 381-390; Hornberger 1994 (see also below 2.2./3.).

[6] For the traces of this contact to be found in the vocabulary of Romance languages, cf. Koch 1993b, 231 s.

[7] Think of the *Iliad*, OE. *Beowulf*, OIr. *Táin Bó Cuailnge*, OHG. *Hildebrandslied*, OIcel. *Edda*; OF. *Chanson de Roland*; OSp. *Cantar de Mio Cid* (cf. Lord 1960; Zumthor 1983; Foley 1990; Parry 1971; Kullmann 1984; Schaefer 1992; Tristram 1988; Wolf 1991; Kellogg 1991; Rychner 1955; Duggan 1973; Montgomery 1977).

[8] Cf. Koch 1993a, 53; Oesterreicher 1997, 213 s. –Cf. also the - partially - analogous case of bodies of customary law on the Iberian Peninsula: Koch 1993a, 59 s.; 1993b, 232.

[9] Cf. Chaytor 1945, 135-137; Febvre and Martin 1971, 17-37; Eisenstein 1979, 12, 22. For the general expansion of literacy, especially in the 12th/13t centuries, cf. Graff 1987, 53-74; Koch 1993b, 232; Raible 1994, 7 s.

[10] This insight contradicts the thesis of several authors as, e.g., Chaytor 1945, 5-21; McLuhan 1962; Eisenstein 1979, 10 s., 698; cf. the critical remarks in Saenger 1982, 367-369; Raible 1994, 7 s.

[11] Cf. for instance Chaytor 1945, 10-21, 52 s., 135-147; Ong 1982, 26, 41, 61; as for references to the situation of performance, cf. also the discussion in Scholz 1980, 35-103, and Green 1990.

[12] Cf. Dante, *De vulgari eloquentia*, II, vi, 4: *dictatores illustres* 'famous poets, i.e. troubadours'; cf. also Germ. *dichten* 'to write poetry' < Lat. *dictare*; see Ernout 1951.

[13] Note that rhetoric is not simply "speaking", but the art of planned distance type communication in the phonic medium (cf. Ong 1982, 9 s., 108-111, 116; Koch and Oesterreicher 1994, 593).

[14] Cf. Ong 1982, 106 s.; Mattheier 1988; Koch/Oesterreicher 1990, 134-136, 169-172, 201-204; 1994, 598 s. - For the role of printing in cultural, economic and linguistic history cf. Eisenstein 1979; Schlieben-Lange 1983, 49 s., 89; Giesecke 1991.

[15] For the conservatism of written language cf. Chafe 1985, 113-116. Certainly, 'innovative' vs. 'conservative' as overall qualifications for orality and literacy deserve a more detailed discussion: cf. Koch and Oesterreicher 1996, 64-68.

[16] Cf. Ferguson 1959; Browning 1982, 52-56; Bauer 1996; Koch/Oesterreicher 1990, 129 s., 133, 166, 199; 1994, 596, 599 s.; Coulmas 1994, 739-743 (note that Coulmas's larger concept of 'diglossia' includes cases of different languages functioning as H and L).

[17] Cf. Harris 1980, 6; Koch 1988, 342-348; Koch and Oesterreicher 1990, 18 ss.; Olson 1991, 258 ss.; Ehlich 1994, 20, 29. –Note that we are speaking here about systematic reflection on language and not about metalinguistic consciousness in general, that certainly exists even in primary oral societies (cf. Finnegan 1988, 45- 58; Feldman 1991). For the exceptional case of systematic reflection on language in the primary oral culture of Ancient India cf. Falk 1990, 116-118.

The Graphic Space of the School Exercise Books in France in the 19th-20th century*

Jean Hébrard

Reading, writing and counting have not always been the core of popular education. At the end of the 16th century, the ability to read seemed to be the only aim of Christian teaching and it was only at a later stage that the teaching objectives of Catholic and Protestant Reform schools developed any further (Hébrard, 1988).

The teaching of writing for the purposes of keeping accounts or for producing the commercial letters that were essential for the correct management of shops or workshops was not guaranteed by schools, and it was only due to the foresight of such organisations as the Brothers of Christian Schools that the offer of writing became one of the most effective ways of attracting urban children from the suburbs into schools. These children had been exposed to protestant propaganda, or they were already "de-christianized" and needed to be lured back to the catechism (Poutet, 1970).

In rural areas, which were still reliant on an oral culture, there was widespread interest in a more complete kind of literacy as a result of the liberal, philanthropic ideas that developed out of the Revolution (Weber, 1976). This time it was not simply a question of christian education but of ridding the rural population of the emotions, fears and passions on which the agrarian revolts had been based. The latter were still part of the collective memory of the nobles or élites of the Revolution or post-Revolutionary period. Through instruction, writing could undermine the old, peasant culture and open up the French countryside to modernisation and social peace[1].

---

*A first enlarged version of this chapter has been published in the book edited by Q. Antonelli and E. Becchi, *Scritture bambine. Testi infantili tra passato e presente.* (Children's writings in past and present times.) Bari: Laterza, 1995. We thank the editors and publisher for permission.

However, in order to be able to produce a simple text one must first learn to write. In a world where paper was expensive and the only instrument was the quill pen, which children's clumsy fingers had trouble in sharpening, learning to write took time and money. It was only at the beginning of the 19th century that the teaching of the complexities of writing began to escape the clutches of the specialist corporations of writing and mathematics teachers (Métayer, 1990). Originally, these teachers only taught writing to older pupils whose parents agreed to pay. It was an expensive, individual training involving the use of handwriting and arithmetic exercise books (Chassagne, 1989). Even though a school teacher was fully qualified to teach handwriting, this teaching was only for children who had not left school after the two or three years required for the reading programme. In 1833, however, school programmes had become sufficiently generalised (each district had to open at least one boys school) for rural families to demand more than the straightforward christian literacy teaching (reading only) that had been sufficient until then.

Thus, from the 18th century, France had a school system based on reading and writing and finally on counting. It was only after the major school reforms of the early 19th century that this new *trivium* became the essential instrument for teaching both urban and rural populations in schools.

However, the explicit formulation of supply and demand was not sufficient for writing to become widespread. First, it required teachers to be able to teach it - this was the aim of the first *écoles normales* that sprung up here and there after the Guizot laws (Gontard, 1963). It also required a pedagogical system which regulated learning processes efficiently. The school grammar book, which was produced at about the same time and was devoted entirely to spelling, was used for this purpose as were the new methods combining reading and writing that were published during the July Monarchy by Louis Hachette, the semi-official editor for the Ministry of Education (Chervel, 1977). Finally it required instruments that would enable the old, apprentice-style 'training' to become institutionalised. These were the individual slate, the beginner's slate, the exercise book for those whose hand was steadier, and, from the 1860's onwards, the metal pen, which freed pupils and teachers from the limitations of the quill[2].

The exercise book (*cahier*) was a normal, post-16th century learning instrument. In the *ratio studiorum* it was often referred to as "the blank book" and was used in alternation with the lined text - the spacing in the lined text enabled pupils to note down the teacher's explanation above the text (Latin or Greek) being studied[3]. Although almost non-existent in the *petites écoles* (elementary school) until the 19th century, the exercise book was, from the start of the 17th century, the necessary support for the handwriting model supplied by the teacher of writing and arithmetic (Chassagne, 1989). When in the classroom some pupils were tought to write, they usually did their writing exercises on loose-leaf sheets of paper. These exercises involved pupils copying examples of handwriting (or etchings) from pages put in front of them (Rulon and Friot, 1962). The 17th century educational reformers' insistence on the need to use more than just loose leaf sheets of paper are the demonstration of what was current practice in schools[4].

The widespread use of the exercise book in elementary schools became established in 1800-1830 and is certainly an important event in the development of school literacy. However, existing sources cannot establish a definite history of the school exercise book. Though the exercise book is shown to be present in a considerable number of classes from 1833[5], there are only sufficient collections for a big enough corpus from 1860. This deficit can perhaps be explained by the events of previous eras: the major international exhibitions, which would have included didactic innovations, only began during the Second Empire[6]. However this does not explain the existing numbers of exercise books that were produced in 18th century boarding schools - there are a good many of these in public collections[7] and they are increasingly available in special private sales. The contradiction between documentary evidence for the existence of elementary school exercise books and the actual numbers that have been preserved needs leads one to prefer an anthropological approach rather than a historical one.

Since the exercise book only is accessible since the time when pedagogical practice unified its use, it can be regarded as a documentary source for the period from 1860[8] to 1960[9]- a particularly important period for school instruction. During this period, the school exercise book is the support for a kind of writing practice that is the framework for the school literacy which enabled rural France to enter 'modern' writing culture.

Historically, the teaching of writing and composing has not always involved the exercise book. Egyptian papyrus, clay tablets from Mesopotamia and Greek pottery fragments (*ostraka*) all show signs of school work (Goody, 1977). The use of wooden tablets covered with wax, frequent in the schools of ancient Greece and Rome, continued in Medieval times - we have examples of them from monastery schools (Riché, 1979). From ancient times school pupils have also used fine sand for writing. Only in the 18th century the slate (Brouard, 1882) replaced this cheap ancestor of the rough version that was still being advocated by supporters of the mutual teaching method.

Each of these objects deserve a full scale study in their own right. The blackboard, a collective erasable surface, enabled simultaneous teaching, which had been invented by the Brothers of the Christian Schools (de la Salle, 1994), to become widespread. The slate was the last in a series of teaching aids for both written calculation (division and subtraction need a number of trials and thus a number of erasures) and manual skills at a time when paper was expensive.

This article concentrates on the exercise book[10] for a number of reasons: firstly, both for its importance in the history of the school and the considerable care taken in its conservation, the exercise book is important evidence of past and present school writing practices; secondly, exercise books are the only documents available in large quantities for a sufficiently long period of time and from the mid 19th century to the present day their use takes up a considerable part of school time; finally, at the very moment that the exercise became the centre of school literacy practice, the exercise book not only acted as a support for it but gives it its essential meaning.

1. Varieties of exercise

When analysing piles of exercise books one notes the extraordinary consistency of writing throughout the century: the work of Saint-Just P., a Norman pupil, in 1893 is very similar to that of Marguerite B from Ansois-dans-la-Nièvre, who at the beginning of the school year in 1914 decorated her moving dictation, entitled *The Mobilising of the Army*, with a garland of flowers. These two exercise books are also similar to that of an unnamed pupil at a school in Castres in 1956.

One's attention is particularly caught by the consistency of the exercises. The most used is the dictation or, in the first grades, writing exercises; these are often followed by grammatical or logical analysis and vocabulary exercises (word families, homonyms, synonyms, antonyms, definitions). The second most frequent exercise type is the problem or, in the first grades, operations and lists of numbers. Problems almost always involve the same subjects - expenditure, weights and measures, sales and discounts, and calculation of surface and volume. There are occasionally two other types of exercise - composition (style exercises in the older books) and the drawing of maps (usually regional). This list of exercise-types shows that the contents of exercise books do not reflect the way school subjects are divided in schooltime. Some subjects such as history are under-represented in as much as there are no exercises for them.

There is thus a permanent doubling-up of the aims of each school practice - everything is used and nothing is wasted. This operation may even become circular when the content of a particular exercise defines the way in which the next exercise is used - for example, this is what happens with dictations designed to improve letter-writing or holding the pen properly in order to write more clearly. The school came to produce an infinite variety of exercises from a limited content and know-how.

This relative mobility of exercise content might lead one to suppose that what is specific to it is not subject matter. If we ignore the standard lesson and exercise headings in the exercise books, what is particularly striking is their layout. Letters are spread out on the page according to a relatively stable set of conventions. Paragraphs are distinguished by handwriting of different thicknesses; margins are structured so as to frame complex, regular spaces; headings are organised into hierarchies by different kinds of underlining. Any description of school exercise books must involve an analysis of the way exercises are presented in the books.

2. Copying

There is a kind of zero level of layout which involves the conscientious filling up of every line on every page. The writing is of maximum density and, in terms of word spacing and punctuation, reminiscent of medieval manuscripts in which the copyist was more concerned with showing the regularity of graphic space than with making the text easy to read. One guesses that here "making pages" is essential, as stated by some pedagogues concerned with banishing what they consider to be illegitimate practices. Nonetheless, it is clear that the exercise of copying lies at the very core of literacy, when this intends to teach not only to read but also to write[11]. Lines of writing are copied and recopied with a clever or a rough hand. In July 1907, for example, Mathilde tirelessly repeats on every line of a long page "nul bien sans peine" ("nothing is done well without hard work") and, since the line is not finished after the full stop, she adds "Nul b" and sometimes "Nul bi".

Educationalists and inspectors have generally examined the quantity of this recopying, which is the centrepiece of the exercise books. However, their quality should not be overlooked: teachers are mainly concerned with writing and spelling and, judging by the exercise books that have been saved, they get good results. One can easily imagine the dedication - and the supervision - that went into these efforts, whether recopying from the rough version or the slate, recopying a model sentence written directly in the exercise book by the teacher or even transcribing a 'summary' from the blackboard or textbook.

It is in the quality of copying that the clearest diachronic development can be seen. In an 1873 exercise book which has been rebound and approved by a school inspector, correct copying is the core activity - there is not a single mistake or crossing-out. Correction by the teacher is highly discreet as though to avoid any sign that might be different from what is written within the page frame. The writing is elegant, even and totally legible. If we ignore the subject matter of what was being copied for 2 or 3 pages per day, the model for writing was the book. At a time when writing was rare (particularly in rural areas) and only a few members of the middle class could afford Hetzel and Hachette's children's editions, the teacher knew that, apart from the reading manual, the exercise book was probably the only 'book' that the child would have access to and be able to keep when school was over. The exercise book, a book without illustrations, thus follows a model that resembles the manuscript reading manuals published during the Restoration after the invention of the lithograph - same economy of layout, use of heading, single and double underlining, and, above all, the same content - a miscellaneous collection of notions supplied by the school.

At the end of the 19th century, illustration became more frequent (see Figure 1) - a decorated heading, a drawing (which might be coloured in the bigger books), a mark for the end of the day. Such an illustrated book for reading was the famous *Tour de la France par deux enfants* (Bruno, 1877; Ozouf and Ozouf, 1984). The image occupied a privileged place in those *leçons de choses* that in the name of empiricism were introduced first in kindergarten and then in schools. Publishers of school books used wood engraving - a technique which was perfected in the large illustrated magazines like *Magasin pittoresque* or *Illustration*. It was less expensive than copper engraving that had been used for the magazines of the Restoration and it could be integrated with the text itself. Thanks to the evocative power of images, the book was no longer the austere object that it had been up till then. It could transmit as much through the image as it could through the text. The pupil, fascinated by the abundance of engraving, included drawings from real life and illustrations in their own exercise books (see Figure 3).

Between the two World Wars illustrated dictation became a means for the pupil to show his skill. At the beginning, exercises in style used a sequence of images for the pupil to build a written narrative on. These exercises naturally led the pupil to recopy the engravings from the school textbook into his own exercise book. The poetry exercise book, in which a small anthology of national poetry has been lovingly put together, is an example of how text and illustration are interlinked[12].

At the beginning of the 1950's, photographs, postcards and cut-out magazine pages began to be used in exercise books. A teacher in Clermont-Ferrand writes in the margin of one of these: "The exercise book is very well kept. Complete the documentation." The exercise book no longer had to be the substitute for the book (Choppin, 1986, 1990) that was freely distributed to pupils but, as often happens in school, it evolved as its model evolved, though conserving its own identity as a handmade product even when its model had long been industrialised.

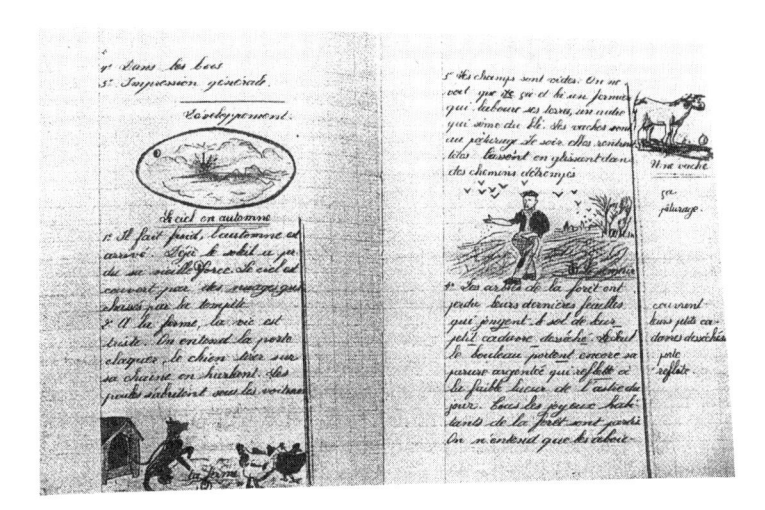

Figure 1. Anonymous notebook without date: "The sky in Autumn"

3. Making lists and tables

Writing space was not entirely taken up by the pages of copied writing described above. There are other types of writing, less economical on paper but perhaps more constraining, namely lists and tables. Although these still involve rewriting in terms of words, sentences and operations, the pupil still has to carry out a transformation in the graphic representation. For instance, in a grammatical exercise, the pupil first has to copy the sentence on the line and then has to rewrite it vertically (see Figure 2), by decomposing it in each single word.

Almost all grammar and vocabulary exercises use the *mise en liste* (listing) in this way (see Figure 4). It might be the starting point or the aim of the exercise. However it is often preceded by a ritual sentence to explain it or to start the process off, e.g. in logical analysis (1914) - "This sentence contains three propositions because it contains three finite verbs" - or in 1956 - "This

180   JEAN HÉBRARD

sentence contains three finite verbs and therefore three propositions". Starting from this statement, the three propositions are separately transcribed. The vehemence of the corrections show clearly that although a mistake in analysis can be excused, an error in the transcription of the introductory sentence is a "mistake".

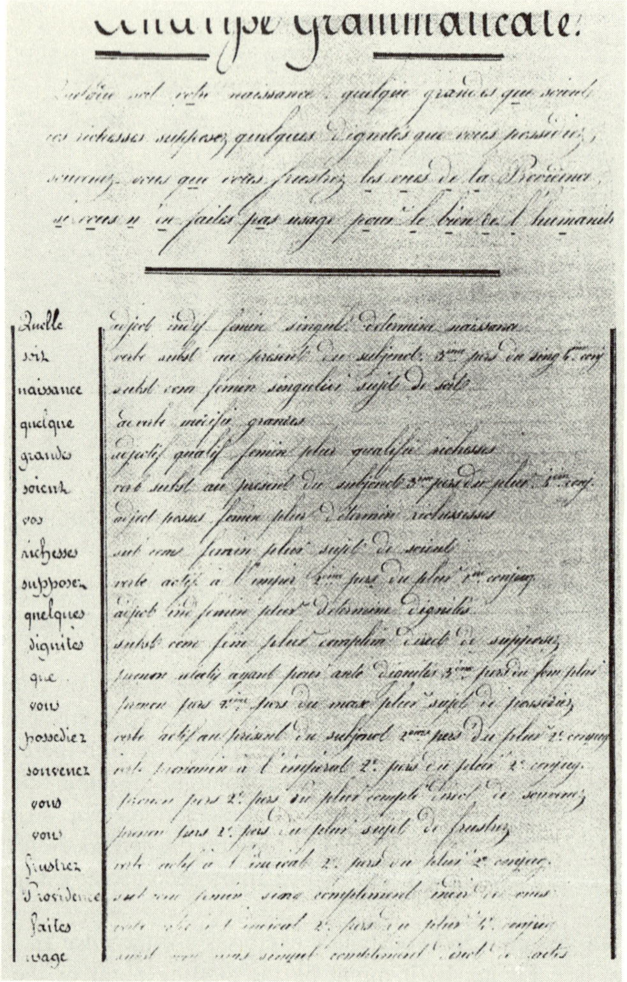

Figure 2. Notebook of Anna Gauthier made at Montigny-sur-aube (Cote d'Or) without date: Analysis of grammar (MNE, box 3.4.01, doc. 79-11833f)

Figure 3. Notebook of Cyr Bigot made at the school of Saint-Prest (Eureet-Loire): "The scale" (MNE, box 3.4.01, doc. 35089-6)

The reproduction of a formula, almost in the meaning of the liturgy, which is both the obligatory start to an exercise and the plan for the subsequent *mise en liste*, produces an automatic kind of writing. In grammar analysis there are also ritual expressions for grammatical class and function in the right hand column:

la | definite article, feminine singular, defines "robe" (dress)

Although the child does a considerable amount of writing, *mettre en liste* is not just a different kind of writing, it means a complete reorganisation of the writer's relationship to language. Copying only involved transcription. *Mise en liste* involves taking words out of context, separating them, rearranging them and somehow objectifying them by writing. These words are thus a specific part of learning through writing: they no longer speak but are objects of knowledge.

In his classic book, Jack Goody (1977) notes how the introduction of writing within a society produces a restructuring of its ways of thinking. *Mettre en liste* seems to him to be the starting point for this restructuring because the linear, one-dimensional word is replaced by a space in which other structures, particularly written classification procedures (alphabetical order, subject areas etc.) are possible. Following Goody, the exercise books may suggest that the school is trying to introduce children to the written word through this 'spatialisation' of language.

Arithmetic problems are also affected by graphic constraints. After the mid-19th century, teachers appear to be looking for the best possible way to organise work on arithmetic within the confines of the exercise book. At first problems were arranged over the whole page as dictation was. Subsequently they came to be divided into two columns but without any of the spaces having a specific function. At the end of the 19th century, teachers arrived at a perfectly organised system of page layout which came to be a model for the organisation of space in the exercise book. First, the problem was written out across the whole line. The page was then divided into two unequal columns (one third/two thirds): additions, subtractions and multiplications were put down in the narrow column under the heading "Operations"; these problems were written out using conventional formulae in the wide column under the heading "Solutions" (or sometimes "Reasoning" or even "Reasoned solutions"). Here, for example is a problem from 1893:

Operations	Solutions
300	300 l of wine were mixed with
+200	200 l of wine
500	= 500 l of wine

On the last line of the "Solutions" column, or sometimes even right across the page, the answer is given using the same terms as those used in the introductory sentence. Here, for example, is the solution to a problem of tailoring:

> Answer: the length of the thread on the spool is 39 metres and 270 millimetres

This layout is the same for all exercises involving calculations whatever their subject or difficulty. If the columns became longer over the years the procedure still remained the same. From 1882 to the present day we found the same visual presentation for different aspects of the child's work - reading the sentence and applying the four operations (see Figure 5). These two aspects are mediated by a third aspect - the 'design' of the procedure.

Since the 1970's the exercise book has often been replaced by the loose-leaf file in which the pupil no longer has to organise the layout. Yet the loose-leaf file still belongs to the same tradition of knowledge organisation: *mise en liste* and graphics. In this sense files of mathematics and grammar are more alike than the arithmetic and grammar exercises of a few decades ago: each answer is to be given in the place allotted to it among a host of other tables.

Thus, when the exercise book started to be used for exercises, a new intellectual technique or way of thinking came into being. The standardised, two-dimensional frame which excluded ambivalence as much as possible shows a need for order and completeness which is typical of writing. As Goody suggests, "One of the features of the graphic mode is the tendency to arrange terms in (linear) rows and (hierarchical) columns in such a way that each item is allocated a single position, where it stands in a definite, permanent, and unambiguous relationship to the others. Assign a position, for example, to 'black' and then it acquires a specific relationship to all the other elements in the 'scheme of possible classification'" (1977:68). Perhaps we are now better able to understand the recurrence of comments like "Badly presented", "Badly arranged", "Badly written"etc.

These are not signs of a teacher's particular obsession or of a teacher who does not look at the important aspects, i.e. whether the result is correct or not. They show how important it is to follow specifically graphic techniques in order to assimilate a particular intellectual process - the ability to record, organise and classify.

4. Keeping daily records

The construction of pages, lists and tables is not the only activity to be found in exercise books. The keeping of daily records is a frequent and functionally important type of graphic organisation since it is chronological order which is the organising factor of graphic activity on the page.

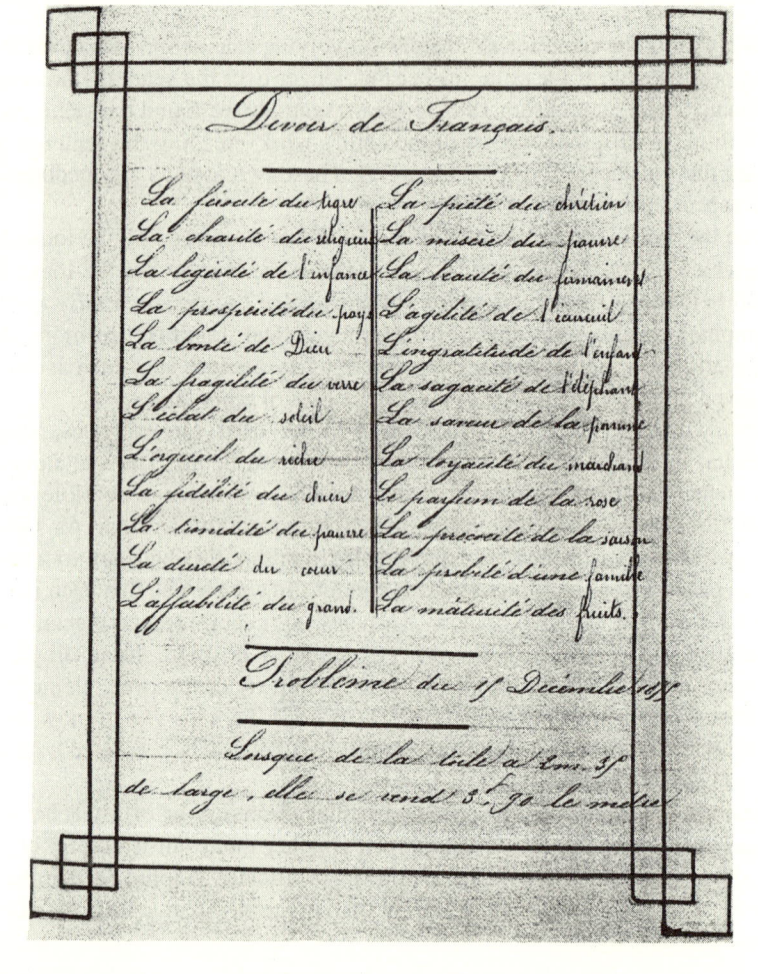

Figure 4. Notebook of Eugenie Marine made around 1873 at the school of Malesherbes (Loiret): Vocabulary exercise (MNE, box 3.4.01, doc. 79-37794-2, photo by Robert Cahen).

It quickly became conventional to write the date at the start of each set of exercises and after 1914 the writing of the date, day, month and often the year was obligatory with some particularly conscientious teachers even including the time of day. Sometimes there are structural subdivisions, e.g. *Morning class* (1907), or a distinction between homework and schoolwork, e.g. *Daytime Monday 19 January* and *Evening homework* (1948).

At first the function of these headings seemed to be to show how much work had been done in the school day, but from 1900 onwards a new item became more influential in the organisation of the exercise book. This was a memorandum of school life describing the lessons that had taken place without exercises and if necessary a brief summary or just a heading (see Figure 6). Initially only the "major subjects" appear to be described, e.g. on 12 April 1893 under the main heading *Moral instruction* is the subheading *Examples of patriotism in ancient Greece*.

All school subjects, even the most recent ones, were soon included in this practice. On 17 July 1907 there are references to "home economics" and "geometry"; there follows a writing exercise and a problem (these are all morning classes). The issue is clear. Writing is still involved but its function is now to organise school time, mapping it out step by step and getting the child used to this kind of daily repetition. As Ch. Defodon, chief editor of the *Manuel Général de l'Instruction Primaire*, writes in 1868, "everything - pages of dictation, analysis, summaries, maps, arithmetic problems with calculations and solutions - is in order and in the right place". If we add, in addition to Defodon's exercises, the references to each lesson, the school day has an overall consistency - there are no empty spaces and the pupil gets used to thinking of the school day as a regular sequence of working periods of time and of the school week as a regular sequence of working days. The child's exercise book becomes the equivalent of the widely admired, 19th century diary, in which the 'gentleman of leisure' kept records of his daily occupations[13].

The other important function of the exercise book-record is to act as proof of work done. This also explains the significance of the frequent pedagogical discussions from 1860-1890 concerning the usefulness of having one or more than one exercise book. One exercise book for each subject means copying the system used in boarding schools but above all it means dissipating the attention not only of pupils and teachers but also of inspectors (who supervised the teacher's work at school) and families (who supervised the pupil's). If there is already a register - the "class journal" or more recently the "exercise-book diary" - in which the teacher writes down what has been done, the single exercise book is the ideal way of checking up on the work the teacher has been doing with each pupil. Charles Defodon is not wrong when he writes in 1887:

"The class 'journal-diary' which is currently being used in all the schools of the Yonne region, shows day-by-day and hour-by-hour the nature of lessons and exercises; the single exercise book shows the date and the hour in which an exercise was done and thus acts as a check of the class journal"[14].

From the First World War to the 1970's this controlling function is shown by the recommended but not compulsory use of the "exercise book by turns", in which pupils took it in turns to record class activities each day. An "exercise book by turns" from Paris in 1948, for example, shows that Fridays were used for singing (with a specialist teacher), arithmetic (the problem is set, answered and corrected), drawing (with a specialist teacher), geography (the topic was "the distributions of continents and seas") and reading (title: *La sagesse d'un bouffon* by Rabelais).

As regards checking on pupils, the "monthly work exercise book" for example, which was compulsory from 1882, contained every composition that had been done by a pupil throughout elementary school and thus enabled the pupil's progress in that area to be easily checked.

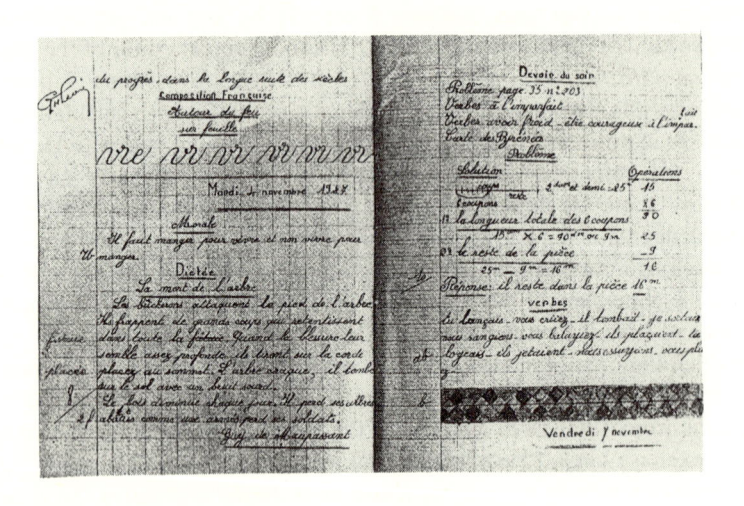

Figure 5. Anonimous notebook, made in 1947: Problem (presented on two organized columns) MNE, photo by Robert Cahen.

The daily exercise book was sufficient for a connection between the school and the family. J.Tronchère in a 1967 *Guide du débutant*, writes: "Our pupils' parents do not come to your lessons. The meeting point between them and you, through their children, is the exercise book." The exercise book enables school work to be "presented" for checking. Its management and upkeep were in themselves an exercise, whose quality could be evaluated by anyone.

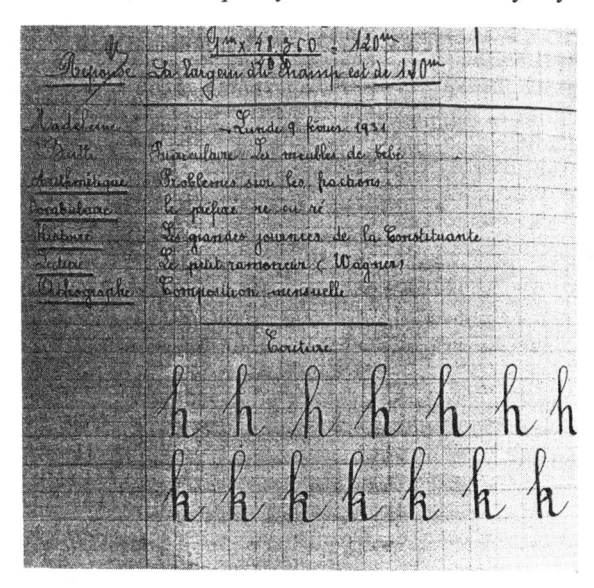

Figure 6. Notebook made by Madeleine Butti in 1931: list of the classes of the day and writing exercise. (MNE, photo by Robert Cahen)

5. The intellectual function of the graphic exercise

The exercise book is not simply a paper support for learning to write. The organisation of the space and time of school work in its three dimensional pages[15] enables the pupil to get used to the continuous practice of both writing down what he is learning and of the writing skill itself. The exercise book is thus what gives school writing its meaning and specific character: it is above all an exercise.

The study of school exercise books seems to show that doing an exercise involves not only a physical skill but also a specific intellectual skill based on graphic knowledge. Doing exercises means learning to present, which involves the consistent use of neatness and naive or affected elegance to turn the exercise book into a small theatre of school knowledge. The teacher checks closely that each child is acting as the craftsman of his pages, in which everything is to be visualised. Doing exercises also means organising, i.e. training oneself in the classifying, recording, indexing etc. skills, which are acquired through graphic techniques. The lists and tables that the child produces at school on a daily basis both define and organise a particular knowledge area, which may be limited but, as a result of its graphic expression, is nonetheless exhaustive.

By allowing all its pupils access to this new practice of writing, the school was compelled to justify it. However, this could not be the traditional justification in terms of rhetoric as practised in the boarding schools. Thanks to the exercise book, the elementary school provided itself with a way of working with writing which was in line with its conception of knowledge: an elementary kind of knowledge with no empty areas and characterised essentially by completion and perfection.

Notes

[1] The debate on the role of writing for the integration of the countryside in the national space between the July monarchy and the 3rd Republic was reopened in 1977 by Françoise Furet and Jacques Ozouf, 1977). Their conclusions, which minimise the impact of 19th century school policy, do not imply that they were not deliberately thought out and put into practice by numerous governments of the period (Hébrard, 1980: 66-80; 1990:95-109).

[2] For 19th century school material see the corresponding articles in Buisson, 1882.

[3] On the "blank book", see for example the *ratio studiorum* of the Messina collegio of 1548 or 1553 or the Collegio Romano of 1564 and 1565. I thank Dominique Julia for these references). For the edition and spacing, as well as the regulations of the boarding schools, see Grafton, 1981, which examines a collection of classical texts commented by a student from the *collège* of Reims, in Paris, in 1572-73.

[4] In *L'Ecole paroissiale*, Jacques de Batencourt (1654) writes: "the teacher will require each pupil to bring him a quire (25 sheets) of paper suitably bound and covered by a folder; the paper should not be in the least wet but absolutely dry and well-waxed so as to accept the ink without absorbing it; the teacher will severely punish whoever does not keep their paper clean, tidy, and unmarked"(1654:256). Half a century later, J.-B. de La Salle (1706) warns: "The teacher will take care that all pupils have white paper at school. He will require pupils to ask their parents for paper as soon as they are down to only six sheets. He will also be careful that if a pupil neglects to bring paper, he does not take away what he has already written before the new paper arrives. All pupils will bring at least half a quire of good paper (...) It is not acceptable for any pupil to bring paper which is not bound or folded into squares;

sheets of paper should be bound right along the edge". One should note that until this time the term 'exercise book' is not used.

[5] When at the start of 1883 Francois Guizot, Minister for Elementary Education, set up a major inquiry into the state of elementary teaching, he was attempting to evaluate the modern teaching system which his new educational laws had been designed to develop. The use of exercise books was one of the symptoms of this development. The researchers asked teachers if their pupils wrote in the exercise books. The results of this enquiry, which are currently being examined at the Service for the history of education at Institut National de recherche pédagogique shows that even in a school district (*académie*) as backward as that of Nîmes (departments of Gard, Ardèche, Vaucluse and Lozère) more than half the classes used exercise books.

[6] The first collections of exercise books from the Musée pédagogique (founded in 1879 by Jules Feny) come from these exhibitions. They are now at the Musée National de l'Education.

[7] The Musée National de l'Education has an excellent collection of exercise books from the collegi of the Ancien Régime. A number of libraries also have them in their archives.

[8] This first date is explained in our research on the introduction of the dictation in the elementary school (Chartier and Hébrard, 1993)

[9] This second date is explained by the appearance throughout the 1960's of new kinds of writing instrument, paper support and above all by the association of the exercise book with the archaic teaching practices that the educational changes of the 1970's will be sweeping away.

[10] The present study elements of research whose previous results have already been published in collaboration with Ch. Hubert (Hébrard and Hubert, 1979).

[11] A 'theory' for this kind of entrance in school writing through copying is given in the pedagogical literature of the 19th century. (See Chartier and Hébrard, 1993).

[12] A trace of the poetry exercise book can be found in the song book, one of the most typical written works of the military service period and very fashionable at the start of the 20th century. It too was illustrated with naive coloured drawings. (See Roche and Roche 1997).

[13] An excellent collection of diaries (*agendes*)of this type is in the archives of the Museé des arts et des tradition populaires in Paris.

[14] When the rule that obliged the teacher to have the pupils keeping an exercise book of the month's *devoirs* was confirmed (in 1877), the inspector W. Marle-Cardine outlined the progress made by this innovation and the resistance it encountered (1888). It provides an interesting overview of the use of this kind of exercise book in late 19th century France.

[15] The exercise book is a vertical collection of sheets of paper. It is thus not two-dimensional like the blackboard, the slate or the single sheet of paper. Its thickness gives it a third dimension, exemplified by the fact that it can be 'leafed through'. In this it resembles the codex (Chartier 1993).

PART III

Written language competence in monolingual and bilingual contexts

Production and Comprehension of Connectives in the Written Modality
A Study of Written French

Michel Fayol, Serge Mouchon

Connectives are text cohesion devices used by authors to tie clauses or sentences together in the linearization process of translating a coherent multidimensional representation (i.e., a mental model) into a strictly linear and time dependent format, in oral or written language (Fayol, 1997; Halliday and Hasan, 1976). These devices enable the organization of word knowledge into information blocks of variable sizes to take place. They govern or control the application of the nextness principle because they indicate what linguistic items go together, and why (Heurley, 1993). They thus show the strength of the link between two statements or utterances. In addition to this primary function, within certain limits, they also help make explicit the nature of the links between the information blocks (i.e., *if* marks a logical link, *then* a chronological link, and so on) (Braunwald, 1985).

The experiments reported here are aimed at studying two problems dealing with the use of connectives in written language. First, connectives exist in speech well before they are used in writing. Thus, acquisition of the linguistic paradigm does not appear to be a problem. Nevertheless, studies of written narratives produced by 6- to 10-year old children have shown that children who are able to use connectives such as *mais* (but) or *soudain* (suddenly) in speech do not use them until the third or fourth grade in the written modality (Fayol, 1991). A first investigation was designed to test the hypothesis that the lag between connective use in oral and written modalities is due to the characteristics of the reported event chains, and not to linguistic difficulties. Second, connectives are marks available to readers, but we know little about the way they are used and even whether they are useful at all, especially for children. The second series of investigation was aimed at exploring if and how children and adults use some connectives when reading short stories for comprehension.

1. Producing connectives in written texts

Over the past two decades, most studies on connectives have dealt with children in situations of oral production (Nelson, 1986; McCabe and Peterson, 1991). These studies have shown that preschool children are able to appropriately employ words such as *if, and, before, after,* and *but*. For example, French and Nelson (1985) observed that preschoolers used these connectives provided that they were talking about situations familiar to them. The order in which these connectives appear during development is the same in all languages (Bates, 1976; Brown, 1973; Jeruchimovicz, 1978; Peterson and McCabe, 1987) and their use depends both on pragmatic conditions and on the child's developmental level (Bennett-Kastor, 1986).

Studies on written production have indicated that writing follows similar tendencies to those observed in speech, with the order of appearance (*and, afterwards, then, but*) being the same, but with a lag of 3 or 4 years for the spoken language (Fayol, 1981). Such a delay is hard to explain. Taking into account the fact that 4- to 5- year-old children use connectives easily and regularly in their oral productions, it seems impossible that 7- to 9-year-old children do not know them. Therefore, there must be another explanation for the delayed occurrence of such connectives in written text production.

We put forward the hypothesis that the lack or scarcity of connectives in the written production of 7- to 9-year-old children is due to the (weak) organization of event-chains they are reporting. Indeed, we observed that 7-to 9-year-olds tended to produce written texts made up of juxtaposed facts and/or highly predictable events (Fayol, 1991). In order to produce such texts, children need no other connective except *et* (and). This hypothesis predicts that connectives such as *mais* (but), *après* (then), *soudain* (suddenly), and so on will occur in written texts as soon as the complexity of the event-chains justifies their use, i.e. when the event-chains contain at least one complication and one resolution. The following experiment was aimed at verifying this hypothesis.

Six event-chains were constructed in such a way that for any given beginning (6) there were three corresponding possible endings. For example, one of the chains began with the three facts (setting): "Eric found his room sad/He decided to repaint it/He took a paint-pot and a brush". Three different series of three states or events (corresponding respectively to the Event/Result/End constituents) possibly followed this setting. In one case, the events were highly predictable (script-like event-chain; Fayol and Monteil, 1988): "He climbed the stepladder (Event)/He painted all day (Result)/ Eric did not find his room sad any more (End)". In another case, an obstacle hindered the realization of the event-chain leading to the goal. This obstacle was either a state, i.e. "The color of the paint seemed too sad to him (Event)/He did not repaint his room (Result)/Eric still found his room sad (End)", or an unexpected event, i.e. "He spilt the paint climbing up the stepladder (Event)/He no longer had enough of it to paint (Result)/Eric still found his room sad (End)" (Table 1). The six chain-beginnings were thus each crossed with three endings, giving a total of 18 six-sentence stories: six script-like stories; 12 with-obstacle stories (6 with a state-like obstacle and 6 reporting the occurrence of an unexpected event). None of the stories contained any connectives.

Thirty six children (18 third graders and 18 fifth graders) took part in the experiment. Each child was presented with the six event-chains, each of them under one story-version (i.e., with each presented beginning having only a single ending for a given child). Therefore, each child saw two script-like stories, two stative-obstacle stories, and two stories reporting an unexpected event. The stories were first presented orally by the experimenter. The same stories were then presented again (orally), with one picture being associated with each of the sentences. In the third phase, the pictures previously associated with each sentence were used as cues for recall. Each child was given the series of pictures corresponding to each story one by one and asked to recall the stories in the written modality.

The room
1. Eric found his room sad.
2. He decided to repaint it.
3. He took a paint-pot and a brush.

WO
4. He climbed the stepladder.
5. He painted all day.
6. Eric did not find his room sad any more.

SO
4. The colour of the paint seemed too sad to him.
5. He did not repaint his room.
6. Eric still found his room sad.

DO
4. He spilt the paint climbing up the stepladder.
5. He no longer had enough of it to paint.
6. Eric still found his room sad.

Table 1. Example of a text with a common beginning (propositions 1, 2, and 3) and three versions (WO=without Obstacle; SO=Static Obstacle; DO=Dynamic Obstacle)

The number of connectives was used as a dependent variable in a series of analyses of variance (ANOVAs). The effect of story versions was significant: The children added more connectives when the event chains included an obstacle (.83) than when no obstacle was present (script-like versions: .62). Significantly more connectives were put at the beginning of the Event (i.e., the first sentence of the three-sentence ending: .97) than at the beginning of the Result- (.84) and End- (.47) constituents. No other effect or interaction was observed.

The analysis of the distribution of the different connectives as a function of the different versions showed that:

- *et* (and) was the most frequent under the script-like versions, mainly occurring just before the End constituent;

- *mais* (but) and *alors* (then/so) were the most frequent when a stative obstacle was mentioned. Most of the time, the children associated these two connectives, putting *mais* before the Event constituent and *alors* before the Result constituent (i.e., "but the car broke down so they walked home");

- *et* (and), *mais* (but) and *soudain* (suddenly) were the most frequent when an unexpected event occurred, mainly being put before the Event constituent.

As expected, the data from the cued (with pictures) recall test showed that third as well as fifth graders systematically added relevant connectives to texts where such connectives were lacking. This result is in agreement with those of previous studies dealing with the oral modality (Esperet and Gaonac'h, 1986; Goldman and Varnhagen, 1983; Mouchon, Fayol and Gombert, 1989; Pearson, 1975) and provides evidence that 7 to 9 year-old children insert the same connectives as adults, and at the same place, provided that the events being recounted justify their use. Our hypothesis is thus verified: children use relevant connectives in the written modality as easily as in the oral modality when the organization of the event chain is previously controlled. It thus appears that subjects spontaneously establish relationships between events, which is reflected in their use of connectives.

2. Comprehending connectives when reading texts

The question is whether connectives act as signals to get the addressee's attention and to suggest potential interpretations or processing modes (Bestgen, 1992). We examined this possibility in several experiments. Our aim was to determine if and how connectives contribute to narrative comprehension during reading.

Some studies have shown that connectives play a role in comprehension, whereas others have shown just the opposite (Segal, Duchan, and Scott, 1991).

Certain experimental results indicate that the impact of connectives is negligible or negative (Irwin, 1982; Roen, 1984). Most of these results are from studies which focus on the conceptual and/or macrostructural aspects of the event sequences being described (Bower and Morrow, 1990; Fayol and Lemaire, 1993; Fayol and Monteil, 1988; Schank and Abelson, 1977). By contrast, studies which have examined microstructural processing and its effect on the construction of mental models (Fayol, 1992) have led to contradictory conclusions (Irwin, 1980 a and b; Irwin and Pulver, 1984; Ziti and Champagnol, 1992). Finally, some theories predict that the impact of connectives is positive (Corbett and Dosher, 1978; Haviland and Clark, 1974; Mann and Thompson, 1980; Rayner and Pollatsek, 1989, pp.287-289).

Unfortunately, most experimental work dealing with the effect of connectives on comprehension has been conducted using insufficiently controlled materials. Connectives have often been inserted or deleted from texts systematically, without consideration of their relevance to the text and/or the reader's goal. Owing to the presence of confounding variables which make it difficult to detect potential effects, it is not surprising to find discrepancies between the various results. The impact of connectives can only be correctly analyzed by examining the interaction between the events described and the presence/absence of certain marks (Haberlandt and Kennard, 1981; Keenan, Baillet, and Brown, 1984; Mouchon, Fayol and Gaonac'h, 1995; Townsend and Bever, 1978). The nature of the events in the sequence determines whether or not inferences are needed to ensure the continuity of the chronological-causal chains. Whenever continuity is not achieved or is difficult to establish, connectives are useful (Noordman, Vonk and Kempff, 1992). By contrast, when the continuity of the facts is obvious, the very same connectives may be superfluous and thereby hinder processing.

At least two hypotheses can be proposed concerning the role of connectives. The first would be that appropriate connectives facilitate the semantic integration of information into the mental model currently being constructed. This hypothesis predicts that connectives will mainly have an effect during the integration phase, perhaps throughout the processing of the proposition following the connective, but more probably at the end of that proposition (Carrithers and Bever, 1984; Green, 1977; Haberlandt and Graesser, 1989). According to the second hypothesis, connectives, like punctuation marks, serve as processing indicators which supply the reader/listener with information on how to treat subsequent items (Caron, Micko and Thuring, 1988; Fayol, Gaonac'h and Mouchon, 1992; Gernsbacher, 1985; 1989; Townsend, 1983). This hypothesis predicts that the impact of connectives will occur on the segment immediately following the connective, regardless of the nature of that segment. Our aim was to determine which conception best describes the impact of connectives.

Short narrative texts were constructed while controlling the predictability of the endings in relation to the beginnings (Mouchon, Fayol, and Gaonac'h, 1991; Mouchon, Fayol and Gombert, 1989) (see Table 2).

Paul / était / heureux/ (Paul was happy.)
Il / venait de poser / du papier-peint / dans sa chambre /(he just finished putting up new wallpaper in his room).
Il / était / content de son travail/ (He was satisfied with his work).
Event (Experiments 1 and 2):
[no connective] [mais (but)] [soudain (suddenly)] une porte / cogna / contre le mur/ (a door hit against the wall).
Event (Experiment 3):
[no connective] [mais (but)] [soudain (suddenly)] une porte / cogna / contre le mur / (a door hit against the wall).
Result
Elle / déchira / le papier-peint / (It tore the wallpaper).
C'était / un courant d'air / qui avait provoqué / l'ouverture /
(It was a breeze that caused it to open).
Paul / était / très en colère / (Paul was very angry).
Comprehension questions:
Pourquoi Paul était-il heureux? (Why was Paul happy?)
Pourquoi Paul se mit-il en colère? (Why did Paul get angry?)

Table 2. Example of the type of text presented in all three experiments. The marks used (in brackets) varied across experiments and versions. Finer segmentation (shown between slashes) was used in Experiments 2 and 3 only.

The texts were displayed on a computer screen using a self-paced technique. Reading Exposure Time (RET) was measured as a function of the presence/absence of an appropriate connective. In Experiment 1, RET was measured on the propositions immediately preceding and following the connective. In Experiment 2, smaller linguistic segments were defined in order to determine the exact location of the facilitating effects observed in Experiment 1. RETs were compared between connectives. In Experiment 3, three connection modes were examined: no connective, presence of *mais* (but), and presence of *après* (afterwards), which introduces a deictic change (Segal, Duchan, and Scott, 1991).

Two predictions were tested. First, it was predicted that connectives like *mais* (but) and *soudain* (suddenly) would facilitate the processing of the subsequent items relative to a control condition (without connective; Expt 1). This facilitating effect was expected to be connective-dependent. Facilitation was not expected to occur with *après* (afterwards) (Expt 3) due to the deictic change (in the time frame of the event sequence) this connective introduces. Facilitation was expected with *mais* (but) and *soudain* (suddenly), which express the occurrence of an unexpected event.

Second, concerning the locus of the connective effect, two alternative hypotheses are plausible. The semantic-integration hypothesis states that the impact should occur at the end of propositions because the reader no longer needs to infer the link between the statement being treated and the mental model being constructed. The processing hypothesis states that the function of connectives is to tell the reader what to do (i.e., to keep the information in its literal form or process it semantically). This hypothesis predicts that the connective effect will occur on the segment immediately following the connective.

The aim of these experiments was to determine whether the introduction of a connective (*mais* (but) or *soudain* (suddenly) in Exprt 1) would facilitate processing of the subsequent items, relative to a control condition without a connective. Such a result would be consistent with the hypothesis that whenever the nature of the logical-semantic relationship between two propositions is stated, the processing of subsequent information by the reader will be facilitated.

We also attempted to determine whether this potential facilitation would be the same for all connectives. According to Townsend (1983), using the connective "but" only facilitates processing near the end of the proposition or the sentence immediately following the connective. In contrast, the facilitation is thought to be immediate when the connective announcing the occurrence of an obstacle is "suddenly". Thus, in a given text, a change of marker should lead to a change in processing. In a narrative containing a complication introduced by *mais* (but) or *soudain* (suddenly) (e.g., *Mais/Soudain la porte cogna contre le mur*, But/Suddenly the door hit against the wall), the facilitating effect of *soudain* (suddenly) should be observed on the next constituent (the Event constituent), whereas the facilitating effect of *mais* (but) should not appear until the Result constituent which follows (*"Elle déchira le papier-peint/* it tore the wall paper).

The materials were the same for all the experiments reported here, and consisted of six narratives containing an obstacle (the occurrence of an unexpected event) (Fayol, 1985). The appropriateness of the connectives *mais* (but) and *soudain* (suddenly) in these narratives was verified via two preliminary tests used to assess the predictability of the narrative sequences and the appropriateness of certain connectives. The first test ensured that the script-like texts were actually considered by adults to be highly predictable and that the narratives containing obstacles were indeed judged to be highly unpredictable. The second test assessed the appropriateness of the connectives. Each of the texts previously selected was presented to a group of children and a new group of adults. The first three propositions were clearly separated from the remaining ones. A series of connectives was given at the bottom of the page for each text. The participants were asked to state which of these connectives they *would* employ and which they *would not* employ to link the two parts of each text. The results were used to define a series of appropriate connectives and a series of inappropriate connectives for each event sequence.

Six narratives with unpredictable endings were presented in three connective modes (*mais* (but), *soudain* (suddenly), no connective, in Expts 1 and 2; *mais* (but), *après* (afterwards, no connective, in Exprt 3), giving 18 texts in each experiment. When present, the connective was located before the Event constituent. Thus, a given version of a text only differed from the two corresponding versions by the link preceding the Event constituent (cf. Table 2).

Each participant processed all six narratives and all three versions, but only saw one version of a given narrative. Fifty-four participants divided into three groups (18 third graders, 18 fifth graders, and 18 university students) participated in the first experiment. A French variation of the *moving window* technique was used (Just, Carpenter and Wooley, 1982; Gaonac'h and Passerault, 1990). The text first appeared in crypted format so that the reader could get an overall view of the text. The text was decrypted by pressing any key. When the first key was pressed, the first constituent appeared where it would normally appear in the text. The pressing of a second key re-encrypted this constituent and decrypted the next, and so on until all text constituents had been viewed. If present, the connective appeared alone and was re-encrypted as soon as the target constituent (which immediately followed) was displayed. The time separating two consecutive pressings corresponded to the RET (Reading Exposure Time) for that constituent.

University students read significantly faster (1865 ms) than fifth graders (2309 ms), who read faster than third graders (2828 ms). The interaction between connection mode and constituent was significant and did not interact with the school level, suggesting that the effect was the same for all three populations considered.

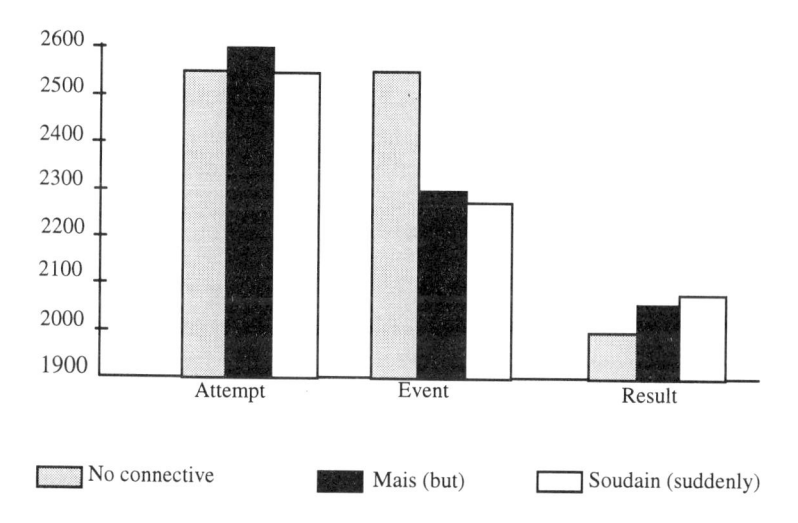

PRODUCTION AND COMPREHENSION OF CONNECTIVES 201

Figure 1. Mean ETR by level, type of mark, and constituent (Experiment 1).

Analysis of the interaction between connection mode and constituent revealed that the shorter RETs occurred on the proposition immediately following the connective, and only at that location. Shorter RETs were observed with *mais* (but) (2307 ms) and *soudain* (suddenly) (2286 ms) relative to the control condition without a connective (2551 ms).

All in all, for all levels considered, the use of *mais* (but) or *soudain* (suddenly) in unpredictable sequences led to faster reading speed relative to the condition without a connective and the locus of the acceleration did not vary across connectives: the faster reading speeds were always found for the proposition (relating the unexpected event) immediately following the connective.

These data suggest that the reading of texts is facilitated by the presence of certain connectives. These connectives may either give the reader specific expectations by indicating the existence and/or nature of a relationship between adjacent propositions or provide the reader with processing instructions. In both cases, connectives would facilitate the construction of an overall representation of what the speaker/writer is trying to say. However, the facilitation would not be based on the same processes. In one case the facilitation would be triggered by the specification of the inter-event relationship, which would free the reader of inference making and decrease the task demands. In the other case, the facilitation would not - or not solely - result from the specification of the semantic relationship, but rather from the information given to the reader about how to process the information. These two views of the role of connectives lead to different predictions as to the locus of their impact.

The aim of the second experiment was to locate the facilitating effects of the connectives *mais* (but) and *soudain* (suddenly). The sentences were segmented into units so that the location of the facilitation could be determined. The place where the processing was facilitated (i.e., where shorter RETs were obtained) would indicate whether their function was semantic (end of proposition) or procedural (beginning of proposition).

Fifty-four subjects divided evenly into three groups of 18 (18 third and 18 fifth graders and 18 university students) participated in the experiment. The materials were the same as in Experiment 1, except that the propositions were segmented into three syntactic components (see Table 2).

RETs were measured at four different places: on the segment preceding the connective or its theoretical location for the versions without a connective (noted P0), and on the three segments that made up the Event constituent situated before the connective or its theoretical location (noted P1, P2, and P3, respectively).

University students read faster (705 ms) than third (1172 ms) and fifth (1168 ms) graders, whose performance did not differ significantly.

The interaction between connection mode and segment was significant. The lack of a three-way interaction between level, connection mode, and segment suggests that the connection mode by segment interaction was not affected by the subjects' school level. Analysis of the data for this interaction showed that:

(1) The RETs of segments preceding immediately the connective or its location (P0) were never significantly different;

(2) The RETs on the Event constituent (P1 + P2 + P3) decreased significantly when a connective was present compared to the condition without a marker (2820 ms with *mais* (but) and 2830 ms with *soudain* (suddenly) vs. 2950 ms without a connective);

(3) Of the three segments in the Event constituent, only the RETs on the segment located immediately after the connective (P1) were significantly shorter. The decrease in RETs (880 ms for *mais* (but) and 850 ms for *soudain* (suddenly) vs. 1000 ms in the no-connective condition) was significant.

(4) The impact of the two markers did not differ significantly.

Of the three segments (P1, P2, and P3) in the Event constituent (which followed the inter-event link marker), only the first (P1) had significantly shorter RET's than in the control condition. This acceleration did not vary across connectives (but and suddenly). These results are consistent with the hypothesis that, in narratives with unpredictable endings, the facilitating effect of these connectives is immediate. The facilitation occurred at the very beginning of the proposition following the connective (cf. Haberlandt and Kennard, 1981). These results suggest that *mais* (but) and *soudain* (suddenly) are interpreted as instructions telling the reader what action to take with the information that follows. This interpretation of the role of connectives argues in favor of the hypothesis that these terms aid the construction of substructures by indicating to the reader whether or not the elements of upcoming segment(s) belong to the same substructure as those which precede the connective (see Gernsbacher, 1989).

The third experiment was designed to show that the increase in reading speed was not dependent upon the mere fact that a connective was present. We wanted to demonstrate that RET does not decrease with *après* (afterwards) as it does with *mais* (but). *Après* (afterwards) was selected because it expresses a deictic change (Segal et al., 1991): it indicates a change in the frame of reference of the event sequence and most likely leads to the construction of a new substructure (Gernsbacher, 1985, 1989). If *après* (afterwards) signals the beginning of a new substructure, it should not trigger any acceleration on the next text segment, contrary to what occurs with *mais* (but).

The materials and procedure of Experiment 2 were used once again but the connective *soudain* (suddenly) was replaced by *après* (afterwards). Eighteen fifth graders who had not participated in the other studies served as subjects.

As expected, the interaction between connection mode and segment was significant. This interaction was due to the fact that RET on segment P1 decreased with *mais* (but), whereas it did not with *après* (afterwards) or with no connective. Closer examination of the interaction showed that, of the three segments in the Event constituent, only the first (P1) was significantly affected by connection mode (1060 ms without a connective, 890 ms with *mais* (but) and 1070 ms with *après* (afterwards)). In addition, the acceleration on P1 was only significant for *mais* (but) (890 ms).

This third experiment thus showed that the only connective that led to an immediate increase in processing speed was *mais* (but), compared to the control condition where no connective was used. On the other hand, *après* (afterwards) did not lead to shortening or lengthening of processing time. Because the moving window displayed the segments one by one, the reader could not, at the time the connective *après* (afterwards) was encountered, determine whether it was appropriate or inappropriate to the subsequent text segment. From the subject's point of view, the presence of this connective could have been perfectly justified. This result suggests that *après* (afterwards) is treated by subjects as indicative of the fact that the upcoming information should not be integrated into the substructure currently being formed. This result very clearly opposes what has repeatedly been observed for *mais* (but). Indeed, with the latter connective, the faster processing of the segment immediately following suggests that the reader interprets *mais* (but) as an instruction to continue building the current substructure.

Thus, the data obtained in this last experiment support the hypothesis that facilitated processing in unpredictable narratives is immediate, provided certain connectives are used as markers.

6. Concluding remarks

The four experiments reported here show that: (1) When the organization of the event chains of texts are controlled (i.e., when they include at least one complication), 8- to 10-year old children spontaneously add the same connectives, i.e., *mais* (but) and *suddenly* (soudain) and at the same places (i.e., at the beginning of the complication) when they recall the texts. The connectives concerned are thus available and seem to be automatically triggered when their conditions of use are fulfilled. These results reinforce French and Nelson's (1985) conception; (2) the use of the connectives *mais* (but) and *soudain* (suddenly) in narratives brings about an increase in reading speed on the linguistic segment immediately following the connective. This speed increase takes place even when the presentation mode of the segment does not allow the event which is taking place to be understood. This increase therefore does not correspond to a semantic integration process. It is more likely to correspond to a particular mode of processing: advancing the construction of the sub-structure already initiated (Gernsbacher, 1989). The absence of reading speed increase in the presence of *après* (afterwards) reinforces this conception: *après* (afterwards) introduces a deictic change and therefore triggers the construction of a new sub-structure. As a consequence, the incoming information is not integrated into the previous sub-structure and no reading speed increase occurs.

The data reported here thus show that third and fifth graders use at least some connectives both in production and comprehension of written narratives. In production, these connectives are regularly associated with certain kinds of events. In comprehension, they lead to a special mode of processing. These facts can be interpreted within the conception of the Structure Building framework developed by Gernsbacher (1989).

Towards a Better Understanding of Biliteracy

Georges Lüdi

1. What is biliteracy ?

In the textbook on bilingualism, Grosjean (1982:288) presents Samuel Beckett and Vladimir Nabokov as "the proof that one person can write literature in two languages". In fact, the ability to read and write in two languages was part of the myth of 'true' or 'perfect' bilingualism. Writers like Samuel Beckett, Vladimir Nabokov, Elias Canetti and Joseph Conrad were certainly highly esteemed (even if their biculturalism aroused the scepticism of certain nationalistic critiques), but they were exceptional cases. And those who professionally translate from one language to another are simultaneously the object of envy and distrust or even suspicion. They are potential traitors not only in the figurative sense of the Italian proverb "traduttore - traditore", but also more fundamentally because (a) multilingualism has weighed on mankind like a divine curse since the building of the tower of Babel; any one who belongs to two or more cultures is considered not entirely reliable because human beings should be monolingual, and because (b) nations should coincide "naturally" with monolingual language territories - and to be a member of two nations simultaneously seems suspicious (see Griego-Jones, 1994 for references to the situation in the US).

Fortunately, these stereotypes are largely out of date. Today, bilingualism (as a particular case of multilingualism) is defined functionally as the ability to communicate in two (or several) languages independently of the relative level of competence, of the modes and ages of acquisition and of the psycholinguistic relations between the different languages of the speakers' repertoire. Bilingual competence, even an asymmetric one, is increasingly viewed and valued as a resource rather than as a deficit. Indeed, according to this definition, most world's population may be called bilingual.

In the same way, biliteracy (or multiliteracy) can no longer be confused with an exceptional capacity for reading or even writing literary texts in two (or several) languages, but refers to "any and all instances in which communication occurs in two (or more) languages in or around writing" (Hornberger, 1990:213). As in the case of bilingualism, one must therefore look for a functional definition. Following Levine's (1986, 1994) view of 'functional literacy', one should define biliteracy in terms of possession of, or access to, the competences and information required to accomplish literacy tasks in everyday situations in two languages.

(Bi-)literacy is in itself a highly complex competence. Firstly, its acquisition means much more than just the appropriation of one or various graphic codes. Indeed, written language is a specific mode of communication that requires new skills and may even lead to a fundamental reorganisation of communicative competence. In order to be able to use written language to communicate, children have to acquire new ways of controlling their language production. This control is not necessarily needed in everyday oral interaction where they communicate very efficiently, partly because the responsibility for the interaction is shared between the interlocutors (Schneuwly, 1988). The restructuring of the repertoire also has consequences for oral activities such as story telling, explaning etc, and the formal means for doing this may differ from language to language.

Secondly, biliteracy comprises more than just the technical skills required for reading and writing in both languages; it subsumes all the capacities needed to produce and understand written information in the speaker's everyday life. According to Olson (1994), this even leads to changes in the perception of the world and of oneself. In the same way, Street (1994:96) reminds us that literacy and personhood are intertwined in many cultural discourses and "literacy practices are constitutive of identities". This holds even more for biliteracy.

Thirdly, this means that describing universal linguistic and cognitive skills is not sufficient to explain the acquisition of biliteracy, because these capacities are context-bound and linked to specific social situations in either language community (Häcki-Buhofer, 1995). Thus, Street (1994) claims that understanding literacy practices is a matter of describing and interpreting specific cultural processes and epistemologies.

As may have become clear from this introductory lines, biliteracy is an enormously complex phenomenon and we still lack a comprehensive theory that integrates its linguistic, cognitive and social dimensions. Furthermore, Street (1984, 1994) argues convincingly against "one single, unified thing called literacy". As written language is used in many different ways in different domains of daily life, readers and writers are engaged in a variety of *literacy practices*, which leads Street to postulate a *multiplicity of literacies* even in a monolingual society. This leads us to a broad concept of biliteracy, which we might define as *the possession of, or access to, the competences and information required to accomplish literacy practices which an individual wishes to - or is compelled to - engage in in everyday situations in two languages, with their corresponding functions and in the corresponding cultural contexts, independently of the degree of mastery and the mode of acquisition.*

2. Contexts of biliteracy

Acquisition of biliteracy and biliteracy practices always takes place in multiple and complex social situations. They depend on variables such as the status of the languages involved, the values attached to literacy in each culture, the educational policy and instruction models, literacy support in the home environment, etc.

Most research on biliteracy - and most biliteracy programmes - appear to have been drawn up in three contexts:

(1) The biliteracy of immigrant or refugee populations. One of the best known is the Canadian Heritage Language programme established as early a, 1971 in some provinces (Cummins, 1983, Danesi, 1989). In the US, too, bilingual programmes were developed to serve non-English speaking children, mostly speakers of Spanish or, in a few cases, of Chinese, Vietnamese, or Hmong. Their aim is to lead non English-speaking students to academic success through a large variety of types of instruction such as family literacy (Mulhern et al. 1994), ancestral language training (Danesi, 1989), two way bilingual classrooms (Griego-Jones, 1994), etc. As for Europe, different solutions have been chosen in different countries (e.g. Kroon and Sturm, 1989 and Verhoeven, 1994c for the Dutch situation and Perregaux, 1994 for the acquisition of reading by migrant children in Switzerland).

(2) The biliteracy of national minorities in bilingual education models which promote education both in the minority and the majority language. Bilingual education programmes exist for example for Swedish speakers in Finland and for speakers of American Indian languages (see McCarty, 1994 for the latter). Developing countries that chose a language of wider communication as their main educational language and give access to literacy in indigenous languages provide other examples (e.g. Harris, 1990 for the Australian case and Hornberger, 1994 for the situation in Peru).

(3) The biliteracy of majority language populations through second language acquisition, namely in the framework of immersion and of two way bilingual

education programmes, with the linguistic aim of making students bilingual and biliterate so that they can function in and draw benefit from pluralistic societies (Skutnabb-Kangas, 1995). Canadian immersion programmes provide a good example of this.

In the case of students from minorities, the reasons given for biliteracy programmes are both psychopedagogical and social, because the promotion of L1 literacy increases the potential for full literate development and fuller social participation of marginal sectors of the population (Hornberger, 1994).

In many cases, literacy in the language or origin is conceived of as transitional, i.e. it is not a goal in itself because it is a valuable good in the bilingual society; rather it is a route to easier and fuller access to literacy in the dominant host language. Thus, the Bilingual Education Act o, 1974 in the US urged the use of the primary language and culture "to the extent necessary to allow children to progress effectively through the school system" (Mc Carty, 1994). In all these cases, children start with literacy in L1; when they become fluent enough in the dominant language, instruction continues through this medium and the students are later compelled to transfer their competences from L1 to L2. Baker (1996) would call this a "weak" model of bilingual education.

In other cases, on the contrary, "strong" biliteracy programmes for minority populations aim at a more balanced bilingual competence and, politically, at minority language maintenance. This means a shift away from compensatory, deficit-driven approaches and a move to orientations which consider minority or heritage languages as a valuable resource. Where "strong" models of bilingual education exist, biliteracy is valued as a symbolic capital and the adequate use of this competence as a profitable management of resources. In various Southwest Indian communities, bilingual education led to tribal policies designating the tribe languages as official on their respective reservations; and biliteracy took on a new meaning as representative of children's identities (Watahomigie, 1992, quoted by McCarty, 1994). In the case of national minorities, maintenance programmes are frequently seen as the natural kind of education in the sense of a basic human right (Skutnabb-Kangas, 1995), whilst this is usually not the case for immigrant and refugees who are in most cases not accepted as members of language minorities (Lüdi, 1990b).

In bilingual societies, a bilingual's and biliterate's decision to use one or the other language of his or her repertoire - or both at the same time in the case of code-switching - follows regular patterns. In most cases, these choices are not idiosyncratic but governed by a socially motivated, supraindividual "grammar of language choice", where social, linguistic and cognitive factors interact in determining which is the appropriate language choice in a given situation (with an important degree of freedom for the interlocutors to negotiate the choice and, eventually, to break the "rules"). Biliterates thus use various written languages with different functions in different types of "literacy events" (defined by Barton (1994: 187) as activities in everyday life where the written language has a role).

This leads us to the question of the relations between biliteracy and diglossia. In the original conception of Ferguson (1959), the 'high' variety was, by definition, the medium for literacy practices. More recent definitions understand diglossia as a superimposed concept for any forms of socially regulated complementary use of multilingual repertoires in a multidimensional "diglossic space" (Lüdi, 1990a). This includes the case where people have different literacies, i.e. clusters of literacy practices, in both their high and their low variety, associated with different domains of life and embedded in networks of support (Verhoeven, 1994a, 11, with reference to Heath, 1982 and 1983; Barton, 1994). In Switzerland, for example, literacy in the vernacular Swiss German dialects is normally limited to the domains of private life, folklore and advertising.

Where ethnic minorities are biliterate, the two written languages are also often attached to complementary functions, e.g. the heritage language to religious education and personal communication inside the family and the host language to vocational training (e.g. Verhoeven, 1994a, 11). As in the case of bilingualism in general, where very strong links exist between the possession of a bilingual repertoire and a plural identity (Lüdi, 1992, Lüdi, Py et al. 1994), literacies in different languages or varieties are "associated with different personhood and identities" (Street, 1994, 98).

Subsequently, the use of literacy practices in one or the other language has to be interpreted as "acts of identity" (Le Page and Tabouret-Keller, 1989), i.e. as a commitment to a "literate world" the individual wants to belong to. On the other hand, literacy practices in the two languages most probably relate to dominance and differences in power between both groups (Barton, 1994) and corresponding attitudes toward the two languages and communities (Danesi, 1989).

In migrant communities, the functions of the language of origin and the host language respectively may change very rapidly due to insufficient social power of the immigrants and sometimes also in default of a strong will to bear a linguistic value system of their own. What is more, these groups are sharply heterogeneous with important differences between the repertoires of individual immigrants, of groups that migrated together, of parents and children, of children born in the host regions and those following their parents, etc. The family is, then, a place of mediation, but also of tensions between both "worlds" (Lüdi and Py, 1984). This does not mean that biliteracy cannot be functional in the compass of social networks that include members of the host region and other members of the migrant community; however, it may impede the establishing of strong shared norms and, consequently, of bilingual educational programmes and force children into an untutored and idiosyncratic acquisition of literacy in their L1.

3. Aspects of individual biliteracy

The acquisition of literacy is a very important domain of research. Viewed as marginal, biliteracy has received very little attention and empirical studies on the emergence and development of biliteracy with bilingual children outside the context of instructional programmes are almost non-existent. In most research, biliteracy is seen as a pedagogical problem (mainly in the framework of specific models of bilingual education like the Heritage Language model, immersion classes, the two way dual language model or the language shelter model) and/or as a result and product of learning rather than as a learning process.

Much research for example has addressed the question of the degree to which literacy knowledge and skills in one language promote or inhibit the learning of literacy knowledge and skills in the other. Indeed, the most important argument for promoting L1 literacy in bilingual programmes for language minorities - that it facilitates the development of literacy in the socially dominant L2 - is controversial (see Cummins and Swain, 1986 for ethnic minority students in Canada, Goldman and Trueba, 1989 for literacy acquisition in English as second language in the US and Krashen, 1991 for a critical discussion of current research). The main subject of the discussion are the advantages and disadvantages of educational models in a specific social, political and economical setting (e.g. Hornberger 1989, 1990 and 1994, Verhoeven, 1987 and 1994b, Painchaud, 1992). This primarily involves addressing the question of whether bilingual education yields better results than dominant-language-only education[1]; secondly, it questions the validity of the option between:

(a) the "educational human right for any ethnolinguistic minority to use its own language as the main medium of education" (Skutnabb-Kangas, 1995:227) and the understanding that "bilingualism can be a positive force in the intellectual development of immigrant children when their heritage language is promoted at school; (...) by enhancing children's perceptions of themselves and their heritage, the school system can help ensure their academic success" (Danesi, 1989:50), and

(b) strong beliefs about the well-being and/or the professional prospects of the next generation as illustrated by the question "Why isn't my child learning

English?" asked by parents in bilingual classes (confused with 'Spanish' classes) in the US.

Some studies have dealt specifically with the acquisition of literacy by migrant children, but usually from the perspective of the L2 or majority language even if bilingual classes are involved (e.g. Verhoeven, 1987, 1991, 1994b). There is an urgent need for this kind of research because "certain types of bilingualism can become 'problematic' when a society perceives certain complexes of skills to be 'inadequate' or 'inappropriate' relative to the things that have to be done and the conventionalised linguistic means for doing so." (Romaine, 1989:252). This is particularly the case for bilingual but monoliterate migrant children whose oral competence in the language of origin (or heritage language) is not valued in strongly scriptural Western societies - and whose "deficient" competence in the host language represents a serious disadvantage on the labour market. In this context, other studies address the role of negative attitudes toward the minority language in bilingual classrooms (Griego-Jones, 1994).

However, compared with what happened in the case of monolinguals, the cognitive and linguistic dimensions of the development of biliteracy have barely attracted the interest of researchers (the publications of Titone on early bilingual reading since 1977 are an exception).

Before going more deeply into the development of biliteracy, let us recall what the acquisition of literacy generally means in terms of cognitive development. To take the example of production of extended texts, it is well known that children have to learn to manage new and specific situations of communication with a high degree of decontextualisation and without the possibility of relying on the prosodic and non-verbal cues that are common in oral communication. In other words, they have to produce text with a much higher degree of autonomy - what Schneuwly (1988) calls "production autogérée". And they must learn to anticipate the reader's knowledge and to accept the entire responsibility for the coherence and the cohesion of specific types of texts in concrete situations of daily life. In this perspective, (bi)literacy is conceptualised "in general terms of human cognition, enacted as processes of mental problem-solving that integrate discourse, language and semantic information to interpret written documents as reading or to produce them as writing" (Cumming, 1994:5). This means, among other things, constructing new linguistic and cognitive abilities which are part of discourse competence (cf. Bronckart and Schneuwly, 1984; Hickmann, 1987, 1991; Bamberg, 1987; Berman, 1988; Berman and Slobin, 1994; Schneuwly, 1988; Reichler-Béguelin, 1988; de Weck, 1991; etc.). We may assume that the development of literacy occurs in the same way as second language acquisition does, i.e. through interaction, by understanding messages and obtaining comprehensible input with the help of background knowledge (Krashen, 1991). In order to do this, children have to make sense of the literacy practices in their environment (Ferreiro and Teberosky, 1982; Pontecorvo, 1994).

Let us admit that these abilities differ more or less from one language - or social community - to the other. Simultaneous acquisition of literacy in both languages thus means constructing the abilities needed to read and write competently in each language and social context - and to learn to distinguish them. In the case of successive acquisition of two literacies, an important part of the cognitive work has been already done when acquiring literacy the first time. In other words, learners have to construct abilities of a type they already possess, building on existing linguistic, cognitive and socioaffective resources in order to acquire a new set of literacy practices associated with another part of their multilingual identity, in the framework of another linguistic system and along with other social rules.

This can obviously not be done by a simple transfer[2]; on the other hand, the necessary knowledge does not need to be constructed from the beginning because there are interdependencies in the acquisition of biliteracy. The interdependency hypothesis (cf. Cummins, 1993) actually presupposes an underlying common proficiency across languages and predicts "that literacy instruction in one language not only leads to literacy in that language, but also to a deeper conceptual and linguistic proficiency which is strongly related to literacy and general academic skills in the other language" (Verhoeven, 1994b, 217). On the other hand, one may extend the "interlanguage hypothesis" in second language acquisition (e.g. Corder, 1967; Selinker, 1972; Krashen, 1981; Klein, 1989) and hypothesise that elements of literacy already acquired combine in a complex cognitive effort with the "intake" of elements of literacy practices in the target language to form an original "approximate" competence which has its own regularities and differs significantly from either system (cf. Py, 1989).

In the case of significant differences between literacy practices at home, in the minority language, and at school, in the dominant language[3], the child also has to learn to differentiate the specific practices in either language and to acquire the rules for using either literacy appropriately in its contexts. This effort of learning what constitutes legitimate literacy practices in either sociolinguistic group takes place in the interaction where these competences are constructed, ratified and transformed. The process of acquiring literacy is, thus, always situated socially and contextually; and interaction is constitutive of literacy acquisition - as is the case for language acquisition in general (cf. Wertsch, 1985; Salomon, 1993). The concept of formats (Bruner, 1990) helps to understand how the cognitive effort of acquiring literacy practices is supported by interactional routines.

A comprehensive theory of biliteracy has to take account of all these factors and also the multiple relations between bilingualism and biliteracy. On the one hand, biliteracy is not a necessary prerequisite of bilingualism: many bilinguals are not literate at all; and if they are in one, the other or both of their languages, their degree of literacy can be variable. On the other hand, 'partial' or 'unbalanced' bilingualism is more the rule than the exception and depends on the distribution of the languages in the individual's repertoire (see Romaine, 1989:244 ff.). Thus persons or groups can be characterised as being more or less functionally literate in each of their languages and these degrees of literacy do not necessarily follow their overall degree of bilingualism[4].

This leads to the question of assessing biliteracy. Needless to say, polar opposites such as illiterate in L1/literate in L2 are too crude. In fact, opposites of this kind are the theoretical endpoints of what is in reality a continuum. This was one of the starting-points of Hornberger's hypothesis that there may be *continua of biliteracy* (Hornberger, 1989, 1990, 1994). She suggests explaining the multiple configurations of biliteracy in terms of a series of nine interrelated continua. Three of them define the contexts of biliteracy, three the extension of the individual's communicative repertoire and the last three the media through which the biliterate individual communicates.

These continua help to understand the enormous complexity of biliteracy. In order to measure it, we need to define, for each individual, his or her ability to read and/or write more or less complex texts of more or less heterogeneous types in L1 and/or L2 with more or less accuracy or mastery (lexical richness, orthographic correctness etc.) i.e. his or her ability to participate successfully in the corresponding literacy events.

Note that when assessing bilinguals' (and biliterates') abilities, one should not just measure their control over the categories and rules of the monolingual code and practices, some of which do not exist in their own speech (Romaine, 1989:252). Where two languages are in a diglossic relation, an individual's competence in those languages simply reflects their unequal distribution. In order to assess biliteracy, we must take into consideration the social context in which the biliterate skills have developed, the patterns of use of both languages and, more generally, the extent of the literacy resources and needs of the bilingual community (cf. Doets, 1994, for a battery of everyday written language tasks for achieving this).

5. Research needs

As we have already mentioned, an important part of research on biliteracy concerns educational contexts. A question which is almost never addressed concerns situations where literacy is taught in the dominant language to bilingual students who nevertheless feel the need to become literate in their minority home language, as is the case with most migrant communities around the world.

Many migrant children construct, often without formal instruction, a literacy in their L1 (heritage language, language of origin) starting from elements acquired at school in L2 and data in L1 to which they are exposed and that they are able to "take in". Hudelson (1987) claims that literacy develops naturally in learners in a literate environment. This holds not only for the acquisition of orthography - a very popular stereotype fails to distinguish literacy in an additional language from the mastery of its orthography[5] - but also, and to even greater extent, for discursive and textual competences[6].

In this kind of situation, the acquisition of literacy in the language of origin despite a "local-language-only" educational environment is naturally linked to a "heritage language-as resource" orientation. However, it has been hypothesised that there is a significant relation between parents' support for their children's biliteracy in the language of origin and the achievement of these children in the host language acquired at school (Sneddon s.d., Egli, 1995b).

Generally, "not enough attention has been paid to (...) everyday or vernacular learning" (Barto, 1994:193). In these cases, literacy in the language of origin is almost exclusively developed within the context of daily family life, along with the personal goals and language values of the parents who serve as models for using literacy in the language of origin (or biliteracy). As already stated, there has been very little research addressing the linguistic, cognitive and social processes of children's construction of literacy outside the framework of bilingual instructional programmes[7]. In a Vygotskian approach to development, this means the child has to engage in literacy tasks in social interaction with more skilled relevant others (parents, skilled peers or siblings) in order to expand his or her repertoire (cf. Wells, 1990).

In such a context, one might wish to address different types of questions:

(1) A first set of questions addresses the *learning of specific skills*: What form does biliteracy development take in a context of exclusive formal education in the dominant literacy? To what extent is the acquisition of L1 literacy guided (private schooling, parents' help) or spontaneous and unguided? Are there differences between reading and writing and between domains of acquisition (orthography, cohesion, textual organisation, etc.)? To what extent do chil-

dren develop individual learning strategies in answer to personal needs and to what extent are generalisations possible? What are the parents' and the children's attitudes towards each language and biliteracy and to what extent do these representations affect the development of literacy in L1?

(2) Secondly, one might address the question of the steps to be taken in building up the cognitive ability of producing and understanding cohesive and coherent texts in L1 after these abilities have been acquired in L2.

(3) A third set of questions relates to the *social context* of this form of successive acquisition of biliteracy: What type of 'literacy events' do we find in either language and through what type of literacy events does the learning of literacy in L1 take place? What types of literacy practices emerge in this context and how do they develop?

(4) Finally, there are questions of a *comparative nature*: are there differences between the two literacies in terms of degrees of competences, types of literacy events and practices involved, in reading and/or in writing? Are there differences between oral and written capacities and/or practices? To what extent do better knowledge (in the language of origin) and better literacy training (in the local language) determine these differences? Are there traces observable at the surface of texts of divergent courses of acquisition, asymmetric competences and differences in the literacy practices in the family context? Do literacy practices of bilingual children differ from those of their monoliterate pairs and, if so, how?

A research project that started in Switzerland on French-German bilingual children is aimed at addressing a number of these questions with reference to an oral and written narrative production task[8]. In order to reduce the number of variables, we are studying two socioeconomically privileged bilingual communities (German speakers in the French speaking part of the country and French speakers in the German part) that we know well from different previous research projects (Lüdi and Py, 1984; Lüdi, Py et al., 1994). In both contexts, the home language has no official status, but is used daily by an important part of the population of the host region and thus constitutes a valuable resource in the "linguistic marketplace" not only in the value system of the migrant community itself, but also in the eyes of the speakers of the dominant language (see Lüdi, Werlen et al., 1996, for further details). There do exist some institutions which use the home language (associations, parishes), but education is provided strictly on the basis of the local language only and the development of biliteracy takes place outside the framework of formal education, depending less on an analysis of children's needs as on the language loyalty of the family towards the language of origin.

The first results of our research are very promising (Egli and Lüdi, 1994, Egli, 1995a, 1995b). But they call for more research on similar situations but with other linguistic and social variables, with the overall aim of discerning elements of an integrated theory for the acquisition and use of biliteracy practices.

Notes

[1] See Baker and de Kanter, 1983 for a sceptical view; however, Cummins, 1986, Danesi, 1989, Fillmore, 1991 and others argue that native language development offers important cognitive, psychological, and social foundations for the development of non English speaking children, including acquisition of English, with the conclusion that "by developing some degrees of proficiency in their home language, immigrant children will usually have little difficulty acquiring high levels of proficiency in the dominant language" (Danesi, 1989, 48).

[2] It is noteworthy, however, that Krashen (1991) mentions "literacy development in the first language, which will transfer to the second language" as a characteristic of a well-designed bilingual programme. For his part, Verhoeven (1994b, 217) claims that, both in a L2 submersion and a transitional approach of biliteracy instruction, "literacy skills developed in one language turned out to be easily transferred to corresponding skills in the other language." Roberts (1994) convincingly argues that the question of transferability of literacy skills is in large measure related to how literacy is defined: "Encoding and decoding skills and functional abilities generally involve rather low-level skills and are generally agreed to transfer". But this does not hold true for "the values and uses associated with literacy" if we consider the latter as a "way of processing information which will affect ways of interacting".

[3] See Michaels and Collins (1984) for the consequences of such a difference inside monolingual classrooms with students from different social backgrounds. They refer to "sharing times", "a daily classroom activity where children were called upon to give a formal description of an object or a narrative account about some past event. (...) Sharing time served as an interface between oral and literate discourse, incorporating aspects of both informal home-based communication and formal discursive prose. On the one hand, it involved face-to-face interaction, thus resembling communicative events in the home and neighbourhood, with their highly contextualised quality, including the richness of kinetic and intonation cues and the immediacy of audience feedback. On the other hand, children were expected to assume a non-face-to-face stance with respect to their audience and incorporate features of discursive prose into their discourse. Hence, nouns were preferred to gestures or deictic pronouns; shifts between topics were to be lexically or syntactically marked; and no background or contextual knowledge was to be assumed on the part of the audience." (Michaels and Collins, 1984, 221].)

[4] His or her competence in one or the other language may indeed be restricted to oral/aural skills, reading and/or writing may only be present in one language and the relation between orality and scripturality may well be asymmetric. As Baetens Beardsmore puts it: "Since many biliterate bilinguals who regularly use their two languages do so in clearly differentiated circumstances, it is perfectly feasible to envisage the productive bilingual who speaks language A better than he writes it and writes language B better than he speaks it." (Baetens Beardsmore 1986:19)

In a project on early German-French biliteracy in Switzerland a little girl told us she was not able to write *after* having written wonderful texts (certainly in a highly idiosyncratic orthography) because she felt very insecure with regard to the orthography (Egli and Lüdi, 1994).

[6] Notice that even motor abilities are not automatically transferred from one language to the other. Although the scripts are very similar, one of our informants uses a very different handwriting writing for German (where she uses the handwriting learned at school) and French (where her use of block letters reflects her unguided approach to literacy through reading).

[7] See also Cumming (1994:5): "Considerable interest remains in defining the general, psychological dimensions of biliteracy among individual school age learners."

[8] In this project, thirdgraders had to retell the 'frog story' and a similar story about a rabbit in written and oral mode in both languages. Extended questionnaires for parents and children aim at collecting date on their representations and literacy practices in both languages.

Acknowledgments

I would like to thank my research assistants Mirjam Egli and Regula Schmidlin for their comments on an earlier version. My gratitude goes also to David Allerton who carefully read the manuscript and invested a lot of time in turning my prose into understandable English.

Acquisition of Literacy by Immigrant Children

Ludo Verhoeven

The migration of people around the world has a profound effect on literacy education in host countries. When a speech community moves to a new environment the schools in that environment will have to help the immigrant children acquire literacy. Literacy can be taught in the children's mother tongue and in the language spoken in the new environment. Whether one or more languages are used for instruction at school and which language and literacy abilities are taken as educational objectives for immigrant children depends on language education policies.

Ethnic communities are often faced with the task of communicating in the dominant language of a majority environment in order to cope with daily life. Usually, this language is learnt as a second language. From a linguistic point of view people from ethnic minorities are often conceived of as 'second language learners'. However, this conception is problematic for at least two reasons. First of all, not all members of ethnic minority groups acquire the dominant language of the majority environment successfully. In fact, L2 acquisition may come to a halt at a stage that is nowhere near native competence. Secondly, the first language is regarded as a potential source of (un)successful transfer in L2 acquisition, rather than a language variety in its own right. Language varieties of the countries of origin, being learnt in the process of primary socialization, can be a vital instrument for in-group communication. These language varieties may therefore act as valuable symbols of ethnic identity.

Hornberger (1989) proposed a framework for understanding biliteracy development in the individual by defining three continua: oral language-written language, reception-production and L1-L2 transfer. To a large extent progress along these continua is dependent on the instructional alternatives offered to the learner. Different models of literacy instruction in a bilingual context may result in different skills on the part of the learner (cf. Hornberger, 1990). The effectiveness of several instructional alternatives has been discussed in many studies.

It can be assumed that children who receive literacy instruction in a second language are faced with a dual task: as well as the characteristics of written language, they will have to learn an unfamiliar language, referring partly to an unfamiliar cultural background. An essential question is to what extent the development of first and second language literacy skills proceeds interdependently. The interdependency hypothesis, put forward by Cummins (1983; 1984), predicts transfer from L1 to L2, and also from L2 to L1, given positive conditions of exposure and motivation.

This chapter deals with the acquisition of literacy by ethnic minority children. Throughout the chapter references will be made to the results of current and recently completed studies on immigrant communities in the Netherlands. The first generation of these communities moved into the Netherlands during the seventies as foreign workers. The children of these immigrants are rarely given initial literacy instruction in their first language. In the vast majority of cases, instruction is conducted in Dutch from the first year of primary school. In the course of the curriculum some additional instruction is offered in their native language for a few hours a week.

In the first part of the chapter the early acquisition of bilingual proficiency in minority children is examined. Special attention is given to the relationship between oral language acquisition, the development of metalinguistic awareness and emergent literacy. In addition, the processes of learning to read in a second language are explored, particularly the extent to which the processes of learning to read in a second language and in the native language can be compared. The relationship between bilingual development and school success is also discussed, focusing on the notion of transfer in bilingual development throughout schooling. Finally, a perspective on literacy education for ethnic minority children is given.

1. Early bilingualism and emergent literacy

1.1. Acquisition of bilingual proficiency

For many ethnic minority children, their first language development (L1) starts from a favorable position. Its development benefits from rich input from the family and the neighborhood, but later the conditions of exposure to L1 may become very poor. At school the L1 is often banned; at best it constitutes only a minimal portion of the curriculum. Depending on the channels of language input in the home environment, a large variation in first and second language acquisition patterns among ethnic groups can be expected. In a recent study

(Narain and Verhoeven, 1993; Verhoeven, et al., 1993; Verhoeven, 1994a) we examined the patterns of first and second language development of 91 Turkish, 111 Moroccan and 104 Antillean children living in the Netherlands. For an overview of the sociolinguistic background of these ethnic groups, see Extra and Verhoeven (1993b).

Turks form the largest minority group in the Netherlands. In 1990 they numbered 185.000, and there were 33.700 Turkish children in Dutch primary schools. Moroccans, numbering 144.000, constitute the second largest minority group. In 1990 there were 33.000 Moroccan children enrolled in Dutch primary schools. Turkish and Moroccan children are from the second generation: the children of immigrants who moved into the Netherlands over the past few decades. The language patterns of these children can be characterized as follows: they live in primarily ethnic group language-speaking homes with mothers who are almost always monolingual speakers of the ethnic group language. The early language input of the children is restricted to this language, and the Dutch language enters into their lives only gradually, through Dutch playmates and school.

The language situation of Antillean children in the Netherlands, on the other hand, is totally different (cf. Narain and Verhoeven, 1993). The children originate from the islands of Aruba and Curaçao which are part of the Dutch Antilles, a former colony. Whereas in Aruba and Curaçao Papiamentu is used officially and unofficially in almost all domains, in the Netherlands the use of Papiamentu is restricted to intragroup communication. Dutch is becoming the language of intergroup communication and the only language used in school. At present there are about 70,000 people from the Dutch Antilles living in the Netherlands. The profile of the Antillean immigrant in the Netherlands has changed drastically over the past decade. Until the sixties, most of the immigrants were élite students eager to be admitted to Dutch society and willing and able to exchange their mother tongue for the Dutch language. Nowadays the greater part of the Antillean ethnic minority in Holland is made up of young Papiamentu-speaking Antilleans with hardly any education who left their home country because of economic deterioration on the islands. The families consist mostly of single mothers with young children. The low level of schooling in Curaçao generally results in a low proficiency in Dutch.

In a longitudinal study language data were collected at three different times: at the beginning of kindergarten, and after one and two years of instruction in school. Starting from a hierarchical structure of language proficiency, separate tasks were administered, measuring equivalent phonological, lexical, syntactic and textual abilities in L1 and L2: a sound manipulation task requiring children to repeat 25 dyads of monosyllabic words with minimal phonemic differences, a cognitive categorization task in which the child had to select the correct label for color, shape, quantity, space and cause-effect relations (65 items), a receptive vocabulary task in which children had to select the correct referent for a spoken word from four pictures (98 items), a productive vocabulary task requiring pictures to be labelled (40 items), a sentence imitation task in which the reproduction of 40 critical morphosyntactic cues was checked, and a text comprehension task in which children had to answer questions about texts which had been orally presented (20 items). The internal consistency of these measures turned out to be reasonable. In all cases the value of Cronbach's alpha was above .84. Moreover, One-Parameter-Maximum-Likelihood analyses (cf. Verhelst and Eggen, 1991) were carried out on the same tasks to test the homogeneity of the measures taken. In no cases did the assumption of fit of the OPML-model need to be rejected.

Turkish children were found to be most dominant in L1 (especially at lexical, syntactic and textual tasks). Analysis of variance showed that the effects of Time and Language were significant for each task. For Sound Manipulation, Cognitive Categorization and Receptive Vocabulary interaction between Time and Language was also significant, showing that there is a tendency for scores to converge over time.

The Moroccan children also turned out to be dominant in L1, although not to the same extent as the Turkish children. Moreover, the differences tended to become smaller over time. Analysis of variance showed that the effects of Time and Language were significant in all cases. Except for the sound manipulation task the same was true for the interaction between the two factors.

For the Antillean children we found a more or less balanced proficiency level in the two languages. From analysis of variance we learned that the effect of Language was only significant for Sound Manipulation. The effect of time was significant for all measures. The interaction between the two effects was significant for all measures, except Receptive Vocabulary.

We conclude from this study that patterns of bilingual development may be very different for different ethnic groups. An important question is what factors are responsible for these differential patterns of development. Verhoeven (1991a) found that the bilingual proficiency level of 6-year-old Turkish children in the Netherlands was highly related to socio-cultural variables. The children's first language proficiency was primarily related to the cultural attitudes developed by the child and its parents. Their second language proficiency was related to both cultural attitudes and second language input measures.

1.2. Bilingual proficiency and metalinguistic awareness

With respect to cognition, it is also important to evaluate the consequences of bilingual development. It has been shown in several studies that children who learn to use two languages at an early stage enjoy an advantage in a number of cognitive domains (for an overview see Bialystok and Ryan, 1985; Hakuta, 1986; Cummins, 1989). One particular domain is metalinguistic awareness, the conscious understanding and manipulation of the units of language. The awareness of linguistic form and content is crucial for grasping the written code.

In Narain and Verhoeven's study (1993) we also explored the effect of bilingual development on Turkish, Moroccan and Antillean children's phonological awareness in Dutch. For each ethnic group the children were divided into three subgroups according to their L1/L2 proficiency: children with above average scores in both languages, children with above average scores in either L1 or L2, and children with below average scores in two languages. In addition, the mean scores of children in the three subgroups on the following phonological awareness tasks, each consisting of 10 items, were compared: phonemic segmentation, phonemic synthesis, and rhyme. Instructions for these tasks were given both in L1 and L2. All three tasks turned out to be internally consistent: Cronbach's alpha was higher than .84. The results are presented in Table 1.

	phonemic segmentation	phonemic synthesis	rhyme
Turks			
Above average L1 and L2	4.67	7.67	6.41
Above average L1 or L2	2.53	4.24	4.94
Below average L1 and L2	1.55	2.95	4.41
Moroccans			
Above average L1 and L2	5.65	5.12	8.35
Above average L1 or L2	5.08	5.85	8.38
Below average L1 and L2	4.48	4.46	7.14
Antilleans			
Above average L1 and L2	3.21	4.46	8.54
Above average L1 or L2	2.23	2.91	7.23
Below average L1 and L2	0.44	1.06	6.13

Table 1. Mean scores of Turkish, Moroccan and Antillean 6-year-old children with varying language proficiency levels on metalinguistic tasks

The table shows that for each ethnic group the children with a balanced level of bilingual proficiency tended to obtain the highest scores on metalinguistic tasks. Within the Turkish and the Antillean group the differences in scores were significant for all the tasks under consideration and within the Moroccan group for phonemic segmentation and rhyme. This part of the study seems to support the hypothesis that a more or less balanced level of bilingual proficiency enhances children's metalinguistic awareness. As such, there is evidence for the assumption that the development of a high proficiency in two or more languages at an early stage may lead to an advantage in the metacognitive domain.

1.3. Emergent literacy in a bilingual context

Multicultural studies of early literacy show that in spite of differences in cultural background and language diversity, children are able to learn the essentials of literacy at a very early age. Studies from Hanson (1980), Mino Garces (1981), Kupinsky (1983) and Moore (1990) have shown that bilingual children in collaboration with teachers or peers who speak and write are able to acquire literacy skills spontaneously. However, it turns out that there are large differences in the knowledge of, and the desire for, literacy among ethnic minority children entering school. This can be explained by a large variation in literacy support in the home environment. Wells (1985) and Snow and Ninio (1986) have shown that success in early literacy acquisition is related both to the values attached to literacy in the home and to the steps that parents take to explain this value to their children. It is clear that the role of parents in helping their children to (re)discover the principles of literacy is crucial.

In many cases there is a mismatch between the linguistic abilities ethnic minority children bring to the classroom and the language and literacy curriculum at school. Downing (1984) has claimed that the essential features of a writing system will be more readily developed, when literacy instruction is based on familiar exemplars from the mother tongue than in less familiar exemplars from a second language. He suggested that the cognitively confusing effects of teaching literacy in a second language will involve both structural and functional aspects. In a recent study (Verhoeven and Van Kuijk, 1991; Verhoeven, 1995) the acquisitional pattern of linguistic and metalinguistic skills in Dutch as a first and second language was compared. The informants were divided into three groups: high SES Dutch children (1), low SES Dutch children (2), and ethnic minority children (of Turkish and Moroccan origin), all of low SES (3). At age 4, 5 and 6 a battery of tasks, measuring a variety of (meta)linguistic skiills was administered with 298 4-year-old children. For present purposes we will present the results of children's development in receptive vocabulary, nar-

ACQUISITION OF LITERACY BY IMMIGRANT CHILDREN   225

rative skills, phonemic segmentation and phonemic synthesis. In the vocabulary task children had to select the correct referent for a spoken word from four pictures (98 items). In the narrative task children were asked to describe two series of events on the basis of pictures. The coherence of retellings were measured by counting the number of relevant idea units and inferences produced by the child (16 items). The phonemic segmentation task and the phonemic synthesis task consisted of two different series of 10 monosyllabic words. All measures were shown to be internally consistent: Cronbach's alpha higher than .86.

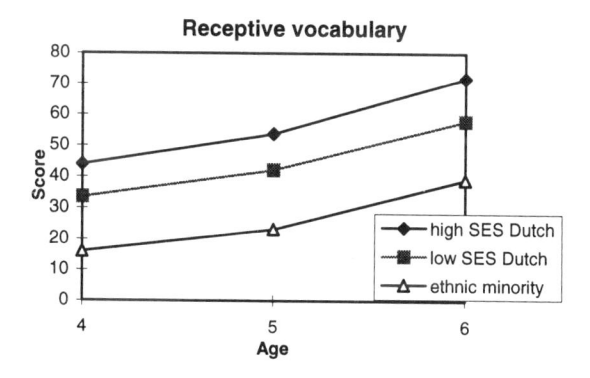

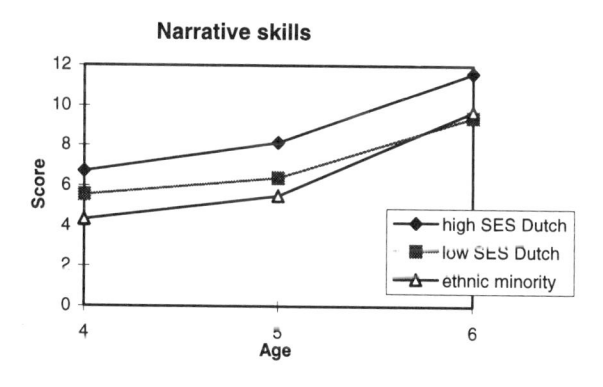

Figure 1. Mean proportion correct scores for high SES and low SES Dutch children and ethnic minority children on the receptive vocabulary task and the narrative task at age 4, 5 and 6.

The results of the receptive vocabulary task and the narrative task are displayed in Figure 1. It shows that that there are large differences in vocabulary development between the three strata: the differences in scores between high and low SES Dutch children are moderate, those between Dutch children and ethnic minority children are large. Analysis of variance showed that the effects of Time and Stratum are significant, whereas the interaction between the two effects is not. Thus it can be concluded that the differences in vocabulary size between the strata remain more or less constant over time.

With regard to narrative competence it can be seen that at age 4 there are substantial differences in scores between the three strata. The differences between high and low SES Dutch children remain more or less constant over time. However, the ethnic minority children seem to make up the initial arrears. The main effects of Time and Stratum turned out to be significant. There was also a tendencial interaction between the two effects.

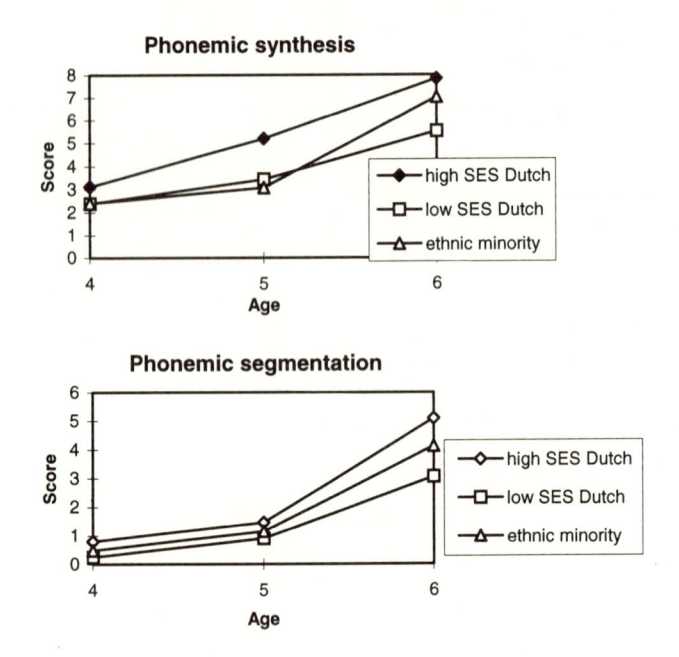

Figure 2. Mean proportion correct scores for high SES and low SES Dutch children and ethnic minority children on the phonemic synthesis task and phonemic segmentation task at age 4, 5 and 6.

Figure 2 presents the results on the phonemic segmentation task and the phonemic synthesis task. It can be seen that there are marginal differences in performance on the two tasks at age 4. The scores tend to diverge in an unexpected way over time: the ethnic minority children outreach the Dutch low SES peers. Analysis of variance showed significant main effects and interactions between effects for each task.

It can be concluded from this study that at the onset of kindergarten there are big differences in proficiency on a variety of (meta)linguistic tasks in Dutch between children of different SES and varying ethnic background: Dutch children from high SES obtain higher scores than Dutch children from low SES, and ethnic minority children obtain lower scores than do Dutch children. In the course of kindergarten, however, some striking developmental patterns take place. While the differences in vocabulary skills tend to remain constant, the differences in narrative skills and metalinguistic skills tend to diminish, or even fade. Apparently, instruction in kindergarten is successful in bridging the gap between children from different strata in narrative skills and metalinguistic proficiency levels but not in L2 vocabulary skills.

1.4. Role of the environment

Research has shown the crucial influence of the home and family on the language literacy development of children. Fantini (1985) showed that various channels of language input in the home environment, such as communication between and with family members and communication with people outside the family, may influence ethnic minority children's language development. According to Tosi (1979, 1984), lack of reinforcement of accepted language norms and exclusion from exposure to the standard language can be responsible for weakening L1 development.

With respect to early literacy acquisition four home factors turn out to be crucial (Teale, 1980, Sulzby and Teale, 1991): the range of printed materials in the home (i.e. written language input), the accessibility of writing materials, the frequency of shared reading and the responsiveness of parents. With respect to the latter, Wells (1985) has demonstrated that the rate of language and literacy development in children is associated with specific characteristics of adult speech. He found that the manner and extent to which adults adjust their speech to the immaturity of their conversational partners affects the ease with which children master the language system(s) under consideration. In functional interaction terms he proposed four broad types of intention to be extremely relevant: (a) maintenance of intersubjectivity, (b) expression of understandable propositions, (c) ensurance of successful communication and (d) stimulation of further interaction.

As to family intervention the media may play a significant role. Television programmes (e.g. Sesame Street), periodicals and public libraries can be seen as possible mediators of the oral and written language input in the family. Furthermore, specific programs can be initiated to help parents collect resources in L1/L2, such as good quality children's books and instruments for drawing and writing. In the same programs the parents' responsiveness can be trained. 'Scaffolding' is seen as a crucial concept associated with parental assistence in children's language and literacy learning. The concept of scaffolding draws on Vygotsky's idea of the 'zone of proximal development', or the distance between the actual developmental level of problem solving and the potential developmental level under guidance of an adult or a more capable peer.

With respect to institutional care, day care, kindergarten and subsequent schooling play an important role in children's early language and literacy learning. These institutional contexts give ethnic minority children the opportunity to use language in a meaningful way and to receive feedback from professional caretakers. It is clear that the instructional approach and the responsivity of teachers play a crucial role. The scaffolding metaphor introduced with family interaction also applies to teacher training. Gaffney and Anderson (1991) underline the importance of an integral relationship between the processes used to prepare experts (both parents and teachers) and the methods they use to teach novices.

In Verhoeven and Van Kuijk's study mentioned above, we examined the extent to which a kindergarten curriculum based on storybook reading and phonological awareness games as a routinized activity had a beneficial effect on children's language and literacy development. We found that in all skills tested the children in the experimental classes did better than in the control classes. The differences were significant for narrative skills and phonological awareness.

Furthermore, in a study by Verhoeven and Van Elsacker (1995) the effect of group setting on interactive storybook reading was explored in multilingual kindergarten classes. 73 children from four schools took part in this study: 20 children were of native Dutch origin, 22 originated from ex-colonial groups (Surinam, Dutch Antilles), and 31 from Mediterranean countries (Turkey, Morocco). The children in these classes heard stories read in two settings: traditional class vs small groups. Two stories with a similar structural pattern were selected from current trade storybooks. For each story 16 comprehension questions were devised. Moreover, a scoring procedure based on current story grammars was provided in order to evaluate children's retellings of the story. Cronbach's alpha, as a measure of reliability, yielded values of .80 and .81 for the story comprehension tasks, and values of .77 and .79 for the retelling evaluations. In two of the schools story A was used in the whole-class setting, and story B in the small-group setting; in the two other schools it was the other way around. The order in which the two conditions were presented was counterbalanced. In both whole-class and small-group settings the children were sitting in a circle around the reader. In the small-group condition there were five children. All storybook reading, both in whole-class and in small-group settings was done by one and the same research assistant, who had previously worked as a kindergarten teacher. The number of probes on the part of the researcher was held constant over stories and over conditions. Each story was introduced by an announcement that interaction during reading of the story was encouraged. On-line observations and audio recordings determined what differences in patterns of verbal exchange there were in the two group settings. Furthermore, analysis of variance with Setting and Ethnic Group as main effects examined to what extent the two group settings led to differences in story comprehension and story recall for both first and second language learners.

The results showed that in general there is much more interaction in small groups whole classes. Both first and second language learners are more engaged in verbal interaction in small groups. The differences in interaction patterns turn out to be consistent over different parts of the story lines. Moreover, both on free recall and on story comprehension it was found that children performed better in small-group settings than in whole-class settings. The effects were equally strong for native Dutch and ethnic minority children. It can be therefore concluded that small-groups tend to promote the language development of both first and second language learners to the same extent.

2. Learning to read in a second language

2.1. Processual characteristics

Bilingual learners bring with them a quite specific information processing system containing two subsystems that are somehow geared to each other, aimed at the comprehension and production of oral and written information in L1 and L2. Starting from this bilingual language user system, the question is in what ways the process of learning to read in a second language may be different from the process of learning to read in a native language. Three possibilities arise: by restricted background knowledge, by interference from L1 and by limited proficiency in L2. However, at the onset of literacy acquition the influence of restricted background knowledge may be considered weak because narratives are highly emphasized in the initial reading curriculum. Two possibilities remain. The question of interference has traditionally been investigated by contrastive analysis. Similarities and differences between two or more languages were taken as a starting point for the interpretation of second language learning problems. However, the debate on the role of interference in second language reading turned out to be far from conclusive (Shuy, 1979; Hall and Guthrie, 1982).

A newer way of looking at L2 learning problems is to refer to substantial similarities between the strategies employed in first and second language learning. Such a design was used in a longitudinal study in which the processes of literacy learning of Turkish children in L2 Dutch were documented and compared with those of Dutch children in their mother tongue during the first two grades of primary school (see Verhoeven, 1987a, 1990a/b). The results of this study show that second language learners are less efficient in various subprocesses of reading and writing than their monolingual peers. Differences in efficiency were found both at the lexical and discourse level of literacy tasks. It can be tentatively argued that owing to limited proficiency in the target language, second language learners have difficulty in both lexical access and context use. With respect to lexical access, it is interesting to note that the nature of such difficulties changed at different stages of development. At first, L2 learners had problems in recoding graphemic strings, then in using orthographic constraints, and finally in attaining direct recognition.

Analysis was also made of whether second language learners learn to profit from contextual facilitation as first language readers do while reading text. In order to answer this question, the word decoding performance of both groups of learners while reading isolated words versus words in context was compared. The orthographic complexity of words in the two conditions was kept constant. For each condition the numbers of words correctly read in one minute were computed after 5, 10 and 20 months of formal literacy instruction. The results are presented in Figure 3.

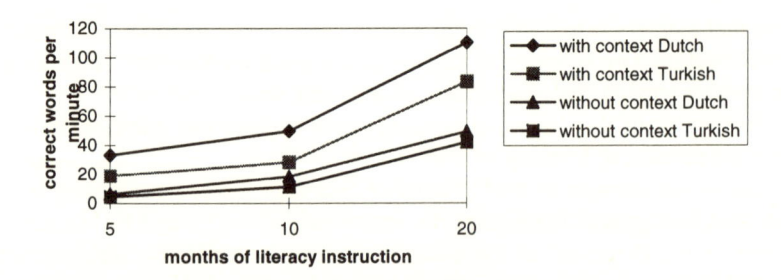

Figure 3. Mean scores of Turkish and Dutch children on reading efficiency with and without context after 5, 10 and 20 months of literacy instruction.

Three-way analysis of variance indicated that the main effects of ethnic group, presence of context and period of instruction were all significant. It can thus be concluded that in text reading Dutch children are more efficient than Turkish children; there is a gain in reading efficiency if words are presented in context, and there is also a gain in reading efficiency as a result of instruction. The interaction between ethnic group and presence of context was significant as well, indicating that Dutch children make better use of context in word recognition than Turkish children.

In addition to the finding that second language learners are less efficient in various subprocesses of reading Dutch, I found that in the acquisition of both lexical abilities and discourse abilities first and second learners relied on highly comparable strategies. At the lexical level it was concluded that the strategies first and second learners use in decoding and encoding isolated words are based on the graphonological structure of the target language Dutch. Moreover, the patterns of misreadings and misspellings in the two groups of learners turned out to be highly comparable. General characteristics were also found with regard to the children's processing of discourse. An analysis of oral reading revealed no evidence of interlingual patterns. Moreover, it was found that semantic complexity does show comparable developmental features in first and second language learners with regard to the understanding of coherence, anaphoric and inferential devices in text.

2.2. Individual variation

In order to explain individual differences in second language reading in an L2 submersion context, the reading comprehension results of the 74 Turkish children were related to various learner variables. Groups of measures of the children's metalinguistic awareness, oral language proficiency, nonverbal cognitive skills and cultural orientation were separately related to their second language reading comprehension results. An attempt was also made to account for bottom up and top down factors in the second language reading process by relating reading comprehension abilities to the children's word reading abilities, their lexical knowledge and their syntactic knowledge.

The longitudinal relationship for reading comprehension was moderate, those for word reading ability, lexical knowledge and syntactic knowledge were strong. From a cross-sectional point of view, the children's word reading abilities strongly predicted reading comprehension. At the end of grade 1, lexical knowledge and syntactic knowledge could also be seen as substantial predictors of L2 reading comprehension. At the end of grade 2, the predictive power of syntactic knowledge increased, while that of lexical knowledge decreased. Apparently, syntactic processing is extremely relevant in the intial stage of L2 reading when lexical knowledge is still minimal. However by the end of the second grade lexical abilities became a significant predictor of word decoding ability. It can thus be concluded that children succeed better in word decoding as more lexical entries are available.

In conclusion, during the first two years of reading acquisition in L2 bottom-up influences seem to be partly replaced by top-down influences. In comparison with research on L1 reading acquisition it seems that the transition from bottom-up to top down processes passes relatively fast. Juel, Griffith and Gough (1986) found a low correlation between the abilities in listening comprehension and reading comprehension with monolingual children in the second grade. The early influential role of top-down processes in L2 reading can tentatively be ascribed to the large individual variation of learners as regards their oral L2 proficiency.

2.3. Causes of class repeating

Children's oral L2 proficiency also turned out to be significantly related to school success. Neither the age level nor the cognitive growth of children explained the teacher's decision that the child should repeat first grade. The teacher's classification of successful and unsuccessful second language learners was much better explained from the children's (meta)linguistic proficiency in L2 at the end of the first grade. The children who were advised to repeat first grade scored significantly lower than the other children on a variety of oral and written proficiency tasks in L2 Dutch. In a discriminant analysis, metalinguistic measures related to literacy, together with global L2 oral proficiency measures, were the most crucial factors in distinguishing between the two groups of children. It was also found that the classification of first grade repeat of second language learners could already be predicted from several L2-related measures at the onset of literacy instruction. Of these, phonemic discrimination and vocabulary size in L2 Dutch turned out to be the best predictors.

An important practical implication of this research is that the acquisition of literacy in a second language requires a certain level of oral proficiency in that language. A minimum level of competence in these two variables seems to be a prerequisite at the onset of literacy instruction for grasping the alphabetical principle in an L2 submersion context. Children with limited L2 oral proficiency should be given the opportunity to build up elementary literacy skills in their mother tongue first.

2.4. Instructional alternatives

With respect to children's cognitive and social development, it can be argued that the acquisition of literacy will be facilitated if the instruction links up with his or her linguistic background. From a cognitive point of view, the transition from oral to written language can be seen as a critical event in the development of children. As Olson (1980, 1991) has pointed out, logical and ideational functions are primary in written communication, whereas oral communication has more informal characteristics. In oral communication the listener has access to a wide range of contextual cues which may clarify the intentions of the speaker, while in written communication such cues are almost completely absent. In a subsequent study Verhoeven (1991b) found that a transitional L1/L2 approach to literacy instruction may have benificial effects. In two small-scale experiments it was found that a strong emphasis on instruction in L1 leads to better literacy results in L1 with no retardation of literacy results in L2. On the other hand, there was a tendency for L2 literacy results in the transitional classes to be better than in the regular submersion classes. Moreover, it was found that the transitional approach tended to develop a more positive orientation toward literacy in both L1 and L2.

3. Bilingualism and school success

3.1. Attaining functional biliteracy

Research conducted in the United States and Europe on the L2 literacy levels of ethnic minority children indicate that they frequently lag behind their monolingual peers (cf. Cummins, 1991). Reports on National Assessment provide evidence that ethnic minority children in the Netherlands attain significantly lower literacy levels in Dutch than native Dutch children. In a study by Triesscheijn, Van den Bergh and Hoeksma (1985) it was shown that ethnic minority children scored lower on a variety of reading and writing tasks. The comprehension of informative texts turned out to be particularly difficult. In a recent assessment study it was estimated that about 15 percent of ethnic minority children can be called functionally illiterate in Dutch (Zwarts, 1990).

An interesting question is what level of first language proficiency will be attained by ethnic minority children in an L2 submersion environment. Owing to a restriction of language models in the community and lack of support for the mother tongue through educational institutions, a stagnation in L1 development can be expected. In a recent study we discovered that this does not necessarily need to occur (Aarts, De Ruijter and Verhoeven, 1994). In this study we collected oral and written language data from Turkish and Moroccan children at the end of primary school. The L1 proficiency of 263 Turkish and 222 Moroccan children in the Netherlands was compared with that of a reference group of 276 Turkish and 242 Moroccan peers in Turkey and Morocco respectively. Six linguistic tasks were administered. In the receptive vocabulary task children had to select the correct referent for a spoken word from four pictures. In the decoding task children had to select the correct referent for a spoken word from four written representations. The spelling task required children to select the right spelling, the sentence judgement the right syntactic construction, and the reading vocabulary task the right meaning from four alternatives. In the reading comprehension task the children had to answer multiple-choice questions along with written texts. The internal consistency of all measures can be called reasonable: Cronbach's alpha was greater than .80 in all cases. The overall results are presented in Table 2.

Tasks	N items	Turkish children in NL	Turkish children in T	Moroccan children in NL	Moroccan children in M
receptive vocabulary	31	77	85	60	91
decoding	35	96	96	79	95
spelling	35	57	76	30	64
sentence judgement	31	70	75	-	-
reading vocabulary	36	66	79	34	77
reading comprehension	19	59	53	50	91

Table 2. Mean percent correct scores on Turkish and Arabic language tasks of Turkish and Moroccan children in the Netherlands and in Turkey and Morocco at the end of primary school

In addition to these tasks we introduced the Functional Literacy Task, which was designed to measure the abilities and knowledge required for the performance of literacy tasks in everyday life. In recent literature it has become evident that the literacy tasks generally taught in schools may not include these everyday tasks. Spratt et al. (1991) developed the so-called "Household Literacy Assessment". This instrument was composed of a series of tasks representing the sorts of literacy activities that are commonly practiced in Moroccan households. The Household Literacy Assessment measured children's ability to make sense of the written features of four items: a letter, a newspaper, an electricity bill and a medicine label. Likewise we developed the Functional Literacy Task, which consists of a letter, a page of a television guide, the frontpage of a newspaper

ACQUISITION OF LITERACY BY IMMIGRANT CHILDREN 235

and an application form. These items are commonly found in Turkey, Morocco and the Netherlands. Children encounter these items in everyday life, so the literacy activities they ask of the children are functional everyday ones. We gathered authentic material in Turkey, Morocco and the Netherlands. The tasks were constructed in a parallel fashion in the three languages concerned: Turkish, Moroccan and Dutch. The questions involved the addressee and the sender, the time a certain program starts, the date of the newspaper, the place to sign the form, etc.

In order to uncover the impact of a first or a second language environment on functional literacy skills, we compared the results of pupils in the Netherlands with those of pupils in Turkey. The results are given in Table 3.

Group	n pupils	Mean	Sd	% correct
Netherlands	155	31.20	4.5	78
Turkey	209	32.97	4.1	82

Table 3. Differences on the functional literacy task between pupils in the Netherlands and pupils in Turkey

The table shows that the pupils in the Netherlands are reasonably successful on the functional literacy task. They seem capable of solving functional tasks which they might encounter in their native language. However, the pupils in Turkey perform significantly better on the functional literacy task than the pupils in the Netherlands (t=3.90, p<.001). This finding indicates that growing up and going to school in Turkey not only has an impact on school literacy skills, but also on functional literacy skills. The results of the Turkish children on a comparable task for functional literacy in Dutch turned out to be more or less similar (mean = 32.47) and just below the functional literacy level of their Dutch peers (mean = 33.22). The latter difference was significant.

In order to explore the impact of a first or a second language environment on functional literacy skills, we compare the results of pupils in the Netherlands with those of pupils in Morocco. The results are presented in Table 4.

Group	n pupils	Mean	Sd	% correct
Netherlands	151	4,44	5,8	19
Morocco	242	18,95	2,8	79

Table 4. Differences on the functional literacy task between pupils in the Netherlands and pupils in Morocco

The Moroccan children in the Netherlands perform very poorly on the Arabic functional literacy task. The majority of the pupils could not answer any of the questions. Sometimes they indicated that they could understand the texts and the questions but were unable to produce the answers. Productive tasks in Standard Arabic seem to be quite difficult for the Moroccan children in the Netherlands. The same tasks were not a great problem for the children in Morocco, who performed well. These results correspond to the results of Spratt et al. (1991), who found the same percentage of correct answers on their Household Literacy Assessment for pupils in grade six in Morocco. The Moroccan children did much better on the functional literacy task in Dutch (mean = 28.89). However, their scores were significantly lower than those of their Dutch peers.

It can be concluded from this part of the study that the pattern of literacy development in distinct ethnic groups can be markedly different. In our case the Turkish children attained a biliteracy level with native-like performance in the mother tongue, and only a slightly lower literacy level in Dutch in comparison with their Dutch peers. The Moroccan children, on the other hand, obtained a relatively low literacy level in the ethnic group language and a moderate literacy level in Dutch. The results can partly be explained by different literacy practices in the two groups. Among first generation Turkish immigrants it was estimated that about 15 percent of the men and 45 percent of the women were illiterate. Among the first generation Moroccan immigrants the estimates were 66.4 and 90.2 percent. Moreover, within the Turkish community a much greater number of written media are used in the native language than in the Moroccan community.

3.2. Bilingual proficiency and school progress

In the study by Aarts, et al. an attempt was also made to explain individual differences in first and second language literacy levels of Turkish and Moroccan children in terms of learner, family and educational characteristics. For the Turkish group it was found that the variables of children's self-esteem, parental support, and the proportion of immigrant children in school explained about 38 percent of the variance in literacy scores. About 12 percent of the variance in their first language literacy scores was predicted by the variables of self-esteem and parental support. The L1 instruction variable turned out to be another relevant predictor. For the Moroccan group parental support was the most relevant predictor, explaining 26 percent of the variance in Dutch literacy scores. About 34 percent of the variance in first language literacy scores was explained by the cultural orientation of the child and parental support. Out-of-school instruction in Arabic turned out to be another relevant predictor.

In the same study we found that the first language proficiency of Turkish and Moroccan children by the end of primary school correlated positively with their success in secondary school. There were positive correlations between factor scores of oral and written L1 proficiency and level of schooling after one and two years of secondary school. In addition, multiple regression analyses were carried out with the children's success in secondary school as dependent variable and their level in L1 proficiency, L2 profiency and mathematics at the end of primary school as independent variables. It was found that along with the L2 proficiency and mathematics scores, written L1 proficiency predicted the success of Turkish and Moroccan children at school.

3.3. Transfer in bilingual development

With respect to the individual variation in literacy success and literacy motivation in bilingual instruction models, the notion of interdependency is highly important. With respect to the acquisition of cognitive/academic language skills such as reading and writing, Cummins (1983) has put forward the interdependency hypothesis which says that:

> To the extent that instruction in a certain language is effective in promoting proficiency in that language, transfer of this proficiency to another language will occur, provided there is adequate exposure to that other language (either in the school or environment) and adequate motivation to learn that language.

The hypothesis not only predicts transfer from L1 to L2, but also from L2 to L1, unless the exposure and motivation conditions are negative.

In a bilingual program, the interdependency hypothesis would predict that reading instruction in one language not only leads to literacy skills in that language, but also to a deeper conceptual and linguistic proficiency which is strongly related to literacy and general academic skill in the other language. In other words: although surface aspects of linguistic proficiency, such as orthographic skills, fluency, etc. develop separately, an underlying proficiency is presupposed which is common across languages and which is said to facilitate the transfer of cognitive/academic skills such as literacy-related skills across languages.

Cummins (1984) attempted to conceptualize language proficiency in such a way that the developmental interrelationships between academic achievement and language proficiency in both L1 and L2 can be more fully understood. He integrated his earlier distinction between basic interpersonal and cognitive/academic language skills in a new theoretical framework by conceptualizing language proficiency along two continua. The firstl continuum relates to the range of contextual support for expressing or receiving meaning. The extremes on this continuum are described as 'context-embedded' versus 'context-reduced'. In context-embedded communication, meaning is said to be actively negotiated by participants who give each other feedback and supply paralinguistic cues in case meaning is not fully understood. In context-reduced communication, learners are said to be entirely dependent on linguistic cues for meaning and in some cases to suspend knowledge-of-the-world in order to interpret the logic of the communication.

The second continuum in Cummins' framework is intended to address the developmental aspects of language proficiency in terms of the degree of active cognitive involvement necessary for appropriate performance on a task. Cognitive involvement is conceptualized in terms of the amount of information which must be processed simultaneously or in close succession by the individual. As such, the upper part of the vertical continuum refers to tasks in which language processes become largely automatized, while at the lower end active cognitive involvement is required.

According to Cummins (1984), the above framework permits the developmental interrelationships between proficiency in L1 and L2 to be conceptualized. First, he proposed that such interrelationships can predominantly take place in the case of performance on academic tasks. A task is defined as progressively more academic as context-reduction and cognitive demands increase. Cummins suggested that the transferability across languages of many of the proficiencies involved in reading and writing is obvious because they strongly incorporate context-reduction and cognitive demands. In a review of studies on bilingual development, Cummins (1989, 1991) concluded that research evidence shows consistent support for the principle of linguistic interdependency in a variety of linguistic domains, including literacy.

In the mentioned study by Narain and Verhoeven (1993) the role of interdependency in the early bilingual development of Turkish, Moroccan and Antillean children was explored. Linear structural analysis on factor scores of L1 and L2 tasks provided evidence of substantial transfer taking place from one language to the other. Verhoeven (1991a/b, 1994b) also found empirical evidence for the interdependency hypothesis in a study on biliteracy development of Turkish children in the Netherlands. Word decoding skills and reading comprehension skills being developed in one language turned out to predict corresponding skills in another language acquired later. Interdependency for word decoding could be explained by the cognitively demanding nature of the metalinguistic skills required. For reading comprehension, the decontextualized nature of text handling seemed the best explanation.

Both studies are more or less in line with earlier research. As such, they provide a cross-validation of the hypothesis that biliteracy education entails no negative consequences for children's linguistic and academic development.

4. Final remarks

In a multi-ethnic society, ethnic communities may use various written codes serving at least partially distinct sets of functions. The written code with the highest status will primarily be used in societal institutions, whereas the written code of the ethnic group language will be used for intragroup communication and expressing one's ethnicity. A further written code may be used for religious identification. In order to do justice to the literacy needs of ethnic minorities, the competence of functional literacy should be defined in terms of their multilingual and multicultural background. With an eye on assessment it is important to evaluate to what extent people belonging to an ethnic community are literate in the ethnic group language, in the language of wider communication, or in another language. It is essential to assume that literacy skills in all these languages are seen as relevant human resources. With respect to the acquisition of literacy, there is clear evidence that the motivation of children to learn to read increases as they become more familiar with the language and as they find themselves more competent at accomplishing school tasks in that language (see Gillmore and Glatthorn, 1980; Trueba, Guthrie and Au, 1981).

Whether one or more languages are used at school and which language and literacy abilities are taken as educational objectives for ethnic minority children have been extensively discussed (cf. Verhoeven, 1994c). In evaluation studies the position of the L2 submersion approach to literacy instruction has been complicated by strongly conflicting results in different settings. In experimental bilingual programs in Canada (immersion programs) it was found that children speaking English as a majority language reached a high level of L2 French literacy skills without their L1 literacy skills lagging behind (e.g. Lambert and Tucker, 1972; Genesee, 1984; Kendall, et al., 1987). Opposite results were obtained in studies of direct literacy instruction in L2 in the United States and Europe when L1 was an ethnic community language with a low level of societal prestige. This contradiction may be resolved by assuming that in the latter context the learning of L2 reflects the loss of L1. Poor results in both languages will then be the consequence, because of feelings of ambivalence on the part of the ethnic community toward the majority group and the majority language.

The debate on bilingual education should be evaluated against the background of a restricted perspective of ethnic minority children in terms of socio-economic and second language 'deficits' rather than ethno-cultural differences. Policy makers in both Northern America and Europe have looked upon home language instruction as a temporary facility for low SES ethnic minority children. Their focus was on bridging the mismatch in language use in the home and the school while aiming at higher results in the majority language. However, home language instruction can also be conceived of in terms of affirmative cultural policy (cf. Extra and Verhoeven, 1993). From a cultural perspective home language instruction can be defined as a structural facility for children with a non-native home language, independent of socio-economic background. Contribution to first language learning is then defined as an autonomous goal. As such, first language proficiency is seen as a school subject and being evaluated accordingly.

With respect to the use of language and literacy two world-wide trends can be observed. On the one hand, there are processes of unification and internationalization through mass media, trade, labor migration and tourism. On the other, there is a growing awareness of the significance of cultural and linguistic diversity. A basic policy question in the area of institutional support is how to reconcile the opposing trends of unification and diversification of different communites in multi-ethnic societies. This question also dominates the language debate, given the fact that languages are prominant features of both trends and also that, within educational contexts, languages are relatively easy to promote or neglect.

It is important to note that a second-language-only approach to literacy teaching does not fit very well with the linguistic and socio-cultural background of ethnic minority children. Research data show that simultaneous and successive literacy instruction in two languages is feasible. Such programs appear to be capable of improving students' academic proficiency and not to result in any retardation of second language literacy skills. Moreover, ethnographic studies make clear that literacy in the L1 ethnic language may help to enhance community and cultural identity. Thus, both cognitive and anthropological arguments speak in favor of a biliteracy curriculum. However, educational programs for ethnic minority communities are not generally determined by psychological arguments or evaluation studies, but rather by political factors. The language policies of regional and national authorities determine whether or not ethnic communities will be in the position to become literate in the majority language, as well as in the ethnic group language.

PART IV

Writing systems, brain structures and languages:
A neurolinguistic view

Domain-Specificity and Fractionability of Neuropsychological Processes in Literacy Acquisition

Giuseppe Cossu

1. Introduction

Unlike most of the contributions to this book, the analysis to be presented here examines the acquisition of written language from a peculiar standpoint. It concentrates upon the biological side of literacy, aiming to outline some of the architectural constraints that shape the development of reading and writing.

The study of the cognitive/biology interface presupposes a distinction between levels of analysis (Marr and Poggio, 1977) and a specification of the principled constraints that relate the cognitive dysfunction (or the normal function) to the underlying neural architecture. Although it is not in dispute that some relation holds between particular parts of the brain and a particular cognitive function, the nature of the interface is far from uncontroversial. In the first place, even the simplest cognitive function is mediated by a cluster of distinct computational components, so that any impairment in the sequence suffices to disrupt the processing of the system. Second, the neural representation of each component of the function can hardly be localized within one circumscribed neural site, as it involves more than one cortical (or subcortical) area.

Two major consequences follow from these architectural constraints: 1) we cannot map a cognitive function directly onto the neural anatomy; 2) the relation between biology and cognition cannot be addressed unless some specification of the cognitive system has been set out in advance. Unfortunately, these methodological concerns have rarely surfaced in the analysis of literacy acquisition.

Whenever research into developmental dyslexia has turned its attention to the biology of literacy, the main target of inquiry has been either the location of brain damage, or the detection of qualitative neural alterations. In the first case (Hinshelwood, 1917), and despite Jackson's protest (Jackson, 1874), the location of the brain damage that impairs a particular function has been mistaken for the location of the function. When a qualitative analysis of the brain became available (Galaburda and Kemper, 1979; Galaburda, Sherman, Rosen, Aboitiz and Geschwind, 1985), no reference to a specific cognitive architecture was made, thus leaving unspecified the question of whether the documented neuronal anomalies were primarily involved in the orthographic processes or were simply correlational. Furthermore, the evidence for a causal role of genetic variables, though admittedly relevant, is usually left in the uncertain domain of the nature/nurture controversy (Smith, Kimberling, Pennington and Lubs, 1983; Scarborough, 1981).

The interface issue is not clarified any better by the cognitive analysis of reading acquisition, since it tends to widen the distance between biology and literacy. Within the standard view, reading acquisition is recognized as a cultural and intellectual enterprise, whose fundamental variables are deemed to be an adequate educational environment and access to phonemic awareness. As a consequence, the role of the biological components in reading acquisition is usually neglected and when the issue emerges, it is claimed that no pre-specified brain structures can exist for the computation of the reading processes. Thus it is no surprise that an "unconventional" hypothesis purporting pre-specified biological components for literacy (Marshall, 1984; Marshall, 1989) has provoked more than the mere raising of eyebrows (Ellis, 1985).

The pre-eminence of the "cultural" view notwithstanding, some clinical dissociations suggest that the child's biological endowment may be playing a more direct role in shaping the growth of the reading architecture than hitherto suspected.

In this chapter I will approach the study of the biology of reading by examining those developmental dissociations that selectively impair distinct computational components of reading (and spelling), or, conversely, leave one single component (or the whole function) selectively spared, in the face of a general cognitive impairment. The preliminary data from this "decompositional" approach reveal the functional independence of the core components of reading (and spelling), thus suggesting that a specific neural architecture is subserving the process of literacy acquisition.

2. Historical digression and clinical paradoxes

Approaching the acquisition of literacy from a biological perspective meets with substantial criticism, since the dominant view holds that reading is an essentially "unnatural" learning task. At first sight, the argument sounds convincing. Literacy is generally regarded as a "cultural invention" (Harris, 1986) of recent origin and it is credited with having evolved through stages of environmental adaptation (Gelb, 1963).

Historically, the emergence of literacy can be traced back to 8.000 BC if we posit a continuity between partial and full writing systems. Earlier notational systems, like the oldest clay pebbles (around 8.000 BC) and the inscriptions of the Uruk IV period (around 5.000 BC) have been regarded as precursors of writing (Schmandt-Besserat, 1978). Current historical analysis, however, suggests that no filiation can be postulated between the pre-existing limited notational systems and the full systems of writing (DeFrancis, 1989). The earlier inscriptions represented picturable objects or numbers and were confined to the domain of economic transactions. Most important, those notational systems retained no trace of the language, whereas all full writing systems were (and are) based upon the transcription of sub-lexical components of the language (be they morphemes, syllables, phonemes, or a combination thereof) into corresponding visual characters.

Scholars of the history of writing acknowledge that the earliest full system of writing was developed by the Sumerians around 3.000 BC, when pictograms were used for their phonetic value, thus marking a crucial shift from earlier notational systems.

The oldest existing writing system, the Chinese script, was highly developed by around 1.200 BC. The case for a recent origin of literacy is further strengthened if we consider that the alphabetic system made its appearance around 500 BC. This digression into the history of writing marks the chronological cornerstones of literacy and implicitly delineates the arguments advocated by the standard view on reading acquisition. 1) An extremely short time (from an evolutionary perspective) has elapsed since the appearance of writing; 2) Until very recent times, elitist access to literacy was the rule; 3) The invention (and the individual acquisition) of literacy implies awareness and explicit computation of the phonological structure of the word; 4) The acquisition of reading requires formal teaching and dedicated learning.

The implications from these premises are straightforward. As Ellis asserts: "Given writing's late entry into the evolutionary stage, there is no way that the genetic endowment of the Homo Sapiens neonate can include a Language Acquisition Device containing protomodules specifically ear-marked for the processing of the alphabetic scripts". Therefore, "..when developmental dyslexia is concerned, such deficits as exist cannot be component specific to reading or writing" (Ellis, 1985).

In clinical experience, however, several paradoxes appear which cannot be accommodated within such a "cultural" view of reading acquisition. Some children show a persistent impairment of reading, in spite of motivation, educational opportunity and normal (or above normal) levels of intelligence. Other children, though affected by severe mental retardation, may nonetheless become fluent readers within a few months of school and without special teaching. Furthermore, at least in transparent orthographies, good mastery of reading is achieved within a few months; after six months of teaching, Italian first graders can read correctly 92.1% of words and 81.7% of non-words (Cossu, Gugliotta, and Marshall, 1995). Finally, the dissociation between reading and spelling of the same words and non-words suggests that distinct processing components may be involvesd in the two tasks. The convergence of these paradoxes weakens the role of general intelligence and of intellectual learning in reading acquisition, and gives pre-eminence to the role of pre-specified biological components.

3. The "extrinsic" factors

Further evidence against the hypothesis of domain-specificity for literacy acquisition is to be found in the heterogeneity of reading disorders. A cohort of multiple cognitive impairments, ranging from mental retardation to language disorders, motor disabilities and impairment of representational space, is often concomitant with reading and writing disorders. The occurrence of this "extrinsic" symptomatology is so common that, for a long time, its causal role has been taken for granted: the associated symptoms were held responsible for the disorders of reading and writing acquisition (Benton and Pearl, 1978). Although no principled explanation was provided for how the concomitant deficits interfered with the orthographic processes, the association was accepted as a criterion for the dichotomic taxonomy of specific vs. general reading disabilities. The distinction was however reduced to a mere fiction, since the same extrinsic factors (in a "subtle", or a manifest form) were pre-theoretically assumed as causal variables for both specific and general reading disabilities.

A first attack against some components of the extrinsic factors hypothesis was launched 17 years ago by Vellutino (1979) who showed that neither the visual-spatial nor the perceptuo-motor or rhythm hypotheses survived critical scrutiny. Children with specific reading disorders and normal readers performed at identical levels of accuracy on non-verbal tasks, whereas the linguistic tasks occasioned lower performances by poor readers (Vellutino, 1979).

The linguistic hypothesis gained increasing consideration, as experimental research confirmed the discrepancy between good and poor readers in the linguistic domain. The linguistic approach to reading disorders was further strengthened by a sophisticated theoretical framework: orthography was viewed as parasitic to language and interpreted as a secondary linguistic activity (Mattingly, 1972). Unlike natural languages, reading was viewed as an "unnatural" act and interpreted as a kind of problem solving, based upon acquired knowledge of the alphabetic principle.

Within this framework, reading acquisition requires access to phoneme awareness, i.e. an explicit knowledge of the constituent phonemes of the language and the ability to manipulate the phonological structure of the word. Experimental evidence has been collected showing that an increase in orthographic proficiency is systematically related to corresponding degrees of efficiency in tasks of phonemic awareness: poor readers of normal intelligence lag behind their age-mates in metaphonological tasks (Goswami and Bryant, 1990). The principal obstacle to reading acquisition is therefore held to derive from difficulties in gaining conscious access to and in the explicit manipulation of the phonological string.

The intellectual approach to reading finds further support in a line of research that postulates a strict (indeed a causal) relationship between general cognitive development and reading acquisition. One such model of reading acquisition (Marsh, Friedman, Welch and Desberg, 1981) maintains that any new achievement in the orthographic "process sequence" stems from a corresponding change in general cognitive development.

In a similar vein, Ferreiro and Teberosky pioneered a line of research aimed at revealing the hidden world of the child's conception of reading. They found that the early reader may have peculiar conceptions of the written word: "Writing *papa* is more difficult than writing *my brother goes to school*, because papa is taller " (Ferreiro and Teberosky, 1985:220). As the authors state "the written names of people are expected to be related to (physical) dimension, or to age, but not to the length of the corresponding name" (Ferreiro and Teberosky, 1985:221). These notions and the rich contributions by Ferreiro and Teberosky document the preschool-child's strategies in differentiating semantics from phonology, as well as scribbles and pictures from printed words. It should be noted, however, that improvements in the conceptualization of the writing system may not necessarily correspond to an increased efficiency in the specific (and automatic) processes actually subserving the transcoding processes of reading and writing.

All the diverse approaches to reading acquisition that I have outlined share the common feature that no component (or process) is ontogenetically specific to reading. According to these conceptions, the architecture of reading is assembled from the outside, either by relying upon other functions (extrinsic to reading), or by an explicit and intellectual manipulation of the phonological structure of the word. In neither case is there consideration for specificity of the reading processes. As mentioned earlier, however, there are clinical paradoxes that raise doubts as to the validity of the "extrinsic" hypothesis

4. External boundaries

Explanations by association imply an axiomatic proposition of the kind: "If A, then B". The logical interdependence between two synchronically occurring events explains why any dissociation thereof undermines the proposition with disruptive effect. It may be for precisely this reason that the clinical evidence for dissociations between reading and other cognitive functions has gone totally unnoticed or banished to anecdotal reports, until recent times. The "hyperlexic" child was merely a clinical curiosity, devoid of any scientific relevance. However, it is sufficient to cast the events within a developmental frame to immediately pose two relevant questions: 1) What prevents an intelligent (dyslexic) child from acquiring orthographic skills?; 2) How can a hyperlexic child, in spite of mental retardation and neuropsychological disorders, achieve mastery of reading qua transcoding skills? A tentative answer to these questions emerges from the inspection of some clinical cases.

4.1. Motor impairment and reading

Pre-natal brain damage may sometimes produce congenital tetraplegia and anarthria. In this clinical condition, children are unable to plan and execute any purposeful movement: they cannot walk, move their arms and utter any sound. Usually, motor impairment and absence of speech is associated with mental retardation and severe comprehension deficits. In some cases, however, these young patients may reveal striking dissociations between motor impairment and cognitive-linguistic development.

F.C. was a 15 year old boy at the time of first testing (Cossu, Urbinati and Marshall, 1987). No purposeful movements were available to him except partial turning of the head to the right and the eye movements. This limited motor repertoire allowed F.C. to push a single all-purpose key, which in turn activated a special computer program for writing. Through this laborious procedure, he was able to communicate. On oral presentation of the PPVT he earned a score of 117 correct responses, corresponding to a verbal IQ of 120. On the WISC verbal scale, F.C. obtained a verbal IQ of 95. Reading words and non-words was tested by presenting him with 80 cards, each containing four printed items; for each card, F.C. had to point to the corresponding item (40 words and 40 non-words) pronounced by the examiner. Correct responses were 80 out of 80. By means of the special computer, we were able to test his writing skills as well. In writing the same list of words and non-words to dictation, F.C. obtained a correct score of 62 out of 80 and all of the 18 errors were single letter substitutions, or elisions. He also succeeded in producing the sentences needed in interactive conversation. Metalinguistic skills were likewise excellent, as appeared from a phoneme segmentation and a phoneme deletion task, where F.C. earned 80% and 85% correct responses respectively (the responses were printed on the screen by F.C.). It appears that congenital motor impairment is neither a necessary nor a sufficient condition to prevent the acquisition of full literacy skills.

4.2. Mental retardation and reading

Reading and writing acquisition can also circumvent mental retardation, clumsiness and disorders in space representation. T.A., a 9 year old boy, who attended the third elementary class is one such case (Cossu and Marshall, 1990). His full scale IQ is as low as 45 and his clumsiness and constructional apraxia is so severe that not one of the drawings he makes reveals the slightest resemblance to the target. T.A. fails to reproduce simple geometric figures with sticks and, on the PPVT, he obtains a raw score of 45; this corresponds (on American norms) to a mental age of 4.6 years. On the Token test, T.A. scored 10/36. In the final syntactic section he scores 0. His verbal memory span for digits is 2 forwards and 0 backwards. No phonological and no morpho-syntactic deficits were detectable in his spontaneous speech.

These pervasive neuropsychological and linguistic disorders notwithstanding, T.A. is an excellent reader. His teacher confessed in embarrassment that he was the best reader in his class. For each reading task T.A. was presented with, the reading scores were systematically 100% correct for both words and non-words.

4.3. Outstanding intelligence and reading

The prototypical dyslexic reader is a mirror (and paradoxical) image of the hyperlexic child. This contrast is vividly rendered by the case of M.F., a 12 year old boy with outstanding cognitive skills a full scale (WISC) IQ of 136 and a verbal scale IQ of 144 (Cossu, Maggetti and Marshall, 1996). His auditory and visual discrimination, as well as praxic skills are excellent, whereas marked deficits appear when M.F. is required to read and write. At the age of 8.6 years, for example, in reading a list of complex words and non-words (5 and 7 letters length, containing geminates and other consonant clusters), his error percentages were 21% (11 minutes) and 19% (14 minutes), respectively. An age matched control group showed corresponding error percentages of 2.5% (2 minutes, 10 secs.) for words and 3.7% (2 minutes and 40 secs.) for non-words. In writing the same list to dictation M.F.'s error scores were 19% (23 minutes) for words and 28.1% (27 minutes) for non-words. The control's error scores were 3.1% (6 minutes and 50 secs.) and 4.3% (8 minutes and 30 secs.) for words and non-words, respectively. No impairment of purely phonological discrimination and phonological output (repetition of words and non words) was evident.

4.4. Phoneme awareness and reading

In summarizing the cases of hyperlexia and developmental dyslexia, I have deliberately omitted consideration of phonemic awareness. The argument deserves treatment of its own since, in the current literature, phoneme awareness is recognized as a prerequisite for reading acquisition. The data to be presented here, however, raise some doubts about the commonly held view of a causal relation between reading acquisition and phoneme awareness.

T.A., the hyperlexic child, fails in metalinguistic tasks in spite of his excellent reading and writing skills. In a Phoneme Segmentation task he performed 5/45 correct; in a Phoneme Deletion task, T.A. gave 18/42 correct responses. A control group matched for age (and reading level) gave 43/45 and 37/42 correct responses in Phoneme Segmentation and Phoneme Deletion tasks respectively. Similar discrepancies between poor phoneme awareness and excellent reading skills were reported in two other hyperlexic children (Cossu and Marshall, 1986).

A systematic investigation of the dissociation between reading and phonemic awareness has recently been reported in a homogeneous sample of Down's Syndrome children (Cossu, Rossini and Marshall, 1993). Ten Italian children with Down's Syndrome (mean age 11.4 and mean IQ 44) and ten chronologically younger normal children (mean age 7.3 and mean IQ 111) were matched for reading ability. In one of the reading tasks (Sartori, 1984), the correct percentage for words (n=40) were 93.8% and 92.8% in the Down's and the control group, respectively. In reading non-words (n=40) the Down's syndrome children and the normal children were 88% and 82.5% correct respectively. No statistically significant difference for reading ability was detectable between the groups. The two samples were then presented with four distinct metalinguistic tasks. The mean percentage correct responses were the following for the Down's patients and the normal children: 1) Phoneme Segmentation: 31.9 vs. 95.7; Phoneme Deletion: 8% vs. 76.5%; Oral Spelling: 8.6 vs. 88.1%; Phonemic Synthesis: 21% vs. 74.5%.

Further evidence for a dissociation between reading achievement and phoneme awareness emerges from developmental dyslexia in both transparent and deep orthographies. M.F., the Italian dyslexic boy mentioned earlier, revealed brilliant mastery of metaphonemic skills, in spite of his severe reading disorders. Phoneme Segmentation for orally presented words was 45/45 correct. Phoneme Synthesis (into words) of 4,5,6,7,8, phonemes was 25/30 correct. A developmental case of phonological dyslexia and dysgraphia was reported by Campbell and Butterworth (Campbell and Butterworth, 1985). In a deep orthography like English, the patient acquired an above average sight vocabulary without efficient command over sublexical processing and phonemic awareness skills.

Overall, these results undermine any hypothesis claiming a causal link between reading and other cognitive functions and, in particular, they undermine the notion of phonemic awareness as an essential prerequisite for reading acquisition. Therefore, by ruling out the causal relevance of the "extrinsic" variables, inside and outside the verbal domains, the explanations of reading disabilities are left with only one logical possibility: a modular architecture disorder.

5. A fractionable edifice

The phylogenetic assembling of a functional system must conform to the restrictions of a modular design. Complex computations, as Marr pointed out, "should be split up and implemented as a collection of small sub-parts that are as nearly independent of one another as the overall task allows" (Marr, 1976). The advantages of this evolutionary "tinkering" (Jacob, 1978) are clear: damage to one of the processing components may not result in lethal consequences for the functioning of the whole system. Similarly, the additive inclusion (in phylogeny) of a new component will not require concomitant compensatory adjustments in the whole system.

The advantages of a "tinkered" function are likewise relevant in ontogeny. An orthographic system implemented by an "additive architecture" (Marshall, 1989), with independent processing components, can benefit from compensatory strategies if one of the components is selectively impaired. Furthermore, if "the processing components involved in normal fluent adult reading become available to the child at different ages" (Marshall, 1989), damage occurring at stage S in ontogeny can disrupt (or delay) the related (orthographic) growing component. The remaining "blocks" of the orthographic architecture are left intact, thus leading to a partially efficient function, but not to an absent function.

Reading acquisition in normal and pathological conditions amplifies these architectural idiosyncrasies and reveals the fractionability of the system. Evidence for this comes primarily from developmental dissociations between reading and writing. Some children as young as 3.6 and 4 years are able to print messages "representing English words with the standard alphabet, though employing an orthography of their own invention" (Read, 1971). These children, however, were unable to read back the messages they had just printed. Bradley and Bryant (1979) described young English school children who spelled words correctly they were unable to read. A reversed pattern was reported by Frith (1980), who documented children with good reading and poor spelling. Similar dissociations were further reported in Spanish-speaking (Carbonell de Grompone, 1974) and in German-speaking school children (Valtin, Jung and Scheerer-Neuman, 1981). Recently, Wimmer and Hummer have shown that for German-speaking children "reading was easier than spelling and real words elicited higher performance than pseudo-words" Wimmer and Hummer, 1990).

Dissociations between reading and writing were also documented in a highly transparent orthography like Italian. The cases of two mentally retarded Italian children were reported in whom the severe inability to read contrasted strikingly with a relatively spared spelling ability (Cossu and Marshall, 1985). A reversed discrepancy between reading and writing has recently been documented in normal first and second grade Italian children (Cossu, Gugliotta and Marshall, 1995). These findings have been confirmed in a subsequent longitudinal study of 95 normal Italian first graders (Cossu, Gugliotta, Villani and Marshall, 1996).

Developmental asynchronism, however, does not solely apply to reading and writing but involves the molecular components (i.e. vowels and consonants) within each separate system as well. In a recent study (Cossu, Gugliotta and Marshall, 1995) it has been shown that the asymmetry in error-rate for consonants and vowels follows an identical pattern in both reading and spelling; in each task, consonant errors outstrip vowel errors by some 40%. Further analysis of errors reveals similar sensitivity to syllable position in both reading and writing: final syllables are prone to error some 40% more frequently than initial syllables in both reading and spelling. These data suggests that in the orthographic system the graphemic representations specify an autonomous level for CV structure and letter identity. The consonant/vowel ratio in reading has been recently confirmed in a sample of Italian first and second grade Italian school children (Cossu, Shankweiler, Liberman and Gugliotta, 1995), whereas the reversed pattern has been documented in American-speaking children (Fowler, Liberman and Shankweiler, 1977). Finally, in acquired agraphia the vowels can be selectively impaired (Cubelli, 1993); when writing to dictation, the patients appropriately insert the consonants, but omit all of the vowels.

To sum up, reading and writing appear to be non-parallel processes and their developmental asynchrony suggests structural independence of the two systems. Furthermore, each system is organized into distinct processing components which can be developmentally fractionated.

6. A domain-specific architecture

The dissociations between literacy acquisition and other neuropsychological functions mark the cognitive boundaries of the orthographic system. The data show that impairments in a wide range of non verbal domains, though frequently correlated with disorders of reading and writing, have no detrimental effects on the reading thereof. The data also rule out a number of linguistic and metalinguistic variables which are currently taken as a bench-mark for literacy acquisition. Congenital anarthria, for instance, does not prevent the acquisition of phoneme awareness and mastery of reading and writing skills (Cossu, Urbinati and Marshall, 1987). Moreover, (some) mentally retarded children can read (and spell) efficiently in spite of failure on tasks of phonemic awareness (Cossu and Marshall, 1990; Cossu, Rossini and Marshall, 1993), whereas intelligent dyslexic children, though improving their metaphonological skills through specific training, fail to convert them into the reading domain (Cossu, Maggetti and Marshall, 1996).

To grasp the full range of implications from these data, we should finally consider that (at least in a transparent orthography) normal first graders achieve straihgtforward control of the orthographic principle within a few months of teaching (Cossu, Gugliotta and Marshall, 1995). The functional independence (and other related properties) of orthographic skills reflects an underlying modular architecture and suggests that domain specific mechanisms are responsible for the acquisition of literacy. Within a modular hypothesis, an appropriate educational environment suffices to trigger the child's orthographic competence, which includes pre-specified processing components, specifically tuned to reading and writing computation (Marshall, 1989).

Before addressing the inevitable objections to the hypothesis of domain specificity for reading acquisition, let me outline the components of a (hypothetical) modular architecture, as conceptualized from the data I have presented (see Figure 1).

The core component of the orthographic system is a transcoding processor which automatically performs a cross-modal computation of the segmented phonological string. Following adequate exposure, the system assigns a sublexical value, be it a phoneme, a syllable, a morpheme, or a combination thereof, to an arbitrary visual (or haptic) token and computes the association in both directions.

From inside the transcoding processor, two separate transcoders are activated, which compute the processes of visual-phonological and phonological-visual conversion, for reading and writing, respectively. The transcoding processor is thus conceived of as an autonomous system, with a specific computational domain. However, since the processor is an interface between phonology and the perceptual systems, its computation is constrained by the integrity of the phonological system. Accordingly, the model keeps the language system separate from the transcoders, though they have primary connections to the phonological sub-component. The "extrinsic" cognitive systems that cooperate in processing phoneme awareness, explicit verbal memory and general intelligence are also kept separate from the transcoding processor, since they are assumed not to have any effect on the intrinsic computation of the orthographic system.

In the early stages of reading (and spelling) acquisition, the construction of the orthographic architecture is documented by the increase of correct performances with non words (or any new word). The two transcoders are supposed to have an ontogenetic priority over the construction of the orthographic lexicons. Acquisition of reading and spelling in a transparent orthography (Cossu, Gugliotta and Marshall, 1996) shows that the growth of the two orthographic lexicons is concomitant with the accuracy in non-word processing, thereby suggesting that the stabilization of the orthographic lexicons requires at least some degree of sublexical processing from the implicit processor.

The increased efficiency of the transcoding systems is assumed to foster a clustering of the orthographic units (and their phonemic correspondences), thus leading to the recognition of morphemic units. This strategy speeds up the computation by reducing the possibility of errors and somehow stabilizes a separate orthographic lexicon.

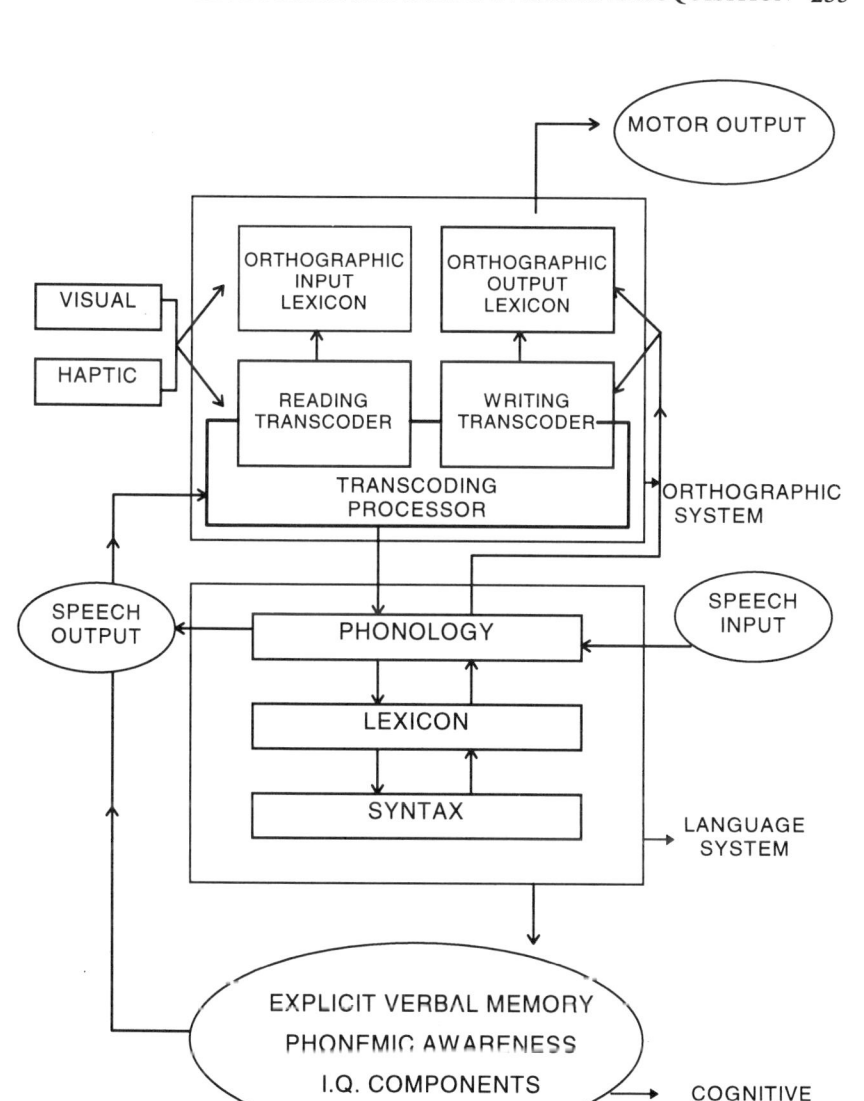

Figure 1. Modular Architecture of the Reading and Writing System

The alternative hypothesis (i.e. an original independence of the orthographic lexicons) should allow, at least in principle, for the acquisition of reading and spelling skills for words in the absence of sublexical processing. However, a primitive complete dissociation of the visual-route has not hitherto been documented. In the reported cases of developmental phonological dyslexia (Temple and Marshall, 1983; Campbell and Butterworth, 1985) only a relative impairment in non-word reading was detected and even an extreme case, such as R.E., scored 60% correct in non-word reading tasks (Campbell and Butterworth, 1985). In the acquired forms of phonological dyslexia, where the two orthographic lexicons were fully established prior to brain damage, there is a selective and (almost) complete impairment of the sub-lexical route, as for the patient W.B. who, after his stroke, was able to read around 90% of words correctly, but completely failed to read the simplest of non-words (Funnell, 1983).

These speculations about the developmental architecture of the orthographic system can be submitted to empirical scrutiny and modified accordingly. The crucial issue, however, concerns the theoretical plausibility of the hypothesis underlying the model: domain specificity for reading implies, in the first place, a phylogenetic history for the transcoding processor.

From the perspective of the standard view, the fundamental objection to the modular hypothesis is that no domain specific architecture for reading can be postulated. The late emergence of literacy makes evolutionary adaptation an unlikely candidate for restructuring the genetic endowment so as to produce a specific "Reading Device". The blind watchmaker, it is objected, needs evolutionary intervals of time to do the job.

I agree wholeheartedly with this objection. The domain specificity hypothesis of reading maintains, in fact, that the phylogenetic emergence of the transcoding processor was independent of the "invention" of the writing systems. The specificity of the biological architecture was not a consequence of an evolutionary adaptation to reading; rather, it was recruited a posteriori and the task of reading was adapted to its architecture. A system of this kind may have emerged as a property of the functional integration of the nervous system (Kauffman, 1993) and as a particular consequence of refining the process of cross-modal integration among different sensory systems. Ultimately, this strategy is not uniquely human, as it extends across different species, aiming to increase the efficiency of a highly integrated nervous system (Stein and Meredith, 1993).

The domain specificity assumption has several implication. By reducing the process of reading acquisition to the computation of a specific biological system, we can account for a number of otherwise contradictory findings. For a school child, the act of reading (and spelling) any novel word is *sensu strictu* a task of (implicit) metalinguistic computation, regulated by the child's exposure to orthographic instructions. Indeed, I suspect, it is the very existence of this largely automatic system that makes reading acquisition an easy task for more than 90% of school children, including a number of severely mentally retarded children. It is the inefficiency of the transcoding processor (to be considered as part of the child's biological endowment) that leads even the brightest child to struggle for decades with an otherwise overly simple task.

The transcoding processor, however, can be accessed for an explicit computation of the segmented phonemic string, as required by a phoneme-awareness task. For this reason, any normal child learning to read usually shows a synchronized increase in accuracy in both reading *and* phoneme awareness tasks. However, the latter task makes significant demands upon attentional, numerical and explicit verbal memory resources, as well as involving the transcoding processor. As a consequence, (some) children with mental retardation, but provided with an efficient (implicit) transcoding processor, can easily acquire reading and spelling skills, while failing in explicit metaphonological computation, due to the overwhelming cognitive and attentional demands raised by the phonemic awareness task.

We can account for the systematic correlation between low levels of reading and poor metaphonemic skills by assuming that reading failure reflects the inefficiency of the transcoding processor. We can also explain the effects of high levels of intelligence in developmental dyslexia, where metaphonological training improves the performance in metaphonemic tasks, but fails to improve the dyslexic's reading skills (Cossu, Maggetti and Marshall, 1996).

A biological view of literacy acquisition also has implications for a general theory of writing systems. The assumption of a domain-specific computation for reading and spelling implies a structural identity (at a very abstract level) of all present and past orthographies. John DeFrancis has recently advocated a similar view by pointing out that the "diverse oneness" of all writing systems stems from the fact that they are "a graphic extension of the uniquely human attribute of speech" (DeFrancis, 1989: 215). Accordingly, the phonological patterns of the language appear to limit the range of solutions for an optimal orthography by constraining the correspondences between the sublexical units (or combination thereof) and the arbitrary graphic symbols by which they are represented. However, assembling a near-optimal orthography is not a purely natural process and History always presents the bill, as particularly evident in the Japanese and Serbo-Croatian writing systems.

7. Conclusions

The dissociations between literacy and neuropsychological functions suggest the functional independence of the reading and writing processes. High levels of intelligence and excellent linguistic skills are insufficient prerequisites for the acquisition of reading and writing. The control of phoneme awareness skills is similarly insufficient. Severe mental retardation, congenital speech disorders and inability in phonemic awareness tasks, on the other hand, do not prevent mastery of orthographic skills. Furthermore, reading can be developmentally dissociated from writing.

These clinical pictures can be coherently accounted for within a modular architecture framework and suggest that a domain specific mechanism underlie the acquisition of orthographic processes. It is hypothesized that an automatic transcoder between phonology and perceptual domains is the core component underlying the process of reading and writing acquisition. It is further assumed that the transcoding processor is part of the child's biological endowment.

Reading Difficulties among English and German Children: Same Cause - Different Manifestation

Heinz Wimmer, Uta Frith

1. What is dyslexia?

For about 100 years there has been scientific awareness that some children have enormous difficulties in learning to read and to spell and that these difficulties are not due to mental deficiency or lack of adequate instruction. Originally, a visual defect was assumed to be the cause of the reading difficulty, as evident from the term "congenital word-blindness" (Hinshelwood, 1917). At present, dyslexia is included in the International Classification of Diseases (ICD-10, World Health Organization, 1992) as one of the Specific Developmental Disorders of Scholastic Skills. In line with recent evidence reading/spelling disorder is characterized as resulting from a language- and not from a visual impairment. Thus it is stated that children with reading/spelling difficulties have often suffered from a developmental language disorder in pre-school years . In cases without gross signs of such a disorder, it is noted that there are often subtle difficulties in auditory processing as evident from rhyme recognition or phoneme categorisation. Also, phonetic spelling errors are considered a characteristic symptom of reading/spelling disorder.

The nature of the reading difficulties of dyslexic children and adults has been intensively explored in recent psychological research (see Stanovich, 1994, for an overview). One of the most consistent findings is that the primary reading problem of dyslexic children is slow and inaccurate word recognition. In contrast, they have no problems in reading comprehension. Within the problem area of word recognition the difficulty has been narrowed down to one particular component, phonological coding. The phonological coding component of word recognition transforms letters and letter patterns into phonological codes.

These codes then allow access to word pronunciation and, also, to meaning. One of the main diagnostic indicators of the impaired phonological coding component of word recognition in dyslexic individuals is a specific difficulty with the reading of nonwords (e.g. *theart, snaligu*).They often fail to pronounce them accurately. Clearly, nonword reading depends on phonological coding to a greater extent than word reading. With nonwords, pronunciation has to be assembled from the letter patterns. There is no help from stored word forms and meaning. A review by Rack, Snowling and Olson (1992) brings together the surprisingly consistent research in this field and underlines the importance of nonword reading as a diagnostic tool.

Phonological coding in word recognition was also postulated as a major step in developmental models of reading acquisition (e.g. Frith, 1985; Jorm and Share, 1983). The acquisition of phonological coding in word recognition - termed alphabetic stage in Frith's model - allows the child to use grapheme-phoneme correspondences in a systematic way to read the many words which are encountered the first time in print by the child. This ability to tackle new words is critical for further reading development, because it functions as a self-teaching device for building up memory representations (i.e. word recognition units) for word spellings. For children with a phonological deficit as part of a manifest or subtle language problem, the acquisition of phonological coding in reading development must pose quite evidently a major hurdle. Accordingly, Frith (1985) characterized dyslexia as developmental arrest at the logographic stage, which in her stage model precedes the alphabetic stage.

The main limitation of psychological research on reading development and dyslexia is its focus on English orthography. This is a serious limitation since English differs from other alphabetic orthographies in terms of its atypically low grapheme-phoneme consistency (Venezky, 1970). It seems obvious that acquisition and execution of phonological coding is much more demanding for an orthography with exceptionally low grapheme-phoneme consistency than for more typical orthographies with consistent grapheme-phoneme correspondences. To illustrate, any phonological coding mechanism must run into difficulties, when confronted with inconsistencies such as hear - bear - heard - beard. One could then further hypothesize that children with a phonological language impairment may be less penalized in acquiring phonological coding for a transparent orthography. It follows that the phonological deficit account of dyslexia may be specific to English and may not apply to children who have difficulties in learning to read and spell in a language with a consistent orthography. In the following we will examine these issues by presenting evidence on how German children acquire phonological coding in reading development. We will also address the question whether German and English dyslexic children exhibit a similar phonological coding impairment. First, however, we present some information on German orthography and on the typical form of initial reading instruction for German children.

2. German orthography and reading instruction

German orthography, like English orthography, tends to represent the morphophonemic level of language, but does so more consistently than English. To illustrate, in the German words Hand, Ball, Garten, and Katze the grapheme a is always pronounced the same way, while in the corresponding English words hand, ball, garden, and cat the pronunciations differ. The umlaut signs of German contribute to consistency, since - besides broadening the orthographic means for vowel representation - they allow preservation of morpheme identity and mark changes in the vowel associated with morphological processes such as pluralization (e.g. Hand - Hände). The main complexity of vowel representation in German has to do with length. For example, there is more than one orthographic device for explicitly marking the fact that a vowel is long: doubling of the vowel grapheme (e.g. Boot, Aal), the silent-h after the vowel grapheme (e.g. Bohne, Bahn) and the long i (e.g. Biene, viel). It should be noted that such complexities have more effect on spelling than on reading. For example, despite the various options for explicitly representing long vowels, there is still consistency in the direction from graphemes to phonemes (but not vice versa) and even when orthographic markings of vowel length are neglected in phonological coding, there is still enough information for correct word recognition, since only in a few cases does vowel length distinguish between words.

Initial reading instruction for the German children, who participated in our studies, makes use of the consistency of German orthography by relying on a slowly advancing phonics program in the first year of school. In Kindergarten there is no reading preparation at all. Critical features of the phonics program are as follows: the main grapheme phoneme correspondences - including all multi-letter graphemes (e.g. sch, ch, ck, au, eu, ei, ie) are directly presented and immediately used for word recognition, and there is direct modelling and training on how to recognize words via grapheme-phoneme translation and blending. This training starts with words like Mimi and Mama, for which blending is easy to demonstrate and to practice, and uses graphical devices to mark syllable boundaries. In the beginning, the blending ritual results in word preforms, which characteristically have artificially lengthened phonemes and incorrect stress assignments. However, due to the consistency of German orthography these preforms are usually close enough to the target pronunciation to allow recognition. A reasonable expectation is that this combination of an "easy" orthography and a systematic phonics teaching approach should make the acquisition of phonological coding in word recognition much less of a hurdle for German than for English children.

3. The acquisition of phonological coding in young German and English readers

Here we will report the main results of two studies which compared word and nonword reading in young German and English readers. A first study by Wimmer and Goswami (1994) examined how 7-, 8-, and 9-year old English and Austrian children read numberwords and analogous nonwords. (As the Austrian children were learning to read in German, they are referred to as German children throughout this paper for ease of exposition). Number words between two and twelve were used because these words have similar pronunciation and spelling in the two orthographies (e.g. two - zwei, nine - neun). Nonwords were derived from the numberwords by exchanging the graphemes that denote the consonantal onsets (e.g. sen was created from seven and ten). For this reason one, eight and eleven had to be omitted. Therefore, the nonwords in both orthographies consisted of the very same letters and letter clusters (for word-onsets and word-rhymes) as the words. Because of the latter feature (preservation of onset- and rhyme- clusters), reading of these nonwords could be based on analogies to the numberwords and gives a conservative estimate of any difficulties of phonological coding. The reading task was simply to read aloud lists of numberwords or nonwords, each list consisting of 6 items. Reading time and accuracy were measured.

A further German-English reading comparison study (Wimmer and Frith, 1994) extended this first study by using a different and enlarged list of words and nonwords.The task format (reading aloud a list of items) was the same as in the Wimmer and Goswami study. Again, only words with identical meaning and similar pronunciation and spelling in the languages were chosen (e.g. hand - Hand, word - Wort, green - grü n). Again the nonwords were derived from the words by exchanging the consonantal word-onset graphemes. The results of these two studies are presented in Table 1 which shows the mean percentages of correct readings of words and nonwords. For each study, only the results for the youngest and the oldest age group are shown in order to illustrate the developmental trend.

		English			German	
Data from: Wimmer and Goswami, 1994		7-year-olds	9-year-olds		7-year-olds	9-year-olds
Number words	'ten'	96	100	'zehn'	99	100
Nonwords	'sen'	66	77	'then'	87	91
Data from: Wimmer and Frith, 1994						
Words	'hand'	69	94	'hand'	92	100
Nonwords	'nand'	47	79	'nand'	85	96

Table 1. Mean percentage read correctly by English and German children (normal readers)

3.1. German-English differences in word and nonword reading

The main finding evident from Table 1 is that young German readers had little difficulty with phonological coding compared to their English counterparts. After only one year of reading instruction they read nonwords - the relevant measure for phonological coding - with realtively high accuracy. In contrast, the young English readers, with about one year more of reading instruction, - they begin school about one year earlier- , did experience a certain amount of difficulty with phonological coding. This difficulty was observed for the nonwords derived from the numberwords, where about a third of the readings were incorrect, and even more so for the nonwords derived from the words, where slightly more than half the readings were unacceptable. The first finding is particularly astonishing. Clearly, the English children had little difficulty in reading the number-words correctly from which the nonwords were derived, and, since only nine different word and nonword items were used, it should have been easy to base nonword reading on analogies to the numberwords.

A striking observation from Table 1 is that the youngest group of German readers, with about one year of schooling, tended to commit fewer errors on nonwords derived from words than the oldest group of English readers, with about 4 years of schooling. English children showed not only impaired reading accuracy for nonwords, but also enormously impaired reading speed on the lists of nonwords. An important further observation was that English children differed markedly from each other (and to a much larger extent than German children) in their ability to read nonwords. Quite a number of the youngest English readers had no difficulty in producing acceptable nonword readings at fast speed, while some children in this group were hardly able to produce any correct response at all.

For the interpretation of the poor nonword reading of the English children it is important to note that reading refusals occurred very rarely and that the scoring of their readings was very liberal. In fact, any pronunciation was accepted, as long as existing grapheme-phoneme correspondences were observed. For example, in the case of theart (analogous to heart), four different readings were obtained taking into account only the pronunciation of the vowel: 8 times the e̱a̱ corresponded to he̱a̱rd, 4 times to he̱a̱rt and in 2 times each to he̱a̱r and to be̱a̱r. All four pronunciations were counted as correct. Of course, no such liberal scoring was used for children's reading of real words. For example, the 8 readings of heart as "hu̱rt" were counted as incorrect. Inspection of errors showed that the errors of the German children tended to be closer to the grapheme sequence than the errors of the English children. For example, to the nonword glinken erroneous responses of the German children were blinken, lingen, gliken and glink. In all these errors the grapheme sequence was observed and the main problem was that graphemes were omitted (e.g. in glink), or, that wrong grapheme-phoneme rules were applied, or, that a grapheme was visually misidentified (e.g. b for g in the first error). Among the errors of the English children more instances occurred where the grapheme sequence was not observed and where phonemes were added. Examples for sequence deviations in the case of the nonword glink were gelk, gilk and garlic, where the l of the onset cluster gl- was moved towards the end of the syllable. Examples for additions were grink, groos and grikin where a wrong phoneme appeared in the initial cluster.

3.2. Conclusions about normal acquisition

The main conclusion from these findings for young German readers is that phonological coding in word recognition poses little difficulty. Apparently the combination of an easy consistent orthography and a phonics approach to initial reading instruction means that after only a relatively short time, children are able to assemble quite reliably pronunciations for any pronounceable letter pattern. The ease with which the German children mastered phonological coding stands in marked contrast to the difficulty posed by phonological coding for many of the English children. These orthography-related differences in the acquisition of phonological coding skills were found for children who were not selected for exhibiting specific reading difficulties. The next section will examine whether similar differences in the ease of phonological coding exist between German and English dyslexic children.

4. Phonological coding in German and English dyslexic children

Here some findings of Karin Landerl's PhD project (supervised by the two authors of the present paper) will be presented. Landerl used the numberword-nonword reading task of Wimmer and Goswami (1994) and also constructed a word- nonword single item reading task, where item length (one-, two- , three-syllables) and frequency (within the one- and two- syllable words) were factors besides lexicality. In this latter task, again, words with identical meaning and similar spelling and pronunciation in the two orthographies were used. Again, for the one- and two-syllable words analogous nonwords were derived by exchanging the consonantal onset graphemes. Examples for the word items were milk - Milch, butter - Butter, examples for analogous nonword items were bilk - Bilch, sutter - Sutter. For the three-syllable items nonwords were created by rearranging the syllables of the words with the constraint that the position of the syllable in the word was preserved in the nonword. Examples for three-syllable words are radio - Radio, paradise - Paradies, examples for nonwords are inlio - Inlio and posidise - Posidies. Scoring of the nonword readings of the English children was again done liberally.

The 18 German and 18 English dyslexic children (mostly boys) were about 12 years old.

		English	German
Number words	'ten'	99	100
Nonwords	'sen'	55	82
Frequent short words	'milk'	81	97
Nonwords	'bilk''	42	92
Infrequent long words	'paradise'	48	89
Nonwords	'posidise'	27	77

Table 2. Mean percentage read correctly by English and German dyslexic children (aged 12 years)

Most of the English dyslexic children were recruited from a special school for dyslexic children. The German dyslexic children came from two longitudinal studies and were diagnosed at least twice as showing specific reading and spelling difficulties before participating in Landerl's study. Both the English and the German dyslexic subjects read at the level of 8 to 9 year old children.

Table 2 shows mean percentages of correct readings for the numberword-nonword task and for word- nonword tasks (i.e. one- or two-syllable words and corresponding nonwords, and three-syllable words as well as their corresponding nonwords).

One interesting observation from Table 2 is that on the numberword-nonword task, the dyslexic children from both orthography groups performed at a level very similar to the normally learning children at the age of 7 years (as shown in Table 1). That is, the numberwords were read nearly perfectly by both the English and the German dyslexic children, while the analogous nonwords were read quite accurately by the German, but not by the English dyslexic children. The difficulty of nonword reading for the English dyslexic children was also confirmed by a mean reading time of 2.6s per item for the nonword list compared to 1.6s per item for the German dyslexic children.

The word-nonword task offered additional observations. One is that the nonword reading difficulty reached dramatic dimensions for the English dyslexic children in the case of the three-syllable nonwords where the large majority of the items were read incorrectly and where the mean reading time for the correctly read items was 5.6s. Another finding was that reading accuracy of the English dyslexic children was strongly influenced by word frequency: Accuracy dropped from the numberwords to the frequent one- and two-syllable words and decreased further for the long and infrequent words. In contrast, German dyslexic children tended to read even the infrequent three-syllable words rather accurately. They also mastered the vast majority of corresponding nonwords.

The comparison of reading errors of German and English dyslexic children shows that the few errors of the German dyslexic children were close to the grapheme sequence, while a substantial number of the errors of the English dyslexic children were far off. For the simple German nonword *bilch* (analogous to Milch) the only error was *bich* with one grapheme omitted, while for the corresponding English nonword *bilk* (milk) readings were *blink* (8 times), *blank* and *brink*. In each of these errors at least two deviations from the grapheme sequence occurred in that the initial simple consonantal onset /b/ was always replaced by a cluster with one phoneme added and the final cluster -lk was always replaced by -nk. For the three-syllable nonword *posidise* the English children produced 12 errors, typical examples being *posdens*, *posdis*, *proisid* and *prodisais*, while the two German errors to the corresponding nonword *posidies* were *positivs* and *prosidies*. For *paradise* English children also were often far off target with readings such as *pardon, proudest, president, paper-disc, pa:d, pepikel, predi* and *parti:s*. In contrast, the only error of the German children to Paradies was par`adi:s with all phonemes correct, but with wrong stress assignment on the second syllable.

4.1. Differences in reading strategies

These differences in reading errors suggest that the word reading strategy of the dyslexic German children differed from that of the dyslexic English children. For this analysis it has to be remembered that the children had to read aloud. This implies that pronunciations had to be accessed as whole sounds (possible in the case of words) or newly assembled (in the case of nonwords). German children apparently solved this pronunciation task for nonwords predominantly in a bottom-up mode by relying on more or less complete grapheme-phoneme coding and by using the resulting phonemes to activate existing syllable-onsets and - rimes, which then were assembled into pronounceable syllables. The English children apparently solved the pronunciation problem in a somewhat different way. Given the nature of the task, they also had to activate phonological structures such as syllable-onsets and -rimes to arrive at pronounceable syllables. However, the activation of these phonological structures was not based on systematic sequential grapheme-phoneme coding as in the case of the German children, but on partial grapheme - phoneme coding only. Errors such *blink* or *brink* for *bilk* are quite indicative for this reading strategy of activating phonological structures such as syllable-onsets and -rimes from partial grapheme-phoneme coding. Obviously, in the case of the three-syllable nonwords the bottom-up information provided by partial grapheme-phoneme coding is so insufficient, that the errors become wild guesses. If such guesses are checked against the grapheme sequence and rejected, then several cycles of partial grapheme-phoneme codings may be required before a pronunciation can be assembled with some certainty. This explains the enormous reading time of about 5.6s per item for the correct readings of the three-syllable nonwords.

4.2. Conclusions about dyslexia

The comparison of German and English dyslexic children reaches a conclusion that is similar to the comparison of young German and English normal readers. Again, the difficulty of phonological coding was confirmed specifically for the English children. This finding is certainly in line with the initially raised doubts on the generality of the phonological deficit conception of dyslexia, which is based on findings from English dyslexic children. However, it would be wrong to conclude that the phonological impairment account does *not* apply to German dyslexic children. This conclusion would be based on the erroneous assumption that poor nonword reading is the only possible manifestation of a phonological coding impairment. It may well be that poor nonword reading can serve as a useful diagnostic indicator of a phonological coding deficit only in the case of English, where grapheme-phoneme coding is a particularly demanding task due to the complexities of grapheme - phoneme correspondences. For German dyslexic children a nonword reading test would not be such a good diagnostic tool. Instead, we have to look for other indicators. Actually, there are now several converging findings suggesting that German dyslexic children exhibit a specific speed deficit in phonological coding.

5. Evidence for a specific speed deficit in phonological coding among German dyslexic children.

There were indications for such a speed deficit in Landerl's PhD project. For example, the 12-year-old German dyslexic children were found to read the nonwords derived from the numberwords more slowly than the 9-year-olds of the reading-level-matched control group. A similar - but not always reliable - tendency was found for several nonword categories of the word-nonword task. In a study of reading impairments and cognitive deficits among German dyslexic children at grade levels 2, 3 and 4, Wimmer (1993) found that these children suffered from a pervasive speed deficit for different types of reading tasks, including text, high frequency words and nonwords. This speed deficit, particularly in the case of nonwords, speaks for an impairment in phonological coding. Another main finding, also suggesting a deficit in speed of access to phonological codes, was that the dyslexic children scored lower than reading-level control children on *rapid naming tasks*, and that *numeral-naming speed* turned out to be the most important predictor of reading speed differences. In contrast, the performance of the dyslexic children on a phonemic segmentation task was high in absolute terms, and phonetic spelling errors were almost absent.

A follow-up study by Wimmer (1994a) tried to establish that the speed deficit of German dyslexic children for nonword reading systematically exceeds the speed deficit for word reading. This is important for theoretical reasons, since nonword reading involves phonological coding to a greater extent than word reading. In this study the grade 4 dyslexic children were carefully matched on a one-to-one basis with grade 2 normal readers on reading speed for frequent short words. Then reading speed was assessed for analogous nonwords derived from the frequent short words by the usual procedure of changing consonantal onsets between the words. In addition, the 'Japanese' nonwords of Wimmer (1993) were also used. These nonwords have little similarity with German words and consist of two or three simple syllables without any consonant cluster. Examples are toki, filuno, and torukim. Table 3 shows the mean reading time per item and mean error percentages for the two types of nonwords.

	Reading level controls (8-year-olds)	Dyslexics (10-year-olds)
Time (Sd) in seconds		
Frequent words	0.98 (.21)	0.98 (.20)
Analogous nonwords	1.70 (.41)	1.99 (.56)
'Japanese' non words	2.40 (.58)	2.84 (.68)
Error percentage		
Frequent words	3	4
Analogous nonwords	5	9
'Japanese' non words	9	16

Table 3. Mean reading time per word and mean percentage of errors in German dyslexic and reading-level-matched control children

From Table 3 it is evident that grade 4 dyslexic children - although reading the frequent words at exactly the same speed as the grade 2 normal children - were slower at reading analogous nonwords and the 'Japanese' nonwords than the control group. The difference in reading time between the two groups was reliable for both types of nonwords. In addition, it is evident that the slower reading time of the dyslexic children was also accompanied by more errors. A further interesting finding was that on a *visual* matching task - instances of a given Chinese target logogram had to be detected in a long series of similar logograms - the dyslexic children performed as fast and as accurately as age-matched control children. This rules out that the dyslexic children may have suffered from a general processing speed deficit.

6. Conclusions from German-English comparisons

One main conclusion from the German-English reading comparison studies is that differences in grapheme-phoneme consistency influence reading development in a profound way. So it was found that the acquisition of phonological coding in word recognition was much easier for German than for English children. This conclusion is based on the findings showing that German children in the early phase of learning to read have little difficulty in reading nonwords accurately in comparison to their English counterparts. We also found phonological coding in word recognition was much less of a hurdle for the German dyslexic children. Given the importance of phonological coding for further reading development, it follows that the risk of serious reading failure is smaller for children learning to read a consistent orthography. The different consistency of German and English apparently also affects the organization of word recognition. The differences in reading errors both between young German and English readers, but also between dyslexic German and English readers, suggest that German children rely heavily on complete phonological coding in word recognition, while English children often use only partial grapheme-phoneme translation with a high risk of erroneous word reading, particularly for longer words.

The second conclusion from the presented findings is about the manifestation and causation of dyslexia in German and English children. The main difference in manifestation was that German dyslexic children show accurate if slow nonword reading. In contrast, the English dyslexic children, in agreement with many other studies (review by Rack et al., 1992), were found to exhibit high percentages of nonword reading errors as well as being slow. Accurate nonword reading was documented previously by Wimmer (1993) for dyslexic German children from the end of grade 2 onwards. However, in the very early phases of learning to read, German children who later exhibited persistent reading difficulties, were found to have difficulties with accurate phonological coding in word recognition (Wimmer, 1994b). Thus, the difference seems to be that most German dyslexic children can quickly overcome their difficulties with phonological coding and achieve a remarkable degree of competence with phoneme - grapheme translation, while most English dyslexic children show their difficulties more glaringly and for much longer.

German dyslexic children showed a general reading speed deficit, which was particularly marked for nonwords. This finding indicates a persistent impairment in the efficiency of phonological coding in word recognition. This finding is highly important for theories of dyslexia; It shows that the very same reading mechanism, - namely phonological coding in word recognition -, is affected in

English and in German dyslexic children. For English dyslexic children the faulty mechanism manifests itself in lower accuracy, for German dyslexic children the faulty mechanism manifests itself in slow speed. This slow speed of the phonological coding mechanism among the German dyslexic children constitutes strong evidence for the phonological deficit account of dyslexia. It is complemented by findings with adult English dyslexics who also show high accuracy in nonword reading, but pronounced slowness in various phonological awareness tasks (Paulesu et al, in preparation). The present German children were learning to read an easy (i.e. consistent) orthography and experienced a strict phonics teaching approach, which directly introduced them to phonological coding in word recognition. The expectation was that such a combination of orthography and instruction would give even phonologically impaired children a good chance to acquire phonological coding skills successfully. With respect to a basic coding competence this actually seems to be the case. Nevertheless, despite this advantage, speed of phonological coding in word recognition remained persistently impaired. This persistent speed impairment is in agreement with findings suggesting a biological hardware problem in the language areas of the brain as ultimate cause of developmental dyslexia.

Neural Organisation and Writing Systems

Brian Butterworth

My aim in this paper is to suggest ways in which knowledge of the brain structures used in reading may help our understanding of literacy skills and why some people have trouble acquiring them. I start with an unusual question: to what extent does brain organisation reflect the social practices of reading? That is to say, to what extent is the the neural substrate of reading determined by the kind of writing system that the child acquires? My question make strike you as unusual since, on the one hand, it is trivial that all differences in experience will lead to differences in neural substrate, and, on the other, these differences can scarcely be systematic, and hence interesting. To begin with, there will be enormously different learning experiences associated even with the acquisition of a single writing system. Secondly, reading and writing cannot be the kinds of things that specific neural systems have evolved to deal with: in evolutionary terms, there has not been enough time for selective pressures to have done their work. Moreover, if we had been endowed special reading and writing bits of the brain - as Chomsky (1972) has claimed we are endowed with special language bits - then one would have expected, perhaps, that writing systems should all follow the same pattern. However, most scholars agree that there are at least four, and probably six, independent orthographic traditions based on distinct ways of representing the spoken language. (According to Gelb, 1963 and Mattingly, 1992 these are. 1. Mesopotamian cuneiform; 2. Cretan, including Linear B; 3. Chinese; 4. Mayan; 5. Egyptian; 6. West Semitic - Phoenician, Hebrew, Greek, Roman.) These facts make the study of the neural substrate of reading very different from, and apparently less rewarding than, the study of, for example, visual processes, where there is a clear evolutionary line of development of a system whose structure is tightly linked to its function.

I shall use the term "writing system" in Sampson's (1985) sense of a set of graphemic units used to represent a language, not the graphemic units themselves, which he calls the "script". Thus, English and Italian use largely (but not completely) the same script - the Roman alphabet - but uses the graphemes in the set in different ways to represent the their respective languages.

Any writing system involves three mappings: between graphemic units and sounds; between graphemic units and meanings; and, this must not be forgotten, between meanings and sounds. This triangular arrangement is represented in Figure 1, where G stands for graphemic units, S stands for sounds and M stands for meanings.

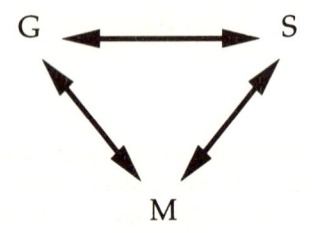

Figure 1

Different writing systems use different types of graphemic unit, and different mappings between the types. In the English writing system, letters are the basic unit type, and these are mapped in a rather inconsistent way onto phoneme sound units. In the Italian writing system, letters are mapped in a more regular way onto phonemes, and phonemes onto letters. It is not quite true than there is a one-to-one mapping between letters and sounds (t <-> /t/, b <-> /b/; s<->/s/ or /ʃ/ depending on context; g <-> /g/ or /d / or /lj/ depending on context). However, instead of taking the letter as the basic unit, we can take graphemes, in alphabetic scripts, these are elements realising single phonemes, so pairs of letters, like TH in English, would count as a grapheme. Notice that TH realises two separate phonemes in English, the one in *the* and the one in *thought*. In Italian, there is almost a one-to-one mapping between graphemes and phonemes (sc <-> /Ú/; ga, go, gu <-> /g-/; gli <-> /lj-/). Moreover, different words in Italian or English are generally distinct in their sounds, with a small number of well-known exceptions (see below). Thus, for these languages, using alphabetic scripts, the route from graphemic units to meaning could plausibly go via sound - G -> S -> M - since once the reader has worked out that the string HINT is pronounced "hint", the meaning will be clear providing of course the word was already a part of the reader's spoken vocabulary.

Writing systems use inventories of different kinds of unit - corresponding to sublexical sound units, or to more word-like units. Now, it has been frequently pointed out that mappings from letters to sounds operate at two levels at least:

at the level of individual grapheme units and at whole word levels, and possibly intermediate levels. Clearly, a whole word mapping is necessary in English to achieve the correct pronunciation of many words. This means that the mappings in Figure 1 have to be supplemented by a mapping that utilizes the reader's knowledge of lexical items, denoted by the letter "L" in Figure 2.

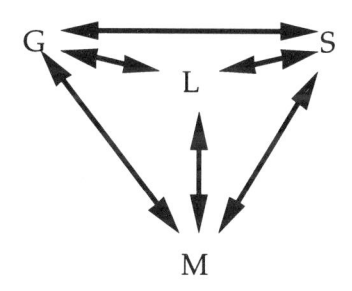

Figure 2

In addition to units at different levels - phonemes, words, etc. - we can distinguish types of *mapping relation* between graphemic unit and sounds: a mapping is *consistent* if the graphemic unit always maps on to the same sound; it is inconsistent if it maps on to more than one sound. Given that there may be more than one level at which the mapping can happen, then an inconsistent mapping is said to *congruent*, in a particular word, if mappings at all levels yield the same sound for the unit. It is incongruent if it does not.

For example, the letter D is always pronounced /d/ in English, I think. It therefore has a consistent mapping, and ipso facto, it will be pronounced /d/ whatever word it appears in. B, on the other hand is inconsistent, since in some words, like *limb, crumb,* it is silent. Now it may be possible to construct a non-lexical level of representation for the sequence, specifying a contextual rule that does have a consistent mapping. A rule such as -MB- -> /m/ will not suffice, because of words like *ambit,* but a rule such as -MB# -> /m/ probably will. However, as is well-known, there are letters in English, like G, whose pronunciation is determined by the word in which it appears. There seems to be no rule that captures the pattern: compare *lager* with *larger,* not to mention *rough* and *bough.* Given that -GE is usually pronounced /d /, the -GE is incongruent in *lager,* but congruent in *larger.*

The question I want to pose in this paper is the extent to which neural organisation of reading is shaped by these mapping properties of the writing system. Will all the mappings shown in Figure 2 be utilized by the readers of widely different writing systems, or utilized to the same extent by readers of different writing systems?

Now Katz and Feldman (1981) some time ago argued that reading processes are shaped by what they call "orthographic depth." This will determine how the reader carries out lexical access.

> The kind of code used for lexical access depends on the kind of alphabetic orthography facing the reader. Specifically, it depends on how directly the orthography reflects the phonetic surface. Languages [they mean writing systems] in which the spelling-to-sound correspondences are simple and invariant (as in Serbo-Croatian) will readily support information-processing structures for reading that utilize the language's [writing system's] surface phonological features. On the other hand, in an orthography that bears a complex relation to speech (a deep orthography such as English), phonologically structured mechanisms for processing words will be less developed. (Katz and Feldman, 1981:85-86)

What they meant by this was that Serbo-Croatian readers would rely on processes involving mappings from letters to phonemes (G->S) to achieve lexical access and hence meaning. They would not use the mapping G->L, but rather G->S->L.

Now Katz and Feldman's idea of "simple and invariant" correspondences does not make the distinction between consistency and congruency, nor between the levels at which these correspondences can occur. Therefore, they really have no account of character-based writing systems like Chinese or Japanese Kana syllabary, where there is clearly invariance in mappings from G->S - the same character is always pronounced in the same way. However, this way is not predictable on the basis of grapheme-sound rules (unless one rule per character is allowed).

The orthographic depth hypothesis has been extensively tested on normal adult subjects, with conflicting results. One of the key problems is the finding of *lexicality effects* in reading aloud words written in shallow orthographies. That is, effects that depend on a sequence of graphemes being an identifiable word - for example, word frequency effects, and the effects of preceding the target word with a word that is related to it meaning, or is an associate of it (like DOCTOR-NURSE, DOCTOR-HOSPITAL). It has been repeatedly demonstrated that this manipulation, called "priming", facilitates and speeds naming of the target word. Baluch and Besner (1991) showed that Persian readers, under some circumstances, would name Farsi words (with vowels marked) more quickly when the words were frequent, and when they were primed by preceding words Now if the readers were operating solely with the sublexical mappings this should not have occurred. Similar results have been found for Spanish (Sebastián-Gallés, 1991) and Italian (Tabossi and Laghi, 1992). More worrying for the orthographic depth hypothesis, are related findings that the presence or absence of lexicality effects depends on whether or not the task involves the reading of *non-words*. In all the studies mentioned here, lexicality effects disappear when non-words are in the target list. Besner and Smith (1992) argue the presence of non-words induces subjects to adopt the strategy of reading by the sublexical process using the G->S mappings which can be applied to both words and nonwords, while, obviously, the whole word route only applies to words. This kind of strategic manipulation of lexicality effects has even been found in Japanese (Wydell, 1991).

Clearly, these results pose serious problems for the orthographic depth hypothesis. They also pose problems if we are seeking to establish the processes for getting from print to sound in the heads of the reader. If the behavioural results seem to depend critically on strategy - here determined by the composition of experimental lists - how can we be sure that the strategy has not been specially devised for the experiment, and is not part of the usual apparatus used in everyday reading?

Our way of answering this is to look at the neuropsychology of reading. We can, in general, tell from neuropsychological studies of higher cortical functions in brain-damaged patients that very specific functions can be impaired - or spared - indicating that these are supported by highly specialised neural structures. By studying a range of relevant patients, it is sometimes possible to discover from the pattern of impaired and spared functions, the cognitive architecture into which the component functions fit. If a function has been seriously damaged, then patients' strategies cannot restore it, in general, though some compensatory processes may be invoked or developed. Suppose, for example, that an English reader, following brain damage, can no longer make use of his knowledge of the whole word mappings, G -> L. He should be poor at reading irregularly spelled words, whatever the task. No list manipulation, apart from excluding irregular words should make any difference.

The question I want to raise is this: to what extent are the components and their interrelations determined by experience? In particular, to what extent are they determined by what the brain has to learn about the social practices in which it develops? Will you get different components or different relations between the components if these experiences are different.

Let us return to the mappings used by the English writing system. I wish to draw attention to three of its main properties.

1. Elements (letters) stand for meaningless speech sounds (phonemes) in a more or less systematic way:
   e.g. D -> /d/; I -> /I/; M -> /m/; N -> /n/ ; T -> /t/
2. Letters and sounds can be assembled to form syllables and words
3. Letters can be combined in new ways to make new syllables
   eg. FREON®, YOMP

Table 1. The English Writing System

A small number of elements (that is the letters) stand for speech sounds that are meaningless, and often unpronounceable, on their own.

B --> /b/	L --> /l/
D --> /d/	M --> /m/
F --> /f/	N --> /n/
G --> /g/	P --> /p/
H --> /h/	R --> /r/
I --> /i/	T --> /t/
K --> /k/	W --> /w/

Table 2. Letter-sound correspondences "phonics"

These are some of the letter-sound correspondence rules for English. The letter is on the left of the arrow its pronunciation on the right. The consonants can really only be pronounced with the addition of a vowel, like bI dI etc. I have listed just one vowel for simplicity.

Letters and hence phonemes can be assembled to form syllables and words. That is the point of an alphabetic system: a small number of elements, readily learned, can be used in various combinations and permutations to make up all the words in the language. You don't have to invent new elements. From the assembled sounds you can fairly reliably derive the meaning. HINT - a slight indication.

And hence, you can use new permutations of letters to spell new words. Like these.

ZINT, YIND

Using the rules, you read those novel strings with no trouble, probably as /zInt/ and /yInd/. This ability to map elements onto sounds is the basis of "phonics". As many of you will know, the British government is very keen on children being able to spell correctly. They are also very keen to make phonics basis of teaching reading in schools, rather than the progressive "look-and-say" method. The idea seems to be that once you have mastered the *discipline* of a few basic rules, like those I presented, you can read all the words, pretty well, that are composed by them. Like these:

DINT, FLINT, HINT, LINT, MINT, PINT, TINT.

Or these:

BIND, FIND, GRIND, HIND, KIND, MIND, RIND, WIND.

Well, it is clear, as I mentioned earlier, that readers of English need to have a way of recognising words as a whole, so as to deal with the irregular spellings of many English words. Clearly, it is possible to read all words, and to spell them correctly, by learning each letter string off by heart. But of course some procedure for mapping letters onto sounds will be helpful for reading letter strings not previously encountered.

It is now widely, though not universally, believed that skilled adult readers of English deploy two "routes" in reading (Patterson, 1981). The architecture of the two routes and how they operate with congruent and incongruent words is shown in Figures 3 and 4.

There is a route that uses word *elements*, Route 1 in Figure 3 below. This route depends on *assembling* the pronunciation of each element to produce the pronunciation of the whole word, and only via this pronunciation, access the word's meaning. Patterson calls this the "assembled route". There is a whole word route, Route 2, which makes use of learned patterns of letters - "visual word forms". These can be mapped directly on to word meanings and to the pronunciation of the whole word. Where the word has a regular spelling there is congruence between the output of both routes - as in BERRY. Patterson calls this the "addressed route".

Where the spelling is not regular, there is conflict. If the reader relied on Route 2, the sound /bjuri/ would be assembled and this doesn't correspond to a word. Now the reader does not know whether the string is regular or irregular before he starts, so it is assumed that both routes are deployed simultaneously. For common words the whole word route is likely to be quicker, for uncommon words the part-word route is likely to be quicker. And it has been found that broadly the regularity of spelling helps the reading of the less frequent words.

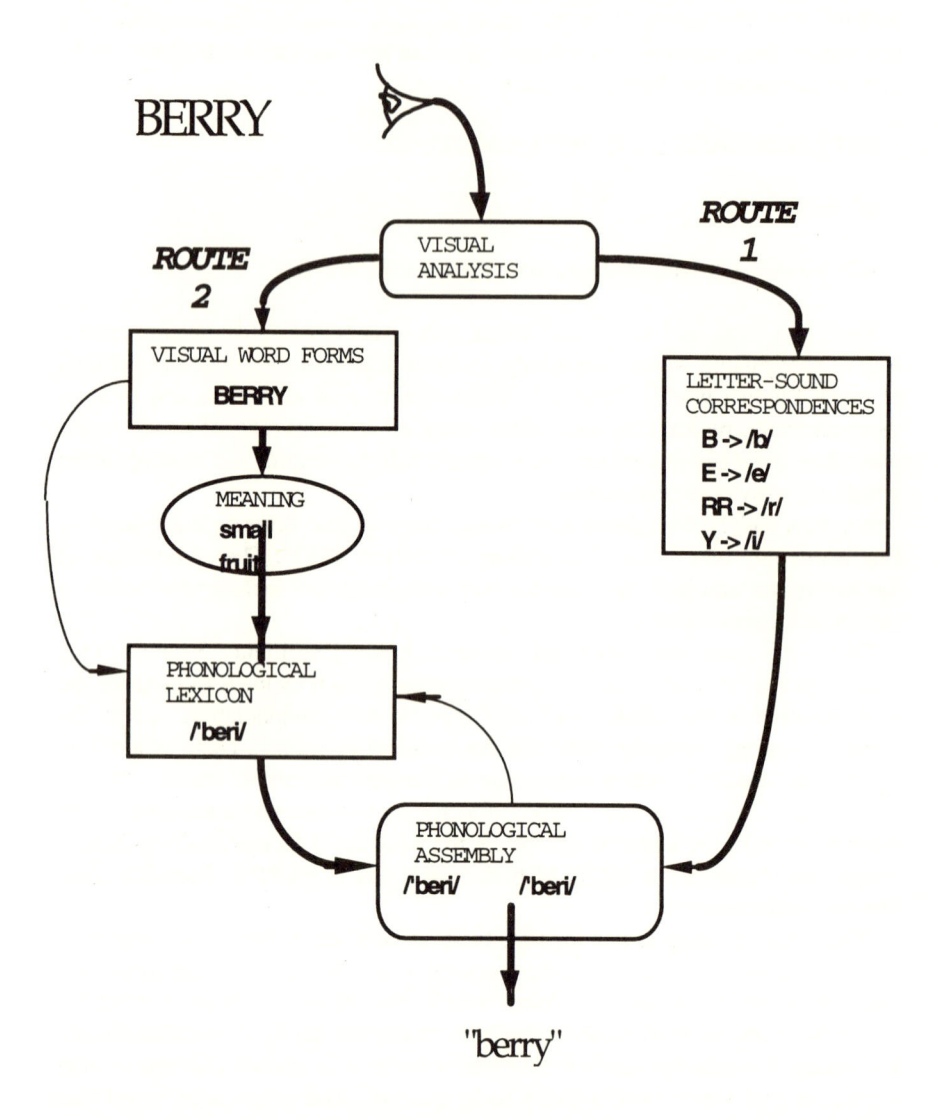

Figure 3. The two-route model of reading English: reading a "congruent" word

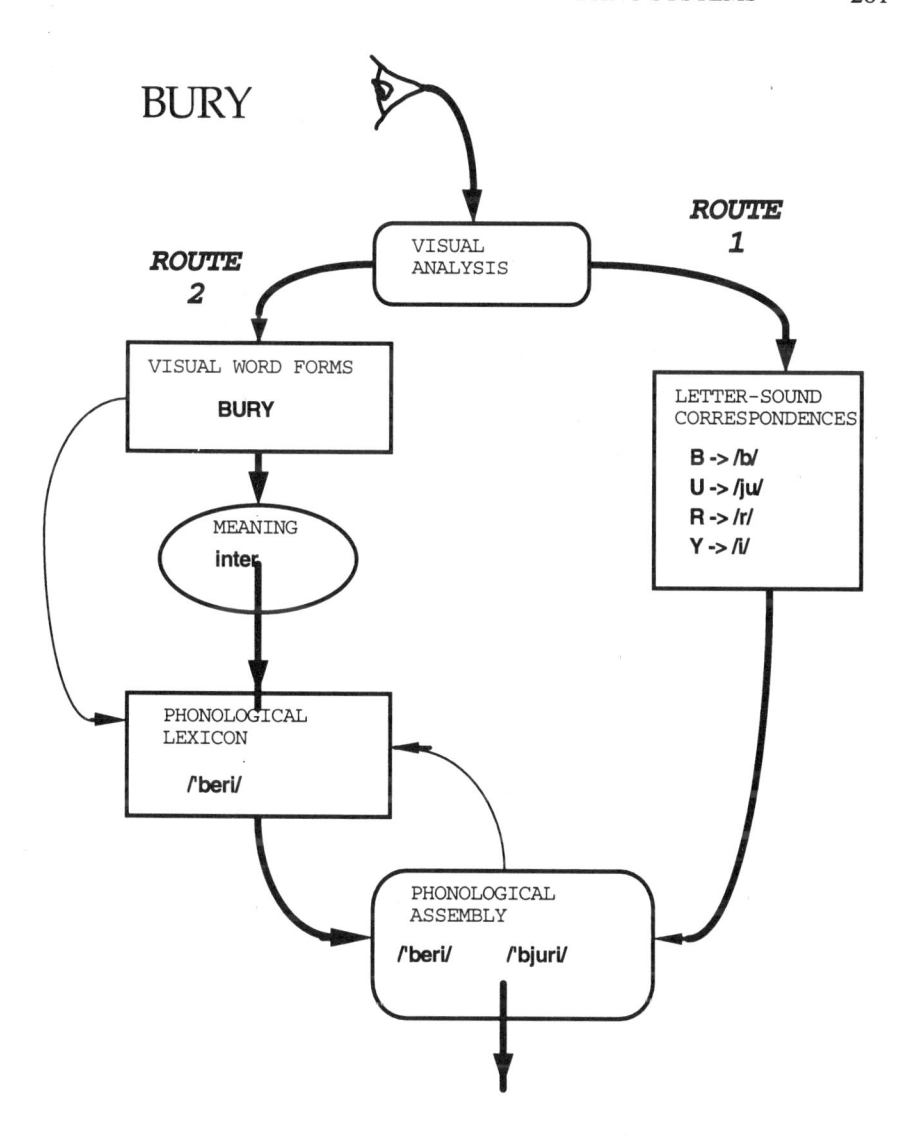

Figure 4. The two-route model of reading English: reading an "incongruent" word

The important point here is that the outputs of the two routes, or processes, are the same: /'beri/. There need be no problem in combining the two outputs, or selecting between them. However in Figure 4, when the word to be read is incongruent, the outputs are different: /'beri/ and /'bjuri/. The important point here is that the outputs of the two routes, or processes, are the same: /'beri/. There need be no problem in combining the two outputs, or selecting between them. However in Figure 4, when the word to be read is incongruent, the outputs are different: /'beri/ and /'bjuri/.

Now if these two routes are reflected in permanent neural organisation, as opposed to being strategies that can be put together as needed, then neural damage may selectively impair one or other route - with predictable consequences

	NORMAL FUNCTION	SYMPTOMS WHEN DAMAGED	DISORDER
ROUTE 1	letter-sound mapping	- new words not readable - no regularity effects - no regularisation errors - semantic errors	"phonological dyslexia" "deep dyslexia"
ROUTE 2	whole word reading	- new words readable - regularity effects reg-regularisation errors	"surface dyslexia"

Table 3. Predicted effects of selective damage to the two routes

You might think that this dual route architecture is demanded by the peculiar nature of English spelling, and it is this that sets up two neurally separable subcomponents in the brain. Writing systems that did not have this mix of regular and irregular mappings should not show a dual route architecture. We should not find it in the brain of readers of Spanish, Serbo-Croatian, Korean HanGul, that use only consistent mappings between letters and sounds. However there is suggestions that even readers of these orthographies might have neurally distinct routes of the right kind. One patient studied by Masterson, Coltheart and Meara (1985) was able to read accurately and fluently, but when confronted by homophones (possible in Spanish, since one phoneme may be represented by more than one grapheme) showed far more confusions as to their meanings than would be expected of normal readers. This suggests that the patient's letter-sound route was working, but his whole word route was not. It must be admitted that neuropsychological data for two routes in highly consistent orthographies has been slow in coming.

If shallow alphabetic orthographies, pose one sort of problem for our approach, then writing systems that don't use letters at all - like Chinese - should pose even more of a problem.

The Chinese system is very different from English.

Far from there being a small number of letters, there are some 50,000 characters, with at least 3000 required for everyday use. These elements, unlike letters, do not stand for sounds that are meaningful only in combination. Each character stands for a syllable, and each syllable is a word (or a meaningful morpheme).

In Chinese Hanzi, or in Japanese Kanji, the smallest graphemic unit, the Hanzi or Kanji, character is mapped onto a whole syllable, and this syllable is a meaningful unit in itself - a word or a morpheme. Now Hanzi or Kanji both map languages that have very small inventories of syllables. In Mandarin Chinese, the national standard language, there are some 1307 syllables (taking into account tones). Japanese there are just 47 basic syllables (strictly, "mora"), and only about 110 including those diacritically marked. However, there are very large inventories of characters: some 50,000 Hanzi, with 3000 in common use; and 50,000 Kanji, with 2500 on the recently officially prescribed list of Jyoyo Kanji, which newspapers and government documents should be restricted to. This means that, unlike European writing systems, each sound unit is mapped onto many, many graphemic units and many, many meanings. The following example in Table 4 from Mandarin Chinese illustrates the point:

(all of these characters are pronounced: **bù**)

NO	不	PLACE-NAME	吥
PLUTONIUM	钚	CLOTH	布
FEAR	怖	BOOK	簿
PLACE-NAME	埗	STEP	步
VASE	瓿	PART	部
WHARF	埠	BASKET	簿
PLACE-NAME	埔		

Table 4. Usefulness of Sound in deriving meaning in Chinese

In English, there are limitless new syllables that could be constructed to make a new word. In Chinese fewer than 1400 syllables are permitted. This means that each syllable has to do duty in many words.This also means that deriving the sound from the writing is a poor guide to the meaning, as we saw above in the case of bù. Unlike English where it's usually one sound one meaning, or set of related meanings; homophones (BEAR-BARE; TOE-TOW) are the exception rather than the rule. Yin (1991) has calculated that each syllable is associated with a mean of some 7.8 characters found in the principal dictionary, each with a distinct meaning, though he notes there are 255 syllables represented by just one character each.

I summarise the relevant aspects of Chinese orthography in Table 5.

1. Elements (characters) stand for meaningful speech sounds (single syllable morphemes) in an unsystematic way

2. Elements and sounds can be assembled to form words

3. Elements cannot combined in new ways to make new syllables. There are fewer than 1400 syllables in Mandarin, and that's it!

Table 5. The Chinese writing system

This is a very different social practice from English. However, a closer inspection reveals *some* similarities. Yin has further calculated that about 80% of characters are "pictophonetic". These characters are not just undifferentiated wholes; they contain two distinct parts, traditionally called radicals. The radical on the left can indicate the meaning, and the radical on the right, the sound. Now the sound radical - sometimes called the phonetic - indicates the sound of the whole character, not some part of it. So it's not like the letter B in BIT, that indicates just the first sound of the word. In Chinese a part stands for the sound of the whole character. So far so simple. There is a tricky bit. Only 36% of sound radicals are a reliable guide to pronunciation - in our terms, consistent. The rest are more or less unreliable. The following figure shows an inconsistent phonetic radical with a congruent and an incongruent pronunciation.

You can see that in the character top left of Figure 5 contains a radical that on its own is pronounced *píng*, the same way as the whole character. If every character in which this radical occurred was pronounced *píng* than we say that the radical is consistent. However, this radical is not. The character top right contains it, but is pronounced *chèng*. The radical is thus inconsistent, but with a congruent reading for *píng* and an incongruent reading for *chèng*.

This property in theory allows Chinese readers to make regularisation errors - comparable to reading PINT as /pInt/. So here we have a potential analogue of irregular English spellings. Of course, there are no letters. But suppose instead of thinking of letter-sound route, we thought more generally of *an analytic route* - a route that takes the parts, be they letters or radicals - and a whole word route - one takes the whole word, be it a letter string or one or more characters.

Congruent character

评

Pronunciation: píng
Meaning: comment

Incongruent character

秤

Pronunciation: chèng
Meaning: steelyard

Phonetic radical in isolation

平

Pronunciation: píng
Meaning: flat, level

Regularization error: 秤 pronounced píng

Figure 5. Congruent and incongruent characters in Chinese

We would then be able to use the same model for Chinese as for English, *mutatis mutandis*. If so, the model for reading congruent characters would look like Figure 6, and for incongruent characters, like Figure 7.

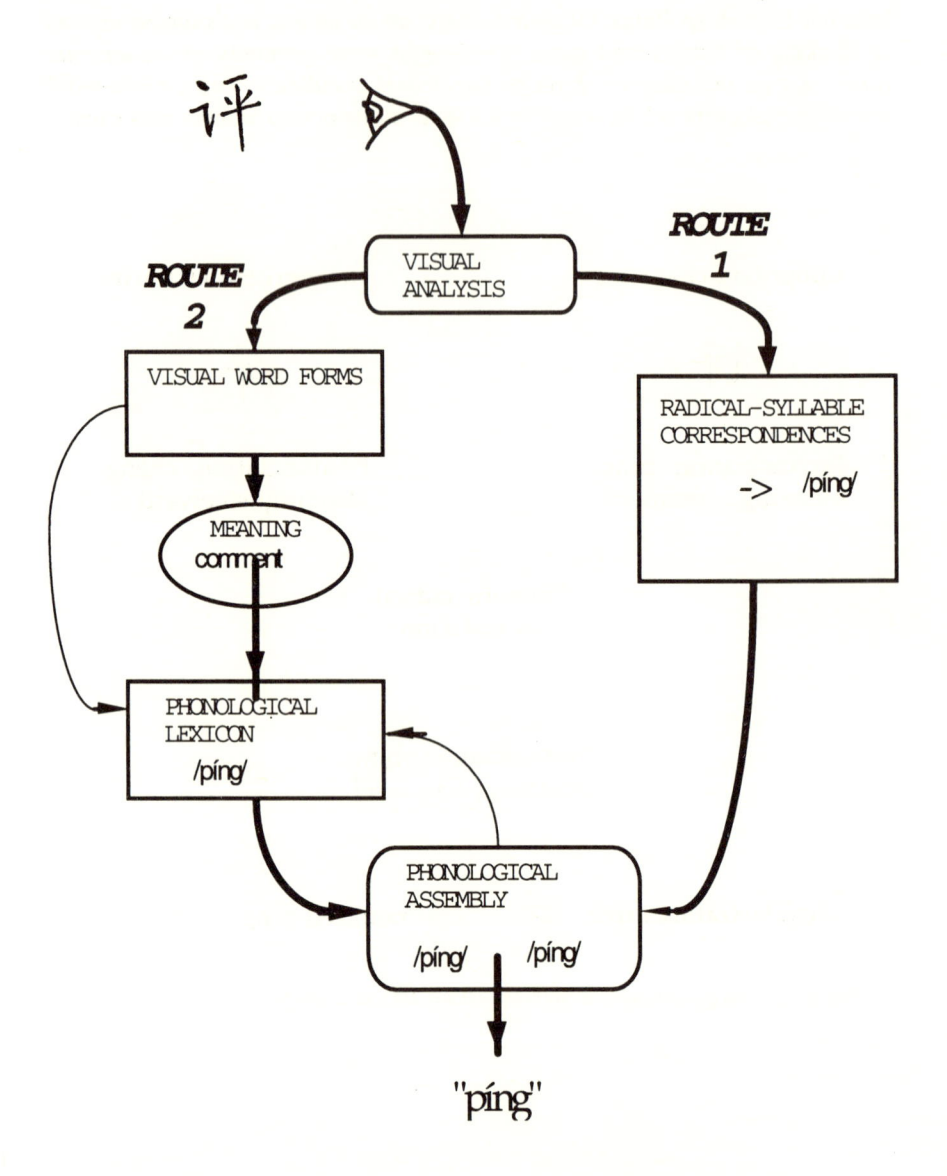

Figure 6. The two-route model for reading Chinese: reading a congruent word

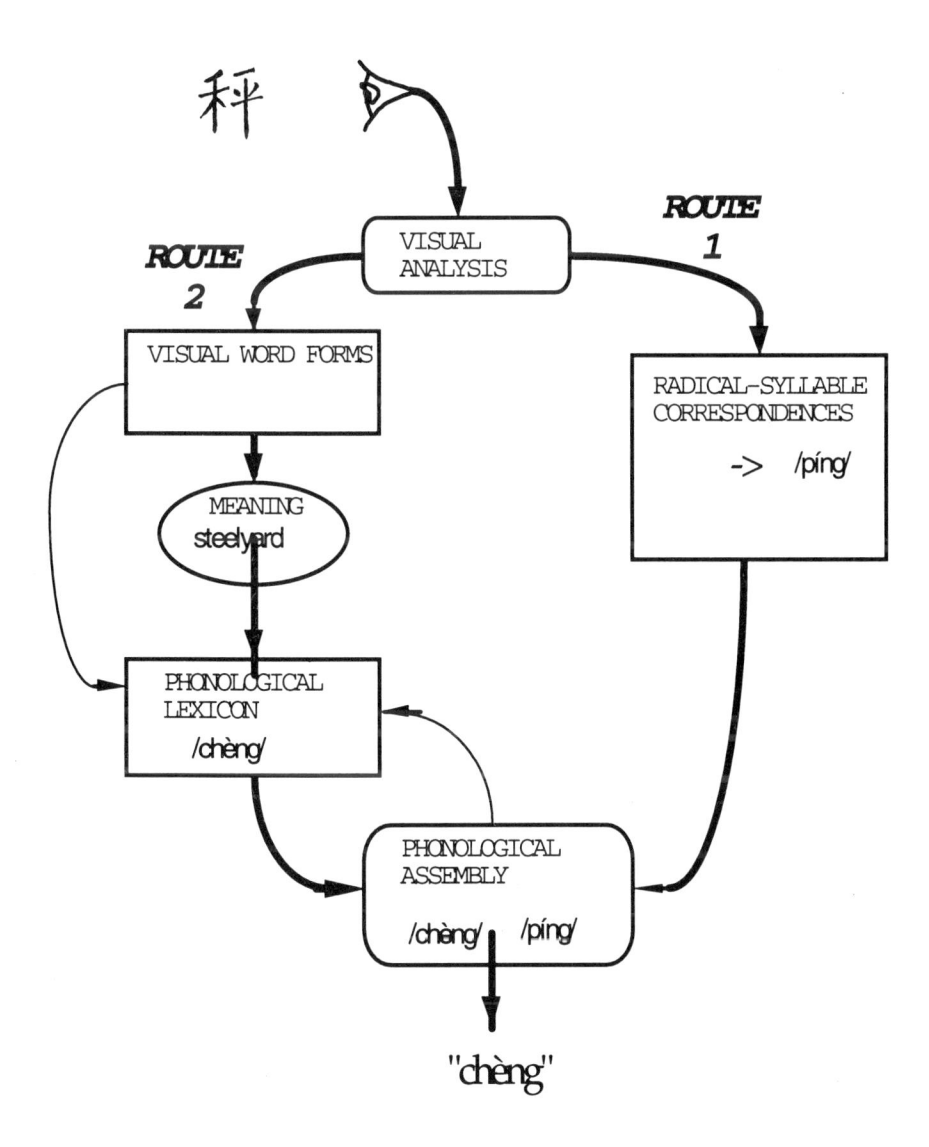

Figure 7. The two-route model for reading Chinese: reading an incongruent word

Is this just procrustean? Are we illegitimately, or over-enthusiastically, applying a known account to an inappropriate case? It would clearly help if we could show that there is a neural basis to it. That is, if we could show that there can be selective impairments of each of the two routes, and, even better, that the selective impairments correspond to separate neural regions. We studied 11 neurological patients with reading disorders. (Butterworth and Yin, 1991)

Now recall two key predictions from deficits to the two routes:

if the analytic route (Route 2) is damaged then you will get semantic errors in reading; while if the whole word route (Route 1) is impaired, then we should find regularisation errors.

types	patients	semantic errors*	regularisations*
deep	QXS	24	0
dyslexia	LYM	45	0
	LLH	54	0
	ZZG	57	0
	LDJ	50	0
	LWY	47	0
	LSJ	41	0
surface	LSH	17	46
dyslexia	LZY	21	53
	LQF	14	25
	WBY	0	75

*percentage of total errors

Table 6: *Semantic and regularisation errors in 11 Chinese patients (from Butterworth and Yin, 1991)*

As we can see from Table 6, the 4 patients at the bottom made regularisation errors, just like the English surface dyslexics, but the first 7 in the table did not make regularisation errors. But they did, however, make far more semantic errors. English patients do not make both kinds, and it is subject of our current research to discover why this difference should be. We therefore classified patients who made regularisation errors as "surface" dyslexics and those who did not as "deep" dyslexics. As you will see below, the distinction made on the basis of this simple criterion turned out to be exceptionally fruitful.

The other key predictions concerns how the two types deal with different kinds of words. Only those with an intact analytic route will be able to read new words, or what in our Chinese experiments we call pseudo words, but at the same time these readers will be much better at reading words that are regular. Those relying exclusively on the whole word route, should be equally good (or bad) on regular and irregular words, but unable to read new words. And this is just what we see in Figure 8.

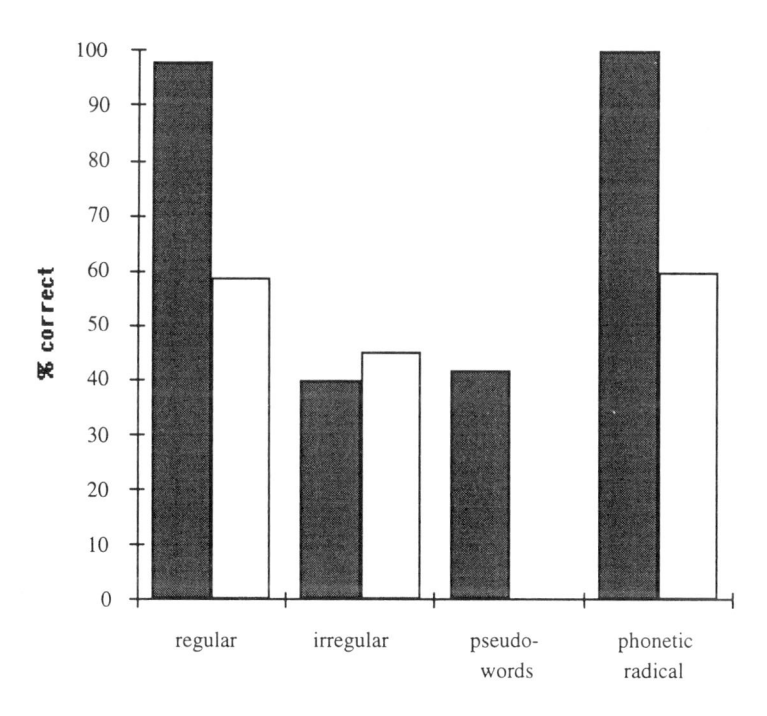

Figure 8: Reading aloud regular words, irregular words, radicals and pseudowords by Chinese deep and surface dyslexics (from Butterworth and Yin, 1991)

So it looks as though the same two components - analytic and whole word processes - characterise Chinese and English readers, each with independent neural substrates, since each can be separately damaged. If that is correct, then the organisation of reading processes in the brain may be determined in their overall architecture not by the social practices the reader acquired, but by some preference the brain has for organising at least some kinds of perceptual work into parallel streams, one global and one analytic.

We have recently gone some way to establishing the anatomical basis of this distinction. With the help of Dr Peter Rudge, a neurologist at the National Hospital for Neurology and Neurosurgery in London, we have been mapping the lesions from our clearest cases of reading disorder. We have seen two Chinese pure alexics: that is, patients with severely impaired reading, but with intact writing or other language skills. These patients show the classical locus in the left occipital lobe described by Déjerine in 1892. Our theoretically ambitious distinction between deep and surface dyslexia turns out to correspond to a very clear anatomical distinction. The three surface dyslexics for whom we have adequate scans all show small areas of damage in superior temporal gyrus near the angular gyrus, and including some of it. Now this is where we would expect it to be. The angular gyrus is thought to be an association linking visual and language functions - it lies between the visual areas in the occipital lobes and Wernicke's area. So potentially a good place to locate the visual forms of words.

The deep dyslexics have much larger lesions, as has been noted for English language deep dyslexics (Marin,1980) than surface dyslexics (Vanier and Caplan, 1985). For our three patients, the common area of damage lies frontally from Wernicke's area on the superior temporal gyrus. There is no region of overlap between the common areas of deep and surface dyslexia. This is, as far as I know, the best currently available anatomical support for our two routes.

Now the two route idea is a claim about the *acquisition* of reading skills. Frith (1985) has shown that children (perhaps I should say English children) learn to read in distinct stages, one of which focuses on words as wholes and another on letter-sound rules. If the brain likes to set up these separate routes, then it is possible that some innate condition will inhibit the development of one or other - with predictable consequences.

Now the child with an inherited impairment of the neural basis of the analytic route will, on this model, have trouble reading new words, but will be able to learn words by rote; while the child with an impairment of the global route will have trouble with irregular words (if he or she is unfortunate enough to be reared in a culture with irrational spelling practices - like Britain's or China's).

As it turns out, Ruth Campbell and I studied a girl, RE, who appeared to have the former condition. She could read and define words that were very uncommon and irregularly spelled, but had the greatest difficulty with even the simplest nonwords.

The complementary condition was reported recently by Goulandris and Snowling. JAS appeared to have an inherited impairment of the global route. She was showed striking regularization errors: like /In'dIktmnt, 'tʃei _s/, like /p_ust/humous, /'kInetic/. On the other hand, she had no problem reading new letter strings. even complicated ones like PLAZJUT.

> **R.E.**
>
> 21 years old, 3 A-levels, degree in Psychology.
>
> **can read:**
> PHLEGM, PUERPERAL, CATACOMB, SUBTLE, IDYLL
>
> **can't read:**
> OWN, OWT, NOO, HOZ
>
> (adapted from Campbell and Butterworth, 1985)
>
> ---
>
> **J.A.S.**
>
> 22 years old, 3 A-levels, degree in Psychology.
>
> **can't read:**
> INDICTMENT, CHAOS, POSTHUMOUS, KINETIC
>
> **can read:**
> MUNT, SEAD, OBTEMP, PLAZJUT
>
> (adapted from Goulandris and Snowling, 1991)

Table 7: Two readers showing selective developmental impairment of the two routes

In evolutionary time, reading is a recent development of homo sapiens, and only very recently indeed has it become a skill that would be relevant to the reproductive success of a large proportion of the population. Therefore, one might have thought that reading would be an ideal candidate for social practice to shape the organisation of the brain. Surprisingly, perhaps, this does not seem to be the case. Rather, the broad neural architecture of reading, at least of the two very different writing systems I have examined, seems to be shaped by the brain's preference for organising perceptual processes into analytic and holistic streams.

Aarts, R., De Ruiter, J., Verhoeven L.(1993) *Tweetaligheid en school succes (Bilingualism and school success)*. Tilburg: University Press
Abu-Mostafa, Y.S. (1995) Machines That Learn from Hints, *Scientific American*, April, 68-73
Adams, M.J. (1991) *Beginning to read: Thinking and learning about print.* Cambridge, MA: MIT Press
Ahituv, S. (1992) *Handbook of Ancient Hebrew Inscriptions* (in Hebrew), Jerusalem
Akinnaso, F.N. (1985) On the Similarities between Spoken and Written Language. *Language and Speech*, 28, 323-359.
Anderson, Stephen R. (1988) Morphological theory. In F.J. Newmeyer (ed.) *Linguistics: The Cambridge Survey, Volume 1, Linguistic Theory: Foundations*, Cambridge, Cambridge University Press, pp. 146-191
Andreewsky E., Rosenthal V. (1990) Alexies-aphasies. Problème des relations écrit-oral. In N.Catach (ed.) (1990), pp. 103-109
Aristotle (1938) *De Interpretatione* (H. P. Cook, Trans. London: Loeb Classical Library)
Aronoff, M. (1985) Orthography and linguistic theory, *Language*, 61, 28-72
Austin, J.L. (1962) *How to do things with words*. Cambridge, MA: Harvard University Press
Badry, F. (1983) *Acquisition of lexical derivation rules in Moroccan Arabic.* University of California, Berkeley, doctoral dissertation
Baetens Beardsmore, H. (1986) *Bilingualism: Basic Principles*, Clevedon: Multilingual Matters
Baker, C. (1996) *Foundations of bilingual education and bilingualism.* Clevedon: Multilingual Matters
Baker, K.A., de Kanter, A.A. (1983) *Bilingual education: A reappraisal of federal policy*. Lexington, MA, Lexington Books
Bally, Ch. (1944) *Linguistique générale et linguistique française*, Berne: A.Francke
Balogh J. (1927) *Voces paginorum*. Philologus 82, 84-127, 202-240.
Baluch, B., Besner, D. (1991) Visual word recognition: Evidence for strategic control of lexical and non lexical routines in oral reading. *Journal of Experimental Psychology: Learning, Memory and Cognition*, 17, 644-652
Bamberg, M.G.W. (1987) *The acquisition of narratives: Learning to use language.* Berlin, Mouton de Gruyter
Barbot, M. (1990) La Structure Du Mot En Arabe Littéral, *Modèles Linguistiques*, XII-2, 7-32
Barr, J. (1989) Hebrew, Aramaic and Greek in the Hellenistic Age, in *The Cambridge History of Judaism*, vol.2. *The Hellenistic Age*, Cambridge pp.79-114
Barton, D. (1994) The social impact of literacy. In L. Verhoeven (ed.) (1994a) pp. 185-197

Baruchson, S. (1993) *Books and Readers. The Reading Interests of Italian Jews at the Close of the Renaissance* (in Hebrew), Tel Aviv

Bates, E. (1976) *Language and context: The acquisition of pragmatics*. New York: Academic Press

Bauer Th. (1996) Die schriftliche Sprache im Arabischen. In H. Günther & O. Ludwig 1994/96, II, 1483-1490

Bäuml F.H. (1980) Varieties and Consequences of Medieval Literacy and Illiteracy. *Speculum,* 55, 237-265

Baurain, Cl., Bonnet, C., Krings, V. (eds.) (1991) *Phoinikeia Grammata, Lire et écrire en Méditerrannée,* Actes du Colloque de Liège, 15-18 novembre (1989) Séminaire d'Histoire grecque, Université de Liège, Société des études classiques, Namur

Bazin L. (1990) Le mot en turc, *Modèles linguistiques* , XII-2, 33-42

Beck, H. (1964) Problems of Word Division and Capitalization. In W.A.Smalley et al., 156-60

Behaghel O. (1899) Geschriebenes Deutsch und gesprochenes Deutsch. In id., *Von deutscher Sprache. Aufsätze, Vorträge und Plaudereien.* Lahr 1927, 11-34

Bennett-Kastor, T.L. (1986) Cohesion and predication in child narrative. *Journal of Child Language, 13*, 353-370

Benton, A. R., Pearl, D., (eds.) (1978) *Dyslexia: an appraisal of current knowledge.* New York: Oxford University Press

Benveniste, E. (1966) Les niveaux de l'analyse linguistique. In *Problèmes de linguistique générale,* Paris, Gallimard, pp.119-131 (= (1964) in *Proceedings of the 9th International Congress of Linguists,* Cambridge, Mas. (1962) Mouton)

Bereiter, C., & Scardamalia, M. (1982). From conversation to composition: The role of instruction in developmental process. In R. Glaser (Ed.), *Advances in instructional psychology* (pp. 132-165). Vol. II. Hillsdale: Lawrence Erlbaum Associates.

Berman, R. (1978) *Modern Hebrew structure.* Tel Aviv: University Publishing Projects

Berman, R. (1985) Acquisition of Hebrew. In D. I. Slobin ed. *Crosslinguistic Study of Language Acquisition.* Hillsdale, N.J.: Erlbaum, 255-371

Berman, R. A. (1986) A step-by-step model of language acquisition. In I. Levin (ed.) *Stage and structure: Reopening the debate.* Norwood, NJ: Ablex, 191-219

Berman, R. A. (1987) A developmental route: Learning the form and function of complex nominals. *Linguistics,* 25, 1057-1085

Berman, R. A. (1988) On the ability to relate events in narrative. *Discourse Processes, 11,* 469-197

Berman, R. A. (1990) Acquiring an SV language: Subjectless sentences in children's Hebrew. *Linguistics, 28,* 1135-1166

Berman, R. A. (1993) Crosslinguistic perspectives on native language acquisition. In K. Hyltenstam & A. Viberg (eds.) *Progression and regression* in language. Cambridge: Cambridge University Press, 245-266

BIBLIOGRAPHIC REFERENCES 295

Berman, R. A. (1993a) Developmental perspectives on transitivity: A confluence of cues. In Y. Levy (ed.) *Other children, other languages: Issues in the theory of language acquisition.* Hillsdale, NJ: Erlbaum, 189-241

Berman, R. A. (1995a) Word formation as evidence. In D. McLaughlin & S. McEwen (eds.) *Proceedings 19th Annual Boston University Conference on Language Development.* Somerville, Ma: Cascadilla, 82-95

Berman, R. A. (1995b) Narrative competence and storytelling performance: How children tell stories in different contexts. *Journal of Narrative and* Life History, 5, 4

Berman, R. A. (1996) Form and function in developing narrative abilities. In D. Slobin, J. Gerhardt, A. Kyratzis, & J. Guo (eds.) *Social interaction, social context, and language*: Essays in honor of Susan Ervin-Tripp. Hillsdale, NJ: Erlbaum, 243-268

Berman, R. A., J. S. Reilly. (1995)-April. *Elements of narrative structure and* narrative development. Child Language Research Forum, Stanford

Berman, R. A., Slobin, D. I. (1994) *Different ways of relating events in narrative: A crosslinguistic developmental study.* Hillsdale, NJ: Lawrence Erlbaum

Berman, R., Clark, E. (1993) *What children know about coining verbs in English and Hebrew.* Paper presented at the Sixth IASCL Congress, Trieste-July

Berman, R.A. (1988) On the ability to relate events in narrative. *Discourse Processes 11*, 469-497

Berman, R.A., Slobin D.I. (1994) *Relating events in narrative: a crosslinguistic developmental study.* Hillsdale/ New Jersey, Lawrence Erlbaum

Berrendonner, A., Reichler-Béguelin, M.(1989) Décalages. Les niveaux de l'analyse linguistique, *Langue française 81*, Février (1989) 99-125

Bertelson, P., de Gelder, B., Tfouni, L. V., Morais, J. (1989) The metaphonological abilities of adult illiterates: New evidence of heterogeneity. *European Journal of Cognitive Psychology, 1*, 239-250

Berthoud-Papandropoulou, I. (1978) An experimental study of children's ideas about language. In A. Sinclair, J. Jarvella, & W. Levelt ((eds.)), *The child's conception of language* pp. 55-64. Berlin: Springer-Verlag

Besner, D, Smith, M.C. (1992) Basic processes in reading: Is the orthographic depth hypothesis sinking? In R Frost & L Katz (eds.) *Orthography, Phonology, Morphology and Meaning.* Amsterdam, Elsevier Science Publishers B.V

Besse, J.M.(1991) Scrivere nella scuola dell'infanzia.In M.Orsolini & C. Pontecorvo eds. *La costruzione del testo scritto nei bambini* . Firenze: La Nuova Italia

Bestgen, Y. (1992) *Deux approches du discours narratif: Marqueurs de la segmentation et profil çmotionnel.* Doctoral thesis. Université Catholique de Louvain, Faculté de Psychologie et des Sciences de l'Education

Bialystok, E., E.B. Ryan (1985) Metacognitive framework for the development of first and second language skills. In: D.L. Forrest-Pressley, G.E. MacKinnon and T.G. Waller eds, *Metacognition, cognition and human performance.* New York: Academic Press

Biber D. (1988) *Variation across Speech and Writing*, Cambridge

Bissex, G. (1980) *GNYS AT WRK. A child learns to write and read.* Cambridge, MA : Harvard University Press

Blanche-Benveniste C., 1982: La escritura del lenguaje dominguero, in E.Ferreiro, M.Gomez-Palacio (a cura di), *Nuevas perspectivas sobre los procesos de lectura y escritura*, México, Siglo XXI Editores.

Blanche-Benveniste C., Jeanjean C. ((1986)) *Le français parlé. Edition et transcription,* Paris, Didier-Erudition

Blanche-Benveniste, C. (1994) The construct of oral and written language. In L. Verhoeven ed., *Functional literacy: Theoretical issues and educational implications.* Amsterdam: Benjamins

Blanche-Benveniste, C. [Article in this volume]

Blanche-Benveniste, C., Chervel, A. (1969) *L'Orthographe*, Paris, Maspéro

Bloomfield L. (1933) *Language.* New York: Holt/Rinehart & Winston

Bloomfield, L. (1927) Literate and Illiterate Speech. In Hockett (ed.) *Léonard Bloomfield, An Anthology*

Bolinger, D. (1975) (2nd.ed.) *Aspects of Language*, New York, Harcourt

Bolotzky, (1978) In Aronson, Berman, R. *Modern Hebrew structure.* Tel Aviv: University Publishing Projects

Boone, E. H. (1994) Aztec pictorial histories: Records without words. In E. H. Boone & W. D. Mignolo, (eds.) (1994)

Boone, E. H. Mignolo, W. D. (eds.) (1994) *Writing without words: Alternative literacies in Mesoamerica & the Andes.* Durham, NC: Duke University Press

Bosch, L., Costa, A., Sebastian, N. (1994) *La estructura interna de las categorias fonéticas: Percepción de vocales e identificación de prototipos en catalán y español.*[The internal structure of phonetic categories: vowels' perception and prototype identification in Catalan and Spanish]. Paper presented at the XII Congress of AESLA, Barcelona, Spain

Bottero, J. (1987) *La Mésopotamie, L'écriture et les dieux*, Paris, Gallimard (Bibliothèque d'Histoire)

Bower, G. H., Morrow, D. G. (1990) Mental models in narrative comprehension. *Science, 247,* 44-48

Bradley, L., Bryant, P. (1979) The independence of reading and spelling in backward and normal readers. *Developmental Medicine and Child Neurology,* 21, 504-514

Bradley, L., Bryant, P. (1983) Categorizing sounds and learning to read: A causal connection. *Nature*, 301, 419-421

Braunwald, S. R. (1985) The development of connectives. *Journal of Pragmatics, 11,* 177-220

Brekle, H.E. (1994) *Die Buchstabenformen westlicher Alphabetschriften in ihrer historischen Entwicklung,* In Günther, Ludwig et al., cit., vol. I, 171-204

Bronckart, J.P. et al. (1985) *Le fonctionnement des discours.* Paris/Neuchâtel, Delachaux et Niestlé

Bronckart, J.P., Schneuwly, B. (1984) La production des organisateurs textuels chez les enfants. In M. Moscato, G. Pierau-Le Bonniec. (eds.) *Le langage -*

construction et actualisation. Rouen, Publications de l'Université de Rouen, 165-178

Brouard, E. (1882) Ardoises. In F. Buisson (ed.) (1882)

Brown, R. (1973) *A first language: The early stages*. Cambridge, MA: Harvard University Press

Browning, R. (1982) Greek Diglossia Yesterday and Today, *International Journal of the Sociology of Language* 35, 49-68

Bruce, D. (1964) The analysis of word sounds by young children. *British Journal of Educational Psychology*, 34, 158-170

Bruner, J. (1990) *Acts of meaning*. Cambridge MA, Harvard University Press

Bruner, J.S. (et al.) (1966). *Studies in cognitive growth*. New York: Wiley & Sons.

Bruni F. (1984) *L'italiano. Elementi di storia della lingua e della cultura*, Torino

Bruno G. (1877) *Le tour de la France par deux enfants*, Paris: E. Belin

Brunot, F. (1967) (rééd.) *Histoire de la Langue Française*, 13 vol., Paris, Colin

Bryant, P., Bradley, L. (1980) Why the children sometimes Write Words which they do not Read, in U. Frith ed. *Cognitive Processes in Spelling*, London: Academic Press

Bryant,P., Goswami, U. (1986) Phonological awareness and learning to read. En J.R. Beech y Colley, A.M. eds. *Cognitive approaches to reading*. London, John Wiley & Sons

Budwig, N. (ed.) (1991) Functional approaches to child language. *First Language*, 11. Special edition

Bugarski, R. (1993) Graphic relativity and linguistic constructs. In R.Scholes (ed.), *Literacy and language analysis* Hillsdale, NJ: Erlbaum, pp. 5-18

Buisson F. (ed.) (1882) *Dictionnaire de pédagogie et d'instruction primaire*, Paris: Hachette

Burns A. (1989) *The Power of the Written Word. The Role of Literacy in the History of Western Civilization*, New York etc. (Studia Classica, 1)

Butterworth, B , Yin, W.G. (1991) Universal and language-specific features of reading: Evidence from dyslexia in Chinese readers. *Proceedings of the Royal Society - Series B*, 245, 91-95

Bybee, J. (1985) *Morphology: A study of the relation between meaning and form*. Amsterdam: John Benjamins

Callebat L, (ed.)(1995) *Latin vulgaire latin tardif IV*. Actes du 4^e colloque international sur le latin vulgaire et tardif. Caen, 2-5 septembre 1994 Hildesheim etc

Camargo A. (1991) *Ars dictaminis, Ars dictandi*, Turnhout (Typologie des Sources du Moyen Age Occidental, 60)

Camean Gorrias, C. (1990) *Las diferencias cualitativas en los periodos previos a la fonetización de la escritura*. Tesis de Maestría no publicada. Centro de Estudios Avanzados del Instituto Politécnico Nacional. Mexico

Campbell, R. (1991) The importance of special cases: or how the deaf might be, but are not phonological dyslexics. *Mind & Language*, 6, 107-111

Campbell, R., Butterworth, B. (1985) Phonological dyslexia and dysgraphia in a highly literate subject: A developmental case with associated deficits of phonemic processing and awareness. *Quarterly Journal of Experimental Psychology*, 37, 435-475

Carbonell de Grompone, M. A. (1974) Children who spell better than they read. *Academic Therapy*, 9, 281-286

Caron, J., Micko, H.C., Thuring, M. (1988) Conjunctions and the recall of composite sentences. *Journal of Memory and Language*, 27, 309-323

Carruthers, C., Bever, T.G. (1984) Eye-fixation patterns during reading confirm theories of language comprehension. *Cognitive Science*, 8, 157-172

Carvalhão Buescu, M.L. (1983) *O Estudo das lìnguas exòticas no seculo XVI*, Lisboa, Conselho da Europa (Biblioteca Breve, série Pensamento e Ciéncia)

Cary, L. (1990) Será a consciência fonológica um todo homogéneo? A evidencia dos iletrados. *Revista Portuguesa de Psicología*, 26, 57-76

Catach, N. (ed.) (1990) *Pour une théorie de la langue écrite, Actes de la Table Ronde internationale CNRS- HESO, Paris 23-24 octobre (1986)* Paris, Editions du CNRS

Cavallo, G. (1995). Introduzione. In G. Cavallo and R. Chartier (a cura di) *Storia della lettura*. Bari: Laterza.

Cavallo, G. and Chartier R. (a cura di) (1995). *Storia della lettura*. Bari: Laterza.

Cerquiglini, B. (1989). *Eloge de la variante. Historie critique de la Philologie*. Paris: Editions du Seuil.

Chafe W.L. (1982) Integration and Involvement in Speaking, Writing, and Oral Literature. In D. Tannen (ed.), *Spoken and Written Language: Exploring Orality and Literacy*, Norwood, N.J. (Advances in Discourse Processes, 9), 35-53

Chafe W.L. (1985) Linguistic Differences Produced by Differences between Speaking and Writing. In D.R. Olson et al. (eds.), *Literacy, Language, and Learning. The Nature and Consequences of Reading and Writing*, Cambridge, 105-123

Chafe W.L., Danielewicz J. (1987) Properties of Spoken and Written Language. In Horowitz, Samuels 1987, 83-113

Chall, J. (1979). The great debate: ten years later, with a modest proposal for reading stages. In L.B. Resnick & P.A. Weaver (eds) *Theory and practice of early reading*, vol.2. Hillsdale, N.J.: Lea.

Chartier A.M., Hébrard, J. (1993) Lire pour écrire à l'école primaire ? L'invention de la composition française dans l'école du XIXe siècle. *Les Interactions lecture-écriture*. Colloque organisé par le Centre de recherche en éducation de Lille, Université Charles-de-Gaulle-Lille III, Villeneuve-d'Asq, 22-24 nov. 1993, Berne: Peter Lang

Chartier R. (1993) Le message écrit et ses réceptions. Du codex à l'écran. *Revue des Sciences morales et politiques*, 296-309

Chartier, R. (1992) ¿Que es un autor? In R.Chartier *Libros, lecturas y lectores en la edad moderna*. Barcelona, Alianza Universidad.

Chartier, R. (1995) *Sociedad y escritura en la edad moderna. La cultura como apropiación*. Mexico: Instituto Mora.

Chassagne, S. (1989) Comment apprenait-on l'arithmétique sous l'Ancien Régime?, *Populations et cultures. Études réunies en l'honneur de F. Lebrun*, Rennes, AFL, 137-144

Chaytor H.J. (1945) *From Script to Print. An Introduction to Medieval Literature*, Cambridge

Chervel A. (1977) *Et il fallut apprendre à écrire à tous les petits Français. Histoire de la grammaire scolaire*, Paris: Payot

Choi, S., Bowerman, M. (1991) Learning to express motion events in English and Korean: The influence of language-specific lexicalization patterrns. *Cognition*, 41, 83-121

Chomsky N (1972) *Language and Mind*. New York, Harcourt Brace Jovanovich

Chomsky N. (1965) *Aspects of the theory of syntax*. Cambridge, MA: MIT Press.

Chomsky N. (1972) *Language and mind*. New York: Harcourt, Brace, Jovanovich

Chomsky N., Halle M. (1968) *Sound Pattern of English*, New York, Harper & Row

Choppin A. (1986) Le livre scolaire, *Histoire de l'édition française*, tome IV, *Le livre concurrencé (1900-1950)*, Paris, Promodis, pp. 281-306

Choppin, A. (1990) *Les Manuels scolaires, histoire et actualité*, Paris: Hachette

Clanchy M. (1992) *From memory to written record*. London: Blackwell (2nd ed.)

Clark E. (1993) *The lexicon in acquisition*. Cambridge University Press

Clark E., Berman, R. (1984) Structure and use in the acquisition of word-formation. *Language*, 60, 542-590

Clark, H. (1965) Some structural properties of simple active and passive sentences. *Journal of Verbal Learning and Verbal Behavior*, 4: 365-370

Cohen, M. (dir.) (1963) *L'Ecriture et la psychologie des peuples*, Paris, Colin

Cole, M., Gay, J., Glick, J.A. & Sharp, D.W. (1971). *The cultural context of learning and thinking*. London: Methuen

Comrie, B. (1988) Linguistic Typology. In F.J. Newmeyer (ed.) *Linguistics: The Cambridge Survey, Volume 1, Linguistic Theory: Foundations*, Cambridge, Cambridge University Press, 551-461

Content, A. (1991) Segmental analysisi abilities constitute a powerful accelerator of reading acquisition. *Mind & Language*, 6, 113-121

Corbett, A.T., Dosher, B.A. (1978) Instrument inferences in sentence encoding. *Journal of Verbal Learning Verbal Behavior*, 17, 479-492

Cornillac, G. (1993) *Le mot en français et en esquimau. Etude de psycho-systématique comparée*. Paris: Peeters (Coll. SELAF N° 341)

Cossu, G., Gugliotta, M., Marshall, J.C. (1995) Acquisition of reading and written spelling in a transparent orthography: two non parallel processes ? *Reading and Writing*, 7, 9-22

Cossu, G., Gugliotta, M., Villani, D., Marshall, J. C. (1996) Developmental trajectory in a transparent orthography. (Submitted),

Cossu, G., Maggetti, S., Marshall, J.C. (1996) A highly specific dyslexia in a child with superior cognitive abilities. (Submitted)

Cossu, G., Marshall, J.C. (1985) Dissociation between reading and written spelling in two Italian children: Dyslexia without dysgraphia? *Neuropsychologia*, 23, 697-700

Cossu, G., Marshall, J.C. (1986) Theoretical implications of the hyperlexia syndrome: Two new Italian cases. *Cortex*, 2, 579-589

Cossu, G., Marshall, J.C. (1990) Are cognitive skills a prerequisite for learning to read and write? *Cognitive Neuropsychology*, 7, 21-40

Cossu, G., Rossini, F., Marshall, J. C. (1993) When reading is acquired but phonemic awareness is not: A study of literacy in Down's Syndrome. *Cognition*, 46, 129-138

Cossu, G., Shankweiler, D., Liberman, I.Y., Gugliotta, M. (1995) Visual and phonological determinants of misreadings in a transparent orthography. *Reading and Writing*, 7, 237-256

Cossu, G., Urbinati, M.L., Marshall, J.C. (1987) Reading without speech and writing without arm movements. Bressanone, Fifth European Workshop on Cognitive Neuropsychology

Coulmas F. (1994) Schriftlichkeit und Diglossie. In Günther, Ludwig 1994/96, I, 739-745

Coulmas F. (1994) *Theorie der Schriftgeschichte*. In H. Günther, O. Ludwig et al. vol. I, 256-264

Coulmas F., Ehlich K. (eds.)(1983) *Writing in Focus*, Berlin etc. (Trends in Linguistics. Studies and Monographs, 24), 31-43

Coulmas, F. (1989) *The writing Systems of the World*, Oxford, Basil Blackwell

Coulmas, F. (1990) Overcoming diglossia: The rapprochement of written and spoken japanese in the 19th century (= Le rapprochement du japonais écrit et parlé au XIX° siècle) in N.Catach (éd.) *Pour une théorie de la langue écrite*, 191-202

Crain, S. (1991) Language acquistion in the absence of experience. *Behavioral and Brain Sciences, 14*, 597-650

Crain, S., McKee, C. (1985) Acquisition of structural restictions on anaphora. In S. Berman, J-W. Choe, J. McDonough, eds, *Proceedings of the 16th North Eastern Linguistics Society Meeting*, [NELS 16], 94-110

Cubelli, R. (1993) A selective deficit for writing vowels in acquired dysgraphia. *Nature*, 353, 258-260

Cumming, A. (ed.) (1994) *Bilingual performance in reading and writing*. Ann Arbor/Amsterdam, John Benjamins

Cummins, J. (1983) *Heritage language education: A literature review*. Toronto: Ministry of Education

Cummins, J. (1984) Wanted: A theoretical framework for relating language proficiency to academic achievement among bilingual students. In: C. Rivera ed., *Language Proficiency and Academic Achievement*. Clevedon: Multilingual Matters

Cummins, J. (1986) Empowering minority students. A framework for intervention. *Harvard Educational Review 56*, 18-36.

Cummins, J. (1989) Language and literacy acquisition in bilingual contexts. *Journal of Multilingual and Multicultural Development 10*, 1, 17-31

Cummins, J. (1991) Conversational and academic language proficiency in bilingual contexts. *AILA Review 8*, 75-89
Cummins, J. Swain, M. (1986) *Bilingualism in education. Aspects of theory, research and practice.* London, Longman
Cutler, A., Mehler, J.,, Segui, J. (1986) The syllable's differing role in the segmentation of French and English. *Journal of Memory and Language.* 25, 385 - 400.
Daiber, H. (1990), *Die Autonomie der Philosophie im Islam.* In, M. Atzalos, J.E. Murdoch, I. Niiniluoto (eds.) *Knowledge and the Sciences in Medieval Philosophy,* Helsinki, pp. 228-249
Daly L. W. (1967) *Contributions to a history of alphabetization in antiquity and the Middle Ages.* Brüssel: Latomus vol. 90
Danesi, M. (1989) Ancestral language training and the development of bilingual literacy. In Zuanelli Sonino, Elisabetta. (ed.) *Literacy in school and society. Multidisciplinary perspectives.* New York/London, Plenum Press, 41-53
de Batencour J. (1654) *L'Escole paroissiale ou la manière de bien instruire les enfans dans les petites escoles par un prestre d'une paroisse de Paris*, Paris: Pierre Targa
De Francis, J. (1989) *Visible speech: The diverse oneness of writing systems.* Honolulu: University of Hawaii Press
de la Salle J.B. (1706) *La Conduite des écoles chrétiennes*, cité d'après le manuscrit de 1706, CE 4,2,2-4,2,5, *Oeuvres complètes*, Rome, Études lasalliennes, EFC, 1994
De Mauro T. (1970) Tra Thamus e Theuth. Note sulla norma parlata e scritta, formale e informale nella produzione e realizzazione dei segni linguistici, *Bollettino del Centro di studi filologici e linguistici siciliani* 11, 167-179
De Weck, G. (1991) *La cohésion dans les textes d'enfants.* Paris/ Neuchâtel, Delachaux et Niestlé
Defodon Ch. (1882) Cahiers scolaires. In F. Buisson, (ed.) (1882)
DeFrancis, J. (1989) *Visible speech. The diverse oneness of writing systems.* Honolulu: University of Haway Press
Déjerine, J (1892) Contribution à l'étude anatomoclinique et clinique des differentes variétés de cécité verbale. *Compte Rendu Hebdomodaire des Séances et Mémoires de la Société de Biologie, 4,* 61-90
Demsky, A. Bar-Ilan, M. (1988) *Writing in Ancient Israel, Part I: The Biblical Period, Part II: Scribes and Books in the Late Second Commonwealth and Rabbinic Period,* in *Mikra* ed. M.J. Mulder, Van Gorcum, Philadelphia
Derrida, J. (1976) *Of grammatology* G. Spivak, Trans.. Baltimore, MD: Johns Hopkins University Press
Desbordes F. (1993) Un element de l'heritage Latin: la notion de l'orthographe. In C. Pontecorvo & C. Blanche-Benveniste, (eds.) (1993) pp. 97-112
Desbordes, F. (1990)a, La prétendue confusion de l'écrit et de l'oral dans les théories linguistiques de l'antiquité. In N.Catach (éd.) *Pour une théorie de la langue écrite,* 27-36
Desbordes, F. (1990)b, *Idées romaines sur l'écriture,* Lille, Presses Universitaires de Lille

Devescovi, A., Orsolini, M., Pace,C. (1990)Consapevolezza linguística nei bambini in età prescolare, *Rassegna di Linguistica Applicata* 153-177
Di Sciullo A.M., Williams, E. (1988) *On the Definition of Word,* Cambridge, MIT Press (Linguistic Inquiry, Monograph Fourteen)
Doane A.N., Braun Pasternack C. (eds.)(1991) *Vox Intexta. Orality and Textuality in the Middle Ages,* Madison
Doets, C. (1994) Assessment of adult literacy levels: the Dutch case. In L. Verhoeven (ed.) (1994), 321-332
Doneux, J.L., (1990) Quand l'ordre des morphèmes vaut l'ordre des mots, Communication au Séminaire de DEA, Aix-en-Provence, avril (1990)
Downing, J. (1984) A source of cognitive confusion for beginning readers: Learning in a second language. *Reading Teacher 37,* 4, 366-370
Downing, J. (1987) Comparative perspectives on world literacy. In D. Wagner ed., *The future of literacy in a changing world* pp. 25-47. Oxford: Pergamon Press
Dubuisson, M. (1991) Lettrés et illettrés dans la Rome antique. L'importance sociale, politique et culturelle de l'écriture. In Cl.Baurain, C.Bonnet & V.Krings (éds.) *Phoinikeia Grammata* 633-648
Duggan J.J. (1973) *The Song of Roland: Formulaic Style and Poetic Craft,* Berkeley etc. (Publications of the Center for Medieval and Renaissance Studies, 6)
Duranti, A., E., Ochs (1997). Syncretic Literacy in a Samoan american family. In L. Resnick, R. Saljo, C. Pontecorvo, B. Burge (eds) *Discourse, Tools, and Reasoning: Essays on Situated Cognition.* Berlin-New York: Springer Verlag.
Egli, M. (1995a) Schriftliches und mündliches Erzählen in der Primarschule: Schriftspracherwerb bei zweisprachigen Kindern in der deutschen Schweiz. *Bulletin Suisse de linguistique appliquée 62,* 233-260
Egli, M. (1995b) L'acquisition de l'écrit chez les enfants bilingues. *Babylonia 2/3,* 21-27
Egli, M., Lüdi, G. (1994) Bilittératie chez des enfants bilingues. In U. Frith et al. (eds.) 1995 (eds.) pp 135-163
Ehlich K. (1994) Funktion und Struktur schriftlicher Kommunikation. In M. Günther & O. Ludwig 1994/96, I, 18-41
Ehri, L.C. (1984) How orthography alters spoken language competencies in children learning to read an spell. In J. Downing & R. Valtin eds. *Language awareness and leaning to read* pp. 119-147. New York: Springer-Verlag
Ehri, L.C. (1985) Effects of printed language acquisition on speech. In D. R. Olson, N. Torrance, & A. Hildyard (eds.), *Literacy, language, and learning: The nature and consequences of reading and writing* Cambridge: Cambridge University Press pp. 333-367.
Ehri, L.C. (1993) English orthography and phonological knowledge. In Scholes ed., *Literacy and language analysis.* Hillsdale, NJ: Erlbaum pp. 21-43.
Ehri, L.C., Wilce, L. S. (1980) The influence of orthography on readers' conceptualization of the phonemic structure of words. *Applied Psycholinguistics,* 1, 371-385

Eisenstein E.L. (1979) *The Printing Press as an Agent of Change. Communication and Cultural Transformation in Early-Modern Europe*. 2 vol., Cambridge usw
Ellis, A. W. (1985) The cognitive neuropsychology of developmental and acquired dyslexia: A critical survey. *Cognitive Neuropsychology*, 2, 169-205
Ernout A. (1951) Dictare 'dicter', allem DICHTEN. *Revue des Etudes Latines* 29, 155-161.
Ernst G. (1985) *Gesprochenes Französisch zu Beginn des 17. Jahrhunderts. Direkte Rede in Jean Heroards 'Histoire particulière de Louis XIII' (1605-1610)*, Tübingen (Beihefte zur Zeitschrift für Romanische Philologie, 204).
Ernst, G. (1980) Prolegomena zu einer Geschichte des gesprochenen Französisch. In H. Stimm (ed.), *Zur Geschichte des gesprochenen Französisch und zur Sprachlenkung im Gegenwartsfranzösischen*, Wiesbaden (Beihefte zur Zeitschrift für französische Sprache und Literatur N.F., 6), 1-14
Esperet, E., Gaonac'h, D. (1986) The role of narrative schema on story production and recall: A longitudinal study, Communication at the 2nd ISSBD European Conference on Developmental Psychology, Rome
Extra, G., L. Verhoeven (1993) *Immigrant languages in Europe*. Clevedon: Multilingual Matters
Falk H. (1990) Goodies for India – Literacy, Orality, and Vedic Culture. In Raible 1990, 103-120
Fantini, A.E. (1985) *Language acquisition of a bilingual child*. Clevedon: Multilingual Matters
Fayol, M. (1981) *L'organisation du récit écrit chez l'enfant*, Université de Bordeaux II, Ph.D. (2 volumes)
Fayol, M. (1985) *Le récit et sa construction*. Neuchâtel-Paris: Delachaux Niestlé
Fayol, M. (1991) Stories: A psycholinguistic and ontogenetic approach to the acquisition of narrative abilities. In G. Piéraut-Le Bonniec M. Dolitsky (eds.) *From language bases to discourse bases*. (pp. 219 - 244) Amsterdam: Benjamin
Fayol, M. (1992) Comprendre ce qu'on lit: De l'automatisme au contrôle. In M. Fayol, J.E. Gombert, P. Lecocq, L. Sprenger-Charolles D. Zagar (eds.), *Psychologie cognitive de la lecture*. Paris: P.U.F
Fayol, M. (in press) On acquiring and using punctuation : A study in written French. In J. Costermans M. Fayol (eds.), *Processing interclausal relationships in the production and comprehension of texts* : Hillsdale, NJ: LEA.
Fayol, M., Gaonac'h, D., Mouchon, S. (1992) L'utilisation des marques de surface lors de la lecture: l'exemple de la ponctuation. *Scientia Paedagogica Experimentalis*, 29, 83-98
Fayol, M., Lemaire, P. (1993) Levels of approach to discourse. Illustrated by story comprehension. In H.H. Brownell Y. Joanette (eds.), *Alternative perspectives on the neuropsychology of narrative discourse* (pp. 3-20) San Diego, CA: Singular Pub
Fayol, M., Monteil, J.M. (1988) The notion of script: From general to developmental and social psychology. *C.P.C., European Bulletin of Cognitive Psychology*, 8, 335-361

Febvre, L., Martin H.-J. (²1971) *L'apparition du livre*, Paris (L'Evolution de l'Humanité, 49)
Feldbusch, E. (1985) *Geschriebene Sprache. Untersuchungen zu ihrer Herausbildung und Grundlegung ihrer Theorie*, Berlin/New York
Feldman, C.F. (1991) Oral Metalanguage. In D. Olson & N.Torrance 1991, 47-65
Ferguson, C.A. (1959) Diglossia. *Word 15*, 325-340.
Ferreiro, E. (1985a) Literacy development: A psychogenetic perspective. In D. R. Olson, N. Torrance, & A. Hildyard (eds.) (1985) pp. 217-228
Ferreiro, E. (1985b) The Relationship between oral and written language: the children viewpoints. In M.Clark (ed.) *New directions in the study of reading.* Sussex-Philadelphia: Palmer Press
Ferreiro, E. (1986) The interplay between information and assimilation in beginning literacy. In W. Teale & E. Sulzby (eds.) *Emergent Literacy: Writing and Reading,*. Norwood, NJ: Ablex, pp. 15-49
Ferreiro, E. (1987) (2nd ed.) *Proceso de alfabetizaciòn. La alpfabetizaciòn en proceso*. Buenos Aires: Centro Editor de América Latina (Bibliotecas Universitarias)
Ferreiro, E. (1988) L'écriture avant la lettre. In H. Sinclair ed. *La production de notations chez le jeune enfant: langage, nombre, rythmes et melodies.* Paris: Press Universitaire de France
Ferreiro, E. (1991) Psychological and epistemological problems on written representation of language. In M. Carretero, M. Pope, R. J. Simons, & J. Pozo (eds.), *Learning and instruction: European research in international context.* Oxford: Pergamon Press
Ferreiro, E. (1995) Diversità e processo di alfabetizzazione. *Età evolutiva*, n.51, 49-57,
Ferreiro, E. (1996) I confini del discorso: la punteggiatura. In E. Ferreiro, C. Pontecorvo, N. Moreira & I. García Hidalgo (eds.) (pp. 147-191)
Ferreiro, E. (in press) La noción de palabra y su relación con la escritura. *Nueva Revista de Filología Hispánica* (México)
Ferreiro, E., Moreira, N. (1996) Le ripetizioni e le loro funzioni testuali. In E. Ferreiro, C. Pontecorvo, N. Moreira & I. García Hidalgo (eds.) pp. 193-236
Ferreiro, E., Othenin-Girard, Ch., Chipman, H., Sinclair, H. (1976) How do children handle relative clauses? A study in comparative developmental psycholinguistics. *Archives de Psychologie*, XLV,3: 229-266
Ferreiro, E., Pontecorvo, C. (1996) I confini tra le parole. In E. Ferreiro, C. Pontecorvo, N. Moreira & I. García Hidalgo (eds.), pp. 39-77
Ferreiro, E., Pontecorvo, C., Moreira, N., García Hidalgo, I. (eds.) (1996a,1996b,1996c). *Cappuccetto Rosso impara a scrivere. Studi comparativi in tre lingue romanze.* Firenze: La Nuova Italia; *Caperucita Roja aprende a escribir.* Estudios psicolingüísticos comparativos en tres lenguas. Barcelona: Gedisa; *Chapeuzinho vermelho aprende a escrever. Estudos psicolingüísticos comparativos em três linguas* . São Paulo: editora Àtica

Ferreiro, E., Teberosky, A. (1982) *Literacy before schooling Los sistemas de escritura en el desarrollo del nino*. Exeter, NH: Heinemann English translation/Mexico DF: Siglo Veintiuno Editors. Original work published (1979)

Ferreiro, E., Teberosky, A. (1979) *Los sistemas de escritura en el desarrollo del niño*. México: Siglo XXI Editores. English translation: *Literacy Before Schooling*. Exeter,N.H. & London: Heinemann, 1982. Italian translation: *La costruzione della lingua scritta nel bambino*. Firenze: Giunti Editore, 1985

Ferreiro, E., Vernon, S. (1992) La distinción palabra/nombre en niños de 4 y 5 años. *Infancia y Aprendizaje*, 58, 15-28

Fevrier, J. (1963) Les sémites et l'alphabet. Ecritures concrètes et écritures abstraites. In M.Cohen (1963) (dir.) *L'Ecriture et la psychologie des peuples*

Fiormonte, D. (1993) *Scrittura, Computer e ipertesto*. Tesi di laurea in Lettere e Filosofia, Università di Roma "La Sapienza",

Filliozat, P. (1990) La notion de mot chez les grammairiens indiens, *Modèles linguistiques*, XII-1, 10-20

Fillmore, L.W. (1991) When learning a second language means losing the first. *Early Childhood Research Quarterly 6*, 323-347

Finnegan R. (1988) *Literacy and Orality. Studies in the Technology of Communication*, Oxford

Finnegan, R. (1977) *Oral poetry: Its nature, significance, and social context*. Cambridge: Cambridge University Press

Fishman, J. (1980) Ethnocultural dimensions in the acquisition and retention of biliteracy. *Journal of Basic Writing 3*, 48-61

Fleisher Feldman, C. (1991) *Oral Metalanguage*. In D.R. Olson & N. Torrance (eds.) *Literacy and Orality*, Cambridge, pp.47-65

Foley J.M. (1977) The Traditional Oral Audience, *Balkan Studies* 20, 470-475

Foley J.M. (1990) *Traditional Oral Epic: The 'Odyssey', 'Beowulf' and the Serbo-Croatian Return Song*, Berkeley

Fowler, C., Liberman, I. Y., Shankweiler, D. (1977) On interpreting the error pattern in beginning reading. *Language and Speech*, 20, 162-173

Fox, B., Routh, D. K. (1975) Analyzing spoken language into words, syllables and phonemes: A developmental answer. *Journal of Psycholonguistic Research*, 4, 332 342

Francis, H. (1975) *Language in childhood: Form and function in language learning*. London: Paul Elek

Frank B. (1994) *Die Textgestalt als Zeichen. Lateinische Handschriftentradition und die Verschriftlichung der romanischen Sprachen*, Tübingen (ScriptOralia, 67)

Freeman, Y, Whitesell, L. R. (1985) What preschoolers already know about reading. *Developmental Psychology*, 13, 84-94

French, L.A., Nelson, K. (1985) *Young children's knowledge of relational terms*. New York: Springer-Verlag

Frith, U. (1979) Reading by eye and writing by ear. In P. A. Kolers; M. Wrolsted and H. Bouma (eds.) *Processing of visible language*. Vol 1. New York: Plenum

Frith, U. (1980) Unexpected Spelling Problems, in U. Frith (ed.) *Cognitive Processes in Spelling*, London: Academic Press

Frith, U. (1985) Beneath the surface of developmental dyslexia. In K E Patterson, J C Marshall & M Coltheart (eds.) *Surface Dyslexia: Neuropsychological and Cognitive Studies of Phonological Reading*. London, LEA

Frith, U. (ed.) (1994) Proceedings of the ESF Workshop on *Contexts of literacy*. Nice, France, 21-24 September 1994

Fruyt, M., Reichler-Béguelin, M. (1990) La notion de 'mot' en latin et dans d'autres langues indo-européennes anciennes, *Modèles Linguistiques*, XI-1, 21-46

Funnell, E. (1983) Phonological processes in reading: New evidence from acquired dyslexia. *British Journal of Psychology*, 74, 159-180

Furet, F., Ozouf J. (1977) *Lire et écrire. L'alphabétisation des Français de Calvin à Jules Ferry*, Paris: Éditions de Minuit, 2 vol

Gaffney, J.S., Anderson R.C. (1991) Two-tiered scaffolding: congruent processes of teaching and learning. In: E.H. Hiebert (ed.) *Literacy for a diverse society*. New York: Teachers College Press

Galaburda, A. M., Sherman, G.F., Rosen, G.D., Aboitiz, F., Geschwind, N. (1985) Developmental dyslexia: Four consecutive cases with cortical anomalies. *Annals of Neurology*, 18, 222-233

Galaburda, A., Kemper, TL. (1979) Cytoarchitectonic abnormalities in developmental dyslexia: A case study. *Annals of Neurology*, 6, 94-100

Galand, L. (1991) Entre l'oral et l'écrit: le berbère. In Cl.Baurain, C.Bonnet & V.Krings (éds.) *Phoinikeia Grammata* , 703-716

Gaonac'h, D., Passerault, J.M. (1990) A.D.F.M.: a technic for the study of reading activities. *Golem, 1*, 11

Garde, P. (1968) *L'accent*, Paris, Presses Universitaires de France

Gauger H.-M. (1994) Geschichte des Lesens. In H. Günther, O. Ludwig et al., vol. I, pp. 65-84

Gaur, A. (1987) *A history of writing* Paperback ed.. London: The British Library. Original work published (1984)

Gee, J. (1990). *Social linguistics and literacies: Ideology in discourses*. London: Falmer Press.

Gelb, I. (1963) *A Study of Writing. (Revised Edn)*. Chicago, University of Chicago Press

Gelb, I. (1973) *Pour une théorie de l'écriture*, Paris: Flammarion

Gelb, I. (1996) *Schrift als Zahlen - und Ordnungssystem - Alphabetisches Sortieren.* In Günther, Ludwig et al. vol. II, 1568-1583

Genesee, E. (1979) Les programmes d'immersion en français du Bureau des Ecoles Protestantes du Grand Montréal. Québec, Etudes et documents du Ministère de l'(ed.)ucation.

Genesee, E. (1984) French immersion programs: A Canadian innovation to bilingual education. In: S. Shapson & V. D'Oyley eds, *Bilingual and multicultural education: Canadian perspectives*. Avon: Multilingual Matters

Gentry, J. (1982) **An** analysis of developmental spelling in GNYS AT WRK. *The Reading Teacher*, 36, 192-200
Gerhardsson, B. (1961) *Memory and Script. Oral Tradition and Written Transmission in Rabbinic Judaism and Early Christianity*, Uppsala
Gernsbacher, M.A. (1985) Surface information loss in comprehension. *Cognitive Psychology, 17,* 324-363
Gernsbacher, M.A. (1989) *Language comprehension as structure building.* Hillsdale, NJ: L.E.A
Gesenius, (1910) Gesenius' Hebrew Grammar, edited by E. Kautzsch, revised by A.E. Cowley. Oxford: Clarendon Press
Gibelli A. (1993) Popular Writing in the 19th and 20th Centuries. In C. Pontecorvo & C. Blanche-Benveniste (eds.) (1993) pp. 255-270
Giesecke M. (1991) *Der Buchdruck in der frühen Neuzeit. Eine historische Fallstudie über die Durchsetzung neuer Informations- und Kommunikationstechniken,* Frankfurt/M.
Gillmore, P., A. Glatthorn (1980) *Ethnography and education: Children in and out school.* Philadelphia: University of Philadelphia Press
Globe & Mail April, (1993) Toronto
Glück H. (1987) *Schrift und Schriftlichkeit. Eine sprach- und kulturwissenschaftliche Studie*, Stuttgart
Goldman, S., Trueba, H.. eds (1989) *Becoming literate in English as a second language.* Norwood, NJ, Ablex
Goldman, S.R., Varnhagen, C.K. (1983) Comprehension of stories with no obstacle and obstacle endings, *Child Development, 54*, 980-992
Gombert, J.E. (1990) *Le développement métalinguistique.* Paris: Presses Universitaires de France
Gombrich, E. H. (1974) The visual image. In D. R. Olson ed., Media and symbols: The forms of expression, communication, and education pp. 241-270. Chicago, IL: The University of Chicago Press
Gontard, M. (1963) *La question des écoles normales primaires de la Révolution de 1789 à nos jours*, Toulouse: CRDP
Goody, J. (1977) *The domestication of the savage mind,* Cambridge: Cambridge University Press
Goody J., Watt, I. (1968) The Consequences of Literacy. In J. Goody (ed.), *Literacy in Traditional Societies*, Cambridge, 27-68
Goody, J. (1979) *La Raison graphique* . Paris: éd. de Minuit
Goody, J. (1987) *The interface between the oral and the written.* Cambridge: Cambridge University Press
Goswami, U., Bryant, P. (1990) *Phonological skills and learning to read.* Hove: Lawrence Erlbaum Associates Ltd., Publishers
Goulandris, N K, Snowling, M (1991) Visual memory deficits: a plausible cause of developmental dyslexia? Evidence from a single case study. *Cognitive Neuropsychology, 8,* 127-154
Graff H.J. (1987) *The Legacies of Literacy*, Bloomington/Indianapolis

Grafton A. (1981) Teacher, text and pupil in the Renaissance classroom. *History of Universities*, tome 1, pp. 37-70
Green D.W. (1977) The immediate processing of sentences. *Quarterly Journal of Experimental Psychology, 29*, 135-146
Green D.W. (1990) Hören und Lesen: Zur Geschichte einer mittelalterlichen Formel. In Raible 1990, 23-44
Green, J. N. (1988) Spanish. In M. Harris & N. Vincent eds.. *The Romance Languages* pp. 79-130. London:
Greene, J. (1972) *Psycholinguistics*. Middlesex: Penguin Books
Griego-Jones, T. (1994) Assessing students' perception of biliteracy in two way bilingual classrooms. *The Journal of Educational Issues of Language Minority Students 13,* 79-93
Grosjean, F. (1982) *Life with two languages*. Cambridge, Harvard University Press
Grossen, M. et Pichon, L. (1997) Interactional perspectives on the use of the computer and on the technological development of a new tool: The case of word processing. In Resnick, Saljo, Pontecorvo and Burge, 1997
Grossman, A. (1988) *The Early Sages of Ashkenaz* (in Hebrew), Jerusalem
Grossman, A. (1995) *The Early Sages of France* (in Hebrew), Jerusalem
Grundmann H. (1958) Litteratus – illitteratus. Der Wandel einer Bildungsform vom Altertum zum Mittelalter, *Archiv für Kulturgeschichte* 40, 1-65
Guillaume, G. (1947)-(1949) *Leçons de linguistique*, Série C, publiées par R.Valin,. Québec-Paris: PUL-Klincksieck (1973)
Günther H. (1988) *Schriftliche Sprache. Strukturen geschriebener Wörter und ihre Verarbeitung beim Lesen*, Tübingen (Konzepte der Sprach- und Literaturwissenschaft, 40)
Günther H. (1994) Aspects of a History of Written Language Processing in the Middle Ages. In U. Frith et al. (eds.), 107-125
Günther H., Ludwig, O. et al. (eds.) (1994)/95. *Writing and its Use. An Interdisciplinary Handbook of International Research*. Berlin & New York: de Gruyter (Vol. I 1994, Vol. II 1996)
Gunther, H. (1994) Aristotle on the relation of speech and writing - a note. In L. Verhoeven & A. Teberosky (eds.), *Understanding early literacy in a developmental and cross-linguistic approach* Vol 2. Proceedings of the Workshop on Understanding Early Literacy in a Developmental and Cross-linguistic Approach pp 283-287, October 7-9, (1993) Wassenaar: European Science Foundation
Haberlandt, K., Graesser, A.C. (1989) Processing of new arguments at clause boundaries. *Memory Cognition, 17,* 186-193
Haberlandt, K., Kennard, M. (1981) Causal and adversative connectives facilitate text comprehension, Annual Meeting of the Psychonomic Society, Philadelphia
Hachlili, R. (1979) The Goliath Family in Jericho, Funerary Inscriptions from a First Century AD Jewish Monumental Tomb in *Bulletin of the American Society for Oriental Research*, 235. pp.31-65

Häcki-Buhofer, A. (1995) Soziale und kulturelle Komponenten der Schriftlichkeit. Funktionen des alltäglichen schriftlichen Ausdrucks. *Babylonia 2/3,* 11-15

Hagège, C. (1982) *La structure des langues.* Paris: Presses universitaires de France (coll. Que sais-je ?)

Hakes, D. T. (1980) *The development of metalinguistic abilities in children.* Berlin: Springer-Verlag

Hakuta, K. (1986) *Mirror of language: The debate on bilingualism.* New York: Basic Books

Hall, W.S., L. F. Guthrie (1982) On the dialect question and reading. In: R.J. Spiro, B.C. Bruce & W.F. Brewer eds, *Theoretical Issues in Reading Comprehension.* Hillsdale, N.J.: LEA

Halle, M. (1969) Some thoughts on Spelling. In K.S.Goodman and J.T.Fleming (eds.) *Psycholinguistics and the Study of Reading,* International Reading Association, Newark, Delaware, Le Tyre Arenne, 17-24

Halliday, M.A.K., Hasan, R. (1976) Cohesion in English. London: Longman

Halliday, M.A.K. (1987) Spoken and Written Modes of Meaning. In R. Horowitz & S. J. Samuels (eds.) *Comprehending Oral and Written Language*, 55-82

Halliday, M.A.K. (1990) *Spoken and Written Language* . Oxford: Oxford University Press

Hamers, J.F., Blanc, M. (1983) *Bilingualité et bilinguisme,* Bruxelles, Mardaga.

Hanson, I.A. (1980) *An inquiry how three preschool children acquired literacy in two languages: English and Spanish. Unpublished dissertation.* Georgetown: Georgetown University

Hanson, V., Fowler, C.A. (1987) Phonological coding in word reading: Evidence from hearing and deaf readers, *Memory and Cognition,* 15, 199-207

Hardy , M., Stenett, R. G., Smythe, P. C. (1973) Auditory segmentation and auditory blending in relation to beginning reading. *Alberta Journal of Educational Research,* 19, 144-158.

Harris R. (1980) *The Language Makers,* Ithaca, N.Y

Harris, J. (1983) Syllabic Structure and Stress in spanish : A Nonlinear Analysis traducc. cast. (1991), La estructura silábica y el acento en español. Madrid: Visor

Harris, R. (1972) Word and word Criteria in French. In *Essays in Honour of Prof. T.B.W.Reid, The History and Structure of French,* Oxford, Blackwell, 117-133. (reprinted in N, Love ed., 1990, pp. 44-59)

Harris, R. (1986) *The origin of writing.* London: Duckworth

Harris, R. (1992) Ecriture et notation. In C. Pontecorvo & C.Blanche-Benveniste (eds.) (1992)

Havelock, E. (1961). *Prologue to greek literacy.* Norman: University of Oclahoma Press

Havelock E. (1976) *Origins of Western Literacy.* Four Lectures delivered at the Ontario Institute for Studies in Education, Toronto March 25, 26, 27, 28, 1974, Toronto: Ontario Institute for Studies in Education, Monograph Series, 14

Havelock, E. (1982) *The literate revolution in Greece and its cultural consequences.* Princeton, NJ: Princeton University Press

Havelock, E. (1991) *The Oral-Literate Equation: a Formula for the Modern Mind.* In D.R. Olson & N. Torrance (eds.) (1991) pp.11-27

Haviland, S.E., Clark, H.H. (1974) What's new? Acquiring new information as a process in comprehension. *Journal of Verbal Learning and Verbal Behavior, 13,* 512-521

Hayes J.R., Flower L.S. (1980) Identifying the organization of writing processes. In: L.W. Gregg & E.R. Steinberg (eds.), *Cognitive processes in writing.* Hillsdale: LEA, pp.3-30.

Heath, C. and Nicholls, G. (1997) Animating texts: Selective readings of News Stories. In Resnick, Saljo, Pontecorvo and Burge, 1997

Heath, S.B. (1982) What no bedtime story means: Narrative skills at home and at school. *Language in Society 11,* 49-76

Heath, S.B. (1983) *Ways with words: Language, life and work in communities and classrooms.* Cambridge MA, Harvard University Press

Hébrard, J. (1980) École et alphabétisation au XIXe siècle. *Annales ESC,* 1, 66-80

Hébrard, J. (1988) La scolarisation des savoirs élémentaires à l'époque moderne. *Histoire de l'éducation,* 38, 7-58

Hébrard J. (1990) L'alphabétisation dans les campagnes françaises au XIXe siècle. *Le Français aujourd'hui,* 91, 95-109

Hébrard J., Hubert C. (1979) Fais ton travail! *Enfances et Cultures,* 2, 47-59

Henderson L. (1985) *Issues in the modelling of pronunciation assembly in normal reading.* In Patterson et al., cit., 459-508

Herriman, M. L. (1986) Metalinguistic awareness and the growth of literacy. In S. de Castell, A. Luke, & K. Egan (eds.), *Literacy, society and schooling.* Cambridge: Cambridge University Press

Heurley, L. (1994) *Traitement de textes procéduraux.* Etude de psycholinguistique cognitive des processus de production et de compréhension chez des adultes non experts.Thèse de Doctorat, Université de Bourgogne

Hickmann, M. (1987) Ontogenèse de la cohésion dans le discours. In G. Pieraut-Le Bonniec (ed.) *Connaître et le dire.* Liège, Mardaga, pp. 239- 262

Hickmann, M. (1991) The development of discourse cohesion: some functional and cross-linguistic issues. In G.Piéraut-Le Bonniec, M. Dolitsky (eds.) *Language Bases...Discourse Bases.* Amsterdam/ Philadelphia, John Benjamins, pp.157-185

Hickmann, M. (1995) Discourse organization and the development of reference to person, space, and time. In P. Fletcher & B. MacWhinney (eds.) *The handbook of child language.* Cambridge, MA: Blackwell, 194-218

Hickmann, M. (in print) Discourse organization and the development of reference. In P.Fletcher, B. McWhinney (eds.) *Handbook of child language.* Blackwell Publishers

Hickok, G. (1993) Parallel Parsing: Evidence from Reactivation in Garden-Path Sentences. Journal of Psycholinguistic Research, 22, 2: 239-250

Hinshelwood, J. (1917) *Congenital word-blindness.* London: H.K. Lewis & Co

Hornberger N.H. (1994) Oral and Literate Cultures. In Günther, Ludwig 1994/96, I, 424-431

Hornberger, N.H. (1989) Continua of biliteracy. *Review of Educational Research 59*, 3, 271-296
Hornberger, N.H. (1990) Creating successful learning contexts for bilingual literacy. *Teachers College Record 92/2*, 212-229
Hornberger, N.H. (1994) Continua of biliteracy: Quechua literacy and empowerment in Peru. In Verhoeven (ed.), 237-256.
Horowitz, R., Samuels, S. J. (eds.) (1987) *Comprehending Oral and Written Language*, New York /London, Harcourt Brace Jovanovich, Academic Press
Hudelson, S. (1987) The role of native language literacy in the education of language minority children. *Language Arts 64/8*, 827-841
Hudson, J. A., Shapiro, L. R. (1992) From knowing to telling: The development of children's scripts, stories, and personal narratives. In A. McCabe & C. Peterson (eds.) *Developing narrative structure*. Hillsdale, NJ: Erlbaum, 89-136
Ibrahim, A. H. (1990) Questions posées par l'arabe à une théorie générale des systèmes d'écriture. In N.Catach (ed.) (1990), pp. 225-234
Ifrah G. (1989) *Universalgeschichte der Zahlen*. Frankfurt: Campus
Illich I. (1984) *Schule ins Museum. Phaidros und die Folgen*, Bad Heilbrunn, Obb. (Schriftenreihe zum Bayerischen Schulmuseum Ichenhausen, 3, 1)
Illich I. (1991) *Im Weinberg des Textes*. Frankfurt: Suhrkamp. English translation: *In the Vineyard of the Text*. Chicago: University of Chicago Press, 1993
Illich, I., Sanders, B. (1988). *The alphabetization of the popular mind*. London: Marion Boyars Publishers Ltd.
Irwin, J.W. (1980a) The effect of explicitness and clause order on the comprehension of reversible causal relationships. *Reading Research Quarterly, 15*, 477-488
Irwin, J.W. (1980b) The effects of linguistic cohesion on prose comprehension. *Journal of Reading Behavior, 12*, 325-332
Irwin, J.W. (1982) Coherence factors in children's textbooks. *Reading Psychology, 4*, 11-23.
Irwin, J.W., Pulver, C. (1984) The effects of explicitness, clause order, and reversibility on children's comprehension of causal relationships. *Journal of Educational Psychology, 76*, 399-407
Isserlin, J.B.S. (1991) The Transfer of the Alphabet to the Greeks: the state of Documentation. In Cl.Baurain, C.Bonnet & V.Krings (éds.) *Phoinikeia Grammata*, 283-292
Jackson, J. H. (1874) On the nature of the duality of the brain. *Medical Press and Circular*, 1, 19-41
Jacob, F. (1978) *Evoluzione e bricolage*. Torino: Einaudi Editore
Jaffré, J. (1990) Graphèmes et idéographie. In N.Catach (ed.) pp. 93-102
Jechle Th. (1992) *Kommunikatives Schreiben. Prozeß und Entwicklung aus der Sicht kognitiver Schreibforschung*, Tübingen (ScriptOralia, 41)
Jeruchimovicz, R.J. (1978) Use of coordinate sentences with the cunjunction and for describing temporal and locative relations between events. *Journal of Psycholinguistic Research, 7*, 135-150

Jisa, H. (1985) French preschoolers' use of *et pis* 'and then'. *First Language*, 5, 169-184

Jisa, H. (1987) Sentence connectors in French children's monologue performance. *Journal of Pragmatics*, 11, 607-621

John-Steiner, V., Panofsky, C.P, Smith., L.W. (1994) *Sociocultural approaches to language and literacy: An Interactionist Perspective.* Cambridge: Cambridge University Press, pp. vii + 402

Joly A., Paris-Delrue L. (1990) Mot de langue et mot de discours: le cas de l'anglais, *Modèles linguistiques*, XII-1, 71-92

Juel, C., Griffith, P.L., Gough P.B.(1986) Acquisition of literacy: A longitudinal study of children in first and second grade. *Journal of Educational Psychology 78*, 243-255

Just, M.A., Carpenter, P.A., Wooley, J.D. (1982) Paradigms and processes in reading comprehension. *Journal of Experimental Psychology: General, 3*, 228-238

Kamii, C., Long, R., Manning, G., Manning, M. (1993) Les conceptualisations du système alphabétique chez les jeunes enfants anglophones, *Etudes de Linguistique Appliquée*, 91, 34-47

Karmiloff-Smith A. (1986)a. Some fundamental aspects of language development after age 5. In P. Fletcher & M. Garman (eds.), *Language Acquisition, revised edition.* Cambridge: Cambridge University Press, 455-474

Karmiloff-Smith A. (1986)b. Stage/structure versus phase/process in modelling linguistic and cognitive development. In I. Levin (ed.), *Stage and structure: Reopening the debate.* Norwood, NJ: Ablex, 164-190

Karmiloff-Smith, A. (1981) The grammatical marking of thematic structure in the development of language production. In Werner Deutsch (ed.) *The child's construction of language.* London, Academic press, 121-147

Karmiloff-Smith, A. (1992) *Beyond modularity: A developmental perspective on cognitive science.* Cambridge, MA: MIT Press\Bradford Books

Karmiloff-Smith, A., Grant, J., Sims, K., Jones, M-C., Cuckle, P. (1996) Rethinking metalinguistic awareness: representing and accessing knowledge about what counts as a word. *Cognition*, 58: 197-219

Katz, L., Feldman, L B (1981) Linguistic coding in word recognition: Comparisons between a deep and a shallow orthography. In A M Lesgold & C A Perfetti (eds.) *Interactive processes in reading.* Hillsdale, NJ: Erlbaum

Kauffman, S. A. (1993) *The Origins of Order.* Oxford: Oxford University Press

Keenan, E. L. (1975) Logical expressive power and syntactic variation in natural languages. In *Formal Semantics of Natural Languages.* Cambridge University Press, 406-421

Keenan, J.M., Baillet, S.D., Brown, D. (1984) The effects of causal cohesion on comprehension and memory. *Journal of Verbal Learning and Verbal Behavior, 23*, 115-126.

Kellogg R. (1991) Literacy and Orality in the Poetic Edda. In Doane, , Pasternack 1991, 89-101

Kendall, J.R., Lajeunesse, G., Chmilar, P., Shapson, L.R., S.M. Shapson (1987) English reading skills of French immersion students in kindergarten and grades 1 and 2. *Reading Research Quarterly* 22, 135-159

Kielhöfer, B, Jonekeit, S. (1983) *Zweisprachige Kindererziehung*. Tübingen, Stauffenburgverlag

Kintsch, W. (1982). Text representations. In W. Otto & S. Whie (eds.), *Reading expository material* New York: Academic Press, pp. 87-102

Kirmeier A. Schütz A. & Brockhoff E. (eds.) (1994) *Schreibkunst. Mittelalterliche Buchmalerei aus dem Kloster Seeon*. München: Haus der bayrischen Geschichte (Catalogue of an exhibition)

Klein, W. (1989) *L'acquisition de langue étrangère*. Paris, Armand Colin

Koch P. (1988) Norm und Sprache. In J. Albrecht et al. (ed.), *Energeia und Ergon. Sprachliche Variation, Sprachgeschichte, Sprachtypologie. Studia in honorem E. Coseriu.* 3 vol., Tübingen (Tübinger Beiträge zur Linguistik, 300), 327-354

Koch P. (1992a and b) Arenga and Ars arengandi. In G. Ueding (ed.), *Historisches Wörterbuch der Rhetorik*, Tübingen, I, col. 877-889 and 1033-1040

Koch P. (1993a) Pour une typologie conceptionnelle et médiale des plus anciens documents/monuments des langues romanes. In Selig et al. 1993, 39-81

Koch P. (1993b) Oralité médiale et conceptionnelle dans les cultures écrites. In Pontecorvo, , Blanche-Benveniste 1993, 227-245

Koch P. (1995) Une langue comme toutes les autres: latin vulgaire et traits universels de l'oral. In Callebat 1995, 125-144

Koch P. (1996) La sémantique du prototype: sémasiologie ou onomasiologie?, *Zeitschrift für französische Sprache und Literatur* 106, 223-240

Koch P. (1997) Graphé. Ihre Entwicklung zur Schrift, zum Kalkül und zur Liste. In id., S. Krämer (eds.), *Schrift Medien, Kognition. Über die Exteriorität des Geistes*, Tübingen (Probleme der Semiotik, 19), 43-81

Koch P., Oesterreicher W. (1985) Sprache der Nähe – Sprache der Distanz. Mündlichkeit und Schriftlichkeit im Spannungsfeld von Sprachtheorie und Sprachgeschichte, *Romanistisches Jahrbuch* 36, 5-43

Koch P., Oesterreicher W. (1990) *Gesprochene Sprache in der Romania: Französisch, Italienisch, Spanisch*, Tübingen (Romanistische Arbeitshefte, 31)

Koch P., Oesterreicher W. (1994) Schriftlichkeit und Sprache. In Günther, Ludwig 1994/96, I, 587-604

Koch P., Oesterreicher W. (1996) Sprachwandel und expressive Mündlichkeit, *Zeitschrift für Literaturwissenschaft und Linguistik* 102, 64-96

Kolinsky, R., Moraise, J., Segui, J. (éds.) (1991) *La Reconnaissance des mots dans les différentes modalités sensorielles. Etudes de psycholinguistique cognitive*. Paris: Presses Universitaires de France

Kötzsche D. (ed.) (1989) *Das Evangeliar Heinrichs des Löwen*. Berlin: Insel

Krämer S. (1988) *Symbolische Maschinen: Die Idee der Formalisierung im ideengeschichtlichen Abriß*. Darmstadt: Wissenschaftliche Buchgesellschaft.

Krashen, S.O. (1981) *Second language acquisisition and learning*. Oxford, Pergamon Press

Krashen, S.O. (1991) Bilingual education: A focus on current research, *NCBE Focus: Occasional Papers on Bilingual (ed.)ucation 3*.

Kroon, S., Sturm, J. (1989) Implications of defining literacy as a major goal of teaching the mother tongue in a multicultural society. The Dutch situation. In E. Zuanelli Sonino (ed.) *Literacy in school and society. Multidisciplinary perspectives*. Ney York/London, Plenum Press, 91-113

Kullmann W. (1984) Oral Poetry Theory and Neonalysis in Homeric Research, *Greek, Roman and Byzantine Studies* 25, 307-323

Kupinsky, B. (1983) Bilingual reading instrcution in kindergarten. *Reading Teacher* 37, 132-137

Labarbe, J. (1991) Survie de l'oralité dans la Grèce archaïque. In Baurain, Bonnet & Krings (éds.) (1991), pp. 499-532

Lambert, W., G. Tucker (1972) *Bilingual education of children: The St. Lambert Project*. Rowley, MA: Newbury House

Larsen, M. T. (1989) What they wrote on clay. In K. Schousboe & M. T. Larsen (eds.), *Literacy and society*. Copenhagen: Copenhagen University, Centre for Research in the Humanities

Lavine, L. (1977) Differentiation of letterlike forms in prereading children. *Developmental Psychology*, 23, 89-94

Le Ny, J.F., Denis, M. (1980) Identification et compréhension du langage naturel. Perspectives cognitives. In J.P.Haton, J.M.Pierrel, P.Quinton (eds.) *Syntaxe et sémantique en compréhension de la parole*, Galf-Gerco, Communication parlée, 3-16

Le Page, R., Tabouret-Keller, A. (1985) *Acts of Identity*, Cambridge

Levin, I., Korat, O. (1993) Sensitivity to phonological, morphological and semantic cues in early reading and writing in Hebrew. *Merrill-Palmer Quarterly.*, 392., 233-251

Levin, I., Korat, O., Amsterdamer, P. (1996) Emergent writing among Israeli Kindergartners: Cross-linguistic commonalities and Hebrew-specific issues. In G. Rijlaarsdam, H. van der Bergh, & M. Couzijn eds. *Theories, models and methodology in writing research* Amsterdam:Amsterdam University Press pp.398-422.

Levine, K. (1986) *The social context of literacy*. London, Routledge & Kegan Paul

Levine, K. (1994) Functional literacy in a changing world. In Verhoeven (ed.), pp. 113-132

Levy, Y. (1988) The nature of early language: evidence from Hebrew morphology. In Y. Levy, I. M. Schlesinger & M. D. S. Braine eds. *Categories and processes in language acquisition*. Hillsdale, N.J.: Erlbaum.73-98.

Levy-Bruhl, L. (1926) *How natives think*. London: George Allen & Unwin. Original work published (1910)

Liberman, I. Y, Shankweiler, D., Liberman, A.D., Fowler, C., Fischer, F. W. (1977) Phonetic segmentation and recoding in the beginning reader. In A. S. Reber and D.L. Scarborough eds. *Toward a Psychology of Reading*, New Jersey: Erlbaum

Liberman, I. Y., Shankweiler, D., Fisher, F. W., Carter, B. (1974) Explicit syllable and phoneme segmentation in the young child. *Journal of Experimental Child Psychology*, 18, 201-212

Lieberman, S. 196 2. *Hellenism in Jewish Palestine*, New York

Lloyd, G. E. R. (1979) *Demystifying mentalities*. Cambridge: Cambridge University Press

Loewe, R. (1994) *Hebrew Linguistics* in G. Lipsky (ed.) *History of Linguistics* London and New York

Lord A.B. (1960) *The Singer of Tales*, Cambridge, Mass. (Harvard Studies in Comparative Literature, 24)

Lowe R. (1981) *Analyse linguistique et ethnocentrisme: Essai sur la structure du mot en inuktitut*, Ottawa: National Museums of Canada/ Musées Nationaux du Canada; National Museum of Man - Mercury Series/ Musée National de l'Homme - Collection Mercure, Canadian Ethnology Service, Paper N°70 / Le Service canadien d'Ethnologie, Dossier N°70

Lüdi, G. (1990a) Diglossie et polyglossie. In *Lexikon der Romanistischen Linguistik*, Holtus, G., Metzeltin, M., Schmitt, Chr.. (eds.), Tübingen, t. V/1, 307-334

Lüdi, G. (1990b) Les migrants comme minorité linguistique en Europe. *Sociolinguistic,a 4*, 113-135

Lüdi, G. (1992) Internal migrants in a multilingual country. *Multilingua 11/1*, 45-73

Lüdi, G., Py,. et al. (1994) *Fremdsprachig im eigenen Land. Wenn Binnenwanderer in B der Schweiz das Sprachgebiet wechseln und wie sie darüber reden*. Basel, Helbing & Lichtenhahn. in French: *Changement de langue-langage du changement*. Lausanne, L'âge d'homme, 1994)

Lüdi, G., Werlen, I. et al. (1996) *Sprachenlandschaft Schweiz*. Bern, Bundesamt für Statistik

Ludwig O. (1983) Einige Gedanken zu einer Theorie des Schreibens. In S. Grosse (ed.), *Schriftsprachlichkeit*. Düsseldorf, 37-73

Ludwig O. (1994) Geschichte des Schreibens. In Günther, Ludwig et al., cit., pp.48-64

Ludwig O. (1996) Vom diktierenden zum schreibenden Autor. In H. Feilke & J. Portmann (eds.), *Schreiben im Umbruch - Schreiben und Schulisches Schreiben*. Stuttgart: Klett, pp. 16-28

Luria, A.R. (1929/1976) *Cognitive Development. Its Cultural and Social Foundations*, Cambridge, Mass./London

Lyons, J. (1981) *Language and Linguistics. An Introduction*, Cambridge

Maas U. (1992) *Grundzüge der deutschen Orthographie*. Tübingen: Niemeyer

Maclean, M. , Bryant, P., V. Bradley, L. (1987) Rhymes , nursery rhymes and reading in early childhood. *Merrill-Palmer Quarterly*. 33, 255-281

Mac-Luhan, M. Fiore, Q. (1967) *The Medium is the Message*, New York, London, Toronto

Magnusson, E., Naucler, K. (1993) The development of linguistic awareness. *First Language*, 37, 93-112

Mair W. (1982) Elemente 'gesprochener Sprache' bei Robert de Clari. Überlegungen zum Problem der Verschriftung im Altfranzösischen, *Zeitschrift für französische Sprache und Literatur* 92, 193-219

Mann, V. Tobin, P., Wilson, R. (1987) Measuring Phonological Awareness Through the Invented spellings of Kindergarten Children, *Merril-Palmer Quarterly*, 33 3., 365-391

Mann, W.C., Thompson, S.A. (1980) Relational propositions in discourse. *Discourse Processes, 9,* 57-90

Mariani J. (1982) *Esope: Un système de compréhension de la parole continue* , Thèse de doctorat d'Etat, Paris VI

Marie-Cardine, W. (1988) *Le Cahier de devoirs mensuels. Textes réglementaires, études sur le cahier de devoirs mensuels, circulaires des inspecteurs d'académie, bibliographie,* Mémoires et documents scolaires publiés par le Musée pédagogique, fascicule n° 43, Paris: Delagrave et Hachette

Marin, O S M (1980) CAT scans of five deep dyslexic patients. In M Coltheart, K E Patterson & J C Marshall (eds.)*Deep Dyslexia.* London, RKP

Marr, D. (1976) Early processing of visual information. London, *Philosophical Transactions of the Royal Society.* B, 275, 483-524

Marr, D., Poggio, T. (1977) From understanding computation to understanding neural circuitry. *Neurosciences Research Progress Bulletin,* 15, 470-488

Marsh, G., Friedman, M. P., Welch, V. and Desberg, P. A. (1981) A cognitive developmental theory of reading acquisition. In MacKinnon, G. E., Waller, T. G. (eds.), *Reading Research: advances in Theory and Practice.* (Vol.) New York: Academic Press. 199-221

Marshall, JC. (1984) Toward a rational taxonomy of the developmental dyslexias. In Malatesha, R. N. and Whitaker, H. A. (eds.) Dyslexia: A Global Issue . (Vol.) The Hague: Martinus Nijhoff. 45-58

Marshall, J.C. (1989) The description and interpretation of acquired and developmental reading disorders. In Galaburda, A. M. (ed.), *From Reading to Neurons.* Cambridge, MA: MIT Press. 69-86

Marshall, J.C., Cossu G. (1991) Poor readers and black swans. *Mind & Language,* 6, 135-139

Martin H.-J. (1975) Culture écrite et culture orale, culture savante et culture populaire dans la France d'Ancien Régime, *Journal des Savants,* 225-282

Martin H.-J. (1988) *Histoire et pouvoirs de l'écrit,* Paris

Martinet, A. (1966) Le mot. In *Problèmes de langage* .Paris: Gallimard, 39-53

Masterson, J, Coltheart, M, Meara, P (1985) Surface dyslexia without;t irregular words. In K E Patterson, J C Marshall & M Coltheart (eds.) *Surface Dyslexia: Neuropsychological and Cognitive Studies of Phonological Reading.* London, LEA

Mattheier K.J. (1988) *Standardisierung europäischer Nationalsprachen seit der frühen Neuzeit,* Tübingen (= sociolinguistica 2)

Mattingly, I G (1992) Linguistic awareness and orthographic form. In R Frost & L Katz (eds.) *Orthography, Phonology, Morphology and Meaning*. Amsterdam, Elsevier Science Publishers B.V

Mattingly, I. G. (1972) Reading, the linguistic process and linguistic awareness. In Kavanagh, J. F. and Mattingly, I. G. (eds.) *Language by Ear and by Eye*. Cambridge, MA: MIT Press. 133-147

Mayroz, O. (1986) Acquisition of derived nominals by Hebrew-speaking children. Tel Aviv University masters' thesis [in Hebrew]

Mazal O. (1994) *Traditionelle Schreibmaterialien und - techniken*. In Günther, Ludwig et al., vol. 1, pp.122-130

Mc Carthy, J. (1981) A prosodic theory of nonconcatenative morphology. *Linguistic Inquiry*, 12, 373-418

McCabe, A., Peterson, C. (1991) *Developing narrative structure*. Hillsdale, NJ: L.E.A

McCarthy, D. (1954) Language development in children. In Carmichael (ed.), *Manual of Child Psychology* New York: John Wiley, pp. 492-630

McCarty, T. (1994) Bilingual education policy and the empowerment of American Indian communities. In *The Journal of (ed.)ucational Issues of Language Minority Students 14*, 23-42

McLuhan, M. (1962) *The Gutenberg Galaxy*, London

Mehler, J., Dommergues, J., Frauenfelder, V. y Segui, J. (1984) The syllable's role in speech segmentation. *Journal of Verbal Learning and Verbal Behavior*, 20, 298 - 305

Meisel, J.(ed.) (1992) *The acquisition of verb placement: Functional categories and V2 phenomena in language acquisition*. Dordrecht: Kluwer

Métayer C. (1990) De l'école au Palais de justice: l'itinéraire singulier des maîtres écrivains de Paris (XVIe-XVIIIe siècles). *Annales ESC*, 5, 1217-1237

Michaels, S., Collins, J. (1984) Oral discourse styles: Classroom interaction and the acquisition of literacy. In Deborah Tannen (ed.) *Coherence in spoken and written discourse*. Norwood/ New Jersey, Ablex, p. 219-244

Michalowski, P. (1994) Writing and Literacy in Early States: A Mesopotamianist Perspective. In: D.Keller-Cohen (ed.) *Literacy: Interdisciplinary Conversations*. Cresskill, N.J.: Hampton Press

Miethaner-Vent K. (1986) Das Alphabet in der mittelalterlichen Lexikographie. *La Lexique* 4, 83-112.

Mignolo, W. D. (1994) Signs and their transmission: The question of the book In the New World. In E. H. Boone & W. D. Mignolo, (eds.) (1994)

Miller, G., McKean, K. (1964) A chronometric study of some relations between sentences. *Quarterly Journal of Experimental Psychology*, 16: 297-308

Mino Garces, F. (1981) *A psycholinguistic analysis of early reading acquisition: six case studies*. Washington, DC: Geogretown University Press

Mittler E. et al. (ed.) (1986) *Bibliotheca Palatina*. Heidelberg (2 vol.) (Catalogue of an exhibition)

Montgomery, Th. (1977) The 'Poema de Mio Cid': Oral Art in Transition. In A.D. Deyermond (ed.), *Mio Cid Studies*, London (Colección Támesis, A 59), 91-112

Moore, A. (1990) *A whole language approach to the teaching of bilingual learners*. Illinois: Center for the Study of Reading

Morais, J., Alegria, J., Content, A. (1987) The relationships between segmental analysis and alphabetic literacy: An interactive view. *Cahiers de Psychologie Cognitive*, 7, 415-438

Morais, J., Bertelson, P., Cary, L., Alegria, J. (1986) Literacy training and speech segmentation. *Cognition*, 24, 45-64

Morais, J., Cary, L., Alegria, J., Bertelson, P. (1979) Does awareness of speech as a sequence of phones arise spontaneously? *Cognition*, 7, 323-331

Morani, M., Pontecorvo, C. (1995). Invenzione e scrittura di storie in coppie di bambini. *Età Evolutiva*, 51, 81-92

Morris, N. (1977) *A History of Jewish Education* (in Hebrew), Jerusalem

Mouchon, S., Fayol, M., Gaonac'h, D. (1991) Impact des connecteurs sur la lecture de textes narratifs. *Bulletin d'Audiophonologie*, 7, 159-174

Mouchon, S., Fayol, M., Gaonac'h, D. (1995) On-line processing of links between events in narratives. Studies of children and adults. *CPC/Current Psychology of Cognition*, 14, 171-193

Mouchon, S., Fayol, M., Gombert, J.E. (1989) L'utilisation de quelques connecteurs dans des rappels de récits chez des enfants de 5 à 8 ans. *L'Année Psychologique*, 89, 513-529

Mulhern, M., Rodriguez-Brown, F., Shanahan, T. (1994) Family literacy for language minority families. Issues for program implementation, *NCBE Program Information Guide Series, Number 17*

Murphy, J.J. (1974) *Rhetoric in the Middle Ages. A History of Rhetorical Theory from St. Augustine to the Renaissance*, Berkeley etc

Naert, P. (1941) Réflexions sur le caractère du mot dans les langues anciennes et dans les langues modernes, *Acta Linguistica*, vol. II, fasc. 4 (1940)-41, 185-191

Nali, F. (1957) Frequency distribution of phones in Hebrew. *Leshoneynu*, 23, 235-241

Narain, G., Verhoeven L. (1993) *Ontwikkeling van vroege tweetaligheid [Development of early bilingualism]*. Tilburg: University Press

Naveh, J. (1982) *Early History of the Alphabet*, Jerusalem

Naveh, J. (1992) *On Sherd and Papyrus. Aramaic and Hebrew Inscriptions from the Second Temple, Mishnaic and Talmudic Periods* (in Hebrew) Jerusalem

Naveh, J., Greenfield J.C. (1984) Hebrew, in W.D. Davies and L. Finkelstein (ed.) *The Cambridge History of Judaism*, vol. 1. *The Persian period* Cambridge, pp.115-129

Needham, J. (1969) *The grand titration: Science and society in East and West*. Toronto: University of Toronto Press

Neisser, U. (1967) *Cognitive Psychology*. Englewood Cliffs: Prentice Hall.

Nelson, K. (1986) *Event knowledge. Structure and function in development*. Hillsdale, NJ: L.E.A

Nencioni, G. (1976) Parlato-parlato, parlato-scritto, parlato-recitato, *Strumenti critici* 10, 1-56

Nida E. (1964) *Orthographic Studies. Articles on new writing systems* . London: United Bible Societies
Nippold, M. A.(ed.) (1988) *Later language development: Ages 9 through 19.* Texas: Pro-Ed
Nissen, H. J. (1986) The archaic texts from Uruk. *World Archeology, 173*, 318-334
Noordman, L.G.M., Vonk, W., Kempff, H.J. (1992) Causal inferences during the reading of expository texts. *Journal of Memory and Language, 31*, 573-590
Nunberg, G. (1990) *The Linguistics of Punctuation*, Stanford/ Palo Alto, CSLI (Center for the Study of Language and Information) Lecture Notes N°18
Nystrand, M. (1987) The Role of Context in Written Communication. In R.Horowitz an S.J.Samuels (eds.) *Comprehending Oral and Written Language* , 197-216
Ochs, E., Taylor, C. (1992). *Family narrative as political activity.* University of California, Los Angeles: Department of Linguistic.
Oesterreicher, W. (1994) El español en textos escritos por semicultos. Competencia escrita de impronta oral en la historiografía indiana. In J. Lüdtke (ed.), *El español de América en el siglo XVI*, Frankfurt, M., 155-190
Oesterreicher, W. (1995) L'oral dans l'écrit. Essai d'une typologie à partir des sources du latin vulgaire. In Callebat 1995, 145-157
Oesterreicher, W. (1997) Types of Orality in Text. In E. Bakker, A. Kahane (eds.), *Written Voices, Spoken Signs. Tradition, Performance, and the Epic Text*, Cambridge, Mass., pp.190-214
Olson, D.R. (1977) From Utterance to Text: The Bias of Language in Speech and Writing. *Harvard Educational Review*, 47. 3. 257-281
Olson, D.R. (1980) On the language and authority of textbooks. *Journal of Education 23*, 186-196
Olson, D.R. (1991) *Literacy and Objectivity: The Rise of Modern Science.* In D.R. Olson and N. Torrance (eds.)(1991) pp. 149-164
Olson, D.R. (1991) Writing as a meta activity. In D. R. Olson & N. Torrance (eds.) (1991)
Olson, D.R. (1993) How writing represents speech. *Language & Communication* 13, 1-17
Olson, D.R. (1994) Literacy and the making of the Western mind. In Verhoeven (ed.) (1994) pp. 135-150
Olson, D R (1994) On the relations between speech and writing. In *Proceedings of Workshop II*, Wassenaar
Olson, D.R. (1994) *The world on paper: The conceptual and cognitive implications of writing and reading.* Cambridge: Cambridge University Press
Olson, D.R. (1996) Towards a psychology of literacy. *Cognition*
Olson, D.R. (ed.) (1987) *Understanding Literacy: A Symposium on the Psychological, Social, and Educational Dimensions of Literacy, Interchange*, Volume 18, Numbers 1/2
Olson, D.R., Torrance, N. (eds.)(1991) *Literacy and Orality*, Cambridge: Cambridge University Press
Olson, D.R., Torrance, N., Lee, E.A. (in preparation) *The young child's concept of text*

Ong, W.J. (1982) *Orality and Literacy. The Technologizing of the Word*, London/New York
Ozouf J., Ozouf M. (1984) Le Tour de la France par deux enfants. In P. Nora *Les Lieux de mémoire*, vol. I, *La République*, Paris: Gallimard, pp. 291-322
Painchaud, G. (1992) "Littératie" et didactique de l'écrit en L2. *Etudes de linguistique appliquée*. 88, 55-66
Paoletti, G., Pontecorvo, C. (1991) Children revising text with and without computer: a system for analysing revision. In M. Carretero, M. Pope, R.J. Simons, J.I. Pozo (Eds) *Learning and Instruction*. (pp. 401-413). Vol. 3. Oxford: Pergamon Press.
Parkes, M.B. (1992) *Pause and Effect - An introduction to the History of Punctuation in the West*. Cambridge: University Press & Scolar Press
Parry, M. (1971) *The Making of Homeric Verse*. The collected papers of M. Parry, ed. by A. Parry, Oxford
Pasques, Li. (1990) Théories de l'écrit dans l'orthographe de l'Académie,. In N.Catach (éd.) *Pour une théorie de la langue écrite* , 35-46
Patterson, K. E. (1981) Neuropsychological approaches to the study of reading. *British Journal of Psychology, 72*, 151-174
Patterson K.E., Marshall J.C., Coltheart M. (eds.) (1985) *Surface dyslexia. Neuropsychological and cognitive studies of phonological reading*. London: LEA
Pearson, P.D. (1975) The effect of grammatical complexity on children's comprehension, recall, and conception of certain semantic relations. *Reading Research Quarterly, 33*, 283-320
Perfetti, C.A. (1987) Language, Speech and Print: Some Assymmetries in the Acquisition of Literacy. In R.Horowitz an S.J.Samuels (eds.) *Comprehending Oral and Written Language*, 355-370.
Pergnier, M. (1986) *Le mot*. Paris: Presses Universitaires de France
Perregaux, Ch. (1994) *Les enfants à deux voix: des effets du bilinguisme sur l'apprentissage de la lecture*. Berne, Lang
Peterson, C., A. McCabe (1988) The connective *and* as discourse glue. *First Language, 8*, 19-28
Peterson, C., A. McCabe (1991) Children's connective use and narrative macrostructure. In A. McCabe & C. Peterson (eds) (1991) pp. 29-54
Peterson, C., McCabe, A. (1987) The connective "and": Do older children use it less as they learn other connectives? *Journal of Child Language, 14*, 375-381
Piaget, J. (1929) *The Child's Conception of the World*. Routledge and Kegan Paul
Piaget, J. (1954) *The Construction of Reality in the Child*. New York: Basic Books
Pick, A. D., Unze, M. G, Brounwell, C. A., Drozdal, J. G. y Hopman, M. R.(1978) Young children's knowledge of word structure. *Child Development*, 49, 669-680
Pierrel, J. (1987) *Dialogue oral homme-machine* . Paris: Hermès
Pines, S. (1986) *Studies in Arabic Versions of Greek Texts and in Medieval Science*, Jerusalem and Leiden
Pinker, S. (1984) *Language learnability and language development*. Cambridge, MA: Harvard University Press

Pontecorvo C., Blanche-Benveniste C. (eds.) (1993) Proceedings of the ESF workshop on *Orality versus literacy: concepts, methods and data.* Siena, Italy, 24-26 September 1992
Pontecorvo, C. (1991) Ecrire et apprendre à écrire aujourd'hui. In Lüdi, Georges. éd.. *L'avenir de l'écrit et du multilinguisme, Die Zukunft des geschriebenen Wortes und der Mehrsprachigkeit. Actes du Symposium du 27/28 juin 1991.* Lausanne, Edipresse, 69-75
Pontecorvo, C. (1993). Developing literacy skills through cooperative computer use: Issues for learning and instruction. In T.M. Duffy, J. Lowyck, D.H. Jonassen (Eds.) *Designing Environments for Constructive Learning* (pp. 133-155). Berlin: Springer Verlag.
Pontecorvo, C. (1994) Emergent literacy and education. In Verhoeven. (ed.), 333-348
Pontecorvo, C. (1994) Iconicity in children's first written texts. In R. Simone (ed.) *Iconicity in Language* (pp. 277-307). Amsterdam: John Benjamins Publishing Company.
Pontecorvo, C., Orsolini, M. (1996). Writing and Written Language in Children's Development.. In C. Pontecorvo et al. (eds) (1996) pp. 3-23
Pontecorvo, C., Orsolini, M., Burge, B., & Resnick, L. (eds) (1996). *Children's early text construction.* Hillsdale, NJ: LEA.
Pontecorvo, C., Paoletti, G. (1991). Planning Story Completion in a Collaborative Computer Task. *European Journal of Psychology of Education*, VI, 2, 199-212.
Pontecorvo, C., Zucchermaglio, C. (1988) Modes of differentiation in children's writing construction. *European Journal of Psychology of Education*, 4, 371-385
Pontecorvo, C., Zucchermaglio C. (1990) Learning text composition in early literacy. In H. Mandl, E. De Corte, S.N. Bennett, H.F. Friedrich (eds) *Learning and Instruction. European Research in an International Context.* Vol.2.2. Oxford: Pergamon Press, pp. 367-384
Porten, B., Yardeni, A. (1986) (1990), *Textbook of Aramaic Documents for Ancient Egypt*, 2 vol. Jerusalem, (1986) (1990)
Poutet Y. (1970) *Le XVIIe siècle et les origines lasalliennes. Recherches sur la genèse de l'oeuvre scolaire et religieuse de Jean-Baptiste de la Salle*, Rennes: Impr. réunies, 2 vol
Prakash, P., Rekha, D., Nigam, R.,, Karanth, P. (1993) Phonological awareness, orthography, and literacy In R. J. Scholes ed., *Literacy and language analysis*Hillsdale, NJ: Erlbaum. pp. 55-70.
Pulgram E. (1970) *Syllabe, Word, Nexus, Cursus.* The Hague-Paris: Mouton (Janua Linguarum, Series Minor Nr. 81)
Py, B. (1989) L'acquisition vue dans la perspective de l'interaction. *DRLAV 41*, 83-100
Rack, J.P., Snowling, M.J., Olson R. (1992) The nonword reading deficit in developmental dyslexia: A review. *Reading Research Quarterly*, 27, 29-53.
Radtke, E. (1984) Zur Quellenlage für die Erforschung des gesprochenen Italienisch in der Sprachgeschichte vor 1860, *Italienisch* 12, 20-28

Raible W. (1991a) *Zur Entwicklung von Alphabetschrift-Systemen.* Is fecit cui prodest, Heidelberg (Sitzungsberichte der Heidelberger Akademie der Wissenschaften. Philosophisch-historische Klasse, Jahrgang 1991, 1)

Raible W. (1991b) *Die Semiotik der Textgestalt. Erscheinungsformen und Folgen eines kulturellen Evolutionsprozesses,* Heidelberg (Abhandlungen der Heidelberger Akademie der Wissenschaften. Philosophisch-historische Klasse, Jahrgang 1991, 1)

Raible W. (1994) Orality and literacy. In: H. Günther, O. Ludwig et al., cit., vol. I, pp.1-18

Raible, W. (ed.)(1990) *Erscheinungsformen kultureller Prozesse.* Jahrbuch 1988 des Sonderforschungsbereichs Übergänge und Spannungsfelder zwischen Mündlichkeit und Schriftlichkeit, Tübingen (ScriptOralia, 13)

Ramat P. (1990) Le mot, *Modèles linguistiques* XII-2, 83-92

Rastier, F. (1990) Signification et référence du mot, *Modèles linguistiques,* Vol.24, XII-2, 61-82

Ravid, D. (1995) *Language change in child and adult Hebrew: A psycholinguistic perspective.* Oxford: Oxford University Press

Ravid, D. (1996) Accessing the mental lexicon: evidence from incompatibility between representation of spoken and written morphology. *Linguistics*

Rayner, K., Pollatsek, A. (1989) *The psychology of reading.* Englewood Cliffs: Prentice-Hall International

Read, C. (1971) Pre-school children's knowledge of English phonology. *Harward Educational Review,* 41, 1-34

Read, C. (1986) *Children's creative Spelling,* London, Routledge & Kegan Paul

Read, C. A., Zhang, Y., Nie, H., Ding, B. (1986) The ability to manipulate speech sounds depends on knowing alphabetic reading. *Cognition, 24,* 31-44

Read, Ch., Zhang, Y., Nie,H., Ding, B. (1986) The ability to manipulate speech sounds depends on konwing alphabetic writing. *Cognition,* 24, 31-44

Reichler-Béguelin, M.J. (1988) Anaphore, cataphore et mémoire discursive. *Pratiques 57,* 15-43

Reichler-Béguelin, M.J. (1990)a, Conscience du sujet parlant et savoir du linguiste. In R.Liver, I.Werlen et P.Wunderli (éds.) *Sprachtheorie und Theorie der Sprache. Festschrift Rudolf Engler,* Tübingen, Gunter Narr

Reichler-Béguelin, M:J: (1994) Perception du mot graphique dans quelques systèmes syllabiques et alphabétiques, *Lallies* 10 (Publications de la Sorbonne Nouvelle)

Reid, J. F. (1966) Learning to think about reading. *Educational Research, 9,* 56-62

Reif, S. F. (1990), *Aspects of Medieval Jewish Literacy* in R. McKitterick (ed.) *The Uses of Literacy in Early Medieval Europe* Cambridge, pp. 134-155

Reilly, J. (1992) How to tell a good story: The intersection of language and affect in children's narratives. *Journal of Narrative and Life History, 2,* 355-377

Resnick, L.B., Saljo, R., Pontecorvo, C. , Burge, B.(eds) (1997) *Discourse, tools and reasoning: Essays on situated cognition.* New York- Berlin, Springer Verlag.

Riché P. (1979) *École et enseignement dans le Haut Moyen Age,* Paris: Aubier Montaigne

Roberts, C. (1994) Transfering literacy skills from L1 to L2: From theory to practice. *Journal of Educational Issues of Language Minority Students 13,* 209-221
Roche D., Roche F. (1979) Le carnet de chansons d'un conscrit provençal en 1922. *Ethnologie française,* IX, 1, 15-28
Roen, D.H. (1984) The effects of cohesive conjunctions, reference, response, rhetorical predicates, and topic on reading rate and written free recall. *Journal of Reading Behavior, 16,* 15-22
Rojo, G. (1991) Frecuencia de fonemas en español actual. In M Brea & F. Fernandez Rei eds. *Homenaxe ó Professor Constantino Garcia.* Departmento de Filoloxia Galega. Universidad de Santiago de Compostela
Romaine, S. (1989) *Bilingualism.* Oxford. GB), Basil Blackwell
Rosat, M.C. (1991) A propos de réalisations orale et écrite d'un texte argumentatif. *Etudes de linguistique appliquée 81,* 119-130.
Rosch E.H. (1978) Principles of Categorization. In B.B. Lloyd (ed.), *Cognition and Categorization,* Hillsdale, N.J., 27-48
Rosetti, A. (1944) Sur la définition du 'mot', *Acta Linguistica ,* IV.
Rousseau, J.-J. (1966) Essay on the origin of languages. In J. H. Moran & A. Gode (eds.), *On the origin of language: Two essays by Jean-Jacques Rousseau and Johann Gottfried Herder.* New York: Frederick Unger. Original work published 1754-91
Rozental D.E., et Telenkova, M.A. (1972) *Spravoçnik lingvistiçeskix terminov,* Moscou, Prosvesçenie
Rulon H.C., Friot, Ph. (1962) *Un Siècle de pédagogie dans les écoles primaires (1820-1940).* Histoire des méthodes et des manuels scolaires utilisés dans l'Institut des frères de l'instruction chrétienne de Ploërmel, Paris: Vrin, 1962
Rychner J. (1955) *La chanson de geste. Essai sur l'art épique des jongleurs,* Genève/Lille (Societé de publications romanes et françaises, 53)
Sabah, G. (1990) CARAMEL: Un système multi-experts pour le traitement automatique des langues, *Modèles linguistiques,* XII-1, 95-118
Saenger P. (1982) Silent reading: Its impact on late medieval script and thought. *Viator* 13, 367-414
Safrai S. (cd.) (1987) *The Literature of the Sages,* Maastricht, Philadelphia
Saljö, R. (1988) *A Text and Its Meaning: Observations on How Readers Construe What is Meant from What is Written in the Written World.* In R. Saljö (ed.) (1988) pp.178-194
Saljö R.(ed.) (1988) *Studies in Literate Thought and Action,* Berlin, Heidelberg, New York, London, Paris, Tokyo
Salomon, G. (ed.) (1993) *Distributed cognition. Psychological and Educational Considerations.* Cambridge, Cambridge University Press
Sampson, G (1985) *Writing systems: A linguistic introduction.* London, Hutchinson
Sampson, G. (1985). Writing systems. Stanford, CA: Stanford University Press.
Sartori, G. (1984) *La lettura.* Bologna: Il Mulino
Saunders, G. (1988) *Bilingual children: From birth to teens.* Clevedon/ Philadephia, Multilingual Matters

Saussure, F. de (1916) *Cours de Linguistique Générale*. Edition critique préparée par Tullio de Mauro, F. Paris: Payot 1974. *Course in general linguistics*. London: Duckworth, 1983

Scarborough, H. S. (1981) Antecedents to reading disabilities: Pre-school language development and literacy experiences of children from dyslexic families. *Reading and Writing*, 3, 219-233

Schaefer U. (1992) *Vokalität. Altenglische Dichtung zwischen Mündlichkeit und Schriftlichkeit*, Tübingen (ScriptOralia, 39)

Schank, R.C., Abelson, R.P. (1977) *Scripts, plans, goals and understanding*. Hillsdale, NJ: L.E.A.

Schlieben-Lange, B. (1983) *Traditionen des Sprechens. Elemente einer pragmatischen Sprachgeschichtsschreibung*, Stuttgart etc

Schmandt-Besserat, D. (1978) The earliest precursor of writing. *Scientific American*, 238, 50-59

Schmandt-Besserat, D. (1986) Tokens: Facts and interpretations. *Visible Language*, 203, 250-272

Schmandt-Besserat, D. (1987) *Oneness, twoness, threeness: How ancient accountants invented numbers*. New York: New York Academy of Sciences

Schmandt-Besserat, D. (1992) *Before writing*. Austin: University of Texas Press

Schneuwly, B. (1988) *Le langage écrit chez l'enfant*. Paris/Neuchâtel, Delachaux & Niestlé.

Scholes, R. (1993) In search of phonemic consciousness. In R. Scholes (ed.) *Literacy and language analysis* Hillsdale, NJ: Erlbaum, pp. 45-54

Scholes, R., Willis, B. J. (1991) Linguists, literacy, and the intentionality of Marshall McLuhan's Western man. In D. R. Olson & N. Torrance (eds.), pp. 215-235.

Scholz M.G. (1980) *Hören und Lesen. Studien zur primären Rezeption der Literatur im 12. und 13. Jahrhundert*, Wiesbaden

Schreiber, P. A. (1987) Prosody and Structure in Children's Syntactic Processing. In R.Horowitz an S.J.Samuels (eds.) *Comprehending Oral and Written Language*, 243-270

Scott, C. M. (1988) Spoken and written syntax. In Nippold (ed.), pp. 49-96

Scribner, S., Cole, M. (1981) *The psychology of literacy*. Cambridge, MA: Harvard University Press

Sebastian, E., D. I. Slobin. (1994) Development of linguistic forms: Spanish. In Berman & Slobin, pp. 239-284

Sebastian, N., Felguera, T. (1992) Detección de fonemas en ataques y coda silábicos. *Cognitiva*, 4, 173-191

Sebastián-Gallés, N (1991) Reading by analogy in a shallow orthography. *Journal of Experimental Psychology: Human Perception and Performance, 17*, 471-477

Segal, E.M., Duchan, J.F., Scott, P.J. (1991) The role of interclausal connectives in narrative structuring: Evidence from adults' interpretations of simple stories. *Discourse Processes, 14*, 27-54

Seguin, H.(1990) L'écriture des mots communs à deux langues de même alphabet: étude comparée du français et de l'anglais. In N.Catach (ed.) (1990) pp. 165-179

Selig M., Frank, B., Hartmann, J. (eds.)(1993), *Le passage à l'écrit des langues romanes*, Tübingen (ScriptOralia, 46)
Selinker, L. (1972) Interlanguage. *IRAL X/2*, 209-31
Serra, E. (1992) *Children's understanding of how writing affects speech.* Unpublished paper, Centre for Applied Cognitive Science, Ontario Institute for Studies in Education,Toronto
Shankweiler, D., Liberman, I. (1972) Misreading: A search for causes. In J. Kavanaugh & I. Mattingly (eds.), *Language by ear and language by eye: The relationships between speech and reading* Cambridge, MA: MIT Press pp. 293-317.
Share, D., Jorm, A. F. Maclean, R., Matthews, R. (1984) Sources of individual differences in reading acquistion. *Journal of Educational Psychology*, 76, 1309-1324.
Shimron, J. (1993) The role of vowels in reading: A review of studies of English and Hebrew. *Psychological Bulletin*, 114, 1, 52-67
Shuy, R.W. (1979) The mismatch of child language and school language: Implications of beginning reading instruction. In: L. Resnick & P. Weaver eds, *Theory and Practice of Early Reading, vol 1*. Hillsdale, N.J.: LEA
Sinclair, A., Jarvella, J., Levelt, W. (eds.). (1978) *The child's conception of language.* Berlin: Springer-Verlag
Sinclair, H. (1978) Conceptualization and awareness in Piaget's theory and its relevance to the child's conception of language. In A. Sinclair, J. Jarvella, & W. Levelt (eds.), pp. 191-200
Sirat, C. (1981a) *L'examen des écritures: l'oeil et la machine. Essai de méthodologie*, Paris, Editions du CNRS (Etudes de paléographie hébraïque)
Sirat, C. (1981b) *La lettre hébraïque et sa signification*, Paris, Editions du CNRS et Jérusalem, The Israel Museum (Department of Judaica)
Sirat, C. (1990a) *A History of Jewish Philosophy in the Middle Ages*, Cambridge and Paris.
Sirat, C. (1990b), *La philosophie et la science selon les philosophes juifs* in M. Atzalos, J.E. Murdoch, I. Niiniluoto, eds. *Knowledge and the Sciences in Medieval Philosophy*, Helsinki, pp.250-261
Sirat, C. (1991) Les rouleaux bibliques de Qumran au Moyen Age: du livre au Sefer Tora, de l'oreille à l'oeil *Compte rendus de l'Academie des Inscriptions et Belles-lettres*, pp.415-432
Sirat, C. (1994) *Du scribe au livre: les manuscrits hebreux au Moyen Age*, Paris
Sirat, C., Irigoin J., Poulle E. (1990) *L'Ecriture: le cerveau, l'oeil et la main* . Turnbout: Brepols
Skutnabb-Kangas, T. (ed.) (1995) *Multiligualism for all.* Lisse, Swets & Zeitlinger
Slobin, D. I. (1982) Universal and particular in the acquisition of language. In E. Wanner & L. Gleitman (eds.) *Language Acquisition: The State of the Art.* Cambridge University Press

Slobin, D. I. (1988) The development of clause chaining in Turkish child language. In S. Koc (ed.), *Studies on Turkish linguistics*. Ankara: Middle East Technical University, pp. 27-54

Slobin, D. I.(ed.) (1985) *The crosslinguistic study of language acquisition. Vol. 1: The data*. Hillsdale, NJ: Lawrence Erlbaum

Smalley, B. (1941) *The study of the Bible in the Middle Ages*. Oxford: Clarendon

Smalley, W. et al. (1964) *Orthographic Studies: Articles on New writing Systems* . London: United Bible Societies

Smith , P. T. (1980), *Cognitive processes in spelling*. London: Academic Press

Smith, M. E. (1973) *Picture writing from ancient southern Mexico*. Oklahoma: University of Oklahoma Press

Smith, S. D., Kimberling, W. J., Pennington, B. F. and Lubs, H. A. (1983) Specific reading disability: Identification of an inherited form through linkage analysis. *Science*, 219, 1345-1347

Sneddon, R. s.d.. Children developing biliteracy at home and at school. Internet document

Snell, B. (1960) *The discovery of the mind: The Greek origins of European thought* T. G. Rosenmeyer, Trans.. New York: Harper & Row

Snow, C. E. (1989) Understanding social interaction a nd language acquisition: sentences are not enough. In M. Bornstein & J. Bruner (eds.) *Interaction in Human Development*. Hillsdale, NJ: Lawrence Erlbaum Associates, pp. 83-103

Snow, C.E., A. Ninio (1986) The contracts of literacy: What children learn from learning to read books. In: W. Teale & E. Sulzby eds, *Emergent literacy: Writing and reading*. Norwood, NJ: Ablex

Söll L. (1974) *Gesprochenes und geschriebenes Französisch*, Berlin (Grundlagen der Romanistik, 6) [1985].

Spencer, A. (1991) A linguist's reflections on 'phonological awareness' and literacy. *Mind & Language*, 6, 146-155

Spratt, J.E., Seckinger, B. & D.A. Wagner (1991) Functional literacy in Moroccan school children. *Reading Research Quarterly 26*, 178-195

Staccioli, G., Andreucci, C. (1989) Il riconoscimento della scrittura in bambini in etá di scuola dell'infanzia. *Etá evolutiva*, 5, 9-14

Stanovich, K.E. (1994) Does dyslexia exist? *Journal of Child Psychology and Psychiatry*, 35, 579-595

Stein, B., Meredith, A. (1993) *The Merging of the Senses*. Cambridge (MA): A Bradford Book, The MIT Press

Stempel W.-D. (1993) La 'modernité' des débuts: la rhétorique de l'oralité chez Chrétien de Troyes. In Selig et al. 1993, 275-298

Street, B.V. (1984) *Literacy in theory and practice*. Cambridge, Cambridge University Press

Street, B.V. (1988) *Literacy Practices and Literacy Myths* In R. Saljö (ed.) (1988), pp.59-72

Street, B.V. (1994) Cross-cultural perspectives on literacy. In Verhoeven (ed.) 95-111

Sulzby, E. & W. Teale (1991) Emergent literacy. In: R. Barr et al. eds, *Handbook of Reading Research vol. 2*. New York: Longman
Swiggers, P., Van Hoeke, W. (eds.) (1986) *Mot et parties du discours*. Paris-Louvain: Peeters
Tabossi, P, Laghi, L (1992) Semantic priming in the pronunciation of words in two writing systems: Italian and English. *Memory & Cognition, 20*, 315-328
Talmy, L. (1985) Lexicalization patterns: Semantic structure in lexical forms. In T. Shopen (ed.), *Language typology and syntactic description. Vol 3. Grammatical categories and the lexicon*. Cambridge: Cambridge University Press, pp. 57-149
Tambiah, S. J. (1990) *Magic, science and religion and the scope of rationality*. Cambridge: Cambridge University Press
Teale, W. (1980) *Early reading: An annotated bibliography*. Newark, DE: IRA
Teberosky, A. (1988). La dictée et la rédaction de contes entre enfants du même âge. *European Journal of Psychology of Education, 3*, (4), 399-414.
Teberosky, A., Tolchinsky Landsmann,L. Zelcer, J. Gomes de Morais, A., Rincon, G. Segmentation phonologique et acquisition de l'ecriture en castillan, catalan et hébreu (1993) *Études de Linguistique Appliquée*, 91,48-59
Teixidor, J. (1991) Lire et entendre en ouest-sémitique. In CL.Baurain, C.Bonnet & V.Krings (éds.) *Phoinikeia Grammata*, 91-100
Temple, C.M., Marshall, J.C. (1983) A case study of developmental phonological dyslexia. *British Journal of Psychology*, 74, 517-535
Templeton, S., Bear, D. eds. *Development of orthographic knowledge: The foundations of literacy*. Hillsdale, NJ: Lawrence Erlbaum
Tene, D. (1968) L'hébreu contemporain. In A. Martinet (1968) *Le Langage. Encyclopedie de La Pléiade*. Paris: Gallimard
Titone, R. (1977) *A guide to bilingual reading*. Rome, Armando
Tobach, E., Joffe Falmagne, R., Brown Parlee, M., Martin, L.M. & Scribner Kagelman, A. (eds) (1997) *Mind and Social Practice. Selected writing of Silvia Scribner*. Cambridge: Cambridge University Press.
Togeby, K. (1949) Qu'est-ce qu'un mot?, *Travaux du Cercle Linguistique de Copenhague*, V. Cf. Michael Herslund (éd.) (1987) *Knud Togeby, Choix d'articles (1943)-(1974)* Numéro Spécial de *Revue Romane*, N° 15, 97-111
Tolchinsky, L., Teberosky, A. The development of word segmentation and writing in two scripts (submitted)
Tolchinsky-Landsmann, L. (1991) The Conceptualization of Writing in the Confluence of Interactive Models of Development . In Tolchinsky-Landsmann ed. *Culture, Schooling, and Psychological Development*, Norwood, New Jersey: Ablex
Tomasello, M., Merriman W.E. (eds.) *Beyond words for things*. Hillsdale, NJ: Lawrence Erlbaum Associates
Torrance, N., Lee, E., Olson, D. (1992), April. *The development of the distinction between paraphrase and exact wording in the recognition of utterances*. Poster presentation at the meeting of the American Educational Research Association, San Francisco, CA

Torrance, N., Olson, D. R. (1987) Development of the Metalanguage and the Acquisition of Literacy: A Progress Report, *Interchange* vol. 18, N°1-2, 136-146
Tosi, A. (1979) Mother tongue teaching for the children of immigrants. *Language teaching and Linguistics: Abstracts 12*, 213-231
Tosi, A. (1984) *Immigration and bilingual education*. Oxford: Pergamon Press
Tov, E. 199 4. *Dead Sea Scrolls in Light of New Research* (in Hebrew) in Jewish Studies, 3 4. pp.37-67
Townsend, D.J, Bever T.G. (1978) Inter-clause relations and clausal processing. *Journal of Verbal Learning and Verbal Behavior, 17*, 509-521
Townsend, D.J. (1983) Thematic processing in sentences and texts. *Cognition, 13*, 223-261
Treiman, R. (1985) Onsets and times as units of spoken syllables: Evidence from children. *Journal of Experimental Child Psychology*, 39, 161-181
Treiman, R. (1992) The Role of Intrasyllabic Units in Learning to Read and Spell, in P. Gough, L. Erhri & R. Treiman eds. *Reading Acquisition*, New Jersey Lawrence Erlbaum
Treiman, R., Baron, J. (1981) Segmental analysis ability: Development and relation to reading ability. In G. E. Mackinnon & T. G. Waller eds. *Reading Research: Advances in Theory and Practice* vol. 3. New York: Academic Press.
Treiman, R., Zukowski, A. (1988) Units in reading and spelling. *Journal of Memory and Language*, 27, 66-85
Triesscheijn, B.H., Bergh, H. van den & J.B. Hoeksma (1985) *Voorstudie periodiek peilingsonderzoek [Pilot study national assessment]*. Amsterdam: SCO
Tristram H.L.C. (1988) Aspects of Tradition and Innovation in the *Táin Bó Cuailnge, Papers on Language and Medieval Studies Presented to A. Schopf*, Frankfurt/M., 19-38
Tronchère, J. (1967) *Guide du débutant et abc de législation scolaire*, Paris: Colin-Bourrelier
Trost V. (1994) "Drei Finger schreiben, aber der ganze Körper arbeitet ..." - Zur Buchproduktion im Mittelalter. InA. Kirmeier et al., cit., pp. 111-122
Trueba, H.T., Guthrie, G.P., K.H. Au (1981) *Culture in the bilingual classroom: Studies in classroom ethnography*. Rowley, MA: Newbury House
Tunmer,W., Pratt, C., Herriman, M. (1984) *Metalinguistic awareness in children.* Berlin: Spinger-Verlag
Vachek, J. (1989) *Written Language Revisited*. Amsterdam: John Benjamins
Valtin, R., Jung, U.O., Scheerer-Neuman, G. (1981) *Legasthenie in Wissenschaft und Unterricht*. Darmstadt: Wissenschaftliche Buchgesellschaft
van Bon, M.H.J., Duighuisen, H.C.M. (1995) Sometimes spelling is easier than phonemic segmentation. *Scandinavian Journal of Psychology*, 36, 82-94
Vanier, M, Caplan, D (1985) CT scan correlates of surface dyslexia. In K E Patterson, J C Marshall & M Coltheart (eds.) *Surface Dyslexia: Neuropsychological and Cognitive Studies of Phonological Reading*. London, LEA
Vellutino, F. (1979) *Dyslexia*. Cambridge: MIT Press

Vellutino, F., Scallon, D. (1987) Phonological coding, phonological awareness and reading ability: evidence from a longitudinal and experimental study. *Merrill-Palmer Quarterly*, 33, 321-363.
Venezky, R.L. (1970) *The structure of English orthography*. The Hague: Mouton.
Verhelst, N., T. Eggen (1989) *Psychometrische en statistische aspecten van peilingsonderzoek [Psychonometrical and statistical aspects of national assessment research]*. Arnhem: Cito
Verhoeven, L. (1987)a. *Ethnic Minority Children Acquiring Literacy Published Doctoral Dissertation*. Berlin: De Gruyter
Verhoeven, L. (1987)b. Literacy in a second language context: Teaching immigrant children to read. *Educational Review* 39, 245-261
Verhoeven, L. (1990)a. Acquisition of reading in a second language. *Reading Research Quarterly* 25, 2, 90-114
Verhoeven, L. (1990)b. Language variation and learning to read. In: P. Reitsma & L. Verhoeven eds, *Acquisition of reading in Dutch*. Berlin: De Gruyter
Verhoeven, L. (1991)a. Predicting minority children's bilingual proficiency: Child, family and institutional factors. *Language Learning 41*, 2, 205-233
Verhoeven, L. (1991)b. Acquisition of biliteracy. *AILA Review 8*, 61-74
Verhoeven, L. (ed.) (1994a) *Functional literacy. Theoretical issues and educational implications*. Amsterdam/Philadelphia, John Benjamins
Verhoeven, L. (1994b) Modeling and promoting functional literacy. In Verhoeven (ed.) (1994a), pp. 3-33
Verhoeven, L. (1994c) Linguistic diversity and literacy development. In L. Verhoeven ed., (1994a) pp. 199-220
Verhoeven, L. (1994d) Acquisition of literacy by immigrant children. In U. Frith et al. (eds.) (1994)
Verhoeven, L. (1994e) Early bilingualism, cognition and assessment. Paper presented at the *19th Annual Conference for the American Association for Applied Linguistics*, Baltimore
Verhoeven, L. (1994f) Transfer in bilingual development. The linguistic interdependency hypothesis revisited. *Language Learning 44*, 3, 381-415
1995, 171-194
Verhoeven, L., Extra, G., Konak, O., Narain, G., Zerrouk R.(1993) *Peiling van vroege tweetaligheid [Assessment of early bilingual proficiency]*. Tilburg: Tilburg University Press
Verhoeven, L., Teberosky, A. (eds.) (1993) ESF Proceedings of the Workshop *on Understanding Early Literacy in a Developmental and Cross-linguistic Approach*, Wassenaar, 7-9 October
Verhoeven, L., van Kuijk J.(1991) Peiling van conceptuele en metalinguïstische kennis bij de aanvang van het basisonderwijs [Assessment of conceptual and metalinguistic awareness at the onset of kindergarten]. *Pedagogische Studiën 68*, 9, 415-425

Verhoeven, L., van Elsacker W.(1995) Effects of storybook reading in small-group settings. Paper presented at *the 45th Annual Meeting of the National Reading Conference*, New Orleans

Vygotsky, L. (1962) *Thought and language*. Cambridge, MA: MIT Press

Wandruszka, U. (1992) Je chantais: Konjugationsthese and suffixe preference, Résumé de communication au Congrès International de Langue et Philologie romane, Zurich, p.159

Wason, P. & Jones, S. (1963) Negatives: denotation and connotation. *British Journal of Psychology*, 54: 299-307

Wason, P. (1961) Response to affirmative and negative binary statements. *British Journal of Psychology*, 52: 133-142

Watahomigie, L. (1992) The power of American Indian communities. Paper presented at the annual meeting of the American Educational Research Association in San Francisco

Weber E. (1976) *Peasants into Frenchmen: The Modernization of the Rural France, 1870-1914,* Stanford (Ca.): Stanford University Press

Weissenborn, J., Goodluck, H., Roeper, T. (1992) Old and new problems in the study of language acquisition. In J. Weissenborn, H. Goodluck, T. Roeper (eds.), *Theoretical issues in language acquisition: Continuity and change in development*. Hillsdale, NJ: Lawrence Erlbaum Associates

Wells, G. (1985) *Language development in the preschool years*. Cambridge: University Press.

Wells, G. (1990) Talk about text: Where literacy is learned and taught. *Curriculum Inquiry 20/4,* 369-405

Wertsch, J. (ed.) (1985) *Culture, Communication and Cognition. Vygotskian Perspectives.* Cambridge, Cambridge University Press

Whorf, B. L. (1956) Science and linguistics. In *Selected writings of Benjamin Lee Whorf*. Cambridge, MA: MIT Press

Wimmer, H. (1993). Characteristics of developmental dyslexia in a regular writing system. *Applied Psycholinguistics*, 14, 1-33

Wimmer, H. (1994a) The nonword reading deficit in developmental dyslexia: Evidence from German children. Manuscript submitted to publication. University of Salzburg, Austria.

Wimmer, H. (1994b) From phonological to surface dyslexia: A longitudinal study of difficulties in learning to read a regular orthography. Manuscript submitted to publication. University of Salzburg, Austria.

Wimmer, H., Frith, U. (1994). Orthographies and Learning to Read: An English-German Comparison. Manuscript submitted to publication. University of Salzburg, Austria.

Wimmer, H., Goswami, U. (1994). The influence of orthographic consistency on reading development: Word recognition in English and German children. *Cognition*, 51, 51-103.

Wimmer, H., Hummer (1990) How German-speaking first graders read and spell: doubts on the importance of the logographic stage. *Applied Psycholinguistics*, 11, 349-368

Wolf A. (1991) Medieval Heroic Traditions and Their Transitions from Orality to Literacy. In Doane, Braun Pasternack 1991, 67-89

World Health Organization (1992) International Classification of Diseases and Health Related Problems. Tenth Revision (ICD-10). Geneva: WHO

Wright, R. (1982) *Late Latin and Early Romance in Spain and Carolingian France*. Liverpool: Francis Cairns

Wydell, T (1991) Unpublished PhD Dissertation. University of London

Yin, W.G. (1991) Unpublished PhD Dissertation. University of London

Ziti, A Champagnol, R. (1992) Effet des connecteurs sur le traitement en temps réel des propositions exprimant des relations cause/effet. *L'Année Psychologique, 92*, 187-207

Zumthor P. (1983) *Introduction à la poésie orale*. Paris

Zumthor P. (1987) *La lettre et la voix. De la littérature médiévale*. Paris

Zwarts, M. (1990) *Balans van het taalonderwijs einde basisschool [Assessment language proficiency by the end of primary school]*. Arnhem: Cito

Analytic index

A
adjective formation 64, 67, 75
Alphabet 118, 119, 120, 121, 124, 125, 127
   Hebrew 104, 106, 112
   Hebrew 78, 89
   Palaeo-Hebrew 102, 103
alphabetic principle 84
   writing 9, 117, 119, 127
   ordering 141, 145, 139, 140
Alphabetic-syllabic mapping 85
Alphabetization 155, 157
Alphabetized 157, 166
analogy 119, 122
and 72, 73, 74
anthropological research xxx
anthropological factors xxxi
après (afterwards) 194, 198, 199, 200, 203, 204
Arabic (mother tongue) 106, 107, 108, 112
Arabic 37, 40, 45
arithmetic 182, 183, 185, 186
assessing biliteracy 213
Auctoritas 127

B
bilingualism 205, 206, 209, 210, 211, 213
Biliteracy 205-217
biliteracy programmes 207, 208
book (history of) 130-134
brain organisation 273

C
children with highly literate parents 53
clause structure 62, 63, 69

clinical paradoxes 245-246
cognitive architecture 244
communicative distance 153, 154, 156
competence/performance distinction 49
complementarity 101, 112
comprehension 162
conception 149, 150, 151, 152, 153, 154, 159, 160, 163, 167, 169
Connectives 72, 73, 193-204
   comprehension of 193-204
   production of 193-204
continuity hypothesis 82
controlling function 185
conversation 149, 150, 151, 154, 163, 168
copying 131, 135, 136, 137, 138, 143, 145, 146, 175 177-179, 182, 185, 189
correction 179, 180
crosslinguistic 68, 71, 75, 76

D
daily records 184-187
Developmental asynchronism 252
   developmental dyslexia (see dyslexia)
diacritics 78, 88, 89, 93
dialect 119
Dictate 159, 160, 161
   dictation 135, 136, 137, 138, 159, 160, 169
Diglossia 68, 165, 169, 171, 209
diglossic 165
discussion 107, 108, 109, 113, 114
dissociations between reading and writing 252
distance 151, 152, 153-154,
domain-specific architecture 253-257

dyslexia 259-261, 267, 268, 270, 271, 273, 288, 290
  developmental dyslexia 243, 246, 250, 251, 257

E
elicitation test 65
epics 154
epos 156
ethnic minorities 219, 239
ethnographic methodology xxix
etymology, 119, 122, 124, 125
European Science Foundation Network xvii
  Network on Written Language and Literacy xvii, xxiii
  Proceedings: Orality and Literacy xvii
  Proceedings: Understanding Early Literacy xvii
  Proceedings: Contexts of Literacy xvii
event-chains 194-195
exercise book (*cahier*) 173-189
expressive options 66, 68, 70, 76

F
face-to-face communication/interaction 151, 154
formal 150, 154, 160
formally constrained writing 85, 86
form-function relations 63-64
frontier age 61, 74
functional literacy (see literacy)

G
Grammar 118-119, 120, 125, 126
  generative 61,62,63
  grammarians 117, 119, 120, 126, 127
grapheme-phoneme consistency 260, 261, 270
Graphic constraints 182
  knowledge 187
  medium (see medium)
  system 3,5,8,9,14,17
Greek (characters and language) 101, 103, 104, 106, 107, 108,112, 114

H
Hebrew 36,40,45,77-97
  alphabet (see alphabet)
  resultative participles 65-68
hellènismos 119
hierarchical structure of the syllable 80
homophones 121, 127

I
ideographic writing 22
illiterate (see literate) 156, 166-169,
illustration 178
immediacy (communicative) 151, 152, 161, 162, 163-169, 170
immersion 207, 208, 210
informal 160
involvement 154, 159, 162
iotacism 119

L
L1 219-240
L1-L2 transfer 219, 220, 237, 238
L2 219-240
Language (history of) 119, 122
  acquisition of 61,63
  second 219-240
  unit 21-45
linguistic hypothesis 247
Latin 38,42,43,45
layout 177, 178, 182, 183
lexical semantics 62
linearization process 193
listing (*mise en liste*) 179
Literacy 101-115, 219-240
  functional 206
  introduction of the word xv
  of immigrant children 219-240
  practices 206, 207, 209, 212, 215, 216, 217
  revolution 51
literate culture/society speech community 149-171
literacy and orality (A literate issue) xxi-xxii

334 ANALYTIC INDEX

Literacy sciences xx-xxiv
  multidisciplinary exchange in xxiii
  as new transdisciplinary domain xxiii

M
mais (but) 193, 194, 196, 198, 199, 200, 201, 202, 203, 204
meaning 22, 23, 25, 26, 27, 28, 34, 35, 37, 38, 41, 43
medium /graphic-phonic 150, 151, 152, 153, 154, 158, 160, 161, 163, 164, 165, 166, 168, 170, 171
migrant children 207 210, 211, 214, 216
minority language maintenance 208
missing letters 120, 124
modular design 251
morpheme 22,32,33,34,35,39,40,44
morphological structure 77, 79, 93
Morphology 62,64,65,66
nonconcatenative 79
multigraphism 112
multilingualism 112
multiplicity 101, 112

N
Narrative 65, 70, 71, 73, 74, 75
comprehension 196, 197, 198
structure 72-75
naturalistic speech 65, 66
neuropsychology of reading (see reading)
nominalizations 64, 68-71, 74
nonliterate 155-156
nonvocalized orthography 78
norm 125-126
notational system 6
null subjects 64, 71-72, 74

O
Oral 149-171
  Law 105, 106, 108, 113
  poetry 156
  production 194
Orality 101-115, 149-154, 155, 156, 158

literate types of xxi
orthoepy 118, 121
Orthography 247, 251, 252, 253, 254, 257
  vocalized 78
orthographers 119, 121
orthographic depth hypothesis 276-277
orthographic proficiency 247

P
passives 65-66
philologists 119
phoneme as conceptual entity 49
phoneme awareness 247, 250, 251, 253, 254, 257, 258
Phonetic transcription 122, 123
  writing 120
Phonic distance 157-161
  medium (see medium)
  units 25
phonics 278
Phonographic 8,9
  writing 130
Phonological coding 259, 260, 261, 262-265, 267, 268, 270, 271
features 77
popular education 173
prescriptive norm 163, 164, 165, 166, 167, 168
primary oral culture/society 53, 154, 155, 156, 161, 164, 170
print, printing 155, 158, 1664, 171
proficiency 62
Psycholinguistic Research 53, 54, 57
  use of reading tasks in 49, 50

Q
quasi-literate 155, 159

R
ratio 122, 124, 125, 127
Reading acquisition 244, 245, 246, 247, 248, 250, 251, 252, 254, 256, 257, 260
  acquisition (standard view on) 245
  aloud 133, 141, 142,143, 147, 151,

158, 169
biology of 244
disorders 246, 247, 251
disorders (heterogeneity of) 246
intimacy offered by silent xxvii
history of xxvii, 129-141
mental retardation and 249
motor impairment and 248-249
neuropsychology of 277
outstanding intelligence and 249-250
phoneme awareness and 250-251
process 141-144
silent 51,158
silent composition and xxvii
two-route model of 280, 281
reception 159, 160
register 66, 67, 68, 69, 70, 76
Representation 118, 119, 122, 123, 125, 126- 128
lexical xxiii
of language xx, xxi
representational system 5, 6
reproduction 126-128
retrospection 64

S
school teacher 174
Script 3-20
Palaeo-Hebrew 106
scriptio continua 51, 133, 147, 142
scriptism 168
second language (see language)
segmentation 12
selective damage 282
selectivity 73, 74
semantic integration 197, 204
semi-literate 155, 161, 162, 166
sequentiality 72, 73
simultaneity 63, 64
Spanish 77-97
speak, speaking, speaker 167, 171
speaker acting as reader 49
speech/writing relation 3-20
spoken 150, 162
sponteneity, spontaneous 149, 150, 151, 152, 154, 159, 160, 162, 163
suddenly (*soudain*) 193, 194, 196, 198, 199, 200, 201, 202, 203, 204
superfluous letters 120
syllabic mapping 84, 85, 86, 89, 92, 95
syllabic period 84
syntactic complexity 150, 159, 160
syntax 8,15,16, 64, 75

T
teaching of writing (see writing) 173, 175
topic elision 71-72
transcoding processor 254, 256, 257, 258
transcription theory 4
transfer 208, 212, 216
transitional 74
transparency 69
typological 67, 68, 70, 75

U
uox scriptiliis 123

V
vernacular learning 214
vocal,vocality 158, 159, 160, 166
vocalized orthography (see orthography)

W
Word
children's concept of 55, 56
children's discovery of the 11-12
division 31,37
notion of 21,30,33
practical existence 54
in the system (*mot de langue*) 23, 32-33, 34, 55
in the utterance 24, 25, 32-33, 36, 55
mapping 275, 277,
segmentation 77-97
unit 21-45
Word processor (use of) xxvii
use of a keyboard of xxviii

Writing
  processes of revision with xxviii
  history of 129, 130, 132, 134
  against the transcription view of xxii
  and cognition 16-20
  ill defined problems 47
  segmentation in 56
  signs as first order signs 51
  signs as second order signs 56
  practice 175, 176
  process 134-141
  teaching of 173, 175
  versus reading xviii, ix
Writing System xxiv-xxvi, 52, 53, 125, 273- 291
  alphabetical 54
  alphabetical (evolutionary view on) 52
  Arabic 35
  Chinese 284
  early 29
  English 274, 277, 278
  Hebrew 35
  lack of theoretical reflection about 47, 48-50
  Latin 41
Written Language 48, 49, 52, 53, 54, 57, 58
  history of 129-147
  mastery of xvi
  sunday language xxv
  representation of xxvi
written Law 104
written narratives 193, 204
written production 194-204

In the STUDIES IN WRITTEN LANGUAGE AND LITERACY the following titles have been published thus far:

1. VERHOEVEN, Ludo (ed.): *Functional Literacy: Theoretical issues and educational implications.* 1995
2. KAPITZKE, Cushla: *Literacy and Religion: The textual politics and practice of Seventh-day Adventism.* 1995.
3. TAYLOR, Insup, and M. Martin Taylor: *Writing and literacy in Chinese, Korean, and Japanese.* 1995.
4. PRINSLOO, Mastin and Mignonne BREIER (eds): *The Social Uses of Literacy. Theory and Practice in Contemporary South Africa.* 1996.
5. IVANIČ, Roz: *Writing and Identity. The discoursal construction of identity in academic writing.* n.y.p.
6. PONTECORVO, Clotilde (ed.): *Writing Development. An interdisciplinary view.* 1997.